**Other History and International Relations Titles
from Potomac Books**

*Napoleon's Troublesome Americans: Franco-American Relations,
1804–1815* by Peter P. Hill

*The First Resort of Kings: American Cultural Diplomacy in the
Twentieth Century* by Richard T. Arndt

*Crisis and Crossfire: The United States and the Middle East
since 1945* by Peter L. Hahn

THEODORE ROOSEVELT

AND WORLD ORDER

THEODORE ROOSEVELT

AND WORLD ORDER

Police Power in International Relations

James R. Holmes

Potomac Books, Inc.
Washington, D.C.

Library of Congress Cataloging-in-Publication Data

Holmes, James R., 1965–
    Theodore Roosevelt and world order : police power in international relations / James R. Holmes.— 1st ed.
      p. cm.
    Includes bibliographical references and index.
    ISBN 1-57488-883-8 (hardcover : alk. paper)
    1. Roosevelt, Theodore, 1858–1919—Political and social views. 2. Roosevelt, Theodore, 1858–1919—Philosophy. 3. United States—Foreign relations—1901–1909. 4. United States—Foreign relations—1901–1909—Case studies. 5. Police power—United States—History—20th century. 6. Intervention (International law)—History—20th century. 7. World politics—1900–1918. 8. World politics—1900–1918—Case studies. I. Title.

E757.H65 2005
327.73'009'041—dc22

2005024062

Printed in the United States of America on acid-free paper that meets the American National Standards Institute Z39-48 Standard.

Potomac Books, Inc.
22841 Quicksilver Drive
Dulles, Virginia 20166

First Edition

10 9 8 7 6 5 4 3 2 1

CONTENTS

1

INTRODUCTION

"Aggressive fighting for the right is the noblest sport the world affords."

Theodore Roosevelt, "Municipal Administration: The New York Police Force"

Why intervene overseas? How should America go about diplomatic and military intervention? These questions vexed practitioners and students of American foreign policy throughout the 1990s, when the collapse of the Soviet Union removed both the primary threat to the West and a stabilizing influence in the less-developed world. The September 11, 2001, terrorist attacks and the ensuing "global war on terror" injected additional urgency into the debate over intervention. Was America now at war with an irregular armed force and its state sponsors, or was the counterterrorist campaign an exercise in global law enforcement, connoting judicial remedies for international violence? By what right could the nation prosecute such a campaign on the soil of sovereign nations? The effort to settle these matters was not merely of academic interest but also carried consequences of the utmost gravity.

The international community—roughly speaking, sovereign states and the organizations pledged to uphold international peace and security—has found it difficult to forge a consensus on the best way to restore a just order in states saddled with failed or abusive governments. Fueling this indecision is a tension within Article 2(7) of the United Nations Charter, which forbids the organization from intervening "in matters which are essentially within the domestic jurisdiction of any state" while exempting enforcement measures carried out under Chapter VII. The inability of the international community to strike a balance between the competing requirements of Article 2(7) has muddied discussions of international intervention. Article 53, which explicitly prohibits regional action without Security

1

Council authorization, presents an additional obstacle to a consensus.[1] Confusion over these articles has inhibited efforts to curb abuses in countries ranging from Bosnia to Rwanda to Sudan. The need for a set of principles to guide American and international decision making in these areas has become abundantly clear.

Outside intervention to shield populations from ineffective or abusive rulers has a long pedigree on the theoretical plane, if not in execution. History thus may be of help in solving today's quandaries. As early as the seventeenth century, Hugo Grotius, building on earlier work by the just-war theorists, sketched a rationale for humanitarian war. "The last and most far-reaching reason for going to war to help others is the common tie of humanity," wrote the great legal theorist. "There is also the problem whether a war is lawful which is undertaken to protect the subjects of another ruler from oppression by him. . . . But where there is manifest oppression, where a [tyrant] uses his power over his subjects in ways odious to every just man, his people will not be denied the right of all human society." Grotius maintained, furthermore, that the principle of intervention remained valid despite the prospect of outsiders using lofty ideals as a pretext to work mischief in neighboring states.[2] Any principle might be misused, he argued; that was no excuse for apathy or inaction.

For the foreseeable future the question of international intervention will remain, by and large, a question of the uses of American power. Yet discourse about U.S. strategic doctrine has been largely bereft of historical content—a striking shortfall considering the impressive collection of minds that has engaged this subject over the past decade. To provide a fresh perspective on the use of American power in the early twenty-first century, this book investigates the diplomacy of the early twentieth century. Theodore Roosevelt, U.S. president from 1901 to 1909, confronted a security milieu that had many traits in common with that of today: rapid economic integration, governments that were unable or unwilling to discharge their duties toward foreigners and their own citizens, and even a loose equivalent of today's terrorist networks, in the form of an international anarchist movement that felled Roosevelt's predecessor, William McKinley. Who better to consult on the proper uses of American power than Roosevelt? Few practical statesmen have written more extensively or more thoughtfully on foreign policy than "TR," or have bequeathed a well-crafted political philosophy for contemporary use. His meditations on diplomacy and military affairs could furnish a model for American strategic doctrine in the present era. In short, the Roosevelt era bears examining as the United States mulls its role in a world awash in religious and ethnic passions, terrorism, the wholesale failure of states, and exotic weaponry.

In an effort to cope with what might be called "failed states," Roosevelt, an avowed interventionist, fashioned an "international police power." Strikingly, he grafted the police power onto the Monroe Doctrine, that venerable principle of U.S. foreign relations that sought to deter European territorial aggrandizement in the New World. His "Roosevelt Corollary" to the doctrine gave the police power both a preemptive and a defensive hue. "Chronic wrongdoing, or an impotence which results in a general loosening of the ties of civilized society," he proclaimed in his December 1904 message to Congress, "may in America, as elsewhere, ultimately require intervention by some civilized nation, and in the Western Hemisphere the adherence of the United States to the Monroe Doctrine may force the United States, however reluctantly . . . to the exercise of an international police power."[3]

What did Roosevelt's words mean? The president, in essence, proposed a humane, disinterested brand of imperialism to displace the self-aggrandizing European variety that drove great-power colonial competition in the late nineteenth century. A former New York City police commissioner, New York state legislator, and U.S. Civil Service commissioner, TR was accustomed to using state power to preserve order and superintend the public welfare. This study argues that he viewed world affairs using the same frame of reference. He asserted that the United States, as the New World's leading republic, was endowed with a quasi-legal right to step in and arrange the repayment of foreign debts for Latin American governments that were unable or unwilling to do so. He also claimed the right to perform police duties within Latin American republics that had egregiously failed to secure the blessings of liberty that were enjoyed by Americans for their citizens. Theodore Roosevelt's supple doctrine required diplomacy, mediation, finance, law enforcement, and armed force to achieve these aims.

Roosevelt's vision of an international police power does not warrant revival in all its details. Forcible repayment of debts, for instance, has been a dead issue for many decades, in part because of TR's diplomatic exertions. The United States needs no longer fear that great-power competitors will use debt collection as an excuse to seize territory in the Americas. This removes the defensive element that prodded TR to shape a doctrine of international policing in the first place. Still, contemporary statesmen are seemingly groping toward an international police power similar to that devised by TR, even though they have far different goals in mind. A useful model of international constabulary duty would be both effective, warding off charges of impotence that are sometimes directed at the international community, and self-denying, to soothe the misgivings of weaker nations fearful of becoming the targets of a latter-day colonialism.[4] Analyzing Roosevelt's concept of the international police power, then, could help statesmen gain intellectual traction on the dilemmas that have bedeviled them since the Cold War sputtered out.

An added benefit of examining Roosevelt's thinking about international police duty will be to clarify the cavalier references to international policing—e.g., "world policeman," "globocop," and other trendy terms—that litter discourses on international affairs today. The Roosevelt Corollary will provide a convenient framework for assessing international police power. Analyzing the corollary and the intellectual milieu in which it was developed could help shape a concept of international police power that achieves decisive results while avoiding the semblance of renewed imperialism. A benevolent, self-limiting doctrine of intervention could command the widespread support needed to buoy efforts on behalf of world order.

The Need for Historical Perspective

The outpouring of literature on intervention since the Cold War contains scant discussion of historical precedent, much less of an international constabulary function along Rooseveltian lines. Nor have the older studies been of much help with TR's police-power concept, despite the existence of an impressive body of work on his diplomacy, including works by Howard K. Beale, Frederick W. Marks III, and Richard H. Collin.[5] Indeed, some eminent scholars have denied that Roosevelt had any lasting impact on American foreign relations. In his *Diplomacy*, for instance, Henry Kissinger specifically denied that TR, despite his enduring personal popularity, had exerted much influence on succeeding generations of policymakers. "Roosevelt lived either a century too late or a century too early," declared Kissinger. "His approach to international affairs died with him in 1919; no significant school of American thought on foreign policy has invoked him since." He attributed this puzzling phenomenon to Roosevelt's defeat in the debate with Woodrow Wilson over U.S. intervention in the First World War.[6]

Whatever the reason, no one has examined Roosevelt's vision of an international police power in any depth or, still less, sought to hammer it into an implement of contemporary statecraft. Most accounts content themselves with quoting the corollary, as though the meaning of "international police power" were self-evident. It is not. One plausible explanation for the dearth of analysis is the disrepute into which American imperialism has fallen.[7] Discussing America's imperial episode dispassionately is nigh on impossible.

Another factor that could help explain TR's virtual absence from discussions of contemporary diplomacy is the gulf between the disciplines of diplomatic history and political science. Some steps have been taken to remedy this defect. The first printed mention of a possible link between the Roosevelt era and present-day foreign-policy debates came in a 1991 working paper titled *Defining a New World Order: Toward a Practical Vision of Collective Action for International Peace and Security*, by Alan K. Henrikson, a professor of diplomatic history at the Fletcher School of Law and Diplomacy.[8] This study builds on the intellectual groundwork laid by previous scholars. It strives to fill a gap in the literature on Rooseveltian diplomacy and, in the process, to illuminate some of the dilemmas besetting statesmen today.

TR left behind a wealth of evidence to aid in this enterprise. The libraries at Harvard University house the nation's largest collection of Roosevelt's letters and personal papers, serving in effect as the TR presidential library. Another sizable cache of material resides in the Theodore Roosevelt Papers at the Library of Congress in Washington, D.C. The most complete edition of TR's letters is an eight-volume set titled *The Letters of Theodore Roosevelt*.[9] Finally, there are two wide-ranging collections of TR's state papers, books, and letters: a mammoth twenty-volume set christened *National Edition: Works of Theodore Roosevelt* and a twenty-four-volume set titled *Memorial Edition: Works of Theodore Roosevelt*.[10] Other useful sources include the redoubtable *Foreign Relations of the United States* (*FRUS*) series, which contains TR's annual messages to Congress and the diplomatic correspondence surrounding all of the cases under study here.[11] Providing support for— and, in some cases, useful counterpoints to—TR's own writings are the writings of figures such as Elihu Root, William Howard Taft, and Leonard Wood, as well as anti-imperialists such as William Jennings Bryan and Carl Schurz.[12]

Layout of the Study

This book starts by examining Theodore Roosevelt's personal convictions and political philosophy, then proceeds outward into the realm of public affairs, examining first domestic and then international politics. Chapter 2 assesses the biographical origins of TR's views about the responsible use of power. Among the key themes derived from this selective biography are Roosevelt's convictions that collective action alone could solve the worst problems facing American society, that government was the proper agent to maintain social equilibrium, and that the middle path in politics was preferable to both utopianism and the amoral pursuit of parochial interests. Chapter 3 examines the police-power concept in American domestic law and shows that, in TR's day, conflicts of police power were increasingly being decided in favor of the federal government. Chapter 4 considers Roosevelt's advocacy of good government, a cause that he championed not only during his service at the U.S. Civil Service Commission and the New York Police Department but also during his conduct of international constabulary missions. Chapter 5 rounds out the discussion of TR's beliefs about domestic politics and law by assessing his handling of capital-labor disputes—the principal threat to the American political system during his public career.

The study next turns its gaze overseas, scrutinizing Roosevelt's approach to diplomatic and military affairs. It identifies the elements of the Roosevelt Corollary, defines the relationship between the Monroe Doctrine and the international police power, and suggests when and how TR believed the police power could lawfully be deployed. It addresses the following questions:

- What constituted "chronic wrongdoing" and "impotence" by a state targeted for intervention? What was a "general loosening of the ties of civilized society"?

- Was the international police power a uniquely American prerogative, or could other nations use it to justify intervention? Could civilized nations intervene with impunity in the affairs of those states deemed barbarous?

- What was the international police power? Was it a legal construct or simply a policy statement? Was it merely an adjunct to the Monroe Doctrine?

- Did the Monroe Doctrine, as modified by the Roosevelt Corollary, bar U.S. intervention outside the Western Hemisphere? Conversely, was the doctrine an absolute injunction against great-power intervention in the Americas?

The process of answering these questions will yield a doctrine of intervention that faithfully reflects Theodore Roosevelt's police-power theory while incorporating data from actual constabulary operations.

Chapters 6 through 9 make up an analysis of Rooseveltian foreign policy. Chapter 6 reviews the theories that molded TR's view of foreign policy. Of particular interest are Alfred Thayer Mahan's maritime theories and TR's own analysis of the symbiosis among justice, peace, and forceful diplomacy. Chapter 7 examines the shortcomings of the international legal order, notably the lack of a sanction of force to bolster international law, and distills principles undergirding the international police power. Chapter 8 weighs several constabulary missions from the Roosevelt presidency and examines how Roosevelt's thinking about an international police power matured. The cases include (a) the extension of the domestic police power to the Philippine Islands during the Philippine War and postwar U.S. military and civil administration; (b) the extension of the police power, under the Platt and Teller amendments, to Cuba in the wake of war with Spain; (c) the U.S. naval response to a European blockade of Venezuela in 1902–3; (d) the U.S. intervention in the Panamanian revolution of 1903 and the legal framework erected to govern the Canal Zone; and (e) the American administration of Dominican finances following the 1904–5 crisis, undertaken pursuant to the Roosevelt Corollary. To help determine Roosevelt's views about policing beyond the confines of the New World, the study examines his discussion of a European exercise of the police power during the Algeciras Conference. Together the cases provide a comprehensive picture of how TR used the international police power in the Western Hemisphere and show that he contemplated a broader exercise of the police power by the advanced nations. Finally, chapter 9 examines the military strategies used for international constabulary missions, focusing in particular on the U.S. Army's experience in the Philippine War and the development of the "small-wars" doctrine by the U.S. Marines in the interwar period.

Theodore Roosevelt's international police-power concept was more ambitious than what has been proposed by even the most enthusiastic present-day proponents of international intervention. He maintained in effect that a power of legislation and regulation was vested in the international community, just as this power was vested in the federal government within the American system. He invoked the police power sparingly and implemented constabulary actions judiciously.

Was Roosevelt credible? Did his deeds match his soaring rhetoric? TR explicitly welcomed the scrutiny of historians in his final message to Congress (December 1908), when he proclaimed that American foreign relations under his presidency had been based on "the theory that right must be done between nations precisely as between individuals." He maintained that "in our actions for the last ten years we have in this matter proven our faith by our deeds."[13] Strong words; if they are borne out by the historical record, Theodore Roosevelt will have handed contemporary statesmen a remarkably useful analytical tool.

2

PHILOSOPHY

"Peace is a goddess only when she comes with sword girt on thigh."

Theodore Roosevelt, *American Ideals*

Theodore Roosevelt was an unabashed interventionist—both by temperament and by philosophy. From manifold sources TR derived a set of precepts that guided his approach to private and public life. During his career he exhorted America to live its national life according to his vision of honor, justice, and righteous strife. For him, power was a tool to be deployed for the common good. Since his vision arose from the nineteenth century's distinctive cultural milieu, it bears reviewing for modern readers. From his principles and experiences, Roosevelt fashioned a vision of government-as-constable, with the police power as the enabling doctrine for a kind of constabulary function.

For Roosevelt the constabulary function seemed to be founded on three elements: (1) preserving public order, in the usual sense associated with police forces; (2) mediating among competing actors in society, especially where this competition threatened American institutions; and (3) nurturing social reform through legislation and regulation. This chapter pulls together material from a variety of sources, including law, economics, and political philosophy, in an attempt to identify the sources of Roosevelt's thinking about the police power. As will be seen in subsequent chapters, TR's notion of the police power also shaped his handling of international diplomacy and warfare. The statesman was vague about the exact intellectual process by which he internationalized the police power. Judging by his reading of American history and his theorizing about the American frontier, he viewed the post-1898 growth of the U.S. world role as simply the latest phase in a natural process of expansion that reached back at least to the days of the Louisiana Purchase, if not beyond, to the westward spread of Anglo-Saxon culture and traditions across the Atlantic.[1] Extending U.S.

authority beyond the confines of U.S. territory probably seemed natural to him. Roosevelt envisioned a great-power exercise of an international police power within geographically circumscribed "jurisdictions." Over the long term, once international society matured sufficiently, he held out the possibility of a broader, multinational exercise of the police power.

Communal Action in Pursuit of Moral Ends

The police-power doctrine dovetailed with the Progressive instincts of reformers like Roosevelt. Roosevelt's sturdy moral sense at times drained his politics of subtlety and guile, but it also clarified his political convictions and provided solid moorings amid the tumult of turn-of-the-century life. Roosevelt attributed his obsession with virtue to his Victorian upbringing. In particular, his adoration for his father, "the best man I ever knew," bred in Roosevelt a powerful sense of right and wrong on which his approach to private and public life stood. Theodore Roosevelt Sr., a moderately wealthy New York businessman and philanthropist, had "combined strength and courage with gentleness, tenderness, and great unselfishness. He would not tolerate in us children selfishness or cruelty, idleness, cowardice, or untruthfulness."[2]

The elder Roosevelt's rigorous moral instruction intensified his son's innate dislike of injustice. "Brutality by a man to a woman, by a grown person to a little child, by anything strong toward anything good and helpless, makes my blood literally boil," he wrote on one occasion.[3] From his upbringing emerged a stern code of personal conduct predicated on honor, honesty, and strenuous exertion.[4] A fighting spirit was essential to any worthwhile endeavor. Righteous strife—meaning hard work in peacetime, martial valor in wartime—was necessary to realize moral ends. Roosevelt credited his father, who helped him to overcome severe physical infirmities, with preparing him to be "both decent and manly" and to take up "the rough work of the world."[5] That work involved using power to counterbalance powerful agents that were able to oppress workers, in the case of the great corporations, or to instigate violent unrest, in the case of the labor unions.

Roosevelt's voracious reading of history reinforced the moral regimen his father imparted.[6] A sickly boy, TR drew sustenance from the deeds of great men. He recalled, "I was nervous and timid. Yet from reading of the people I admired—ranging from the soldiers of Valley Forge, and Morgan's riflemen, to the heroes of my favorite stories—and from hearing of the feats of my Southern forefathers and kinsfolk, and from knowing my father, I felt a great admiration for men who were fearless and who could hold their own in the world, and I had a great desire to be like them."[7] Enjoined by Theodore Sr. to "make" his feeble body by physical labor, Roosevelt fell back on the heroism of ages past. In public life he conjured up great Americans such as Washington, Lincoln, and Grant to inspire and to help defend his policies.

Fiction was another source of inspiration for TR, who favored literature that reinforced the lessons in moral virtue conveyed by his father and other sources of wisdom. Roosevelt thought his favorite poem, Henry Wadsworth Longfellow's epic *Saga of King Olaf,* was an example of meritorious verse. He counseled Martha Baker Dunn, a literary critic for the *Atlantic Monthly* and a partisan of Browning, "Just one word about Longfellow, however. Don't look down on him because he is so utterly different from Browning; so different that he might belong to another world. For all his gentleness he strikes the true ring of courage, the balladlike ring of courage." He maintained, more to the point, that "if a boy or girl likes [the *Saga*] well enough to learn most of it by heart and feel the spirit of it, just as they ought to like Julia Ward Howe's battle hymn, they will always have in them something to which an appeal for brave action can be made."[8] For Roosevelt great literature bestowed on the reader not only pleasure but also beneficent moral effects.

In the *Saga,* Longfellow recounted a tale, replete with Nordic themes of honor and valor, in which barbarism had been quenched, and civilization extended, at the point of a sword.[9] Insists Thor, the Norse god of thunder, in a plaintive show of bravado:

> *Force rules the world still*
> *Has ruled it, shall rule it;*
> *Meekness is weakness,*
> *Strength is triumphant,*
> *Over the whole earth*
> *Still is it Thors-Day!*

King Olaf, a recent convert to Christianity, vows to wean his own vassals from the old faith, by force if necessary:

> *All the old gods are dead,*
> *All the wild warlocks fled;*
> *But the White Christ lives and reigns,*
> *And throughout my wide domains*
> *His Gospel shall be spread!*

And beyond. Mustering a company of champions, Olaf campaigns throughout the Salten Fjord region of Norway, vanquishing heathen deities and imposing the Christian faith.

> *In their temples Thor and Odin*
> *Lay in dust and ashes trodden,*
> *As King Olaf, onward sweeping,*
> *Preached the Gospel with his sword.*[10]

Longfellow considered force a civilizing agent. Roosevelt heartily agreed.

TR praised an unlikely source, his Southern heritage, for shaping his views on diplomacy.[11] "I have always felt that my southern ancestry was responsible for much of my attitude in foreign politics," he confided in 1903. "I do not intend to do injustice to anyone; but I do not intend to be withheld from doing justice to all, including our own people, by either technicality or sentimentality."[12] Antebellum Southerners took a romantic view of the Middle Ages. The Southern strain of chivalry, observed Eugene Genovese in *Sewanee Review*, spurred gentlemen to cultivate a "spirit of honor" that would temper their love of arms and channel their romantic urge to adventure in a more beneficial direction. Protection of women and the weak was a central theme in Southern literature.[13]

For Southern aristocrats, the health of American civilization flowed from the chivalric ideal, not the amoral—as they viewed it—pursuit of wealth.[14] One prominent Virginian, Thomas Roderick Dew, reminded Southern men that knighthood had been created "to arrest the downward progress of civilization; that all true knights must be honorable, courteous, liberal, clement, loyal, devoted to woman, to arms, to religion."[15] Chief among the chivalric virtues were piety, morality, gallantry, and honor.

Ferocity toward enemies was expected; so was gentleness toward those in distress. The Southern code of honor ran counter to the mercantile ethos championed by Northerners. Aspirants to knightly virtue derided the commercial and industrial spirit, which, they claimed, "destroys the ideal and reduces everything to a utilitarian standard." For them the industrial North embodied sterile materialism. Southerners also ridiculed Northern skepticism. Southern gentlemen condemned the "mocking spirit which derides alike religion and honor—and is thoroughly mercenary, sensual, and devilish." [16] Yankeeism, in sum, worked against chivalry. Similar themes reverberate throughout Theodore Roosevelt's political philosophy. TR's love of bold enterprise, distaste for untrammeled individualism, insistence on caring for the weak, and belief that American civilization turned upon individual acts of gallantry surge from his writings. The upshot: private virtue had public ramifications for a nation undergoing wrenching change.

From power flowed a responsibility to maintain order and tend to the public welfare. The scion of a patrician New York family, Theodore Roosevelt imbibed the concept of noblesse oblige, which emphasized the benevolent use of privilege. Wealth and power conferred social responsibility. Theodore Roosevelt Sr., who confessed to a "troublesome conscience," had devoted the bulk of his time outside of business hours to charitable concerns, helping found the Children's Aid Society and the State Charities Aid Association.[17] He frequently enlisted the help of his children in his philanthropic endeavors, acquainting them with the grim realities that accompanied America's waxing economic might.

Roosevelt thus was exposed at a tender age to the hardships that afflicted the urban poor during the Industrial Revolution. He recalled assisting Theodore Sr. at the Newsboys' Lodging-Houses, in the night schools, and in programs designed to resettle orphans from the harsh streets of New York to the homes of families in the West.[18] Close contact with the dispossessed solidified his conviction that the well-off must exert themselves on behalf of the destitute. Noblesse oblige was the medium through which personal morality was transposed to the realm of public affairs. Roosevelt candidly admitted that he lacked the aptitude for his father's hands-on style of philanthropy.[19] Even so, social uplift pervaded his philosophy.

Individual efforts to better American society were all very well, maintained Progressive Americans, but individuals could not stand against the new forces that threatened to dominate society. The U.S. educational system was partly at fault. TR bemoaned the dearth of instruction on communal virtue and responsibility in his own primary and secondary school education and at Harvard College. While American citizens exhibited laudable civic virtue, Roosevelt nonetheless maintained that the educational establishment had acquiesced in "a riot of lawless business individualism which would be quite as destructive to real civilization as the lawless military individualism of the Dark Ages."[20] He denounced the laissez faire doctrine, which formed the orthodoxy for political economists of the day.

For TR, the term "laissez faire" conveyed the impression that self-interest was everything. American society overlooked the danger excessive individualism, particularly among the great captains of industry, posed to democracy. To combat this indifference to the common good—this betrayal of noblesse oblige—Roosevelt preached the ethics of collective responsibility and collective action. Collective action, he believed, could redress some of the shortcomings of American society.

To Theodore Roosevelt it was self-evident that "what is true of the individual is also true of the nation."[21] The virtue of individual citizens channeled political endeavors in the morally correct direction; a collective ethos focused those endeavors on affairs of state. Fighting for the public interest, then, was the core of TR's philosophy. Elevated ideals would not only better social conditions but equip the nation on a cosmic level to withstand the lure of materialism. The temptation to materialism was especially pronounced in prosperous times. Roosevelt proffered the frivolous life enjoyed by the Four Hundred in Newport, Rhode Island, as proof that wealth and ease lent themselves to sloth and "degeneration in character."[22] He deplored the industrialists' habit of subordinating public affairs to business. During the run-up to war with Spain, he wrote to Robert Bacon that "you can scarcely imagine the bitter indignation which one grows to feel at a time like this when all the people of means, all the people to whom one had been accustomed to look up to as the leaders, or should-be leaders, in civic matters, seem to show a callous indifference to the honor of the country."[23]

Although he regarded himself as a strong party man, Roosevelt clearly did not share the Republicans' habitual fealty to wealthy interests. Instead he insisted that fearless, self-denying men should dedicate themselves to realizing grand ideals in the face of soulless materialism. And he matched words with deeds to an uncommon degree. Roosevelt claimed to have little heed for his future in politics. Personal repercussions were secondary when the public interest was at stake. He maintained that he expected every political appointment to be his last, largely because he was willing to stand on principle. While running for reelection in 1904, he declared, "I should like to be elected President. . . . But I shall not do anything whatever to secure my nomination or election save to try to carry on the public business in such shape that decent citizens will believe I have shown wisdom, integrity and courage."[24]

TR was open to horse trading with political foes and mindful of the Republican Party's political fortunes. He was also prepared to confront machine politicians and powerful political interests. His uncompromising stances on the patronage system, graft in the New York Police Department, and the regulation of corporations and trusts stand out. Of his tenure as police commissioner, for example, Roosevelt wrote that "we shall win, in spite of the open opposition of the forces of evil, in spite of the timid surrender of the weakly good, if only we stand squarely and fairly. . . . But if we were to face defeat instead of victory, that would not alter our convictions, and would not cause us to flinch one hand's breadth from the course we have been pursuing. There are prices too dear to be paid even for victory."[25]

Finally, Roosevelt was a fervent nationalist who maintained that "love of country is one of the elemental virtues."[26] He considered outspoken Americanism the conceptual bridge between private virtue and the realm of public affairs. This had manifold implications. First, the United States should conduct its affairs according to individual standards of virtue rather than *raison d'état*. "Alike for the nation and the individual," he declared in *Outlook*, "the one indispensable requisite is character—character that does and dares as well as endures, character that is active in the performance of virtue no less than firm in the refusal to do aught that is vicious or degraded."[27]

Second, TR's muscular brand of Americanism favored individual merit over outward attributes such as political affiliation, social status, race, and creed. "Americanism is a question of spirit, conviction, and purpose," he wrote, "not of creed or birthplace."[28] Nurturing the merit principle and "fellow-feeling" among Americans of all classes, races, and creeds would help the United States surmount the frictions and inequities intrinsic to a multiethnic republic. "[T]he only true solution to our political and social problems lies in cultivating everywhere the spirit of brotherhood, of fellow-feeling and understanding between man and man, and the willingness to treat a man as a man, which are the essential factors in American democracy," he wrote in 1900.[29] In an early iteration of his "Square Deal" philosophy, he vowed that all parties to the great disputes of the day would receive "exact justice" from his administration without regard to superficial characteristics such as class or creed.[30]

Third, Americanism implied a willingness to reform the Founders' framework while preserving its essence. Scoundrels—in his telling, Roosevelt's political antagonists were mentally or morally defective—often lay claim to the mantle of patriotism, but "the man who can do most in this country is and must be the man whose Americanism is most sincere and intense." "The stoutest and truest Americans," he said, "are the very men who have the least sympathy with the people who invoke the spirit of Americanism to aid what is vicious in our government or to throw obstacles in the way of those who strive to reform it." Roosevelt shrouded his appeals for reform in patriotism, entreating his countrymen "to work to find out all we can about the existence and extent of every evil," to "acknowledge it to be such," and then to "attack it" with resolve derived from "an intense and fervid Americanism."[31]

Above all, a great nation, like a man of great soul, should pursue the "strenuous life." Theodore Roosevelt insisted that the United States had been entrusted with a grand mission overseas, whether in the Philippines, Cuba, or other far-flung regions. "Normally the individual rises to greatness only through labor and strife," he wrote in 1899. He asserted with a Darwinian flourish that "this is invariably the case with the species. In the great majority of cases it is also true of the nation."[32] For Roosevelt life was a battle to be waged with vigor and courage, even if the struggle ended in the nation's defeat and downfall. Even the greatest civilization must finally wither and die. Its citizens must nonetheless live bravely and joyously to make their imprint on human history. Rome, he pointed out, had left behind a patrimony that continued to shape Western societies; England's achievements ranked alongside those of the Romans.

Thus the nation must strive toward the right.[33] Responsibilities to other nations accompanied America's prowess in manufacturing and other material endeavors. "Our nation is that one among all the nations of the earth which holds in its hands the fate of the coming years," he prophesied in 1894.[34] Only grand endeavors could offset the deadening effect of material self-interest. At home, government must maintain order, check wrongdoing by powerful new actors in American society, and use its powers of legislation and regulation to improve the lives of the working class. Abroad, the United States must preserve order in its geographic neighborhood, offset any attempts at great-power encroachment in the New World, and work to spread civilization. The police-power doctrine gave the state the legal implements it needed to promote these ends.

The Elusive "Golden Mean"

His avowed idealism notwithstanding, Theodore Roosevelt had no illusions about creating heaven on earth. Idealism divorced from practical concerns, Roosevelt insisted, had led directly to the fanaticism and extreme political programs that disfigured American politics at the turn of the century. The usual suspects, socialists and pacifists, were bad enough, but some of his natural allies in the good-government movement were among the worst offenders. "[T]he greatest help I got [as New York governor] was from genuine reformers, [but when] you came to the lunatic type, they did a great deal more harm than good."[35] For TR, then, virtue meant striking an Aristotelian balance between extremes. His preference for the middle ground found its way into his concept of the police power, by which the state mediated among competing interests and championed the public interest. TR's visceral dislike of extremes grew as much out of his education as out of his temperament. He admired conservative political philosophers such as Aristotle and Edmund Burke, as well as prudent statesmen such as Washington and Lincoln.[36] Alluding to Aristotle, TR once confessed to "an almost Greek horror of extremes." His reflexes, like those of the "wonderful old Greeks," pointed TR onto the middle path.[37]

TR's distaste for political extremism molded his outlook on public affairs in several respects. First and foremost, as noted above, he was an acolyte of Edmund Burke's brand of prudence, which itself represented an adaptation of Aristotle's concept to eighteenth-century English politics. Burke called the middle ground between runaway idealism and shallow pragmatism the "golden mean." The prudent statesman strove to advance grand ideals while acknowledging the boundaries imposed by political reality. Burke christened prudence "the God of this lower world" and insisted that it had claim to "entire dominion over every exercise of power."[38]

Prudent statecraft in a republic made possible a large degree of civil liberty, commensurate with law and order. The degree of liberty varied from nation to nation, depending on reigning history, traditions, and culture. Burke chastised Parliament for acting imprudently toward Great Britain's American colonies, indulging in heavy-handed actions that had antagonized the colonists and triggered a revolution. For Burke there was no obvious way to set boundaries on civil liberty. Only by experimenting cautiously with a nation's institutions could political leaders determine "with how little, not how much of this restraint, the community can subsist. For liberty is a good to be improved, and not an evil to be lessened."[39]

Burke's dual emphasis on civil liberty and judicious experimentation, not to mention his aversion to political programs unmoored from pragmatism, sat well with Theodore Roosevelt. From his meditations on philosophy and history TR derived his own distinctive notion of practical wisdom. Ideal solutions, he observed, were chimerical in a republic that relied on transitory political coalitions.[40] The prudent statesman had a duty to find the golden mean merging the ideal with the practical. Upon leaving the New York governor's mansion in 1900, TR trumpeted his policies, including the first-ever legislation regulating corporations, as "practical and yet decent."[41] Impractical idealists and pragmatists without noble ideals were alike dangerous to the cause of prudent reform. Conversely, "wise radicalism and wise conservatism go hand in hand, one bent on progress, the other bent on seeing that no change is made unless in the right direction."[42]

While no compromise could be reached on matters of principle, in practice there was wide latitude for political give-and-take. The best, TR admonished readers of the *Churchman*, was often the enemy of the good. He elaborated on this pithy formula: "Every leader of a great reform has to contend, on the one hand, with the open, avowed enemies of the reform, and, on the other, with its extreme advocates, who wish the impossible, and who join hands with their extreme opponents to defeat the rational friend of the reform."[43] Doctrinaire advocacy of any political program invited reaction that would likely bring that program to grief. Forging coalitions for reform, across party lines when necessary, was TR's strategy for overcoming the resistance of Right and Left to his proposals.[44]

Political philosophers such as Burke, who had learned his craft amid the rough-and-tumble of parliamentary debate, endeared themselves to TR, who modeled his approach to political warfare on practical statesmen such as Abraham Lincoln, "my hero" and "the kind of chief who can do most good in a democratic republic such as ours."[45] TR declared himself a "radical democrat" in Lincoln's mold, professing his affection for the "plain people"; yet he also shared Lincoln's impatience with the tyranny of mobs, corporations, and individuals.[46] The "great railsplitter" had managed to achieve great ends by shunning extreme abolitionists. (Exasperated at Lincoln's moderate course, doctrinaire abolitionists had nominated a third ticket in 1864 and, according to Roosevelt, provided aid and comfort to the foes of liberty and the Union.[47]) Lincoln's more sober approach had enabled him to rally the public behind a crusade against slavery and the dissolution of the Union.[48]

Roosevelt merrily battled plutocrats, militant socialists, mugwumps, and pacifists, to name a few of his opponents. His electioneering attests to his iconoclastic approach to politics. In 1896, and again in 1900, he reproached William Jennings Bryan, the Democratic contender for president, for premising his campaign on envy of the moneyed classes.[49] TR conceded, however, that Bryan had accurately diagnosed some of the inequities convulsing American society. This gave Bryan's populist platform traction with ordinary citizens. Roosevelt maintained that "these representatives of enormous corporate wealth have themselves been responsible for a portion of the conditions against which Bryanism is in ignorant, and sometimes wicked, revolt." He believed that willfully ignoring nettlesome realities would consign

Republicans to defeat and irrelevance. It was neither wise nor safe, consequently, "for us as a party to take refuge in mere negation and to say that there are no evils to be corrected."[50]

TR strove with varied success to cajole the Republican Party into searching out and assailing these social evils. He distanced himself from the wealthy interests that formed an influential constituency within the party, reasoning that this would bolster the party's appeal with rank-and-file Americans. Predictably, this move did not sit well with the party establishment. In 1900 TR accused New York corporate interests of conspiring to push his nomination for vice president, thereby removing their nemesis from the governor's mansion in Albany. And in the 1904 campaign, said Roosevelt, he had been compelled to beat back an insurrection of the "criminal rich" led by conservative Ohio senator Mark Hanna.[51] Wealthy businessmen, including the railroad magnates, had hoped to unseat TR because he had vehemently advocated regulating corporations and trusts.

Roosevelt worked with unlikely partners during his tenure in Albany. Notwithstanding his dislike of machine politics, he cultivated cordial relations with Senator Thomas Collier Platt, New York's Republican boss. He appeased Platt wherever possible, cooperated with the machine on matters of mutual interest, and refrained from building up a machine of his own that might provoke a backlash from the senator.[52] He parted company with Platt, however, over the Ford Bill, the state government's first effort to regulate corporations. TR implored Republicans not to deny the existence of social ills merely because such maladies provided grist for socialist and populist programs. When the machine proved deaf to his entreaties, he patched together a bipartisan coalition and passed the bill anyway.[53]

Governor Roosevelt also crusaded to remove Lou Payn, an influential but corrupt Republican operative who enjoyed the backing of the machine. TR proclaimed that he had overcome the Republican establishment's stiff resistance by brandishing the Big Stick. "I have always been fond of the West African proverb: 'Speak softly and carry a big stick; you will go far.'" The African maxim, explained Roosevelt, involved being absolutely inflexible on matters of principle while remaining flexible in less critical areas—all leavened with the utmost in tact and good humor.[54]

TR had philosophical reasons for his forceful but temperate perspective on public affairs. Like his conservative forebears, he contended that republican self-government—indeed, civilization itself—depended on taming the passions of the citizenry. Self-restraint would inoculate Americans against demagoguery and mob rule, forces he believed to be as malignant as the depredations of the criminal rich.[55] If, however, Americans could not curb their passions, government would be forced to do it for them. Ordered liberty would shrink as state power grew. Quoting Burke, Roosevelt averred, "Men are qualified for civil liberty in exact proportion to their disposition to put moral chains upon their own appetites; in proportion as they are disposed to listen to the counsels of the wise and good in preference to the flattery of knaves. Society can not exist unless a controlling power upon will and appetite be placed somewhere, and the less of it be within the more there must be without. It is ordained in the eternal constitution of things that men of intemperate minds can not be free. Their passions forge their fetters."[56]

Thus civic virtue was the foundation of a vibrant republic. Conversely, ordinary Americans' inability to tame their passions and withstand demagoguery could subvert the American experiment.

Government as a Tool for Social Equilibrium

Judicious, preemptive state intervention could counter the excessive influence of the labor movement and the great corporations and thus damp the impulse to mob rule and despotism. The lodestars of statecraft, intoned Theodore Roosevelt, were "disinterested sentiment" and "intelligent self-interest."[57] As his public career unfolded, both of these imperatives transfigured his reforming impulse, itself an outgrowth of noblesse oblige, into full-blown Progressivism. Like other luminaries in the Progressive movement, Roosevelt mingled politics and morality freely. As mentioned previously, his understanding of the relationship between private and pubic virtue held that only communal effort could correct the inequities produced by industrialization. How so? First, he believed that government was, by and large, a neutral and wholesome actor capable of advancing moral ends through the legislative and regulatory functions—that is, its police power. If this was possible at the state and local level, well and good; but federal intervention was necessary in certain matters, especially those relating to interstate commerce. Second, he seemed to assume that state and society were coterminous and that, consequently, government should be the primary agent for social action.[58] Roosevelt's vision of a disinterested state's role in bettering social conditions included checking egregious abuses by corporations and, to a lesser extent, unions; enacting programs designed for social uplift; and upholding public order in the face of labor unrest. Only a stable framework that restrained the influential new actors in society could blunt the hardships suffered by workers and thereby nourish ordered liberty in an America that differed radically from the agrarian republic crafted by the Founders.

With respect to "intelligent self-interest," and in keeping with his conservative outlook, Roosevelt's aims were largely defensive. Preserving the institutions bequeathed by the Founding Fathers was his prime object. In 1906 Roosevelt confided to William Howard Taft, "I do not at all like the social conditions at present. The dull, purblind folly of the very rich men; their greed and arrogance, and the way in which they have unduly prospered by the help of the ablest lawyers, and too often through the weakness or shortsightedness of the judges or by their unfortunate possession of meticulous minds; these facts, and the corruption in business and politics, have tended to produce a very unhealthy condition of excitement and irritation in the popular mind, which shows itself in part in the enormous increase in the socialistic propaganda."[59] This flood of propaganda, he predicted, would spawn a political campaign resembling the Free Silver movement of the late 1800s. Attenuating the appeal of socialism was a central objective of his Progressive-minded proposals. Not some impulse to remake society but his predilection toward social equilibrium thrust Theodore Roosevelt into the forefront of the Progressive movement.

The organized interests' burgeoning might, as well as TR's genuine humanitarian concerns over the social problems those interests exacerbated, propelled his sometimes-strident advocacy of government interventionism. Calculations of power underlay the Progressive movement. Progressive intellectuals, including TR and Herbert Croly, feared the industrial barons' virtual life-and-death power over laborers and their families.[60] In the aftermath of the 1894 Pullman strike and other traumas, the Progressives wanted to deploy a countervailing force to ward off similar dangers.[61] Roosevelt brushed aside concerns about the expansion of state power. He claimed to be "a Jeffersonian in my genuine faith in democracy and popular government," but "a Hamiltonian in my governmental views, especially with reference to the need of the exercise of broad powers by the National Government."[62]

Ordered liberty, the Founders' chief objective, now hinged on adjusting their bequest. Only a more muscular government, affirmed TR, could counterbalance the corporations and trusts in an industrial age. Rather than endorsing the approach taken by William Jennings Bryan, who called for restoring competition among numerous small enterprises—a utopian vision in TR's mind—Roosevelt embraced what historian Richard Hofstadter termed "counterorganization."[63] Counterorganization involved augmenting state power to offset that of business and to defend powerless workers. TR shared the common

assumption, accentuated by his Social Darwinist leanings, that organizations evolved toward larger, more complex, and more efficient
forms. He at once accepted business consolidation as a fact of life and
insisted that combinations could be accommodated within the framework of capitalism. He maintained, for instance, that there were good
and bad trusts; it was the job of government to distinguish good from
bad and to discipline the bad trusts. Even symbolic opposition to the
trusts, believed TR and like-minded Progressives, would help mollify
workers angry at the plutocrats' excesses.

To sustain his brief for counterorganization, Roosevelt pointed
out that business firms were creatures of the American legal order.
Their legal personality subjected corporations to government supervision, just as the behavior of ordinary citizens could be restricted by
law and regulation. Yet the obligations of business were even heavier
than those of individual Americans. TR likened the great corporations
to public entities—and corporate executives to public officials—because of their capacity to dominate the lives of Americans, particularly unskilled laborers. He voiced bafflement at the industrial magnates' stubborn resistance to government regulation, pointing out that
corporations relied on a stable legal framework to secure them against
social tumult. The Pullman strike, he declared, should remind the
magnates how precarious their position really was.[64] Nationalization,
meaning the dispossession of the rich, lurked within socialist appeals.
Roosevelt consequently assured the powerful that he had both their
interests and those of the poor at heart.

Government, it followed, needed the authority to check flagrant
wrongdoing by business, to help the weakest members of society, and
thus to sustain a modicum of social amity. TR advocated for the benevolent use of power. As governor of New York, for instance, he chafed
at the work conditions of New York City sweatshops. He pled with
the state labor committee chairman for the authority to appoint fac-
tory inspectors. "We have it in our power," wrote TR, "to partially
abate the misery and wrongdoing of a peculiarly flagrant kind which
bears with peculiar heaviness upon the most helpless class of our population and which results in danger to all classes."[65] This plea succinctly
conveyed the distinct mixture of humanitarianism and self-preservation undergirding conservative Progressivism. Applied to capital-labor relations, Roosevelt's vision of collective action entailed executive, legislative, and even judicial oversight of private actors.

Despite his professed distaste for legalism, Roosevelt justified
the unprecedented extension of state power over business in part with

a legalistic sleight of hand.[66] A self-professed "broad constructionist in constitutional matters," TR was known on occasion to blithely wave away even the exact text of the U.S. Constitution, which fettered state action in matters TR believed to be of overriding importance. He told his friend Leonard Wood, "I am no believer in technicalities" where the public interest was in jeopardy.[67] Under this novel (for the day) school of jurisprudence, the U.S. Constitution could be reinterpreted in light of new social conditions. Only by injecting new meaning into outdated language, reasoned broad constructionists, could the principles underlying the Constitution be preserved. In essence the Progressives argued from the doctrine of the lesser evil. Lawmakers could enact moderate change now or risk a revolution that could utterly shatter the American system—certainly an unpalatable outcome. Roosevelt urged Congress to construe the commerce clause, which empowered the national legislature to regulate commerce crossing state borders, as broadly as possible, justifying federal oversight over the railroads and other concerns. His constitutional theorizing was of a piece with his chivalric refusal "to be withheld from doing justice to all . . . by either technicality or sentimentality."[68] In the debate that marked turn-of-the-century jurisprudence, then, TR sided with those who wanted to expand the federal role in state and municipal affairs.

Impatient at the inefficiencies the Founding Fathers had deliberately built into the American system, Roosevelt maintained that judicial action was an instrument for Progressive reform. The "chief lawmakers of our country," he declared, "may be, and often are, the judges, because they are the final seat of authority." Every time judges interpreted some question of law or liberty, they gave "direction to all lawmaking." Court decisions on economic and social questions depended on judges' prevailing "economic and social philosophy; and for the peaceful progress of our people during the twentieth century we shall owe most to those judges who hold to a twentieth century economic and social philosophy and not to a long outgrown philosophy, which was itself the product of primitive economic conditions." Jurists possessed of a "progressive social philosophy" would be an engine for reforming a Republic whose outworn political institutions had not kept pace with socioeconomic change.[69]

Unlike the Founding generation, then, TR believed in a government less of laws than of men. "To a practical student of government like yourself," he told one colleague, "I do not have to say that the question of who is to administer the laws is always more important than the question of exactly what the law shall be."[70] The letter of the law must not impede the honorable course of action. Enlightened statesmen, steeped in noblesse oblige and the latest in social science, could be relied upon to make correct decisions.

As president, Roosevelt interpreted his constitutional prerogatives expansively. His departure from the tradition of executive restraint turned on his reading of Article II of the Constitution, which laid out the duties and responsibilities of the chief executive. Article II, Section 1 vested the "executive Power" in the presidency and outlined procedures for electing and compensating the president. Section 2 listed the specific duties and responsibilities of the president and was customarily understood as a simple enumeration of the powers allocated to the president under the aegis of the executive power. A president strayed beyond the enumerated powers at his peril during the long era of congressional supremacy in the nineteenth century. TR, in contrast, argued that the initial grant of executive power was separate from the list of responsibilities. By his logic, Article II endowed the chief executive with a *general* grant of power that emanated directly from the American people. The other branches of government, as well as the provisions of Article II, Section 2, were simply checks on the executive. For TR, in short, presidential actions represented a kind of embodiment of the general will.

The statesman's task resembled that of a naval architect. When designing a warship, the naval architect balanced the competing demands of propulsion, navigation, and battle; the statesman adapted the ship of state to the socioeconomic change that accompanied industrialization.[71] In both scenarios, trade-offs among competing goods helped achieve the best overall performance. Roosevelt proclaimed himself "a steward of the people bound actively and affirmatively to do all he could for the people, and not to content himself with the negative merit of keeping his talents undamaged in a napkin." His active outlook demanded that he "do anything that the needs of the Nation demanded unless such action was forbidden by the Constitution or by the laws."[72] By reinterpreting the doctrine of enumerated powers, TR helped free the presidency from its constitutional shackles.

TR waved aside objections from critics disquieted by his perspective on constitutional law. He was prepared to act on his convictions now and face the judgment of Congress, the courts, and public opinion later. The Roosevelt administration spurred Congress to pass legislation intended to improve the lot of working-class Americans and to create administrative organs such as the Bureau of Corporations and the Department of Commerce and Labor to discharge the new oversight functions. These agencies pursued antitrust actions against the Northern Securities Company and other business combinations, earning President Roosevelt the reputation of a trustbuster. His administration also worked with Congress to craft a body of legislation pertaining to workman's compensation, woman and child labor, working hours, minimum wages for women, and old-age pensions.[73] TR hailed the generally positive response to these initiatives as public endorsement of his policies. For him, an active government was the most reliable defender of ordered liberty and, thus, of America's standing as a civilized nation.

3

LAW

The Police Power in U.S. Domestic Law

Activist government lay at the heart of Theodore Roosevelt's ambitious political program. It is useful, consequently, to briefly review the theory of the police power in U.S. domestic law, which formed the template Roosevelt applied to affairs of state. Noted a mid-twentieth-century analyst, "When the Constitution was adopted, the states possessed what lawyers style the 'police power,'" meaning "the power to regulate the conduct and relations of the members of society," and in effect "the general power of legislation."[1] The doctrine of the police power was in rapid flux in Roosevelt's day, partly because of the Industrial Revolution—which for many represented a challenge from private commerce that only government action could meet—and partly because of the perennial power struggle between the states and the federal government. From his legal studies at Columbia Law School (1880–81), his omnivorous reading, and his public service, TR was familiar with this legal concept, which informed his correspondence and public statements and helped mold his thinking about international affairs.

What was the police power? In the early nineteenth century Chief Justice John Marshall described it as "that immense mass of legislation, which embraces every thing within the territory of a State, not surrendered to the general government."[2] Judge Stephen J. Field, one of Roosevelt's contemporaries, supplied the Supreme Court's understanding of the concept in the late nineteenth century, defining it as "the power of the State, sometimes termed its police power, to prescribe regulations to promote the health, peace, morals, education and good order of the people, and to legislate so as to increase the industries of the State, develop its resources and add to its wealth and prosperity."[3]

The police power was clearly a sweeping power. Because it was not specifically mentioned in the U.S. Constitution, it generally fell to the courts to delineate precisely which matters the state and local governments were permitted to legislate or regulate and which matters fell to Congress. The dual structure of American government, then, was one factor driving the police power's evolution. Another factor in play was the Fourteenth Amendment, passed in the wake of the American Civil War, whose contours lawmakers and judges were exploring during Roosevelt's era. Much of the case law of the time involved determining whether police laws or regulations discriminated against particular classes of people and thus ran afoul of the Fourteenth Amendment's due process clause.[4]

A typical case for the period was decided in October 1884 — shortly after TR studied at Columbia Law School and during his service in the New York Assembly — when the Supreme Court ruled in *Barbier v. Connolly*, a police-power case that involved the due process clause. Judge Field, writing for the majority, affirmed a lower court ruling that a San Francisco city and county ordinance forbidding the nighttime operation of laundries and washhouses was "purely a police regulation within the competency of any municipality possessed of the ordinary powers belonging to such bodies." The danger of fire in San Francisco's many wooden buildings had induced the local government to enact the law. The Court found that "precautionary measures against fire and to secure proper drainage must be taken for the public safety. It is not legislation discriminating against any one" and thus was proper — or constitutional, at any rate; the justices did not presume to rule on the law's wisdom, or whether it ran up against the California constitution — exercise of the police power.[5]

Having rebuffed the plaintiffs, Judge Field took the opportunity to elaborate his view of the police power. "From the very necessities of society," laws and regulations designed "to promote, with as little individual inconvenience as possible, the general good" passed constitutional muster so long as "they operate alike upon all persons and property under the same circumstances and conditions." The San Francisco law, concluded Field, represented a lawful exercise of the police power and did not violate the federal Constitution. He helpfully listed some specific uses of the police power: "draining marshes and irrigating arid plains," as well as tending to "general benefits" such as "supplying water, preventing fires, lighting districts, cleaning streets, opening parks, and many other objects."[6]

The public good, then, sometimes demanded that government abridge the liberty of action of private economic interests. Yet making inroads into state and local affairs was no easy task for the federal government. At the Constitutional Convention, strong federalists among the Founders had advocated giving the national legislature a veto over state laws. Others maintained that such a constitutional provision would infringe on the states' prerogative of internal police. The opponents of a congressional veto proposed instead that the federal judiciary be empowered to evaluate the constitutional validity of national and state laws. They prevailed, and the convention ended up giving the U.S. Supreme Court, not Congress, jurisdiction over questions touching "the national peace and harmony," to quote James Madison.[7]

A close reading of the Constitution, then, provides little evidence of a federal claim to wield the police power—that is, a claim to oversee the conduct of and relations among the members of society by means of legislation or regulation. Yet power inexorably gravitated to Washington over the course of the nineteenth and early twentieth centuries, owing largely to the constitutional grant of power (Article I, Section 8) to Congress to "regulate commerce . . . among the several States." The courts often found themselves deducing rules that were nowhere expressly stated in the Constitution from their analysis of the dual structure of American government. The judiciary's widening interpretation of the meaning of "commerce," coupled with the primacy of Congress over state legislatures—one of the fundamental principles underlying the Constitution—allowed federal lawmakers to intervene in a broad range of state and local affairs.[8]

In Theodore Roosevelt's day the process was still at an early stage. Adherents of the burgeoning good-government and Progressive movements applauded the extension of federal power, which they viewed as leverage to implement their vision of good government, rein in corporate abuses, and tend to the collective weal; but the Progressive project was not fully realized until the Great Depression and Franklin Roosevelt's New Deal. To supplement the federal government's ability to exercise police powers, turn-of-the-century reformers entreated judges to interpret the commerce clause of the Constitution more broadly—allowing the legislative and executive branches to interpose themselves in local and state police activities on a hitherto-unthinkable scale.

In the early days of the Republic, Congress generally contented itself with forbidding interstate traffic in commodities deemed injurious to public morals, public health, or economic welfare. The Court sustained regulations prohibiting the interstate transportation of white slaves, stolen automobiles, and kidnapped individuals.[9] As the Industrial Revolution accelerated, however, regulation took on a broader, and more preemptive, hue. Preventing malfeasance was just as important as punishing it after the fact. Adopted in 1890, the Sherman Antitrust Act dealt with conspiracies in restraint of—and monopolies on—interstate trade. Enforcement was left to the courts, either through government-initiated civil suits or criminal prosecutions or civil actions brought by aggrieved parties. The courts rebuffed arguments that such activities were purely local and thus beyond the reach of congressional action under the commerce clause.[10]

Also in 1890, Congress concluded that it could not enact statutes to regulate all of the intricate workings of interstate carriage by rail, especially the rates and practices of the interstate railroads. Instead, in the Interstate Commerce Act, legislators set forth broad principles on this matter and created an administrative body, the Interstate Commerce Commission, to investigate alleged abuses, hear complaints, formulate and promulgate rules, and issue orders prohibiting practices in conflict with the act—subject, of course, to court review. By the end of the nineteenth century, then, the courts had approved three types of regulation: those designed (1) to interdict the interstate transportation of specified persons or commodities; (2) to interdict concerted action, whether it straddled state borders or not, that interrupted free competition in interstate trade; and (3) to regulate the affairs of those engaged in interstate transportation, using an administrative body to enforce the will of Congress as codified by statute.[11]

In practice the federal courts saw fit to set limits on state police power in three situations. First, and most obviously, when Congress had enacted valid legislation to take over the regulation of a given area, that federal legislation both superseded existing state law and ruled out future state attempts to regulate in that area. Second, until the national legislature prescribed a uniform national rule, state and local authorities enjoyed broad latitude to legislate and regulate in matters such as health and safety. In *Barbier v. Connolly*, for instance, the Supreme Court abstained from interfering with San Francisco's statute fixing the hours of operation for laundries and washhouses. Third, in several cases states had regulated matters that clearly fell within the scope of interstate commerce but Congress had failed to enact a national rule. The claim in these cases was that state or local government had infringed on federal jurisdiction, even though Washington had not yet set any national policy. Conversely, Congress may have overstepped its constitutional mandate under the guise of regulating interstate commerce. In such instances the Court adjudicated the respective claims of the state and federal governments.[12]

The *Shreveport* case is a classic illustration of the Court's weighing of the contending claims of Congress and a state government. The Interstate Commerce Commission had prescribed rates it found just and reasonable for interstate carriage by interstate railroads traversing the state of Texas. State law, however, permitted these carriers to set much lower rates for intrastate carriage. The upshot was substantial discrimination against interstate carriage. The railroads sued the federal government after the commission directed them to raise intrastate carriage rates to the same level assessed for interstate carriage. They claimed that Congress was impotent to meddle in the rates charged for purely intrastate commerce, even though discrimination against interstate traffic might result. The Court ruled against the railways, proclaiming, "The fact that carriers are instruments of intrastate commerce as well as of interstate commerce does not derogate from the complete and paramount authority of Congress over the latter, or preclude the federal power from being exerted to prevent the intrastate operations of such carriers from being made a means of injury to that which has been confided to the federal government."[13] The national legislature increasingly sought to go beyond the boundaries of the *Shreveport* case, justifying regulation of local economic interests by asserting that these interests would interfere with interstate commerce if left unregulated. By the 1920s the Court gradually began to relax a series of earlier decisions that had prohibited congressional regulation of enterprises such as manufacturing, mining, and various forms of production.[14]

What lessons did TR absorb from this slow-motion struggle over police power? First, he decided that the state, as the steward of the public interest, could and should exercise its powers to legislate and regulate to tend to the public welfare and morals. This conformed to his own leanings in favor of centralized power as the remedy for disorder and many social ills. Deploying its monopoly of physical force to maintain public order was a fundamental task of government; but there was clearly far more to it than that. The federal role in policing came to the fore in matters where, to borrow from Madison, "the national peace and harmony" were at stake—certainly an overriding interest. Otherwise, the job of finding the appropriate mix of police regulations and statutes was best left to local and state authorities. Second, he determined that in certain circumstances the federal government had a role to play in state, and even municipal, government affairs. Federal supervisory authority was necessary where states proved unable to address social woes. Third, he learned that the federal government, through the medium of the congressional commerce power, could rightfully oversee the activities of private economic interests when the public interest was engaged. Fourth, he found that judicial tribunals were an effective means to adjust disputes surrounding the exercise of police powers. And finally, he found that administrative bodies animated by disinterested officials were an effective instrument for enforcing police laws and regulations. These themes coursed through Theodore Roosevelt's handling of public policy and informed his thinking about whether an international police power should be entrusted to the great powers and, ultimately, the combined action of the civilized world.

Roosevelt's Convictions about Law and Order

All of this dovetailed well with Theodore Roosevelt's own beliefs. For Roosevelt, the police power was the state's way of counterbalancing powerful new actors in society, the concrete expression of the collective action he prescribed. To be sure, maintaining social equilibrium was a delicate proposition. TR was willing to work with all claimants, even the militant socialists he disdained, to strike a balance that reined in business excesses and advanced the cause of social uplift. Interjecting the coercive power of the state into the relations between capital and labor, however, could tip the balance in the opposite direction, fomenting mob rule, paralysis of the business community, and economic stagnation that would be equally harmful to all Americans. "I have just as much difficulty in preventing the demagogues from going too far," he complained in 1905, "as in making those who are directly or indirectly responsive to Wall Street go far enough."[15] The challenge was to address the labor unions' legitimate demands without creating a tyranny of labor that would be likewise inimical to the bequest of Washington and Lincoln. In particular, the U.S. government should mediate among capital and labor interests that impinged on interstate commerce.

A certain detachment from these powerful interests, then, was essential for a statesman entrusted with the authority to make laws or regulations or to enforce the laws and regulations thus made. The Square Deal concept, which pervaded Theodore Roosevelt's political philosophy, was a useful weapon in the battle to sustain equilibrium. Consonant with his sense of Americanism and insistence on absolute honesty, he pledged to mete out "exact justice" to all parties to a dispute without regard to their party affiliations, the likely political repercussions for himself, or other peripheral concerns. Roosevelt professed bewilderment at labor advocates' and industrialists' inability to fathom what was plain to him: that he might side with either labor or capital, depending on how he gauged the merits of each case.

It was apparently incomprehensible to them that a politician would adhere to principle and, as a corollary, refuse to proclaim fealty to influential patrons in business, the unions, or other interests. TR wrote of those baffled at his apparently inconsistent handling of labor cases: They were of "such limited brain power" as to be beyond redemption. "Of course when we get hold of a fool who thinks that my refusing to sanction the tyranny of capital over labor is contradicted by, instead of complemented by, my refusal to allow labor in its turn to tyrannize, why, I don't see that any explanation will make the matter clear to him."[16]

For TR square dealing was not only morally correct but also politically advantageous. Evenhanded conduct in capital-labor disputes, declared Roosevelt, served the Republicans' interests by distancing them from the plutocrats and burnishing their appeal with the masses. Such a posture also reflected his ingrained iconoclastic streak. While serving as governor of New York, he confided his glee at his independence from the Republican machine and wealthy interests. Senator Platt, he asserted, "liked me for the excellent reason that I never deceived him and he always knew I would do exactly as I said I would"—even though that sometimes set him at odds with the Republican machine. For their part, the industrialists, though incensed at his franchise taxation law, had reconciled themselves to the fact "that I cannot be used." While "I will never for a moment yield to the demagogues, . . . it is idle even to propose anything to me on behalf of a corporation merely to benefit that corporation."[17] In the end, the Square Deal doctrine, like most of Roosevelt's politics, boiled down to morality. He insisted that the principle behind the Square Deal bolstered America's claim to stand at the forefront of progressive civilization.

His quest to stamp out lawlessness took on added urgency when he succeeded President William McKinley, who was slain in 1901 by a pistol-wielding anarchist. Civilization was a fragile thing, never more than a generation from extinction. Public order, upheld by honest law enforcement, was the foundation of the ordered liberty that entitled the United States to number itself among the civilized nations.[18] Roosevelt assured his confidants that only muscular government could avert a slide into barbarity. Fending off labor violence, consequently, was his top priority in the many labor disputes that marred the Industrial Revolution. Violent protest inflamed passions on both sides and guaranteed impasse at the bargaining table. Thus government must suppress attacks on capital to give itself a chance to adjust the dispute.[19]

There were, of course, other enemies of an orderly society. In the aftermath of the McKinley assassination, for example, TR vowed to war remorselessly on anarchists and those who sympathized with them. He pronounced the assassination an assault not only on a man but "solely upon free government, government by the common people, because it *was* government, and because though in the highest sense a free and representative government, it yet stood for order as well as for liberty" (emphasis in original).[20] Such a blow against ordered liberty could not be tolerated. On similar grounds, Roosevelt deplored the wave of lynching then engulfing the country and bewailed the lack of intervention by federal authority in local law enforcement. Mob violence, he reminded Americans, was the forerunner of tyranny and must be stamped out.[21]

The implied or actual use of force thus was inseparable from TR's politics. The government's coercive power must be deployed at home, just as U.S. military power was sometimes necessary abroad. Long experience had accustomed Roosevelt to overseeing the use of force. As police commissioner he deployed armed policemen to deter violence against the New York Cab Company.[22] On several occasions during his governorship, he dispatched militia forces to quell labor unrest. In 1899, for instance, he reported activating a full brigade of the National Militia to discourage rioting in Buffalo. He brandished the Big Stick. "I told [the labor representatives] instantly that I should entertain no protest; that the militia would not be called out unless the local authorities stated that they needed them; but that the minute this condition was found to exist, they would be called out, and that I should not consider for a moment the protest that this was 'intimidating the laboring men,' because it would intimidate no one unless he was anxious to commit lawlessness, and that in this case it would be my especial care to see that he *was* intimidated" (emphasis in original).[23]

Yet TR also took pains to show striking workers that he was not a reflexive ally of business. After a strike at Croton Dam he ordered an investigation into working conditions and introduced legislation to ameliorate the worst abuses. TR believed his willingness to rein in corporations enhanced the credibility of muscular actions vis-à-vis labor. By threatening or using force against the unions and deploying its legislative and regulatory functions to keep the corporations in check, the government could act as mediator between these interests. Where legislation or regulation could improve the lot of Americans, Theodore Roosevelt embraced it, but he also did not shrink from taking more forceful measures where circumstances warranted. His thinking about relations between industry and labor set the pattern for his thinking about an international police power, under which he envisaged the United States playing a similar mediating role between the Latin American republics and the European great powers.

4

POLICING LABOR RELATIONS

Government as a Balancer

Strife between capital and labor was a fact of American life during Theodore Roosevelt's career. This strife caused much of the misery with which his childhood and his duties at the New York Police Department had acquainted him. The police power gave TR a way to mediate among parties that were incessantly at odds. The state's response to such upheaval was the nexus where the police function merged with the military function. Anarchism, the other major challenge to an orderly society in Roosevelt's day, was purely a matter for law enforcement, but the burgeoning labor movement had legitimate grievances that could not and should not be solved solely by the operation of the police and the judiciary. TR was determined to use government power to deter or quash violent unrest while reconciling the interests of the great corporations and their workers.

TR's approach to stormy labor disputes flowed directly from his personal philosophy and his outlook on legal affairs. His writings on labor-capital relations—his "rhetoric of militant decency," as one historian described it[1]—convey a distinctly Social Darwinian flavor. Although he distanced himself from some of the more extreme tenets of Social Darwinism, the biological theories of society and state that were fashionable in the late nineteenth century strongly influenced TR. Notions of growth, decay, and equilibrium permeate his letters and speeches. Unlike populists such as William Jennings Bryan, however, Roosevelt accepted big business as a fact of life. Not the existence but the conduct of influential interests concerned him. "The war we wage must be waged against misconduct, against wrongdoing wherever it is found," including among "the wrongdoers of great wealth" who so vexed Roosevelt.[2]

TR believed organizations evolved toward ever larger and more intricate forms. This process was often beneficial for the larger organism, the nation, but in some cases the runaway growth of corporations was akin to a malignancy menacing the American body politic. When private organizations grew powerful enough to threaten the public interest, it was a brawny government's job to deploy its regulatory authority—and in extreme cases its monopoly of force—to check rogue corporations and unions. Endowed with the police power, state and local governments could step in in a variety of ways. The U.S. Constitution, moreover, authorized Washington to intervene in situations, such as massive labor strikes, that confounded state and local authorities or, in the case of interstate commerce, eluded the legislative and regulatory authority of state governments for geographical reasons. With respect to the latter, contended Roosevelt, "I believe that under the interstate clause of the Constitution the United States has complete and paramount right to control all agencies of interstate commerce, and I believe that the National Government alone can exercise this right with wisdom and effectiveness so as both to secure justice from, and to do justice to, the great corporations which are the most important factors in modern business."[3]

Roosevelt vehemently denied that the expansion of federal power he proposed would injure American business. He portrayed this expansion of power as a matter of aligning the American political system with realities that had already come into being. Federal control of interstate commerce, for instance, "does not represent centralization. It represents merely the acknowledgement of the patent fact that centralization has already come in business."[4] In short, no alternative to a national government was muscular enough to counterbalance big business. "The danger to American democracy," he insisted, "lies not in the least in the concentration of administrative power in responsible and accountable hands. It lies in having the power insufficiently concentrated," that is, "among a variety of men who work in secret, whose very names are unknown to the common people," so that "no one can be held responsible to the people for its use."[5] Centralized, democratically accountable power was Theodore Roosevelt's prescription for effective government.

In keeping with his activist nature, Roosevelt used the police power frequently and skillfully. He repeatedly invoked the police power during his terms as New York police commissioner, governor of New York State, and president of the United States. Sometimes this involved the direct use of force to deter or quell violence. As police commissioner Roosevelt assigned armed policemen to deter union attacks on cab drivers who crossed the picket lines. As governor he used New York militia and as president he used U.S. Army troops to quell labor unrest. In keeping with the Big Stick doctrine, these forceful measures were invariably a prelude to government-sponsored efforts such as mediation, investigation of labor conditions, or the enactment of new laws or regulations to ameliorate the dreary conditions characteristic of many industries.

In the spring of 1900, for instance, Italian laborers rioted at Croton Dam, in the process murdering one of the national guardsmen called in to restore order. Then-governor Roosevelt directed the State Board of Mediation and Arbitration to conduct a "most thorough" inquiry into working conditions and to determine whether the immigrant workers were, as they claimed, paid less than their native-born fellows.[6] (Roosevelt confided to Henry Cabot Lodge that management had "decidedly oppressed" the Italian employees, and he fretted that the incident would hurt his chances for becoming the Republicans' nominee for vice president.[7]) TR habitually took a direct hand in the policing process, as when he and Jacob Riis personally surveyed working conditions in New York City sweatshops.[8]

Roosevelt's use of the police power, then, had a preemptive tinge that complemented the more conventional, and reactive, use of the state's monopoly on force to maintain order and punish lawbreaking. Resolving the workers' legitimate grievances, reasoned TR, was preferable to armed confrontation that could spiral out of control and ultimately, in the extreme case, start a revolution leading to the overthrow of the American system. As governor he shepherded the Ford Bill, the first to regulate New York corporations, through the state legislature over the objections of Boss Platt's Republican machine.[9] He trumpeted business regulation as a victory for the public interest, a way to ward off Bryanism, and thus one of his proudest achievements.[10]

His activism in New York induced Senator Platt to discreetly usher Roosevelt out of state politics, using the time-honored formula of promotion into irrelevance. Platt engineered the governor's nomination for vice president in the 1900 election. Yet Roosevelt simply carried his reform crusade to the national level. As William McKinley's running mate, he promptly formulated a Republican plan for state and federal police action against corporate abuses.[11]

The Presidency: Preventive Use of the Police Power

National disaster, in the form of a pistol-wielding anarchist who murdered President McKinley, soon handed TR the chance to enact his vision on a national scale. That he viewed the police power as a tool for realizing his goals had become evident as early as 1899, when

he invoked "the police power of the State" as giving the state government the right to regulate the New York railroads. (In this case the
apparently trivial question was whether the railroads could build four
tracks along one of the city avenues.) The police power was, he
declared fervently, a tool of justice and thus of overarching importance to civilization.[12] Asked by one firm to grant a monopoly on New
York City railway transport, then-governor Roosevelt replied that such
matters were the exclusive province of the Board of Railroad Commissioners, which determined the conditions of operation for the railways. "The police power of the city," admonished TR, "of course is
not and cannot be interfered with." Regulating private contract in the
public interest was a central duty of government.[13] Carried to the international realm, the use of the police power to install good government among subject peoples would give them the institutions they
needed to join the civilized world.

Yet this was not a simple exercise of power for its own sake. "By
the time I became President," Roosevelt proclaimed in his autobiography, "I had grown to feel with deep intensity that governmental agencies must find their justification largely in the way in which they are
used for the practical betterment of living and working conditions
among the mass of the people."[14] In other words, the government's
police powers were the medium by which the ideal—improving the
lot of a population wracked by the effects of industrialization—was
transmuted into reality. For Roosevelt and like-minded Progressives,
the police power entailed not only its most obvious form, the use of
force to maintain order, but also a multitude of regulatory and legislative actions to safeguard American health, welfare, and morals. In international police actions, the United States had to accomplish a variety of things, including establishing a native constabulary to impose
order, enacting and enforcing sanitary regulations, and erecting the
infrastructure native citizens needed to live a decent life.

President Roosevelt framed a compelling rationale for federal
exercise of the police power over big business. "As long as the States
retain the primary control of the police power," declared his 1904 message to Congress, "the circumstances must be altogether extreme which
require interference by the Federal authorities" to safeguard the interests of labor. To be sure, there were other, more clear-cut reasons for
federal intervention. "If there is resistance to the Federal courts, interference with the mails, or interstate commerce, or molestation of Federal property, or if the State authorities in some crisis which they are
unable to face call for help, then the Federal Government may interfere." But in the case of an outbreak of labor unrest, "the interference

itself simply takes the form of restoring order without regard to the questions which have caused the breach of order—for to keep order is a primary duty and in a time of disorder and violence all other questions sink into abeyance until order has been restored." Mob rule was "intolerable in any form."[15] Roosevelt appealed to the overarching principle that a superior authority could step in to restore order before addressing the substantive issues that had spawned disorder.

TR hoped to prevent events from degenerating that far. He planned to deploy the police power *preemptively* to allay the underlying causes of labor unrest. By alleviating human misery, the government would hold at bay the extremists who, thought TR, hoped to overthrow the Republic in favor of a socialist system. While the federal government was not nearly so powerful in Roosevelt's day as it is today, Washington could do much to prevent disorder. First, drawing on his service at the Civil Service Commission and the New York Police Board, he aimed to make the federal government a model employer by hiring on the merit principle and enacting measures such as strict enforcement of the eight-hour day in cabinet agencies. He hoped that state and local governments, as well as private entities, would emulate the example thus set. Second, the national government could enact good labor laws wherever Washington had direct jurisdiction, especially in the District of Columbia and the territories.

Third, an expansive reading of the constitutional provisions on regulating interstate commerce gave Congress and the White House a wedge to interpose themselves in affairs hitherto thought to be the province of state and local authorities.[16] Upon assuming the presidency, Roosevelt almost instantly set about pushing his concept of "social and industrial justice" at the federal level. Corporations, he maintained, were similar to public agencies in that their activities touched intimately on the public interest. Just as government could rightfully regulate public bodies, so too could it compel corporations to "do their duty."[17] For him, public affairs came down to morality and the rigorous demands of the American creed. Roosevelt was abundantly prepared to deploy government power for moral ends. As will become clear in subsequent chapters, this argument bore a strong resemblance to his line of reasoning for an international police power. As creatures of municipal law, the president told Congress, corporations engaged in interstate commerce "occupy the position of subjects without a sovereign, neither any State government nor the National Government having effective control over them." This was unacceptable because it forced ordinary Americans to rely on corporations' uncertain goodwill for fair wages and prices. Experience, said President Roosevelt, had shown "conclusively that it is useless to try to get any adequate regulation and supervision of these great corporations by State action. Such regulation and supervision can only be effectively exercised by a sovereign whose jurisdiction is coextensive with the field of work of the corporations—that is, by the National Government." Consequently, it should be Washington's "steady aim" to "give to the sovereign—that is, to the Government, which represents the people as a whole—some effective power of supervision over their corporate use."[18] Among the instruments the federal government had available to oversee corporate interests were the Interstate Commerce Commission and the Bureau of Labor and Corporations. Federal supervisory activities during the Roosevelt years ranged from enacting pure food laws, to suing combinations guilty of throttling competition, to fixing railroad rates.[19] As his notion of an international police power evolved, Roosevelt for a time envisioned making the United States a sort of distant, benevolent sovereign over the Latin American states, albeit a sovereign with a lighter hand than he had in mind for the federal government at home.

The president touted his domestic regulatory accomplishments. In 1902 he rejoiced in his assault on the trusts.[20] He averred, for instance, that his administration's lawsuit against the Northern Securities Company—a railroad holding company accused of stock transactions constituting an illegal combination under the Sherman Antitrust Act—was important as much for its salutary moral effects as for its benefits to consumers. By March 1904, after a lengthy cycle of litigation and appeals, the Supreme Court had ordered that the trust be dismantled. "To give any color for misrepresentation to the effect that we were now weakening in the Northern Securities matter would be ruinous," he informed George Bruce Cortelyou. "The Northern Securities suit is one of the great achievements of my administration. I look back on it with great pride, for through it we emphasized in signal fashion, as in no other way could be emphasized, the fact that the most powerful men in this country were held to accountability before the law."[21]

Although his reputation as a trustbuster is somewhat overblown—William Howard Taft opposed business combinations more aggressively—Roosevelt did sponsor a variety of legislation designed to deter and punish corporate and labor abuses. To Dr. Lyman Abbott he recounted his battle to create a Department of Commerce, including a Bureau of Corporations to publicize the administration's accomplishments in this area. Roosevelt chuckled when he recalled the futile resistance of Standard Oil, the country's first billion-dollar

firm, to the creation of the new cabinet agency. It bears repeating that President Roosevelt generally did not oppose industrial combinations; he simply wanted to discipline the new behemoths through strict policing of antitrust laws and more far-reaching supervision of big business.

He also pushed through a law, under the aegis of the commerce clause, that prohibited the railroads from offering rebates to preferred shippers. The law threw "the highways of commerce open on equal terms to all who use them."[22] Roosevelt argued that government should be empowered to reset the rates for railroad use where they were deemed unfair and that the federal government could regulate working conditions for railroad employees engaged in interstate commerce. His feud with the railroad magnates, recalled Roosevelt, had been regarded as "frightfully aggressive missionary work"—an apt metaphor for his whole approach to politics. In his autobiography TR denounced federal and state judges who had "invoked the Constitution in a spirit of the narrowest legalistic obstruction" to block Washington's efforts on behalf of labor. He contended that his use of the bully pulpit had largely corrected these misguided views, at least among the "best and most enlightened judges."[23]

Finally, TR overruled the firing of a Government Printing Office employee who had refused to unionize when the office became a union shop. For him it was a matter of simple fairness. "Not by preaching, but by immediate action, I enforced the doctrine that the union man and the nonunion man stand on an exact equality in the eye of the law, and therefore in the Government service."[24] This was vintage Roosevelt. A product of the Victorian era, the president evaluated government actions by their effect on the nation's moral virtue.

The Presidency: Blunting Violent Labor Unrest

What convinced Roosevelt that the state should deploy its monopoly on force to head off violent labor strife? The nation's history, and TR's own tender years, had been pockmarked by uproar ranging from the Molly Maguires incident to the Pullman strike. The clashes seemed to portend a genuine threat to American political institutions, and conditions threatened to worsen barring vigorous government intervention. TR had dealt with labor disputes from his f days in public office. His presidency was equally eventful.

In June 1902, for instance, TR ordered U.S. Army troop Arizona to quell rioting in the wake of a miners' strike. True to TR ordered a swift deployment of force to deter additional vio

then directed the federal authorities to mediate a solution. Decisive action, claimed Roosevelt, had kept the unrest in check. "The miners struck, violence followed, and the Arizona Territorial authorities notified me they could not grapple with the situation. Within twenty minutes of the receipt of the telegram, orders were issued to the nearest available troops, and twenty-four hours afterwards Gen. Baldwin and his regulars were on the ground, and twenty-four hours later every vestige of disorder had disappeared." To the accusations of favoritism flung at him by labor representatives, Roosevelt replied, "While I am President I wish the labor man to feel that he has the same right of access to me that the capitalist has . . . *and no easier*. Anything else seems to me not only un-American, but as symptomatic of an attitude which will cost grave trouble if persevered in" (emphasis in original).[25]

Despite TR's impatience with "technicalities," there were limits—limits, to be sure, that were not spelled out clearly—to his interventionism. Although he believed a broader interpretation of the federal government's constitutional prerogatives was essential, he remained staunchly loyal to the principle of federalism. In 1903, and again in 1904, he denied requests to intervene in a strike by the Western Federation of Miners. During the first incident, Governor James Peabody of Colorado asked the president to dispatch federal forces to the state to suppress local disturbances. After consulting with Secretary of War Elihu Root and Attorney General Philander Chase Knox, Roosevelt decided not to honor the request on constitutional grounds. Federal law implementing Article IV, Section 4 of the U.S. Constitution required that a disturbance amount to an insurrection against the state government if it were to justify federal military action.[26] Peabody had failed to show that an insurrection existed or that the crisis outstripped state capabilities. Thus federal action would usurp local prerogatives before local resources had been exhausted. The president also pointed out that he could not lawfully place federal troops under state command, as the governor had asked; he must exercise personal command of the operation.[27]

In 1904 TR rebuffed the pleas of the attorney for the Western Federation of Miners, who had claimed that a group known as the Citizens' Alliance was threatening striking miners and keeping them from their homes. Roosevelt protested that, whatever the merits of this claim, he could not order military action at the request of private citizens; else "the United States Government would be continually sending troops into particular States or cities, or particular counties, on the assertion of some individual or individuals that either the county authorities, including the sheriff, or the mayor and police, or the gov-

ernor and militia, were unable or unwilling to afford them adequate protection." Assenting to such requests "would render it necessary for the national government generally to displace the local authorities in the preservation of peace and order."[28] To interfere in Colorado, argued TR, would subvert the U.S. federal structure.

Similarly, Roosevelt turned down a joint resolution of the Maryland legislature that requested U.S. Army troops to restore order in Baltimore in the aftermath of a massive fire. TR pointed out, first, that the resolution authorized the governor to determine how long the troop presence would be required. Second, he observed that the governor had already indicated that the state militia could cope with the situation and that he would request the immediate withdrawal of any federal forces sent to the city.[29] Despite his impatience with the inefficiencies built into the American legal order, then, Roosevelt did not indiscriminately override the explicit text of the Constitution and federal law. For him the federal government's role in local and state affairs remained limited. Only extenuating circumstances could justify extraordinary actions such as his mediation of the anthracite coal strike (covered below). His handling of intermittent labor unrest bespeaks a reluctance to interfere until local remedies had been exhausted, combined with a palpable impatience at being bound by the list of enumerated powers granted him in the U.S. Constitution. For Roosevelt, knowing when to step in and when to abstain from these disputes was a matter of prudential statecraft.

The Model for Federal Police Action: Mediating the Coal Strike of 1902

Theodore Roosevelt regarded his handling of the 1902 anthracite coal strike in Pennsylvania as one of his crowning accomplishments and "very much the most important" of his actions involving a labor dispute. That the police power shaped his actions in the conflict between miners and operators was evident from an explicit mention in his correspondence at the time (of which more later). An event of this perceived magnitude warrants revisiting in some detail because it exemplified Roosevelt's view of the proper use of governmental police powers, occasioned a discussion of presidential power, and supplied the conceptual model for his approach to certain international crises.

What stood out so prominently in TR's memories? The sequence of events was straightforward. In May 1902 John Mitchell, president of the United Mine Workers of America (UMW), called a strike in the anthracite regions of Pennsylvania over the dismal pay accorded coal miners. In October, after negotiations between the UMW and mine owners had deadlocked and the owners had refused arbitration, President Roosevelt intervened to impose federal mediation. In March 1903 the commission appointed to investigate the dispute (a body headed by former president Grover Cleveland) awarded the mine workers a 10-percent wage increase but refused to grant the union recognition.

What was it about the coal strike that inspired foreboding in TR? With frosty weather impending, the impasse threatened to incite widespread unrest in the Northeast, possibly even—he shuddered to think of it—"socialistic action." The nation's fuel supply was highly inelastic. The rudimentary home heating systems of the day burned anthracite coal; bituminous coal, the alternative fuel, was vastly inferior as a substitute. Pennsylvania supplied the bulk of the coal to the Northeast. Thus, recalled Roosevelt, "the coal famine became a National menace as the winter approached. . . . In the populous industrial States, from Ohio eastward, it was not merely calamity, but the direst disaster, that was threatened."[30] "I think all competent observers agree," he told Lyman Abbott, "that if the strike had not been settled there would have been within thirty days the most terrible riots that this country has ever seen, with as their consequence the necessity of drastic, and perhaps revolutionary measures, by the state governments, or by the national government."[31]

Alarmed at the prospect of public disorder, the governor of Massachusetts and the mayor of New York City notified President Roosevelt "that frightful consequences might follow" a prolonged interruption of the fuel supply.[32] The situation, reported TR with a martial flourish, "was quite as serious as if they had been threatened by the invasion of a hostile army of overwhelming force."[33] Circumstances—the plight of cold, angry citizens, not to mention the fortunes of the Republican Party in the 1902 congressional elections—seemingly militated for presidential action.

Why federal action? The Pennsylvania state government had been unable to broker a settlement. The governor had few militiamen at his disposal to deter violence or to cope with it once it erupted. Furthermore, the repercussions of a strike that dragged on into 1903 would clearly cross state boundaries—triggering presidential action not by means of the U.S. Constitution, but by the Lincoln-Jackson school of executive power extolled by Theodore Roosevelt. "Owing to the peculiar division of our powers under the constitution," explained Roosevelt to Robert Bacon, "while Boston and New York are as much interested as Philadelphia in the coal famine, only Pennsylvania has immediate power to deal with the situation." The governor should afford as much protection as possible to miners who wished to work in defiance of the strike, as well as to the property of the mine owners. But Pennsylvania should also bring the operators to heel should they maintain their "insolent" and intransigent attitude.

"I do not think I need assure you," continued the president, "that in case I am called upon to act, through the inability of Pennsylvania to keep order and on the demand of her constitutional authorities, I will guarantee that order will be kept and life and property absolutely respected, and all men alike made to yield obedience to the law." Nonetheless, he hesitated to commit federal forces to maintain order. "I wish to feel that I have done everything in my power to bring about a peaceful solution before any such dreadful alternative is forced upon me."[34] He was as good as his word; appointing a commission to look into the dispute ultimately settled the strike without forcible federal intrusion. Here again, TR displayed his characteristic outlook on the use of the police power. The federal government interposed itself between the miners and the owners, then appointed an impartial administrative body to adjust the dispute. Force was kept in reserve to back up the administration's quasi-diplomatic intervention and to step in if events again turned ugly. Roosevelt used much the same combination of diplomacy, force, and public administration in Santo Domingo a couple of years later.

Roosevelt blamed the hardheadedness of capital, which lent credence to the arguments of extreme socialists, for the standoff.[35] The mine operators, said TR, had concluded that they could simply outwait the miners, many of whom subsisted paycheck to paycheck. Consequently, the operators agreed among themselves to take a hard line in the negotiations. They initially rejected the president's offer of arbitration and even, he reported, treated him insolently. But that was not the worst of their misconduct from Roosevelt's standpoint: he was especially indignant when the owners simultaneously denied that the public had a stake in this essentially private matter *and* demanded that the president use force to uphold their interests. "It is amazing folly on their part," he wrote to Bacon, "clamorously to demand by the public the exercise of the police powers, at no matter what expenditure in blood and money, and yet to resent any suggestion that they have duties toward the public of which its governmental representatives must take cognizance."[36]

The notion of a federal police power divorced from the public interest (or, in the case of the coal strike, used in the service of a private interest) was nonsensical for TR. He assessed the Pennsylvania standoff through the prism of his views on capitalism and counter-organization, drawing sweeping lessons from the episode. The coal operators were, he said, "men of unquestionable good private life, and they were merely taking the extreme individualistic view of the rights of property and the freedom of individual action upheld in the laissez faire political economies."[37] The powers apportioned to the U.S. government were the only implement available to offset this extreme individualism in the public good.

Theodore Roosevelt was prepared to wield such power. As mentioned previously, as president he fancied himself the embodiment of America's general will, not simply as a chief executive empowered to carry out a list of constitutional duties. "In vital fashion, this question was that which beyond all others concerned the entire nation; and, as being for the moment the head of the nation, I obeyed the supreme law of duty to the republic in acting as I did."[38] Failure to act, he insisted, would have relegated him to the status of such lackluster chief executives as James Buchanan and Franklin Pierce. The coal strike, he declared, had "illustrated as well as anything that I did the theory which I have called the Jackson-Lincoln theory of the Presidency; that is, that occasionally great national crises arise which call for immediate and vigorous executive action, and that in such cases it is the duty of the President to act upon the theory that he is the steward of the people, and that the proper attitude for him to take is that he is bound to assume that he has the legal right to do whatever the needs of the people demand, unless the Constitution or the laws explicitly forbid him to do it."[39]

This is an extraordinary statement. TR's predecessors had generally regarded the list of presidential duties spelled out in the Constitution as the end-all-and-be-all of their authority; indeed, some had thought of their role as merely executing the will of Congress. Roosevelt inverted this view. To be sure, the ground had been prepared for such a transformation of the chief magistrate's role. After the Civil War the balance of power between Congress and the White House slowly began to shift in favor of the presidency. Rutherford B. Hayes warred against Senate prerogatives in selecting cabinet members. Grover Cleveland transformed the veto into a tool to strike down legislation he opposed, not simply legislation he held to be unconstitutional. The federal government's power, moreover, had grown steadily since the 1870s, preparing the ground for a muscular executive.[40] Still, Roosevelt's outlook on the executive power was unprecedented for his day.

In keeping with the president's musings on Jackson and Lincoln, his role in the anthracite coal strike was basically extraconstitu-tional. First, after waiting several months in hopes that the parties could reach an agreement on their own, Roosevelt injected himself into the dispute, as the agent of the public interest, by appointing a commission and browbeating the owners into accepting its findings.[41] (At the outset he had wished for federal authority to place the mines in receivership pending an investigation and an imposed settlement.) Second, although never driven to such an extreme, Roosevelt later confided that he had been prepared to wring a request from the Pennsylvania governor to use federal troops to seize and operate the mines by force, despite the "evil precedent" this would set.[42] On October 5 he told President Cleveland, who had applauded his stance on the coal strike, that "if ever the necessity arises for my interference to restore order in Pennsylvania on the call of the constituted authorities, or to protect government property by force of the United States regular army, I shall try to use this force with the same firmness that you showed" during the 1894 Pullman strike.[43] (In 1895, commenting on the strike, TR had written in the *Forum* that Cleveland's forceful intervention in the Pullman strike had set a precedent for government's use of arms in labor disputes.[44])

Roosevelt summarized his views on government intervention in labor unrest in his 1904 annual message to Congress. He rued the effects of laissez faire: "No small part of the trouble that we have comes from carrying to an extreme the national virtue of self-reliance, of independence in initiative and action. It is wise to conserve this virtue and to provide for its fullest exercise, compatible with seeing that liberty does not become a liberty to wrong others." To modulate the irresponsible liberty bred by extreme individualism, the Founding Fathers had wisely built a commerce power and other hedges against injustice into the U.S. Constitution.[45]

TR discerned in the anthracite coal crisis a moral imperative to impose additional government supervision on corporations. Yet self-restraint by individual citizens also played a pivotal role in the labor question. To safeguard the public interest, the president exhorted the American people to "continue to show the very qualities that they have shown—that is, moderation, good sense, the earnest desire to avoid doing any damage, and yet the quiet determination to proceed, step by step, without halt and without hurry, in eliminating or at least in minimizing whatever of mischief or of evil there is to interstate commerce in the conduct of great corporations."[46] Mob violence could not be countenanced, even when the mob had worthy objectives.

In short, the government had to be a party to crises that engaged the public interest, especially when public order threatened to unravel.[47] It was "essential," TR wrote to J. H. Woodward, "that organized labor and organized capital should thoroughly understand that the third party, the great public, had vital interests and overshadowing rights in such a crisis as that through which we have just passed."[48]

It bears repeating that 1902–4 was an extremely volatile period in U.S. history. A review of TR's correspondence shows a president grappling with labor unrest in Pennsylvania, Arizona, and Colorado, not to mention a fire in Baltimore and the subsequent request for federal aid. Intermingled with this domestic tumult were the great powers' blockade of Venezuela; revolution in Panama on the heels of a U.S. standoff with Colombia over the isthmian canal; and a collapse of Dominican finances that seemingly imperiled the Monroe Doctrine.[49] Small wonder that Roosevelt, beset by this litany of turmoil, pressed into service a ready-made conceptual tool, the police power, to cope with events not only on American soil but also in the Caribbean littoral.

The rudiments of a police-power doctrine were evident both in Roosevelt's theorizing and in his actual responses to capital-labor disputes. Like other broad constructionists, TR found constitutional sanction for a federal exercise of the police power in a creative reading of the commerce clause and other provisions. Several conditions warranted federal intrusion into state and local affairs. First, chronic wrongdoing by organized interests, an unfortunate byproduct of the Industrial Revolution, could accentuate human suffering sufficiently to provoke civil unrest. The political clout and geographic sweep of these interests often allowed them to evade local and state supervision. Second, a fraying of the ties of civilized society could overwhelm the capacities of local authorities, requiring the federal government to step in. Atrocious living conditions for the working poor, for example, warranted government supervision. Third, private contracts might infringe the interests of the public, which wanted for a champion in such transactions. Statesmen and individual citizens animated by chivalrous ideals should combat these evils, both out of humanitarian concern and in their own interest. The magnitude of these ills and the threat they posed to American institutions justified intervention by a superior authority wielding the sanction of force — namely, the U.S. government.

Some guidelines for police-power deployment were evident in the anthracite coal strike. First, Roosevelt, not normally known for his patience, waited until relations between the miners and the mine

owners had deadlocked before injecting himself into the feud. He preferred to give the antagonists every opportunity to sort things out for
themselves. Second, he genuflected to the principle of federalism by
refraining from the use of force pending a request from the Pennsylvania government. Third, in keeping with his model of forceful diplomacy, he used the threat of force judiciously to nudge the parties toward a settlement that incorporated the findings of President
Cleveland's commission. And finally, he cited his handling of the coal
strike as the model for a doctrine of federal intervention in labor disputes, as well as evidence of a need for federal regulatory powers over
the great corporations. His restraint allowed President Roosevelt to
emerge from the strike with his political fortunes intact.

What implications did his domestic uses of the police power
have for Theodore Roosevelt's diplomacy? Precision was not one of
TR's political virtues, and so he can be tough to pin down. Perhaps
intentionally so: for politicians, after all, public commitments have a
way of becoming shackles on prudential statecraft. Roosevelt refrained
from clearly defining the parameters of the *international* police power,
just as he had for the federal police power, for fear of interfering with
prudential statesmanship. The international police power represented
a way to confront turmoil in America's geographic environs; its use
was reminiscent of the use of federal power within the United States.
In constabulary operations, the U.S. government temporarily arrogated
to itself the authority to discharge some of the functions of the sovereign government, usually relating to law enforcement and finances,
where a foreign government was unable or unwilling to do so. By
mediating between stricken Latin American governments and the great
powers, the United States sought to create an equilibrium that would
allow these governments to put their affairs in order. Such an equilibrium, believed TR, would stave off a threat to American interests in
the Western Hemisphere while improving conditions for the citizens
of beleaguered countries. In so doing the Republic would bring its
interests into greater harmony with its ideals.

5

PUBLIC ADMINISTRATION

Politics Out of the Civil Service

If the state was to fulfill its role as a disinterested steward of the common good, asserted good-government proponents, politics had to be cleared out of its workings. Predictably, then, Theodore Roosevelt's vision of the police power, domestic and international, owed much to his theorizing on upright public administration. At times he defined the role of international constabulary duty as giving less-advanced countries good government along the lines reformers had espoused at home. To do otherwise condemned these countries to oligarchy — or worse. Roosevelt's views were rooted in experience as well as abstract theory. He served for six years as a U.S. Civil Service commissioner, receiving appointments from Presidents Benjamin Harrison, a Republican, and Grover Cleveland, a Democrat.[1]

During TR's tenure as Civil Service commissioner, many of the traits that later shaped his handling of public affairs at the New York Police Department became apparent. First, he contended that centralizing power and responsibility in the hands of one disinterested individual was the best way to produce government that was at once effective and accountable to the American public.[2] He had little patience with administrative bodies that were divided evenly between Republicans and Democrats — often leading to stalemate, though appearing bipartisan — or that were made up of too many officials — preventing anyone from being held responsible for failure by diffusing responsibility. Oddly, for someone who on other occasions had lauded Andrew Jackson's outlook on statecraft (as a student of the Lincoln-Jackson school of muscular executive power), Roosevelt traced the ills of patronage to the Jackson era, when offices began to be "disposed of in the interest of the dominant party."[3]

Second, he took a more or less Aristotelian view of law enforcement, insisting that laws and regulations governing the civil service should be rigorously enforced and that lawmakers and regulators should exercise restraint when modifying the legal framework. To take a lax attitude toward law enforcement, or to continuously tinker with the legal order, encouraged disrespect for American institutions and led citizens to conclude that their leaders were not themselves serious about the substance of, or obedience to, the law. Roosevelt attributed much of his success to "better enforcement of the law," as well as to the extension of the classified service under successive administrations beginning with that of President Chester Arthur.[4] To be sure, enforcing the law was not an easy task. While cabinet secretaries could generally be trusted not to violate the rules personally, it was necessary "to goad them continually to see that they do not allow their subordinates to evade the law"; and persuading the president or the cabinet secretaries to punish those guilty of malfeasance after the fact was difficult. Even under the most auspicious conditions, an "unscrupulous head" of a backwater office or bureau might try to "persecute his subordinates who are politically opposed to him into resigning, or to trump up charges against them on which they can be dismissed."[5]

Third, TR demanded that the spoils system, the practice of awarding government jobs to political supporters ("political pulls," he sometimes called it), give way to the merit principle in government hiring and promotions. He fought to extend the classified service, in which job candidates were evaluated by written examination, to as many federal posts as possible—taking political influence, and the corruption that went hand-in-hand with it, out of the equation.[6] Publicizing wrongdoing and subjecting wrongdoers to public opprobrium were other effective means of deterring repeat offenses.[7] Patronage, declared TR, was little more than a conduit for bribery: "It treats all offices as fit objects wherewith to reward partisan service, as prizes to be scrambled for by the smirched victors in a contemptible struggle for political plunder, as bribes to be parceled out among the most active and influential henchmen of the various party leaders." Those who upheld the merit system, by contrast, maintained that "offices should be held for the benefit of the whole public" and that "the truly American and democratic way of filling these offices is by an open and manly rivalry, into which every American citizen has a right to enter, without any more regard being paid to his political than to his religious creed." Just as a patriotic Americanism demanded that citizens be treated without regard to superficial characteristics, so it was incumbent on the U.S. government to evaluate job applicants objectively, by "honest, common-sense, competitive examinations," rather than by race, religion, or political leanings.[8]

Fourth, and closely related, TR, like other good-government advocates, insisted that the civil-service machinery be cleansed of partisan politics. Both parties were guilty of spoils politics. On numerous occasions TR rebuffed entreaties from Republicans who expected him to make decisions out of party loyalty rather than dispassionate devotion to the public good. For him, a cohort of nonpartisan officials that applied the laws and regulations in a rigid, nonpartisan manner was crucial to assure that government functioned in the public interest. "Of course all the politicians to whom politics is merely a trade and a means of livelihood do everything in their power to hinder the growth" of public revulsion against the spoils system. Consequently, foretold TR, career politicians would attempt to "thwart the progress of the reform, to obstruct and hamper the execution of the law, and to cripple the Civil Service Commission and the other administrative bodies by which the law is executed. Their great aim is to make the law inoperative and bring it into contempt." Occasionally the congressional foes of civil-service reform waxed bolder: under President Ulysses Grant, for instance, Congress had refused to appropriate funds to operate the Civil Service Commission in a bid to decapitate the reform movement. Reformers clearly had to be vigilant.[9]

The postal and customs services were particularly prone to partisan influence—making them a magnet for Roosevelt's attentions. During his tenure at the Civil Service Commission he scourged "spoilsmen" in agencies such as the Baltimore post office. One common practice, as Roosevelt discovered when investigating the Baltimore postmaster general, a Mr. Brown, was assessing subordinates for contributions to their superior's political party and retaliating against them if they balked. The "seemingly almost universal payment of campaign assessments at election time" gave TR ample cause for suspicion. In his defense, Brown told the investigators that the contributions had gone to whichever party was in power, protesting that "it was expected of every man holding a political job." This kind of logic carried little weight with Roosevelt. Another widespread practice (again, in the case of Baltimore) was "the wholesale dismissal of post office employees for political reasons," in what was "known in the spoils vernacular as a 'clean sweep' of the office." (Of the 367 carriers and clerks in the public employ four years previously, only 11 remained—a 96 percent turnover rate.) Pointing to the lack of settled policy on such matters, Roosevelt declined to recommend that the postmaster general be fired or to demand his resignation, but he did urge his fellow commissioners to adopt such a policy for the future.[10]

How did his thinking on public administration influence conduct of diplomacy? As discussed in later chapters, Roos justified U.S. involvement in the affairs of foreign peoples in much the same terms he used to advocate good government within the United States itself. He argued that the job of the United States in nations such as the Philippines, Cuba, and Santo Domingo was to provide less-developed societies with the habits and institutions necessary for good government—just as it was the job of reformers at home to ferret out spoilsmen, buttressing America's own claims to be an exemplar of good government and a bastion of progressive civilization. "No republic can permanently endure," he declared, "when its politics are corrupt and base"; and patronage was sure to bring about that unhappy result in the long run.[11] The spoils system was "essentially undemocratic," and, left unchecked, led inexorably to "corrupt and ignorant oligarchy," in which only the "vile and the dishonest" were permitted to hold office. This was alike true of foreign countries—TR singled out Russian despotism—and of the great American cities where machine politics threatened the workings of democratic society.[12]

A fighting spirit was as critical to civil-service reform, maintained Roosevelt, as it was to other grand enterprises. "The friends of the civil-service law, like the friends of all other laws, would be in a bad way if they had to rely solely upon the backing of the timid good." Because there was "a good deal of rough-and-tumble fighting" to be done in public life, "a man is entirely out of place in it if he does not possess the virile qualities, and if he fails to show himself ready and able to hit back when assailed."[13] A combative spirit was the antidote to timidity.

Combating "Political Pulls" at the New York Police Department

TR's no-nonsense outlook on civil-service reform carried over into his conduct as president of the Board of Commissioners at the New York Police Department. In 1894, fed up with corruption, a loose coalition of Republicans, anti-Tammany Democrats, and reform Independents had ousted Tammany Hall and brought to power a reform mayor, William Strong. Asked to join the newly instituted police board, TR quickly secured election to the board presidency and set out to implement the ideas he had fine-tuned during his years at the U.S. Civil Service Commission. This was no small task, said TR, for civic corruption suffused the police department, spilling over into the wider polity of New York City. This was largely a function of big-city machine politics, with whose workings he had become intimately acquainted while serving in the state legislature.[14] Within the police bureaucracy, for instance, "both promotions and appointments toward the close of Tammany rule were made almost solely for money, and the prices were discussed with cynical frankness." Two or three hundred dollars purchased an appointment as patrolman, while a commission as police captain typically fetched fifteen thousand dollars. Worse, the police force was in the habit of enriching itself through systematic blackmail of business owners and ordinary citizens. "This was chiefly carried on at the expense of gamblers, liquor-sellers, and keepers of disorderly houses [brothels]; but every form of vice and crime contributed more or less, and a great many respectable people who were ignorant or timid were blackmailed under pretense of forbidding or allowing them to violate obscure ordinances and the like."[15]

Roosevelt remained as vehement as ever about rigid law enforcement and the need to shape an effectual legal order. One of his first orders of business was removing Thomas Byrnes, the chief of police, an ally of Tammany Hall, and a staunch defender of the corrupt status quo. To Commissioner Roosevelt's delight, the ouster of Chief Byrnes induced a multitude of senior officers to retire—allowing the Strong administration to fill their slots with officers whose ethics were more to the liking of good-government proponents.[16] Another perennial irritant, and one that was not so easily disposed of, was the composition of the police board. Shortly after the board began its work, Tammany's friends in Albany had pushed through the Lexow Bill, also known as the Bipartisan Police Bill, which, Roosevelt claimed, "was avowedly designed to make it difficult to get effective action."[17] His complaints were four. First, the legislation pegged board membership at four, two Democrats and two Republicans, making it tedious to muster a majority even on routine matters.[18] In the early going, the commissioners worked together amicably in a spirit of bipartisanship. As time progressed, however, personal enmities and shifting coalitions among the board members increasingly held back Roosevelt's efforts to realize his vision of police reform.[19]

Second, the law conferred a veto on each member in "certain very important matters," such as the permanent promotion of senior officers. The veto power was Roosevelt's eventual reason for leaving the police department before the end of his term. Andrew Parker, one of TR's fellow commissioners and a Democrat, chose to flex his veto on numerous occasions in 1896–97, chiefly on personnel decisions. His motivations for deadlocking the board's decision making remained mysterious. Personal envy toward Roosevelt, who invariably grabbed headlines and whose propensity for unilateral action rankled with his colleagues, was probably responsible. Parker's "cunning, unscrupulous and shifty" ways, complained TR to his sister Anna, posed "an almost intolerable difficulty" for the police board.[20]

Third, the law provided that, "even when we were unanimous," the chief of police, "our nominal subordinate, should have entirely independent action in the most important matters, and should be practically irremovable, except for proved corruption; so that he was responsible to nobody." Fourth, and closely related, the mayor "was similarly hindered from removing any police commissioner, so that when one of our colleagues [Parker] began obstructing the work of the board, and thwarting its effort to reform the force, the mayor in vain strove to turn him out." (The flimsiness of the accusations Roosevelt leveled against Parker did not help.) TR viewed the law, in short, as a recipe for administrative deadlock. He reproached the legislature for deliberately spawning "a complete divorce of power and responsibility," which made it "exceedingly difficult either to do anything, or to place anywhere, the responsibility for not doing it." As under other circumstances, he argued that the best way to achieve useful results in an administrative body was to entrust power and responsibility to one person accountable to the public.[21] "I believe in the centralization of power and responsibility in an impersonal organization like a board of police commissioners or jury or anything like that" because otherwise "the responsibility becomes so diversified that a large portion of it is frequently lost. You will find that the people will hold to a stricter accountability one officer about whom they know much, than fifty about whom they know little."[22]

Yet the board had to make do with the police law as it stood. Creating a culture of disinterested law enforcement was one of the keys to police reform; personal oversight of the transformation process was essential. The war to cleanse the police force of corruption had several fronts. First, in the quest for good government, TR sought to expel "political pull," that is, political influence, from hiring, firing, and promotion decisions, just as he had tried to do within the federal civil service.[23] Many Republicans who had expected to enjoy the fruits of patronage under the Strong administration saw their expectations go unfulfilled. As he had in Washington, Roosevelt railed against the spoils system and vowed to make merit the lone standard for personnel decisions.[24]

Second, he sought to reorganize the police department's cultural problem out of existence. That Theodore Roosevelt made little distinction between military and law-enforcement functions is abundantly clear. In this he may have looked to the British example. As early as 1822 Sir Robert Peel had drawn liberally on the military model to create London's Metropolitan Police, famed by TR's day as Scotland Yard.[25] TR averred that "many of the principles . . . which obtain in the army" applied equally to the administration of a police department.[26] He justified the police board's new policy of rewarding "personal prowess as shown in any special feat of daring" by observing that "the police service is military in character, and we wished to encourage the military virtues." Emulating the armed services, the police department instituted "a system of rigid competitive examinations," complemented by "a very severe physical examination" and "a rigid investigation of character." The department even adopted uniforms that had a martial flair to them. As a consequence of this effort to fashion a quasi-military police service, recounted TR, former military men fared boot in obtaining positions as patrolmen. Making "war upon all criminals alike" required the police department to gird itself for battle, much as soldiers girded themselves for combat against foreign enemies.[27]

Third, transforming the police department culture meant stamping out graft among corrupt policemen. Roosevelt made his reputation with newsmen early in his term as police commissioner, when he and acquaintances, including Jacob Riis and Lincoln Steffens, "made frequent personal inspections" of the city streets, dubbed "midnight rambles," in search of official vice.[28] They turned up "anywhere, at any time" to find out "whom among our upper subordinates we could trust and whom we could not."[29] Patrolmen found to be on the take, drinking or whoring on duty, or brutalizing the citizenry were subjected to informal trials by the police board and its crusading president.[30] TR denied that he reflexively sided with citizens who filed complaints against the department during these forums. He reported that he had displayed little "of that maudlin sympathy for the criminal, disorderly, and lawless classes which is such a particularly unhealthy sign of social development." If a mob "threatened violence we were glad to have the mob hurt"; if a "criminal showed fight we expected the officer to use any weapon that was necessary to overcome him on the instant."[31] Once examples had been made of several officers, the frequency of offenses tapered off rapidly. Also helping morale was the police board's parallel policy of using promotions to reward valor.[32]

These themes—good government, disinterested police work, and encouragement of respect for the law—converged in Commissioner Roosevelt's campaign to vigorously enforce the Sunday closure law, passed in the early 1890s. The law forbade saloons to sell alcohol on the Sabbath. Roosevelt characterized it as a product of political cowardice. "In New York," he declared, "we suffer from the altogether too common tendency to make any law which a certain section of the community wants, and then to allow that law to be more or less of a dead letter if any other section of the community objects to it. The multiplication of laws by the legislature, and their partial enforcement by the executive authorities," deadened citizens' respect for the rule of law, degrading civic conditions in the city. In the case of the liquor law, lawmakers and their constituents from rural New York State, especially temperance proponents, "felt that liquor should not be sold on Sunday," while the "larger part of New York City," notably the large German immigrant population, "wished to drink liquor on Sunday."[33] Politicians wanted to please all segments of society. They often did so by winking at lawbreaking.

Roosevelt declined to say whether he personally favored the Sunday closure law. Although he believed drinking wrought enormous harm among the working classes, he hinted that he personally opposed the law. For him that was beside the point: he was less interested in suppressing alcohol consumption than in improving the civic climate, which corroded when laws were enforced arbitrarily or, in the case of the liquor law, corruptly. He turned a deaf ear to arguments that laws not backed by popular sentiment should not be enforced and to not-so-veiled threats that his hardheadedness would cost him politically. "If it meant a hundred political deaths for me to obey my duty," he told one city official, "I would do it. I would not move an inch."[34] In any case, noted TR, the "Sunday liquor law was by no means a dead letter" when he and his fellow commissioners took office; some eight thousand arrests had been made under the Tammany regime the previous year. The problem was that "it was only executed against those who either had no political pull, or who refused to pay money" to escape the law's strictures. And based on a report from his predecessor on the police board, TR alleged that some of the saloon keepers had bartered their political support to Tammany in exchange for relief from the blackmail normally exacted by crooked police officials.[35] Such malfeasance represented a plain abuse of the New York City police power.

What to do? "Under these circumstances," explained Commissioner Roosevelt, "the new police board had one of two courses to follow. We could either instruct the police to allow all the saloon-keepers to become lawbreakers, or else we could instruct them to allow none to be lawbreakers." The police board took the latter course, cracking down on locales frequented by the wealthy and politically well connected as well as the poor and powerless. "After the Saloon Men," read a headline in the *New York Times*, aptly summarizing the strategy of the police board.[36] For a while the police "had a regular fight, and on Sundays had to employ half the force" to implement the liquor law. The crackdown provoked an outcry from immigrant groups.[37] The yellow press and the German newspapers in particular assailed Roosevelt "with a ferocity which really verged on insanity." Still, he declared that a "very wholesome lesson" had been delivered: "a law should not be put on the statute-books if it was not meant to be enforced, and that even an excise law could be honestly enforced in New York," contrary to the conventional wisdom.[38]

A final arena for police reform was the oversight of elections, a task long entrusted to the police department. TR contended that under Tammany electoral fraud had been commonplace, largely because of "the very low character of the men put in as election officers." To improve matters, the police board had created a system of examinations and character references for prospective officials. "We then merely had to make the police thoroughly understand that their sole duty was to guarantee an honest election, and that they would be punished with the utmost rigor if they interfered with honest citizens on the one hand, or failed to prevent fraud and violence on the other."[39] TR later brought this same kind of good-government outlook to the foreign policy realm when the United States oversaw elections in Cuba and the Philippine Islands.

Social Reform as Police Work in New York City

"I have read your book," proclaimed a calling card, "and I am here to help."[40] The book was *How the Other Half Lives*, an exposé of the horrendous living conditions in New York City tenements.[41] The book's author was Jacob Riis, a reformer and a reporter for the *New York Evening Sun*. The self-proclaimed helper was Theodore Roosevelt, newly arrived at the New York Police Department. The post of police board president carried with it ex officio membership on the New York Board of Health—giving Commissioner Roosevelt another venue in which to champion his Progressive ideas. Riis, said TR, was "the man who helped us most," by his "ardent championship of all that was good against all that was evil."[42] For his part, Riis recounted, "It was like a man coming to enlist for a war because he believed in the cause, and truly he did."[43] The martial allusion was not misplaced.

As seen above, the police power connoted far more than the simple maintenance of order, arduous though that was. Paired with order maintenance—the most obvious police function—was a hodge-podge of other tasks: supervising elections, enforcing health and sanitary laws and regulations, overseeing private contracts that impinged on the public interest, and the like. In Roosevelt's day the federal government had little to say in these matters, which were regarded as the province of local and state governments (unless, that is, interstate commerce or a breach of the Fourteenth Amendment was involved). So it was in New York, where the police department had a hand in superintending the health and welfare of the populace. The dual nature of his responsibilities was not lost on TR, who maintained that "there were two sides to the work: first, the actual handling of the Police Department; second, using my position to help in making the city a better place in which to live and work for those to whom the conditions of life and labor were hardest."[44]

Roosevelt's efforts in this enterprise were limited in comparison with the reforms he sponsored within the police department itself. Nonetheless, they provide clues to his thinking about the scope of the international police power. TR credited his and Riis's midnight rambles, for instance, with not only exposing sloth in the police ranks but with giving him "personal insight into some of the problems of city life. It is one thing to listen in perfunctory fashion to tales of overcrowded tenements, and it is quite another to actually see what the overcrowding means, some hot summer night, by even a single inspection during the hours of darkness."[45] The rambles stirred the philanthropist in him, impelling him to join forces with Riis to clean up the tenements. As early as 1886 the New York Assembly had passed a law that required the demolition of some of the worst buildings in Mulberry Bend, where mortality rates among the Italian immigrant population were triple the citywide rate and nearly a third of infants perished in their first year of life. TR brought his influence to bear shortly after taking up duties as health commissioner, and demolitions began in June 1895.[46] His brush with the harsher side of life in New York City, then, gave Roosevelt a foretaste of the rigors of enacting good government and public services in less-developed nations.

6

FOREIGN POLICY

"Diplomacy is utterly useless where there is no force behind it."

Theodore Roosevelt, Naval War College, 1897

Theodore Roosevelt had fused his perspectives on domestic and world order at an early date, when his term as New York City police commissioner coincided with the 1895 crisis over Venezuela.[1] Exactly how he made the intellectual leap from the domestic to the international realm is not entirely clear. On the one hand, TR told one correspondent that there was no analogy between domestic and international law. This suggested a certain skepticism about the prospect of world order. On the other hand, TR declared that the international legal order lacked only the sanction of force, and he held out the possibility that some kind of superior authority would emerge in the international system to take up coercive powers similar to those enjoyed by national governments within their own borders.[2] Some transitional arrangement was necessary to assure a modicum of order and justice until an international confederation could be constructed.

TR anticipated that the advanced nations would use force under certain conditions until then. To bridge the gap between international anarchy and world order, nations like the United States would exercise a quasi-legal police authority beyond their borders. He seemed to view the post-1898 expansion of U.S. political commitments as a direct, if attenuated, extension of the American system beyond American shores. A kind of international police authority would enable the United States to maintain order and nurture good government in its geographic environs—serving both the national interest and the common interest of the American republics. TR also spelled out conditions for the use of this authority. In his postpresidential years, he espoused the formation of a "League of Peace" equipped with an international police power and urged the architects of such a league to model their efforts on the U.S. Constitution.

Roosevelt's personal characteristics reinforced his thinking about America's world role. First, he was gifted with a multidisciplinary mind, able to range across the globe and from naval history to biology to natural history, to name a few subjects on which his nimble mind alighted. For TR it probably seemed only natural to view international politics as an analogue to domestic politics, with certain obvious differences that might be reduced over time. He had served at all levels of government at home, and so it seemed obvious that the United States could and should exercise a limited international authority, both in its immediate geographic vicinity and in territories such as the Philippines that were obtained outside the Americas. Second, he was animated by noblesse oblige. He sincerely believed that the growth of American power would benefit the peoples who fell within the American sphere of action.

Third, his restless temperament came into play. "Aggressive fighting for the right is the noblest sport the world affords," read a sign on Roosevelt's desk at the New York Police Department in the mid-1890s.[3] Roosevelt was not the bloodthirsty firebrand of popular and academic lore.[4] He lusted less for the actual clash of arms—although, should war come, he was eager to take his place in the ranks—than for political warfare that would safeguard the well-to-do while improving the lot of the dispossessed.[5] This required a combative spirit. Roosevelt wove his philosophy of collective action and moderation into an intricate doctrine of war, peace, and justice in which it was difficult to disentangle interest from ideals. This doctrine bore a strong resemblance to his Progressive philosophy of domestic politics. He equated state activism at home with the combined use of diplomacy and military power abroad. Both types of intervention advanced the cause of liberty by promoting order, empowering local authorities to correct the social maladies blighting nations that were undergoing industrialization, and thereby nourishing social uplift. Despite the obvious differences between the domestic and international legal orders, then, his approach to politics in both spheres was much the same.

When Roosevelt discerned an overriding priority in national or international affairs, he was quick to seize whatever lay to hand to support his intuitive course of action. Impatient at "technicalities" that impeded the exercise of power, he revolutionized the traditional view of the presidency at home and argued for an assertive policy abroad. Theodore Roosevelt believed his pursuit of the overarching good would excuse his casual attitude toward legal niceties that might otherwise hold him back. However he arrived at his expansionist conclusions,[6] TR's prescription for upheaval within and without America's borders was the same: righteous strife in the service of interest and collective uplift. Just as he admonished Republicans to embrace change in the domestic context, Roosevelt enjoined his countrymen to cast off the shackles of nonentanglement and throw themselves into what he called "the great world work."[7]

TR, the Frontier, and Foreign Policy

Theodore Roosevelt cited the American West as one precedent for his expansionist program. He praised Frederick Jackson Turner's famous "frontier thesis," which explained the sudden U.S. interest in overseas colonies as a result of the closing of the American West, the latest barrier to Anglo-Saxon expansion. Taming the West impelled restless Americans to turn their gaze across the Pacific Rim in search of an outlet for the frontier impulse.[8] TR credited Turner's influential pamphlet, "The Significance of the Frontier in American History," with shaping the latter volumes in his four-volume account of the *Winning of the West*, which he composed at the close of the nineteenth century. "I have been greatly interested in your pamphlet on the Frontier," he wrote to Turner in 1894. "It came at *the* right time for me, for I intend to make use of it in writing the third volume of my 'Winning of the West,' of course making full acknowledgment. I think you have struck some first class ideas, and have put into definite shape a good deal of thought which has been floating around rather loosely" (emphasis in original).[9] Roosevelt put this newly crystallized analysis of America's destiny to practical use when he burst into public life.

The battle with the anti-imperialists over annexing the Philippines was one forum in which the frontier analysis made a handy cudgel. Roosevelt pointed to the Louisiana Purchase. "The parallel between what Jefferson did with Louisiana and what is now being done in the Philippines is exact," he proclaimed in his letter accepting the 1900 Republican nomination for vice president. The conquest of the Indian nations had never been labeled imperialistic or militaristic; nor should the enterprise in the Philippine archipelago. "The simple truth is that there is nothing even remotely resembling 'imperialism' or 'militarism' involved in the present development of that policy of expansion which has been part of the history of America from the day when she became a nation." U.S. policy in the Philippines was "only imperialistic in the sense that Jefferson's policy in Louisiana was imperialistic; only military in the sense that Jackson's policy toward the Seminoles or Custer's policy toward the Sioux embodied militarism."[10] For TR, expansion beyond North America represented not a "great aberration" but the latest phase in American and Anglo-Saxon expansion.[11]

Yet the forcible subjugation of the Philippine archipelago, complained many anti-imperialists, flew in the face of the "consent of the governed" doctrine that underpinned the American experiment in self-rule. The U.S. flag, they insisted, could be planted only where the inhabitants had freely assented under the Constitution and where constitutional provisions would apply fully. To these critics Roosevelt replied that, after the sale of Louisiana to the United States, most of the territory's inhabitants, "white and colored alike, were bitterly opposed to the transfer. An armed force of United States soldiers had to be hastily sent into the territory to prevent insurrection, President Jefferson sending these troops to Louisiana for exactly the same reasons and with exactly the same purpose that President McKinley has sent troops to the Philippines." Nor had Jefferson deigned to negotiate with the Indian tribes. The Filipinos were unfit for self-government, continued TR, just as those who dwelt in Louisiana had been unfit for self-government in the days of Jefferson. He maintained that equipping the inhabitants of U.S.-occupied territories for self-rule before gradually emancipating them warranted imposing U.S. sovereignty.[12]

"We made a great anti-imperialistic stride," therefore, "when we drove the Spaniards from Porto Rico and the Philippines and thereby made ready ground in those islands for that gradually increasing measure of self-government for which their populations are severally fitted." It would have been disastrous to guarantee the Philippines in particular against European interference while declining to establish a stable government in the archipelago. Freeing the Filipinos prematurely would have led inexorably to the establishment of an oligarchy, possibly under the German yoke. "If we have a right to establish a stable government in the islands it necessarily follows that it is not only our right but duty to support that government until the natives gradually grow fit to sustain themselves."[13] TR's letter accepting the 1904 presidential nomination evidenced his consistency on these points, arguing for continued U.S. administration of the islands in terms virtually identical to the ones he used in 1900.[14]

That Roosevelt equated the pacification of the Philippines (and Cuba) with the imposition of the police power on Indians was abundantly clear. Nor was the evolution of American attitudes lost on Roosevelt's contemporaries. Of the 1899 Hague conference, one observer wrote that the aspect of the conference "which will have interest for American readers more than any other, is the fact that it marks the advent of the United States of America as a leading factor in the international affairs of the world." For this commentator, the conference, no less than the Spanish-American War, exemplified the departure from the Founding Fathers' counsel regarding abstention from European politics. While "Cuba lay at your back door, and even the Philippines came in as a corollary to an operation of domestic police," at The Hague the American delegation had abandoned any pretense at aloofness from world affairs.[15]

When Gen. Nelson A. Miles, a veteran of the Indian wars, asked to be assigned to the Philippines to prosecute the campaign against Emilio Aguinaldo, the Filipino insurgent leader, he informed President Roosevelt that he would like to bring Aguinaldo back to the United States for trial.[16] Roosevelt demurred, reminding the general that "at the time of the Pine Ridge outbreak the Aguinaldo of the period was Sitting Bull; that instead of bringing Sitting Bull here to Washington, the Indian police were sent out to arrest him, and when he resisted he was killed."[17] In the West the United States had established Indian constabulary units to help suppress lawbreaking of the kind committed by Sitting Bull. So, too, should U.S. military forces and their Filipino surrogates handle Aguinaldo, who had defied the police power that the United States had wrung from Spain by right of conquest.

The pacification process might be bloody, as it had been in the West. Roosevelt grudgingly conceded that American troops had at times been guilty of atrocities in the Philippines and other operations, but he reminded his critics that such abuses were unavoidable in counterinsurgency campaigns. He insisted, often stridently, that these lapses were no excuse for withdrawing from newly acquired territories and thereby abandoning the quest to spread republican self-rule. Of one such atrocity he wrote, "it is a lamentable incident of a type that happened hundreds of times in our warfare against the Indians. . . . My doctrine is what I preached in my *Winning of the West*. . . . In a fight with savages, where the savages themselves perform deeds of hideous cruelty, a certain portion of whites are sure to do the same thing." He vowed that U.S. soldiers guilty of war crimes would "be punished with merciless severity; but to withdraw from the contest for civilization because of the fact that there are attendant cruelties, is, in my opinion, utterly unworthy of a great people."[18]

On another occasion TR had made a similar argument, with a strong ends-justifies-the-means flavor, about the events through which the United States had wrested Texas, New Mexico, and California from Mexico. Roosevelt condemned the "feeling of arrogant and domineering race superiority" behind the U.S. raids into Texas. Still, he proclaimed that the annexation of Texas and the conquest of New Mexico and California had furthered the cause of civilization. "From the standpoint of technical right and wrong, it is impossible to justify the American action in these cases, and in the case of Texas there was the dark blot of slavery which rested upon the victors; for they turned Texas from a free province into a slave republic." Still, "it was of course ultimately to the great advantage of civilization that the Anglo-American should supplant the Indo-Spaniard," not least because of the benefits conferred on Indo-Spaniards who dwelt in the conquered lands.[19] For TR the greater good had transcended "technical right and wrong" in the Old West. His commentary reaffirmed his bias toward action.

TR leavened his perspective on Turner's frontier thesis with a moral dimension. Not only would overseas expansion, accompanied in some cases by the U.S. police power, refresh American democracy. He also claimed that it constituted a humane U.S. stewardship over native peoples, typified by energetic efforts to instill the habits and infrastructure needed for self-government. The armed might of the civilized world, concluded Roosevelt, was crucial to spread the benefits of honest law enforcement, dispassionate civil service, and social uplift—just as federal authority had imposed civilization in the American West.[20]

The Concept of Civilization

For TR, the concept of "civilization" gave domestic and foreign policy much of its direction. Consolidating constitutional republicanism at home and expanding the domain of the republican peace abroad was one of his avowed goals. He elaborated his theories on the nature of civilization, and the American role in pushing back the frontiers of the civilized world, with a candor certain to jar contemporary sensibilities. Yet his theories were more humane than the crude doctrine of the white man's burden, which had been used to rationalize European dominion over less-advanced countries.[21] TR's brand of imperialism— which he insisted did not qualify as imperialism at all—was more benign than the exploitative strain practiced by the European great powers. Like some of the most distinguished social scientists of his day, Roosevelt asserted that some societies were less advanced than others and thus could profit from supervision by the civilized powers. Since the most reliable exponents of civilization were the English-speaking peoples, and since the United States—declared patriots of TR's ilk—stood at the forefront of the English-speaking world, it fell to America to spearhead the drive toward a pacific world order.

Roosevelt prescribed a course of munificent, self-denying expansion that would promote the U.S. national interest while diffusing the blessings of ordered liberty. His writings evoke Immanuel Kant's republican peace theory while adding a distinctly martial twist. The great eighteenth-century German philosopher, one of the forefathers of liberal internationalism, had written that constitutional republics were inherently reluctant to fight one another. The citizens of republican societies tended both to discourage adventurism that interfered with peaceful commerce and to demand a higher moral standard of their leaders. Kant concluded that expanding constitutional republicanism across the globe would speed the advent of perpetual peace.[22] Similarly, TR maintained that spreading republican self-government was the key to world order and justice. Yet where the German philosopher had predicted that enlightenment would spread naturally throughout human society, Roosevelt maintained that forceful means were necessary to hasten the process. As early as 1901, he began hinting that the major powers could exercise an international police power under the rubrics of self-defense and civilization. He drew an exact analogy between social uplift at home and abroad. The United States had a great mission in the world. Not only must America defend its tangible interests "forward," consonant with Mahanian sea-power theory (covered later in this chapter), but it had a duty to foster the Western brand of civilization. "Every expansion of civilization makes for peace. In other words, every expansion of a great civilized power means a victory for law, order, and righteousness."[23]

Crucial to Roosevelt's analysis of justice and peace was his conception of the benefits civilization's spread conferred on both civilized and barbaric peoples. While war between civilized nations was and should remain infrequent, he contended, war between civilized nations and bordering savage nations was an unfortunate, but necessary, byproduct of the advance of enlightenment. In his first annual message to Congress, Roosevelt maintained that "of recent years, wars between the great civilized powers have become less and less frequent. Wars with barbarous or semi-barbarous peoples come in an entirely different category, being merely a most regrettable but necessary international police duty which must be performed for the sake of the welfare of mankind."[24] Roosevelt compared the imperial expansion of the great powers to the westward surge of the United States. He concluded that the United States was obliged to expand, not only out of self-interest but also to expand the advanced world.

Roosevelt offered two grand strategies for fashioning a realm of peace and prosperity. He wanted to preserve concord among the advanced nations while reaching out to the less-advanced nations and bringing them into the civilized world. He viewed America's duty toward the civilized world far differently than he did its duty toward the barbarous world. First, consider U.S. relations with the advanced nations. The destruction of a civilized regime could cause the demesne of the republican peace to contract. TR urged America, accordingly, to work to bolster equilibrium within the existing boundaries of civilization. To do so, the United States should discourage war between civilized states, preferably by international arbitration or other methods of pacific dispute resolution. TR lobbied forcefully for the resort to formal and informal tribunals. Holding the line against savagery was his top priority.

Second, the United States must help expand the frontiers of the civilized world by nourishing enlightened standards of conduct in the less-developed world. In extreme cases, cautioned TR, this could require the use of American arms. Roosevelt broke radically with the longstanding doctrine of nonentanglement, altering the ideas propelling American foreign policy. His vision of civilization, nurtured through the judicious use of an international police power, was a constant theme in the muscular foreign policy he espoused.

In keeping with his grand strategy, TR worked diligently to promote pacific relations among the advanced states. He was convinced that the well-being of the United States would be threatened should one power come to dominate a vital region such as Asia, Europe, or Latin America. Upholding a stable balance of power in far-flung regions would prevent the emergence of a serious threat to American interests. There were several means to this end. Roosevelt hoped, for instance, to avert a great-power partition of China that would negate the Open Door and deny the United States access to the China trade. Aligning with Great Britain to resist Russian or Japanese primacy in the Far East featured prominently in his thinking. Close collaboration between the leading Anglo-Saxon powers would foster civilization in East Asia while reinforcing the balance of power.[25]

TR's efforts to thwart great-power fratricide were wide-ranging and, on balance, successful. TR interposed himself between Russia and Japan when their war dragged on, seemingly endlessly; he mediated between France and Germany when the two great powers squared off over Morocco; and he pressed governments to settle their disputes through diplomacy. He favored the Hague system of international dispute resolution as a tool to manage discord in the advanced world. In 1907, for instance, he instructed the American delegation to The Hague to press for an ambitious slate of initiatives: an agreement mandating international arbitration, the establishment of a permanent court to hear such cases, a prohibition on the use of force to collect debts, an agreement on the immunity of private property at sea, a clearer definition of the rights of neutrals, and, insofar as possible, arms limitations. While it fell short of his aspirations in many respects, the conference did agree to renounce forcible debt collection—easing the fears that had led Roosevelt to enunciate the Roosevelt Corollary.[26]

In light of this advocacy, one analyst has suggested that Roosevelt's "second corollary" to the Monroe Doctrine asserted "the right of the United States to interfere in European quarrels that were likely to compromise its security."[27] Roosevelt's behind-the-scenes efforts in the negotiations ending the Russo-Japanese War (1904–5) offer perhaps the best glimpse into his approach to great-power relations. Dismayed at the prospect that Russia or upstart Japan might upset the frail Asian equilibrium, he agreed to secret entreaties from Tokyo to mediate the peace negotiations. He garnered the Nobel Peace Prize for brokering a settlement that ended the bloodletting in the Far East and, in the bargain, helped restore a balance of power in East Asia. Roosevelt labored to head off great-power wars whose baneful effects could endanger the Western Hemisphere.

Closer to home, Roosevelt voiced optimism about the future of Latin America. Argentina, Brazil, and Chile showed particular promise. "The history of most of the South American republics," declared his essay on the Monroe Doctrine in the obscure *Bachelor of Arts* magazine, "has been both mean and bloody; but there is at least a chance that they may develop, after infinite tribulations and suffering, into a civilization quite as high and stable as that of such a European power as Portugal." Because of their potential, he concluded, and because much of the blame for Latin America's misfortunes had to be laid at the feet of Europeans, it was "in the interest of all the people of the western hemisphere" for the United States to dislodge Europeans from their footholds to the south.[28] Great-power intrigues had no place in the New World. These sentiments ultimately metamorphosed into Roosevelt's theory of an activist police power wielded by enlightened American statesmen and prodded him to theorize that the advanced South American republics should themselves be endowed with international police authority.[29]

TR's model of civilization and barbarity had its ambiguities. He conceded that classifying nations was tricky work. A German republic might be friendly to the United States, but Roosevelt maintained that, as a despotism under the erratic Kaiser Wilhelm II, the Reich constituted a menace to civilization.[30] An even more troubling case was Russia, which tottered between civilization and savagery. Roosevelt became increasingly disaffected with the Eurasian behemoth, in which ordered liberty had obstinately refused to take root.[31] In 1905, speaking in the context of the Russo-Japanese War, he asked Secretary of State John Hay rhetorically, "Did you ever know anything more pitiable than the condition of the Russian despotism in this year of grace? The Czar is a preposterous little creature as the absolute autocrat of 150,000,000 people. He has been unable to make war, and he is now unable to make peace."[32] The result was misery for the Russian people that shriveled the national spirit and led indirectly to military defeat at the hands of Japan, whose martial vigor and industrial prowess were beyond dispute.[33]

Indeed, Japan's astonishing victory in 1905 induced TR, who interpreted the debacle and ensuing revolution as evidence of Russian decline, to wonder whether Russian expansion would be a boon or a setback for the cause of civilization. He concluded that the West should welcome Japan's ascendancy while remaining wary of Japanese ambitions.[34] Referring to China, he recalled telling a pair of Japanese dignitaries, "I thought it for the interest of all the world that each part of the world should be well policed."[35] Russia had shown itself unequal to the task of maintaining order, even within its own borders, but Japan had demonstrated both the capabilities and the will to police the Far East. He hoped the Japanese would use their military power for benign ends rather than embarking on a course of aggression that could upset the regional balance.

If being civilized was the quality that entitled a nation to exercise extraterritorial police powers, how should this quality be measured? The example of China showed that the most venerable nation could decay into semibarbarity; the example of Japan showed that a formerly barbarous nation could vault into the ranks of civilization—giving it the right and the wherewithal to police its geographic neighborhood. Because of sharp differences in their value systems, Roosevelt doubted that Japan and America, to take an obvious example, would be able to agree on which nations were entitled to civilized status. Although the evidence on how TR would treat such ambiguities is sparse, it is possible to infer his views from his analysis of Turkey. Although he seemed to assign Turkey to the realm of civilization, he also compared it unfavorably to Japan, which he regarded as an outpost of civilization in the Far East—a sort of honorary Western great power that manifested the manly virtues Roosevelt admired.[36] That he compared Turkey directly with Japan, a leading civilized state that commanded his admiration, implies that he regarded the Turkish nation as at least nominally civilized—worthy, that is, of such a comparison. Yet he deplored the Turkish government's abuse of ethnic

Armenians. He bitterly condemned the European great powers for failing to police their own periphery and chasten the Turks. Indeed, he wished the American people would support him in a crusade to halt the maltreatment of the Armenian population. For TR, the enlightened behavior of the Japanese outweighed superficial affinities linking Turkey to the West.[37]

How did Roosevelt square his thirst for armed intervention against Turkey with his insistence on order and pacific dispute settlement among the civilized powers? He did not say. From what we know of him, he would probably premise his case for intervention on a claim that the Turks had reverted to savagery and needed to be shepherded back into the civilized world. In 1903 he declared, "If the chance comes when I can say or do a deed for the oppressed people in Turkey, I shall do so." But there were prudential grounds for restraint—namely, public apathy and limits on American power projection. "I have a great horror," he confessed, "of words that cannot be backed, or will not be backed, by deeds." Earlier that year President Roosevelt had dispatched the U.S. Mediterranean squadron to Beirut to support U.S. claims in the Magelssen affair, which had involved the assassination of the American minister to Turkey; but TR believed considerations of power and public opinion ruled out anything more ambitious than that.[38]

Third, consider U.S. relations with the less-advanced world. Wars by the major powers against savage nations were necessary at times, if also regrettable. The quest for the republican peace might require application of "the warlike power of a civilized people."[39] TR wove a Darwinian thread into his arguments for "international police duty." Even if great expansionist nations ultimately proved unfit and collapsed, their achievements could still bequeath great benefits to humanity as a whole—witness the Roman Empire, which had left behind a system of law that endured two millennia hence.[40] Thus the prospect of eventual downfall should not deter expansion. Like Longfellow's King Olaf, the United States might on occasion be compelled to impose civilization and peace by force of arms. Roosevelt insisted nonetheless that "Fundamentally the cause of expansion is the cause of peace." While he acknowledged the many faults of imperialism and strove to put some distance between the European and American varieties of imperialism, he also averred that imperial rule had been an efficient method of imposing order on chaos and had, on balance, enhanced development among colonial peoples.[41] He again pointed to the American West. "If we ought to leave the Philippines now," wrote TR in 1899, "then we ought to leave Alaska; indeed we ought to leave [New York] to the Indians."[42] For TR the prospect of retrenchment was absurd.

If America fought against less-advanced nations, its efforts would be judged by their impact on foreign peoples. Roosevelt insisted that his handling of the Philippines marked a break with the European pattern: "the justification for our stay in the Philippines must ultimately rest chiefly upon the good we are able to do in the islands. I do not overlook the fact that in the development of our interests in the Pacific Ocean and along its coasts, the Philippines have played and will play an important part, and that our interests have been served in more than one way by the possession of the islands. But our chief reason for continuing to hold them must be that we ought in good faith to try to do our share of the world's work."[43]

U.S. foreign policy, then, would be tarred by association with European imperialism if it were seen as self-aggrandizing. By 1904 U.S. forces had subdued a stubborn Filipino insurgency, a native constabulary was in place, and efforts were underway to establish an indigenous parliament and foster economic development. TR repeatedly urged Congress to eliminate the tariff on Filipino goods—just as it had authorized reciprocity between the United States and Cuba, another former Spanish territory—to accelerate the development process and thus emancipation day for the archipelago.

Roosevelt meshed moral concerns with the U.S. national interest to define and justify the imperial mission. He compared U.S. deportment favorably with that of the other great powers: "More distinctly than any of these powers we are endeavoring to develop the natives themselves so that they shall take an ever-increasing share in their own government, and so far as is prudent we are already admitting their representatives to a governmental equality with our own."[44] Roosevelt's notion of imperialism as a variety of stewardship, and thus as a temporary expedient, was an innovation that carried the Progressive impulse to a new, global plateau. The United States was obliged to help police the international realm, just as the federal government used the police power to promote order and the welfare of American citizens at home. For TR the advance of morality in the world required vigorous U.S. action, possibly involving military means, to expand the geographical space occupied by constitutional republics—the dominion of peace and prosperity.

Roosevelt, Mahan, and Geopolitics

The United States began to look outward during the 1890s, partly at the urging of expansionists like Theodore Roosevelt and partly under the press of events. Why look outward? To recap: Several factors shaped TR's thinking about U.S. foreign policy. First, his reading of history convinced him that the United States could and should be a force for good in the world while remaining mindful of its own interests. He regarded the American mission in the Philippine Islands as just the latest stage in a process of Anglo-Saxon expansion that went back to the Louisiana Purchase and beyond. For him 1898 represented not an aberration from American traditions but a continuation. Tellingly, each U.S. expansion across North America had featured an extension of American political institutions once order had been imposed by force of arms. Second, the actual course of U.S. history during his own day prodded TR to advocate a direct expansion of American power. Providence had seemingly bestowed the Philippines on the United States—giving the nation an unforeseen chance to project power and implant American institutions in the Far East. For him, history taught an unmistakable lesson: the United States must expand.

Third, maritime theory played a critical role in TR's thinking. He seized on the Copernican revolution in American thought wrought by the Spanish-American War. The United States had sheltered behind its oceanic bulwarks for most of the nineteenth century. That began to change at the urging of expansionists, including TR and naval theorist Alfred Thayer Mahan. By the turn of the century, Americans had come to think of their nation as possessing an extraterritorial dimension encompassing not only Hawaii but also the Philippine Islands and the Caribbean possessions from which Spain had been expelled. Expansionists argued forcefully that an American commercial empire defended by a powerful battle fleet would secure the foreign markets on which the nation's prosperity was believed to depend. While he capably managed the mundane realpolitik tasks of defending the homeland and upholding the nation's foreign commitments, TR also proclaimed that the United States had a grand mission in the world. He exhorted Americans to turn their gaze outward.

TR's brief for expansionism rested to a great extent on concrete interests such as defending the homeland, securing a sizable share of world commerce, and constructing a canal across the Isthmus of Panama. He pled with Americans to acknowledge that the world was a dangerous place for a nation that, in the process of trouncing Spain in 1898, had burdened itself with significant foreign commitments for the first time. These commitments clashed directly with those of the great powers in the Far East and the Caribbean Sea. Roosevelt underlined the imperatives to defend the homeland, expand American trade and prosperity, consolidate the nation's new holdings overseas, and uphold the Open Door in China. These great endeavors, he argued further, represented the strenuous life for the United States; they would renew American democracy and reinvigorate the national character while also advancing material objectives.

Americans of the day were unaccustomed to thinking in the world-historical terms that came as second nature to Theodore Roosevelt, who after all was possessed of a near-photographic memory and whose voracious reading had given him an encyclopedic knowledge of history. The theories of Alfred Thayer Mahan, the renowned propagandist for sea power, armed TR with a potent weapon against the entrenched insularity of American foreign relations.[45] At an early date he had welcomed Mahan's writings, which argued that America should obtain a maritime commercial empire founded on a network of overseas fueling stations and should construct a strong battle fleet to guard its merchant shipping and new bases. Indeed, after reading the navy captain's influential *Influence of Sea Power upon History* (1890), he wrote to Mahan, "I can say with perfect sincerity that I think it very much the clearest and most instructive general work of the kind with which I am acquainted."[46] High praise from someone who himself was an accomplished author in the area of nautical warfare.[47]

As assistant secretary of the navy in 1897, writing confidentially on the subject of annexing the Hawaiian islands, TR offered an even stronger endorsement. "I suppose I need not tell you that as regards Hawaii I take your views absolutely, as indeed I do on foreign policy generally."[48] Indeed, he vowed to implement Mahan's ideas on maritime policy to the extent he could from his position of influence.[49] In 1901, as vice president, TR applauded a subsequent work titled *The Problem of Asia and Its Effect upon International Policies* (1900), declaring himself in "entire agreement" with the book's thesis that the United States should cooperate closely with Great Britain in defense of the Open Door and to maintain great-power equilibrium in the Far East.[50] Mahan's analysis thus accorded with Roosevelt's own views.[51] If TR needed any convincing, the Boxer Rebellion persuaded him that the United States and Great Britain should put aside their differences and cooperate closely to suppress disorder in China. "The stupendous revolution now going on in China is an additional reason why we should work together," he declared in 1900, while the outcome of the combined military expedition still remained in doubt.[52] "The Chinese outrages *had* to be stopped and the Chinese bandits punished," he told George Ferdinand Becker in the aftermath of the Boxer affair (emphasis in original).[53]

What were the concepts that inspired such enthusiasm? The navalists argued in part that America's internal troubles dictated expansion. Because two oceans insulated the United States, a policy of expansion would have an inexorably maritime cast to it. "Sea power," remarked Mahan, "is but the handmaid of expansion; it is not itself expansion."[54] But sea power was not strictly equivalent to naval power. Mahan defined this nebulous concept variously in economic and military terms. Economics provided the main rationale for a powerful navy and overseas expansion. Domestic prosperity seemed to be the central concern for Mahan, although his arguments had a circular quality to them: Economic growth demanded vibrant naval power, which in turn demanded economic growth, which in turn was predicated on overseas expansion. The pillars of sea power and, by extension, of prosperity, were: robust production at home, colonies and markets overseas, and merchant and military shipping.[55] Colonies and foreign markets were required to relieve surpluses produced by the Industrial Revolution, thereby easing social tensions at home.

With commerce, believed expansionists, came the possibility of conflict. Mahan and fellow navalists insisted that the prosperity of a great nation hinged on maritime commerce. They also insisted that there was only so much trade to go around. Navalists predicted that the maritime nations would wrangle among themselves for a share of the fixed pie. This competition would in turn lead to a naval contest to protect the trade.[56] It followed from this zero-sum thinking that the United States needed naval forces to defend its merchant fleet against foreign navies and to prevent bombardment of American ports. Mahan urged the United States to construct a modest fleet of armored battleships able to defeat enemy flotillas far from its coastlines and help make good its claim to a slice of international commerce.

Despite their resignation to international conflict, Mahan's disciples craved not war but a heavily armed peace—or so they said.[57] Roosevelt likewise discerned a symbiotic relationship among the Republic's diplomacy, its economic interests, and the availability of a combat fleet able to stand toe-to-toe with the best Europe had to offer. "Arbitration is an excellent thing," he told students at the Naval War College in 1897, "but ultimately those who wish to see this country at peace with foreign nations will be wise if they place reliance upon a first-class fleet of first-class battleships rather than on any arbitration treaty which the wit of man can devise. Nelson said that the British fleet was the best negotiator in Europe, and there was much truth in the saying."[58] Not bloodlust, then, but a sort of fatalistic, Clausewitzian resignation to conflict stood aback of the expansionists' theorizing. Since "commerce thrives by peace and suffers by war," vouchsafed Mahan, "it follows that peace is the superior interest" of great maritime nations such as the United States.[59] For him the navy was a necessary outgrowth of peaceful maritime commerce.[60] By extension, forward bases were necessary to permit warships to operate "forward," strategically scattered along the sea lines of communication. For Mahan and like-minded individuals such as Theodore Roosevelt, naval power and economic health mingled freely under the aegis of sea-power theory.

In short, Alfred Thayer Mahan made a stalwart ally in Roosevelt's fight against the comfortable isolationism of the American people. TR nearly despaired at the effort to rally public support for expansion. He bemoaned evidence showing that Mahan was more popular in Europe than at home.[61] "I am glad Mahan is having such influence with your people," wrote TR to Hermann Speck von Sternburg, a German diplomat and close friend, as tensions mounted between the United States and Spain, "but I wish he had more influence with his own. It is very difficult to make this nation wake up. . . . I sometimes question whether anything but a great military disaster will ever make us feel our responsibilities and our possible dangers."[62] Among the dangers catalogued by TR was the immediate threat posed by the Spanish navy. More troubling were German designs on the Caribbean and burgeoning Japanese naval might in the Far East, either of which could ultimately threaten U.S. ambitions in Hawaii and elsewhere in the Pacific.

Only some catalytic event could focus the energies of the American populace on the grand enterprise that beckoned overseas. Lord James Bryce, a foreign observer, had observed during his travels in North America in the late 1880s that "the general feeling of the nation [was] strongly against a forward policy" in Hawaii and the other islands that captivated Mahan's followers. Yet Bryce also suggested that the cause of expansion was not hopeless. After talking to a cross section of Americans, gleaning some sense of the national mood, he prophesied that the public "would not stand by and see any other nation establish a protectorate" over the Hawaiian Islands. Nor would Americans tolerate efforts by the great powers to occupy Caribbean islands such as Santo Domingo.[63] No amount of abstract sea-power propaganda would galvanize U.S. public opinion, but a foreign war might.[64]

The events of 1898, consequently, seemed providential to navalists anxious to jolt Americans out of their sluggish attitude toward international affairs. The U.S. Navy defeated the Spanish navy in detail, seemingly vindicating the navalists' advocacy of a battle fleet, while the nation unexpectedly acquired a base to project power into the Far East and reap the supposed bounty of the China trade. The overnight turnaround in Americans' perspective on world affairs dispelled the apathy about which TR had complained. Several annexations followed in short order. The fait accompli of expansion following the Spanish-American War complemented Mahan's persuasive argumentation, which by itself probably never would have wrought a change of such magnitude in Americans' attitude toward the world.

For his part, Roosevelt cleverly threw opponents of expansion on the defensive. In 1898, he observed that the United States *had* expanded. In the wake of victory over Spain, declared his letter accepting nomination for the vice presidency, "the question is now not whether we shall expand—for we have already expanded—but whether we shall contract. . . . To surrender [the Philippines] would be to surrender American territory."[65] Did anti-imperialists such as William Jennings Bryan, who had sought to make imperialism an election issue, really want America to shirk its overseas mission? Did they want to abandon a valuable base, seemingly bestowed by Providence, in the Philippine Islands? Roosevelt dared Bryan to answer in the affirmative—and be branded an ostrich and a coward.[66]

TR and the navalists' chief innovations, then, were broadening the geographic scope of Americans' worldview and altering the assumptions underlying American foreign policy. No longer was nonentanglement axiomatic in American statecraft. Expansionists answered their critics in part by citing the last sentence of Washington's Farewell Address, which promised that, following a period of consolidation on the North American continent, the Republic could choose peace or war based on its own calculations of interest and justice.[67] In essence Roosevelt's contribution to American diplomacy was to help reverse the "polarity" of the nation's foreign policy. Where they had formerly relied on geography to ward off threats to the North American redoubt, Americans now cast their gaze abroad or, in Mahanian parlance, "forward."

Tending to the independence and fostering the well-being of the New World was the first priority of an expansionist U.S. foreign policy. Rallying the people behind an assertive policy was no easy task in a Republic characterized by volatile politics. "I wish we had a perfectly consistent foreign policy," wrote Theodore Roosevelt, "and that this policy was that ultimately every European power should be driven out of America, and every foot of American soil . . . should be in the hands of independent American states, and so far as possible in the possession of the United States or under its protection." The United States, moreover, should "treat as cause for war any effort by a European power to get so much as a fresh foothold of any kind on American soil."[68] Even before the 1898 war with Spain, TR had begun mulling ways to prevent new European encroachment. A U.S. protectorate over the Western Hemisphere seemed an apt solution.

The Monroe Doctrine was the tool he hoped to use to prevent new colonization and, over time, dislodge the imperial powers from their American holdings. Why was it so important to oust the great powers from the New World? The Berlin Conference of 1885 and the realignment of the European balance of power, chiefly by means of German unification, seemed to signal a threat to the Western Hemisphere.[69] The partition of Africa, the seemingly imminent collapse of China, and the weakness of many American republics spelled trouble. Evidence of German ambitions in the Caribbean, punctuated by the onset of a powerful German battle fleet, was particularly worrisome for Roosevelt and Mahan. The potential European menace, then, demanded the change in perspective urged by Mahan. Part of the problem was technological. Steam propulsion had made navies and merchant fleets reliant on foreign coaling stations scattered along the sea-lanes. Bitter competition for island bases had erupted among the European imperial powers. An era of imperial rivalry that could culminate in a partition of the Americas seemed to lie in store.[70]

Competition among the great powers, then, threatened not only to shut the United States out of foreign markets, damaging America's economic fortunes, but also to provoke European attempts to penetrate the Western Hemisphere contrary to the Monroe Doctrine, which Bismarck had deemed an "insolent dogma" beneath Germany's notice.[71] European warships operating from bases in the Caribbean Basin could endanger the approaches to an isthmian canal, and thus a vital interest of the United States. A threat to ports along the U.S. Gulf Coast was even conceivable. Mahan's works contained ominous maps of the Caribbean Sea depicting the sea lines of communication and opportune islands from which to interrupt U.S. shipping en route to the isthmus. The growing threat to U.S. foreign trade induced Mahan to link prosperity to national security and to recommend an offensive naval strategy for the first time.[72]

Not only Americans' habitual isolationism but their allegiance to the Monroe Doctrine—in particular the doctrine's supposed pledge to abstain from European politics—threw up a barrier to the navalists' aspirations. To jar Americans out of what he regarded as an outdated worldview, Mahan used whatever implement lay at hand. He invoked fashionable theories of Newtonian physics, natural law, Social Darwinism, and the biological nature of the state. In *The Problem of Asia* he openly sought to apply the stimulus necessary to overcome inertia, the "force of tradition, of simple conservatism" underlying isolationism and the Monroe Doctrine.[73] He denied the permanence of Washington's injunction against nonentanglement, admonished his countrymen not to make "even this revered doctrine a fetish," and recommended readjusting "our views of its corollary—that concerning apartness from European complications."[74] Because the Monroe Doctrine was a policy statement, not international law, he concluded, it was not legally binding. It could be modified or discarded at need.

A higher law than the Monroe Doctrine commanded overseas expansion. "The first law of states, as of men, [was] self-preservation" in Mahan's Darwinian view. "Growth," for such organisms, was "a property of healthful life," which conferred a "right to insure by just means whatsoever contributes to national progress, and correlatively to combat injurious action taken by an outside agency, if the latter overpass its own lawful sphere."[75] Since all nations were bound to obey the natural law of growth, their expansion resulted "in a corresponding contraction of the ground free equally to all." The struggle over this fixed pie might engender conflict if other states resorted to "the alien element of military or political force."[76] Mahan ascribed the worst intentions to America's rivals and urged the United States to protect itself by undertaking a modest military buildup.[77]

Roosevelt too appealed to cosmic notions of destiny and civilization. Playing up the beneficent influence of the English-speaking peoples, he asserted that it was "for the interest of civilization that the United States themselves, the greatest branch of the English-speaking race, should be dominant in the Western Hemisphere."[78] Indeed, this was the patriotic duty of the American citizenry. Although TR doubted the ability of a democracy to sustain a consistent policy,[79] he declared that "it would be well were we sufficiently farsighted steadily to shape our policy with the view to the ultimate removal of all European powers from the colonies they hold in the western hemisphere."[80]

One point of mild discord among the expansionists was exactly how far the Monroe Doctrine should extend in geographic terms. U.S. "jurisdiction" over American affairs could go only as far as the military might of the Republic would carry it. An experienced military officer attuned to the limitations of naval power, Alfred Thayer Mahan maintained that U.S. power ebbed as the distance from its coastlines increased, especially when there were no forward bases to support power projection. Logistics represented a severe constraint on U.S. Navy operations south of the Caribbean Basin. Massachusetts senator Henry Cabot Lodge, TR's close friend and a kindred spirit on matters military and diplomatic, informed Roosevelt that Mahan "takes the view that we should not undertake to keep Europe out of South America below the Caribbean Sea, that Northern South America and Central America are enough for us to protect."[81] Mahan thus believed that the Monroe Doctrine should apply to the Caribbean Basin alone, along the approaches to the isthmus.

Senator Lodge temporized on this point. He confided that he did "not agree with [Mahan's] view at all, and yet I see the difficulties of enforcing the Monroe Doctrine in Southern Brazil, for example, and in getting our people to understand the importance of doing so at such a distant point." While he quarreled over the minutiae of policy, however, he was in full agreement on the military component. The army was important, but "the navy is the vital point. We must go on and build up the navy as rapidly as possible. . . . You and I agree absolutely as to the importance of this."[82]

At the opposite extreme from Mahan stood William Howard Taft, who declared that Monroe's maxim had extended U.S. military frontiers to encompass the entire Western Hemisphere. "By virtue of this doctrine," Taft informed an audience in Columbus, Ohio, "we in effect and for defensive purposes extend the frontiers of the United States far beyond the actual confines of our territory, to Central America and the islands of the Gulf of Mexico and the Caribbean, to the mouths of the Orinoco and the Amazon, to Magellan and Tierra del Fuego."[83]

Varying opinions on the geographic reach of the Monroe Doctrine, even among TR's closest friends, complicated the effort to determine how widely the president envisioned deploying an international police power. In the end he gravitated toward Mahan's more modest view. The overall drift of TR's writings and actions points to this more limited view that the United States should settle for defending the approaches to the isthmus, site of the future transoceanic canal. He declined to limit the doctrine explicitly—and in effect sketch an American defensive perimeter—for fear of signaling that the United States would tolerate European mischief beyond a certain line on the map. During his presidency, however, the United States refrained from meddling in Latin American affairs outside the Caribbean littoral.

Purposes of American Power

Roosevelt's foreign-policy thinking had a strong moral and philosophical component. What purposes should guide American foreign policy? The keystones of a prudential statecraft worthy of a "world power," maintained TR, were enlightened self-interest and high-minded sentiment. An activist United States could not be expected to act out of pure altruism, just as individuals factored their own interests into any decision.[84] As president he hoped to inaugurate a new and superior brand of diplomacy rooted both in benevolence and in realpolitik. For the United States that implied policing areas of vital interest, such as the Caribbean Basin, to prevent creeping European expansion and to foster a measure of political stability in a region where stability was rare. In essence TR declared that the Western Hemisphere fell under a kind of American "jurisdiction" because of the threat of European territorial aggrandizement contrary to the Monroe Doctrine and because the United States, as the leading "civilized" power in the Americas, was best qualified to help Latin America along the path to civilized status. "While paying heed to the necessity of keeping our house in order at home," wrote Roosevelt in 1900, "the American people can not, if they wish to retain their self-respect, refrain from doing their duty as a great nation in the world."[85]

This duty could involve military force. Roosevelt appealed to moral precepts to fashion a doctrine governing U.S. conduct in diplomatic and military affairs. He linked muscular diplomacy underwritten by military force to justice, peace, and world order—not to mention American security and prosperity. His insistence on the connection between force and peace, as well as his preaching of a patriotic internationalism, distinguished TR from the more legalistic Wilsonian school that dominated American diplomacy after the First World War. And his notion that the major powers should police the world to spread civilization was a call to grand endeavors. Had the United States abstained from the war against Spain, asserted TR, "all mankind would have been the loser." Roosevelt insisted that a just war was a mechanism for realizing grand ideals, albeit by violent means. "Unless men are willing to fight and die for great ideals, including love of country," thundered TR during the First World War, "ideals will vanish, and the world will become one huge sty of materialism."[86]

TR made an argument reminiscent of St. Augustine. He pointed out that even unjust regimes had no intrinsic hatred of peace. They might undertake war to transform the status quo, but once they had achieved their political goals, even tyrants would become staunch advocates of the barren "peace" that would cement their gains. "Tyrants and oppressors have many times made a wilderness and called it peace," said TR, and therefore the "peace of tyrannous terror, the peace of craven weakness, the peace of injustice, all these should be shunned as we shun unrighteous war." Although as a conservative politician he feared the disruptive influence of war, TR also refused to rule out war in the service of his notion of justice. For him political stability was far from an absolute good.

Should the two goods clash, justice was superior to peace. Inaction in the face of wickedness amounted to surrender. Roosevelt offered two historical examples to bolster his case in his 1899 article, "Expansion and Peace." First, what consequences, he asked, would have followed had the United States either permitted the Confederacy to secede or allowed slavery to continue thriving within the Union? He reminded readers that many people of goodwill had opposed intersectional war at its outset, for fear of upsetting the nation's political institutions. But America had "escaped generations of anarchy and bloodshed, because our fathers who upheld Lincoln and followed Grant were men in every sense of the term, with too much common sense to be misled by those who preached that war was always wrong, and with a fund of stern virtue deep in their souls which enabled them to do deeds from which men of over-soft natures would have shrunk appalled."[87] Second, he offered the more recent example of the massacre of ethnic Armenians in Turkey. "The great blot on European international morality in the closing decade of this century has been not a war, but the infamous peace kept by the joint action of the great powers, while Turkey inflicted the last horrors of butchery, torture, and outrage upon the men, women, and children of despairing Armenia. War was avoided; peace was kept; but what a peace!"[88] The Armenian genocide, he observed, had exacted far greater human suffering than the late wars between Prussia and France and between Russia and Turkey. This was TR's rejoinder to pacifists and isolationists who opposed his brawny approach to foreign affairs.

"Anti-Imperial" Imperialism

TR portrayed the Spanish-American War as the first bout in a sustained campaign against European imperialism. Ousting the imperial powers from the New World and preventing new encroachment from the Old would serve the cause of American—writ large— independence. Roosevelt drew a stark contrast between his vision of Caribbean diplomacy and what he regarded as the amoral diplomacy of the great powers. His appraisal reflected his distinctive conception of personal and national honor. He pointed to the withdrawal of American forces from Cuba—the first instance, he contended, of a great power's keeping its word to relinquish foreign territory—as evidence of American trustworthiness and benign intentions.[89] The United States was a worthy steward not only of its own interests but of the interests of civilization; and as such it was entitled to perform the constabulary function in the Americas.

Theodore Roosevelt espoused a mild, fleeting sort of anti-imperial imperialism that was grounded in his meditations on geopolitics and morality and incorporated both the national interest and international philanthropy. The war with Spain represented the first test case for U.S. interventionism. Roosevelt vehemently denied that imperialism or, for that matter, militarism of any kind had typified the McKinley administration. While European expansion had on the whole been a force for good—despite its inarguably baneful effects on native peoples—he was clearly ambivalent about the whole imperial movement and sought to distance the United States from it. He maintained that the American triumph over the Spanish Empire constituted not the beginning of a formal American empire but the "first triumph in what will be a world movement" against European domination of the less-developed world.[90]

There were, to be sure, abundant reasons for war against Spain, ranging from the most high-minded to the purely pragmatic. As relations with Madrid soured in 1897, TR mused, "I would regard a war with Spain from two standpoints: first, the advisability on the grounds both of humanity and self-interest of interfering on behalf of the Cubans, and of taking one more step toward the complete freeing of America from European dominion; second, the benefit done our people by giving them something to think of which isn't material gain, and especially the benefit done our military forces by trying both the Navy and Army in actual practice."[91] He candidly admitted, then, that he expected the Republic to benefit materially: "It seems to me that the time has come for us to fight, and that this fight will be of great advantage of the nation, both from the moral lift it will give us, and because it will mean that we shall acquire both St. Thomas and Hawaii."[92] The latter project, of course, had languished since Grover Cleveland, suspecting some kind of malfeasance, had quashed a congressional bid to annex the Hawaiian archipelago. TR expected that, should the United States vanquish Spain, victory would provide the political momentum needed to restart these stalled annexation movements.

Still, the salutary effects on the American national character seemed to occupy pride of place in his thinking. After a grand crusade against an imperialism that in Cuba had wrought fearful human suffering, the American people, TR believed, would finally be ready to take a station in world affairs befitting their material prosperity and moral stature. "For two years I have consistently preached the doctrine of a resolute foreign policy, and of readiness to accept the arbitrament of the sword if necessary; and I have [always] intended to act up to my preaching if occasion arose." War would wean citizens away from their unthinking allegiance to "the ideas of the peace-at-any-price theorists on the one side, the timid and scholarly men in whom refinement and culture have been developed at the expense of all the virile qualities," and, on the other hand, "the big moneyed men in whose minds money and material prosperity have finally dwarfed everything else."[93]

Roosevelt told Elihu Root, who later served as his secretary of war and secretary of state, "I have all along thought that we ought to intervene for the Cubans. I most severely [criticized] the European powers for not interfering on behalf of the Armenians, and it seems to me that in the first place our duty to humanity requires that we should interfere on behalf of the Cubans, and, in the second place, that it is obviously for the interest of our people as a whole that we should decline longer to allow this hideous welter of misery at our doorsteps, and that we should drive the Spaniard from the new world." Indeed, he bewailed the deafening public outcry over the sinking of the battleship *Maine*, which he feared had obscured the exalted principles at stake in the Cuban affair.[94] He hoped that people would back the war out of fealty to noble ideals, not momentary fury, and would join in the other grand endeavors he had espoused for the nation.

More importantly for the purposes of this book, Roosevelt found in the Spanish-American War a clear precedent for projecting the police power beyond national borders—although he had not yet framed his doctrine in those terms. "I feel that we have been derelict in not interfering on behalf of Cuba for precisely the same reason that I felt you were derelict in not interfering on behalf of Armenia," he reminded his friend Lord Bryce tartly, "and I never preach for others what I don't, when I have the power, advocate doing myself." Pointing to the Spanish *reconcentrado* policy and other brutal tactics, he declared, "For the last three years in Cuba [Spain] has revived the policy and most of the methods of Alva and Torquemada."[95] Halting these abuses, which TR portrayed as reminiscent of the Spanish Inquisition, warranted forceful U.S. intervention—just as the Turkish slaughter of Armenians would have justified European police action in defense of beleaguered populations. In the end the victory over Spanish forces was more convincing than even Roosevelt could have hoped. The peace settlement left foreign territories wrung from Spain in U.S. hands. TR, like many, detected the hand of Providence in this startling turn of events. The American project in Cuba and the Philippines, he proclaimed, marked the culmination of the U.S. surge across the American continent to the Pacific and indeed the latest phase in centuries of westward diffusion of Anglo-Saxon traditions across the globe.

7

INTERNATIONAL LAW

The "Insular Cases" and Extraterritorial Police Powers

How did the McKinley and Roosevelt administrations justify annexing foreign soil and, in the case of the Philippines, waging a sanguinary military campaign to put down the indigenous resistance? Could the police power be extended wholesale to territories won by right of conquest? Did the Constitution follow the flag, as the anti-imperialists insisted? In its famous series of rulings in the 1901 "Insular Cases," the U.S. Supreme Court somewhat tepidly endorsed the imperialist position on extending the police power—ruling, namely, that the extent of American authority should vary on a case-by-case basis. Extraterritorial jurisdiction was established by congressional action, subject as always to judicial review.

In *De Lima v. Bidwell*, for example, the Court found that, upon ratification of the peace treaty with Spain, Puerto Rico had ceased to be a foreign nation and thus that duties could not be levied on goods imported from the island without congressional authority.[1] Conversely, *Dooley v. United States* held that U.S. goods shipped to Puerto Rico were to be free of duty. The Constitution extended to the island, then, giving Congress the right to legislate and regulate for its inhabitants.[2] On the other hand, *Downes v. Bidwell*, the most far-reaching of the cases, asserted the principle that the U.S. Constitution did not *automatically* and *immediately* apply to the people of an annexed territory. Nor did the Court confer on subject peoples the full panoply of rights and privileges accorded American citizens. Rather, Congress was to determine which constitutional provisions would apply to the annexed territories and when such provisions would be extended.

Asked to rule that Puerto Rico had become "a part of the United States within that provision of the Constitution [Article I, Section 8]

which declares that 'all duties, imposts, and excises shall be uniform throughout the United States,'" and thus that "the Foraker
act imposing duties upon its products is unconstitutional" by reason of a violation of the uniformity clause, Justice Henry B. Brown,
writing for the majority, observed that the "Constitution itself does
not answer the question . . . whether the revenue clauses of the
Constitution extend of their own force to our newly acquired territories." The answer to that question "must be found in the nature
of the government created by that instrument, in the opinion of its
contemporaries, in the practical construction put upon it by Congress, and in the decisions of this court."[3]

To determine whether there was precedent for a partial extension of the Constitution to newly won territories, the Court investi-
gated American history, unearthing many relevant cases. *Downes v.
Bidwell* listed a number of instances in which the Constitution had not
been fully applied to U.S. territories. Of particular interest, since
Roosevelt also pointed to the doings of the Jefferson administration,
was the Court's analysis of the debate surrounding the Louisiana Purchase. "Suffice it to say," noted Justice Brown, "that the administration party [the Democratic-Republicans] took the ground that, under
the constitutional power to make treaties, there was ample power to
acquire territory, and to hold and govern it under laws to be passed by
Congress." Since Louisiana had been "incorporated into the Union as
a territory, and not as a state, a stipulation for citizenship became
necessary." As citizens of a full-blown state, the inhabitants of
Louisiana "would not have needed a stipulation for the safety of their
liberty, property, and religion, but as territory this stipulation would
govern and restrain the undefined powers of Congress to 'make rules
and regulations' for territories." Even the opposition Federalists
"admitted the power of Congress to acquire and hold territory,"
but they "denied its power to incorporate it into the Union under the
Constitution as it then stood." The Court concluded that both sides
were in agreement on the main point: that the Constitution need not
apply in full to newly acquired territorial possessions. This was instead a matter for legislative deliberation.

As noted in chapter 3, the judiciary was often called upon to
adjudicate conflicts over the respective powers of U.S. states and the
federal government. So, too, did the U.S. Supreme Court determine
the principles governing police-power allocation between the U.S. government and the territories annexed in the wake of the Spanish-American War. Of the Supreme Court decisions in the Insular Cases, Secretary of War Elihu Root reportedly quipped, "Ye-es, as near as I can

make out the Constitution follows the flag—but doesn't quite catch up with it."[4] Root's sardonic appraisal captured the ambiguity of Roosevelt's own thinking about an extraterritorial exercise of American legal authority. To his credit, Roosevelt believed that international negotiation, sanctified in treaty law, was the best means to give the United States a legal basis for the extraterritorial use of police powers when a sovereign nation was the target of U.S. intervention. This outlook on U.S. prerogatives formed the pattern for his diplomacy in the New World.

Quasi-Sovereignty over the Americas?

In the early stages of his public career, Theodore Roosevelt took an expansive view of how far U.S. authority over the Americas ought to extend. In this he was encouraged by the Cleveland administration's handling of the Venezuela border crisis (1895), which had not only far-reaching political implications but also far-reaching legal implications.[5] The encounter spurred TR to think not only about the Monroe Doctrine but also about the basic deficiencies in the international legal order. To the applause of expansionists such as TR and Senator Lodge, the Cleveland administration had injected the United States, wholly uninvited, into a dispute between Britain and Venezuela over the demarcation of the British Guiana–Venezuela border.[6] Roosevelt found Secretary of State Richard Olney's analysis of the situation particularly compelling.[7] Olney maintained that, despite the fact that the "civilized states of Christendom deal with each other on substantially the same principles that regulate the conduct of individuals," each state "nevertheless, is only too liable to succumb to the temptations offered by seeming special opportunities for its own aggrandizement, and each would rashly imperil its own safety were it not to remember that for the regard and respect of other states it must be largely dependent on its own strength and power."

"Today," asserted Olney, "the United States is practically sovereign on this continent, and its fiat is law upon the subjects to which it confines its interposition." By what right did the United States stake such an extravagant claim? "It is not because of the pure friendship or good will felt for it. It is not simply by reason of its high character as a civilized state, nor because wisdom and justice and equity are the invariable characteristics of the dealings of the United States. It is because . . . its infinite resources combined with its isolated position render it master of the situation and practically invulnerable as against any or all other powers."[8] Its power, then, entitled the United States to make its voice heard in affairs spanning the Western Hemisphere.

A newly industrialized America, maintained Olney, had not only the moral standing but the wherewithal to enforce its will. By his logic, physical might gave the United States virtual control over the New World—and thus a limited form of sovereignty.

In the Americas, the Republic might be able to supply the sanction of force that, as Roosevelt would complain to Carl Schurz, was lacking in the international legal order. The United States boasted a local superiority of naval force that no European power could match— particularly one with Britain's far-flung commitments and a nascent German High Seas Fleet to contend with across the North Sea. The United States had the strength, and thus the right, to prohibit a partition of Latin America by the great powers and to implement its own will.[9] Unable to meet Cleveland's challenge, and delighted at evident U.S. willingness to guard its interests in the New World, Great Britain ultimately acquiesced in this reading of the Monroe Doctrine.

Olney's shrewd blend of personal morality, high-minded rhetoric about civilization, and hardheaded realpolitik found a hearty supporter in Roosevelt, who warmly endorsed the administration's firmness vis-à-vis Lord Salisbury's government.[10] TR professed to be "very much pleased with the President's or rather with Olney's message" to Congress declaring that the United States would defend any Venezuelan claims it regarded as just. "I most earnestly hope he will receive full support from both houses of Congress," added Roosevelt.[11] Henry Cabot Lodge agreed that apparent weakness on the part of the president would "only encourage England in a policy which will surely lead to trouble if persisted in."[12] A show of American strength, on the other hand, would increase the likelihood of an amicable settlement, heading off a needless conflict within the fraternity of advanced states.[13]

Lord Salisbury delivered a tart rejoinder to Olney's message. Salisbury began by observing that the Monroe Doctrine had never been announced "in any written communication addressed to the Government of another nation," leaving its standing under international law shaky at best. Assuming for the sake of argument that the doctrine was a settled rule of international law, "the aspect which it now presents in the hands of Mr. Olney differs widely from its character when it first issued from the pen of its author" in 1823. How so? First, "Great Britain is imposing no 'system' upon Venezuela, and is not concerning herself in any way with the nature of the political institutions under which the Venezuelans may prefer to live." The disputed frontier, consequently, had "nothing to do with any of the questions dealt with by President Monroe." Because Britain was not attempting to colonize Venezuela or extend Europe's political system, the United States had no standing to meddle in the controversy under the Monroe Doctrine. Second, even assuming the United States did have standing in the dispute, it had voiced no opinion on the merits of the border controversy, and the U.S. demand that the British government submit to arbitration found little sanction in the language of the doctrine. Finally, Salisbury pointed out that "international law is founded on the general consent of nations; and no statesmen, however eminent, and no nation, however powerful, are competent to insert into the code of international law a novel principle which was never recognized before, and which has not since been accepted by the Government of any other country."[14]

Salisbury's analysis carried little evident weight with Roosevelt, who let it pass without comment. By their stubborn insistence on U.S. rights and their exploitation of potential force, concluded TR, Cleveland and Olney had brandished the Big Stick masterfully, precluding any British mischief. "I most earnestly hope that our people won't weaken in any way," wrote TR to Lodge shortly after Cleveland's message. He hoped that patriotism would trump material interests. "The antics of the bankers, brokers and anglomaniacs generally are humiliating to a degree," he groused, "but the bulk of the American people will I think surely stand behind the man who boldly and without flinching takes the American view."[15] With palpable glee, he subsequently reported that the *Harvard Graduates Magazine*, which emphatically did not share his enthusiasm for Olney's handling of the situation, was "assailing me with the ineffective bitterness proper to beings whose cult is nonvirility."[16]

The furor over Venezuela encouraged TR to think of the Caribbean Basin as a U.S. preserve, subject to the exercise of the Big Stick. "Temperate but resolute insistence on our rights is the surest way to secure peace," he had exclaimed in the pages of the *Harvard Crimson* during the Venezuela boundary impasse.[17] He next summarized his views in an exposition of the Monroe Doctrine in *Bachelor of Arts*. He proclaimed that his reading of the doctrine constituted not a departure from tradition but an extension of a principle that antedated Monroe's 1823 message: that New World territories could not be transferred from one European power to another.[18]

Venezuela also kindled in Roosevelt the idea that a U.S. protectorate over Latin America would deter European encroachment and thus benefit *all* of the American republics. In 1900 he told his brother-in-law, William Sheffield Cowles, that "if the Monroe Doctrine means anything, it means that European powers are not to acquire additional territorial interests on this side of the water." A joint protectorate between the United States and the great powers might be a prelude to European territorial aggrandizement and likewise could not be countenanced. (TR's discussion harked back to John Quincy Adams's refusal to make the doctrine a joint declaration, issued in concert with Great Britain, placing the New World off limits to the Old.) "I am not afraid of England, but I do not want to see Germany or France given a joint right with us to interfere in Central America, for how can we then refuse a joint right to interfere in the partition of Brazil or Argentine [sic]?"[19]

The no-transfer principle underlying the doctrine had a long pedigree. Even the "timid statesmen of the Jeffersonian era," claimed TR, had invoked this principle to acquire the Louisiana Purchase from Napoleon. John Quincy Adams had used it to hound Spain and Russia into relinquishing their North American possessions; William Seward had reasserted the doctrine to topple the Mexican empire of Maximilian. "The principle which our statesmen then announced was in kind precisely the same as that upon which we should now act if Germany sought to acquire Cuba from Spain, or St. Thomas from the Danes." Under such circumstances the United States would swiftly intervene, "if necessary by force of arms; and in so doing the national authorities would undoubtedly be supported by the immense majority of the American people, and, indeed, by all save the men of abnormal timidity or abnormal political shortsightedness."[20]

Roosevelt stoutly defended the Cleveland administration's actions in Venezuela, which, he asserted, had been primarily based on national self-interest and were therefore a matter of patriotism. Keeping European powers out of the Western Hemisphere allowed the United States to avoid militarism; conversely, to let "the timid and selfish 'peace at any price' men have their way" would invite aggression, forcing the Republic to arm itself to the teeth to fend off war. *That*, said TR, was where the nation ran the risk of militarism—not by the modest arms buildup advocated by the expansionists. Overrefinement, suggested Roosevelt, had blinded large segments of educated opinion to this fact.[21] TR likened American citizens informed by a "milk-and-water cosmopolitanism" to a man who loves other women as much as he loves his wife. He also insisted that national loyalties were in no way incompatible with a laudable desire to remedy the wrongs suffered by other peoples, such as those the Venezuelans had endured at British hands. TR noted that halting European colonial inroads also benefited Latin America, for "the only hope for a colony that wishes to attain full moral and mental growth, is to become an independent state, or part of an independent state."[22] He thus introduced the idea that the Monroe

Doctrine had an altruistic dimension, serving the interests of the southern brethren of the United States. But America came first.

The isthmian canal, representing concrete U.S. interests, was the proximate reason TR urged the United States to appoint itself guardian of the Latin American republics. He mentioned the desirability of a canal as early as 1894.[23] "I believe we should build the Nicaraguan canal at once," he wrote Alfred Thayer Mahan in 1897, "and in the meantime that we should build a dozen new battleships, half of them on the Pacific Coast; and these battleships should have large coal capacity and a consequent increased radius of action."[24] Naval power, embodied in big-gun warships, was the key to defending the approaches to the canal against European flotillas. That power could not easily be concentrated without a transoceanic canal—as shown by the example of the battleship *Oregon*, which in 1898 had to circumnavigate South America before it could engage the Spanish squadron near Cuba.

Roosevelt had the threat posed by Wilhelmine Germany uppermost in mind. The Reich had eclipsed the British threat in the wake of the Venezuelan boundary crisis and the rapprochement with Salisbury's government. "I do not care a rap whether [England] subscribes to the Monroe doctrine or not," TR told Lodge in 1901, "because she is the one power with which any quarrel on that doctrine would be absolutely certain to result to our immediate advantage. She could take the Philippines and Porto Rico, but they would be a very poor offset for the loss of Canada."[25] The United States enjoyed no such leverage over the other great powers. To prevent a countervailing European naval buildup in America's backyard, therefore, the United States should turn Spain out of the West Indies, acquire the Danish islands, and "serve notice that no strong European power, and especially not Germany, should be allowed to gain a foothold by supplanting some weak European power."[26]

While he had indulged in a bit of self-congratulation regarding his influence on the German naval buildup, then, Roosevelt was perplexed now that the Reich's maritime power held U.S. interests at risk. Influencing German perceptions was critical. In 1901 he told Lodge that the Germans would "regard our failure to go forward in building up the navy this year as a sign that our spasm of preparation, as they think it, has come to an end; that we shall sink back, so that in a few years they will be in a position to take some step in the West Indies or South America which will make us either put up or shut up on the Monroe Doctrine; they counting upon their ability to trounce us if we try the former horn of the dilemma." While naval preparation was necessary to ward off a confrontation with Great Britain, "the only power which may be a menace to us in anything like the near future is Germany."[27]

A clear U.S. policy statement, underpinned by American naval might and the willingness to use it, was the key to deterring European expansion in the New World, consonant with the U.S. national interest, thus sustaining peace. In 1901 President Roosevelt recounted telling a German diplomat that he "did not desire to see the United States gain any territory in South America itself, and that as far as I was concerned I would do all in my power to have the United States take the attitude that no European nation, Germany or any other, should gain a foot of soil in any shape or way in South America, or establish a protectorate under any disguise over any South American country."[28] By the time he entered the Oval Office, Roosevelt was primed to exclude great-power expansion in the Americas while claiming the constabulary function for the United States.

Shortcomings of the International Legal Order

How did Theodore Roosevelt bridge the legal gulf between imposing the domestic police power on conquered territories and exercising a truly *international* police power? Many of his contemporaries doubted the wisdom of extending the police power even to the former Spanish possessions. Some questioned administration policy because they loathed the prospect of war. Many entertained misgivings about the former Spanish subjects' capacity for self-rule and worried, accordingly, that the United States had embarked on a perpetual war it could not win. Just before the United States entered the lists against Spain, Senator John Spooner, a conservative Republican from Wisconsin, wrote, "I dread war, and, looking beyond to-morrow, I dread what is to follow war. . . . I fear Cuba having been rescued from Spain, may more than once demand rescue from the Cubans." Others questioned the material benefits of empire. The acquisition of the Philippines, declared Charles J. Bonaparte, one of TR's confederates, had "cost us a great deal of money; and any benefits which have resulted from it to this country are, as yet, imperceptible to the naked eye." Lord James Bryce pointed to the corrupting influence of imperialism on democracy. The United States, said Bryce, would be compelled either to set up "among an inferior and dissimilar population its own democratic institutions" or to "so far depart from all its traditions as to attempt to govern that population and its own citizens abroad by despotic methods." Either course of action would pose "danger to its new subjects and injury" to American institutions.[29]

Roosevelt's most systematic discourse on the legal basis for the international police power came in his 1905 correspondence with Carl Schurz. The two men's protracted debate over the course of U.S. foreign policy ranged freely from politics to culture to military strategy. In the end, however, it revolved around a legal question: might the United States rightfully extend its police power overseas, and would it be wise to do so? Roosevelt viewed the intellectual tilt between himself and Schurz during his second term as significant enough to merit verbatim inclusion in his autobiography—one of few exchanges of correspondence thus honored. And he was so well pleased with his own performance in the exchange that he forwarded the letters to Henry Cabot Lodge.

Schurz was a veteran and exile of the 1848 revolutions in Germany; a Union general and diplomat, not to mention a confidant of Abraham Lincoln, during the American Civil War; a senator from Missouri during the Grant administration; a secretary of the interior under Grover Cleveland; a president of the Civil Service Reform League; and an outspoken vice president of the Anti-Imperialist League. In a word, he was a formidable, resolute antagonist of the expansionists in 1898. During the Cleveland administration, he had befriended Roosevelt, a like-minded partisan of civil-service reform.[30] But the two Progressives parted ways on the future of U.S. foreign relations. At first a supporter of war with Spain, Schurz came to view the McKinley administration's policy toward the island territories as nothing short of "criminal aggression"—the term the president had used to disavow any intention of annexing Cuba.[31] By 1899, when Congress was debating the Treaty of Paris, Schurz had become an increasingly shrill critic of international policing of the type contemplated by Roosevelt.[32]

Schurz was a principled and skilled orator; he was also a strident and inflexible one. He richly deserved the description accorded him by John Hay, a fellow intimate of President Lincoln: "a wonderful land pirate, bold, quick, brilliant, and reckless,—hard to control and difficult to direct."[33] The Prussian expatriate's January 1899 convocation address at the University of Chicago, in which he laid out his most comprehensive case against the imperial enterprise, warrants reviewing here. Some of Schurz's points tell heavily against Roosevelt's own worldview.[34] Even so, TR came out on top in the court of public opinion; little suggests that his expansionist views ever cost him public support. In part this was because Schurz was less a savvy political operator than a political theorist, prone to hyperbole and slippery-slope argumentation. The fatal damage to American democracy that would arise from expansionism, a staple of anti-imperialist rhetoric, never came to pass. The United States did not retain the Philippines permanently, as anti-imperialists foretold. Nor did post-1898 America, its appetite for conquest whetted by the Philippines, hurl itself whole-sale into the contest for empire. The American people, the ultimate arbiters of U.S. foreign policy, evidently found the anti-imperialist case unconvincing or, perhaps, not of sufficient importance to warrant turning against President Roosevelt and his cohort of expansionists.[35]

At the University of Chicago, Schurz raised numerous objec-tions to U.S. annexation of the islands that had been wrested from Spain. Any effort to Americanize inhabitants of the tropics, he declared adamantly, would constitute "a delusion of the first magnitude." Whereas the temperate climate of North America—a climate that "stimulates the working energies [and] nurses the spirit of orderly freedom"—nourished democracy, tropical peoples would be resistant to the "common interests, laws, and aspirations" by which previous waves of U.S. immigrants had been assimilated into a "substantially homogeneous people." Having suffered under the Spanish yoke for centuries, and for assorted cultural reasons, these peoples would find it difficult to integrate with the Anglo-Saxon tradition of ordered lib-erty that had shaped the American system. So the imperial project, even assuming the sincerity of McKinley's professions of altruism, was doomed to failure.[36]

Why the gloom? Schurz ridiculed expansionist analyses that likened the insular acquisitions to the Louisiana Purchase and the other, previous territorial additions to the Union. The new island territories, he pointed out, were not contiguous to the United States; they were not in the "temperate zone, where democratic institutions thrive"; and they were densely settled, preventing Americans from emigrating en masse and creating a critical mass for republican self-rule. For demo-graphic reasons, consequently, the islands would never be admitted to the Union "as self-governing states with populations substantially homogeneous to our own." Last but not least for Schurz, a keen pro-ponent of disarmament, pacifying the previous territories "did not require a material increase of our army or navy, either for their subjec-tion to our rule or for their defense against any probable foreign at-tack provoked by their being in our possession." Whereas the United States could have continued to digest North American territories in-definitely without becoming a militarist nation, "immutable forces of nature" were arrayed against the civilizing mission espoused by im-perialists.[37] Putting the sanction of force behind the police power would be a mammoth undertaking in the Philippines and elsewhere.

The imperial mission would require the United States to maintain a vast standing military. Schurz worried that imperialism would be at once fruitless and harmful at home. Its potential to corrupt American principles, moral virtue, and institutions was his overriding concern. Because of pressure from imperialists, the U.S. government seemed poised to abandon its high-minded stance, embodied in the Platt and Teller amendments and McKinley's disclaimers, and to annex all of the islands. In William McKinley's about-face Carl Schurz found proof that America, if it once yielded to the temptation to acquire foreign territories, would be unable to resist the temptation to embark on that endless "career of conquest" that had ensnared European statesmen [38] Stepping onto this slippery slope would propel the United States wholesale into "that contest for territorial aggrandizement which distracts other nations and drives them far beyond their original design." Entering the imperial competition would expose overseas U.S. possessions to attack and thus demand a ruinous military and naval buildup.[39]

Worse, imperialism would poison American institutions and insinuate destructive habits of mind among the American populace. If the United States plunged ahead and granted statehood to the islands, it would have to grant the new states representation in Congress— thereby allowing an alien political culture, composed of "people utterly alien and mostly incapable of assimilation to us in their tropical habitation," to infiltrate and debase the core of American democracy.[40] Schurz painted an even grimmer picture of the future. Imperialist plans to build an isthmian canal, he claimed, portended a campaign to acquire not only a swathe of Nicaraguan territory adjoining the canal but all of the countries between Texas and the canal. Should these countries be admitted to the Union, the balance of political power would shift even more alarmingly, to the detriment of the original states and the common American culture.[41]

Alternatively, if the United States chose to administer its insular possessions as dependencies, it would erect on a permanent basis "substantially arbitrary government over large territories with many millions of inhabitants, and with a prospect of there being many more of the same kind." Carl Schurz prophesied that arbitrary rule over the islands would corrupt the spirit of liberty and natural equality. In effect America would, "for the first time since the abolition of slavery, again have two kinds of Americans: Americans of the first class, who enjoy the privilege of taking part in the government in accordance with our old constitutional principles," and a large group of second-class citizens ruled "through congressional legislation and the action of the national executive—not to speak of individual 'masters' arrogating to themselves powers beyond the law." This two-tiered system of American sovereignty would inevitably have to be upheld by force of arms.[42]

Erecting such arbitrary governments would be tantamount to surrendering the universal principles, held dear by generations of Americans, that underpinned the Declaration of Independence. Accordingly, Schurz cautioned "the American people that a democracy cannot so deny its faith as to the vital conditions of its being—it cannot long play the king over subject populations without creating within itself ways of thinking and habits of mind most dangerous to its own vitality." This "land greed of the Anglo-Saxon race"—to use Whitelaw Reid's memorable phrase, which Schurz quoted approvingly—should it become the settled policy of the United States, would condemn generations of Americans to entanglement in European affairs, contrary to George Washington's great rule of conduct, and thence to intrigues, international tension, and certain war.[43]

From the vanguard of progressive civilization, said Carl Schurz, the United States would slink back into the rear and, indeed, become an obstacle to international peace and justice. A U.S. arms buildup would contravene the spirit of the Hague conferences, which sought to broker arms reductions. Schurz enjoined Americans to lead by example: not to be laggards but to exercise their "beneficent influences upon mankind, not by forcing our rule or our goods upon others that are weak at the point of the bayonet, but through the moral power of our example, in proving how the greatest as well as the smallest nation can carry on the government of the people, by the people, and for the people in justice, liberty, order, and peace without large armies and navies."[44] He closed his Chicago address by exhorting the United States not to annex Cuba, the Philippines, and Puerto Rico, and thus step onto the downslope toward militarism. While the peoples of the islands might not form governments that lived up to American standards, they deserved the right to try.

Schurz's Chicago address highlighted three philosophical quarrels between skeptics of expansionism and expansionists such as Roosevelt, Lodge, and Taft. First, the debate between imperialists and anti-imperialists was a clash between universal and particularistic worldviews. Imperialists maintained that, schooled by the United States in the habits of self-restraint, any subject people would be capable of republican self-government along American lines. A suitable period of U.S.-supervised education would create a critical mass of citizens able to oversee the workings of their government and ward off oligarchy. Anti-imperialists were more pessimistic, and their arguments were clad in racial determinism. Schurz insisted, for example, that tropical peoples, for reasons of climate and tradition, would never acculturate to Anglo-Saxon political institutions. No amount of international policing would instill in them the traits underlying ordered liberty.

Second, anti-imperialists doubted the durability of American exceptionalism and scoffed at imperialist claims that U.S. foreign policy derived from a superior morality. Such advantages as the Republic did enjoy derived from distinctive political institutions—the very institutions that would be weakened by ruling foreign peoples. Anti-imperialists confidently predicted that the United States would become a typical, amoral great power, perpetually embroiled in balance-of-power politics and the contest for empire, if it once adopted an imperial policy. Schurz fretted that the United States, like other great powers, would never relinquish territory it had won by force of arms. Rather, it would most likely administer its new possessions as dependencies, its newfound taste for arbitrary rule over foreign peoples poisoning the traditions and institutions bequeathed by the Founding Fathers. (Roosevelt, of course, boasted that America had established a new and more enlightened brand of foreign policy predicated on individual standards of morality. He later cited the U.S. withdrawal from Cuba as proof of this claim. Both men, then, viewed Cuba as a litmus test.)

Third, Schurz maintained that the United States would have to defend its imperial policy by force. An onerous military buildup would further coarsen American traditions, drain the national treasury, and distract from vexing social problems at home. A large army would be required to put down native resistance in the Philippines. (He correctly predicted that an insurrection in the islands would ensue should the United States proceed with annexation.) Only a massive navy would be able to defend the American share of the China trade, as well as the chain of coaling stations that would be needed to fuel steam-powered warships operating thousands of miles from home. And taking on territories in remote locations would expose U.S. soil to attack—a danger to which the Republic had not been subjected since 1812. Imperialists, naturally, downplayed the expense of large armed forces within the surging national economy, pointing to the economic benefits of a commercial empire watched over by robust armed forces.

Who won the argument over imperialism? On the first point, the record is mixed. Observers a century removed from Roosevelt's and Schurz's day would have difficulty maintaining that the United

States, even after extending the municipal police power to the islands, managed to fully transplant republican self-rule to Cuba and the Philippines. Carl Schurz may have been onto something when—evoking Edmund Burke's defense of diverse political regimes—he argued that creating Anglo-Saxon institutions in the countries won from Spain would be impossible. Clearly, Roosevelt's blithe insistence that a short period of U.S. tutelage could instill democratic traditions that had taken centuries to evolve in the West was deeply flawed.

On the remaining two points of contention, TR had the upper hand. The United States did show itself to be a great power animated by lofty ideals as well as concrete self-interest. It pulled out of Cuba as promised and ultimately turned the reins of power in the Philippines over to a Filipino government. Acquiring overseas possessions did not enfeeble American institutions, as Schurz had predicted: the United States neither admitted the islands to the Union, nor administered them as permanent dependencies, nor exercised arbitrary rule. And finally, its far-flung holdings did not impel the United States to construct enormous armed forces—although the resulting mismatch between its foreign commitments and its meager armaments, and the impression of weakness this mismatch conveyed, was one factor tempting Japan to strike in the 1940s.[45] In short, while many of Carl Schurz's alarming predictions were well founded in reason, they did not, in the main, come to pass.

That was 1899. Six years later Schurz struck a more conciliatory note, imploring President Roosevelt to place the prestige he had reaped from mediating the Russo-Japanese War at the service of global disarmament.[46] He commended the president for "one of the most meritorious and brilliant achievements of our age, not only bold and noble in conception, but most admirable for the exquisite skill and tact with which it was carried through." Invoking the spirit of the Hague movement, he called on TR to use his influence to bring about "the gradual diminution of the oppressive burdens imposed upon the nations of the world by armed peace." As the leader of the nation that was best equipped to fund a large standing military and navy, Roosevelt would derive a "peculiar moral force" from such an audacious act of self-denial. Schurz concluded, "if there is any man in the world that can give a strong impetus, a real propulsive force, to such a movement, you are that man."[47] As in his Chicago address, he beseeched the United States to lead by example.

Schurz's appeal went for naught. President Roosevelt rebuffed his correspondent's entreaties, pointing to the yawning gap between domestic and international law. Shorn of all the flowery rhetoric of which TR was fond, the problem of world order ultimately boiled down to force. "There is of course no analogy at present between international law and private or municipal law," Roosevelt insisted, "because there is no sanction of force for the former while there is for the latter." No lawgiver stood above national governments. The major powers' ad hoc exercise of the police power was a substitute for a standing international police force, which could suppress disorder much as domestic law-enforcement organs maintained order within national borders. For Roosevelt the parallel between municipal and international police powers was perfect, even though the "persons" who inhabited the domestic and international legal orders—individuals and corporations within states, nation-states in the international realm— were quite different. Yet there was no supranational authority to wield the international police power. "Inside our own nation the law-abiding man does not have to arm himself against the lawless simply because there is some armed force—the police, the sheriff's posse, the national guard, the regulars—which can be called out to enforce the laws. At present there is no similar international force to call on, and I do not yet see how it could at present be created. Hitherto peace has often come only because some strong and on the whole just power has by armed force, or the threat of armed force, put a stop to disorder."[48] The role of the United States and other advanced nations, then, was to furnish the sanction of force that was sorely lacking in the anarchic international realm.[49] As in the domestic context, the threat or use of force by a superior authority was a tool for social equilibrium. Disarmament would be foolhardy under such circumstances; by disarming, the major powers would in effect be abandoning the nascent world order to the barbaric and the frail nations that needed policing.[50]

Roosevelt's innovation was to fuse this legal argument with his expansive concept of the U.S. national interest, his romantic vision of America's grand mission, and the Monroe Doctrine—in effect transmuting the doctrine, a purely defensive policy statement, into a license for a munificent U.S. imperialism. He argued that, as a stopgap solution pending the emergence of a more enlightened world order, the advanced countries should police their geographic neighborhoods. The terms under which the United States exercised its "jurisdiction" could, and preferably should, be set by negotiation and codified by treaty. Roosevelt drew an exact parallel between the civilized world's international constabulary duties and the law-enforcement activities of national authorities within national borders. For the United States this predominantly meant "doing what a policeman has to do" in Santo Domingo and other hot spots.[51] Because it held fast to the principles of 1823, the United States had to undertake police actions itself—preemptively—to foreclose an extension of the European political system to the New World.[52] The police power was not part of the original doctrine, but Roosevelt did use Monroe's precepts to explain why the United States would no longer permit European governments to undertake police actions in the Americas of the sort that had led to a partition of much of Africa and Asia. To make good his words, the United States maintained sufficient forces to bolster its diplomatic efforts and guard against trouble.

As in domestic crises, Roosevelt concluded, a national government's inability to carry out the responsibilities that went with sovereignty justified international mediation, or in extreme cases armed intervention. Roosevelt granted that an international organization might eventually take on the police role, leaving national armed forces with the more mundane task of preserving order within municipal borders. Yet he doubted that a viable organization would emerge any time soon, owing to the immature state of civilization. Should the less-advanced states be admitted to a sort of parliament of mankind, they could simply outvote the civilized world by sheer weight of numbers and erect an oppressive international order. Unlike more pacifist statesmen, TR affirmed that a universal allegiance supplanting patriotism—a necessary ingredient of any world body endowed with the police power—was "eons distant."[53]

What Was an International Police Power?

To fully understand the international police power, it is important to understand what it was not. It was not, first of all, a replica of European great-power diplomacy. Roosevelt's reading of European history, and the recent example of European intervention in the Boxer Rebellion (1900), kept him from endorsing the Old World brand of realpolitik. Mindful of their own and, they claimed, native interests, European diplomats had occasionally invoked the need for international police. But such pronouncements had been used as a pretext for Europe's spasm of foreign annexations. Where European missionaries and business interests first trod, troops soon followed, establishing a permanent military presence. From his training as a historian and his correspondence with British diplomats such as Cecil Arthur Spring Rice, Roosevelt certainly knew that the British Empire had invoked an international police power during the nineteenth century to justify its administration of far-flung territories. And he generally applauded the civilizing effects of Anglo-Saxon expansionism.

But TR acknowledged that even Great Britain's lofty ideals lent themselves to abuse. The mid-nineteenth-century Opium Wars, in which Britain had forcibly upheld the drug trade in China, were perhaps the most egregious example of this. To distance the United States from such disgraceful episodes, Roosevelt strove to strip the international police power of its more self-serving connotations. Most prominently, he disclaimed territorial ambitions in the strongest terms. He voiced optimism that the American victory over Spain had represented the opening fusillade in a worldwide revolt against European imperialism. To distance himself from European diplomacy, he reminded his confederates that the United States was the first great power in history to withdraw voluntarily from the territory of a weaker neighbor, in this case Cuba. The only way to judge American police activities, he maintained, was by the benefits they conferred on subject peoples.

The international police power also was not a reformulated, offensively minded Monroe Doctrine or a warrant to bully weaker neighbors, as historians and many of Roosevelt's contemporaries alleged. Rather, the police power was the common thread that linked the Roosevelt administration's interventions in Venezuela, Panama, and Santo Domingo and connected these operations with the actions in the Philippine Islands and Cuba. It was a legal concept that existed independent of the doctrine, which, Roosevelt proclaimed, was not international law but an American policy statement.[54] The doctrine simply explained why the United States would undertake preemptive diplomatic and military action in the Americas.

Even Dexter Perkins, author of the magisterial *History of the Monroe Doctrine*, was baffled at the apparent lack of a unifying conceptual framework for Theodore Roosevelt's Caribbean diplomacy. Only in the Santo Domingo intervention, observed Perkins, had U.S. action been justified by reference to the precepts of 1823. Perkins thus attributed Roosevelt's conjuring up of Monroe in 1904 to simple political expediency rather than principle.[55] Yet he failed to notice that Roosevelt had invoked the police power to help justify both the Panama and Santo Domingo interventions. Roosevelt also alluded to the police power during the 1902 Venezuela controversy, the other major Caribbean incident of his presidency. He cited the Monroe Doctrine in his 1904 message merely to explain why the United States would police the Western Hemisphere in lieu of European action.

The offhand manner in which TR invoked the police power probably helps explain the lack of attention afforded this aspect of his diplomacy. Even his closest disciples made little mention of the police power; the concept stirred little debate in the academic community, both then and today. A search of the legal and academic literature of the early 1900s reveals no scholarly articles relating to the police power.

Enthusiastic backers of the Roosevelt foreign policy, including Henry Cabot Lodge and Elihu Root—the latter toured Latin America to explain the Roosevelt Corollary—nonetheless did not phrase their defenses of the corollary in terms of the police power.

What else explains this dearth of commentary on the international police power? First, Roosevelt quickly realized that his corollary had appeared to claim a U.S. right to meddle in Latin American affairs. This understandably alarmed leaders throughout the region. To assuage their fears, TR himself downplayed the police power during his second—less eventful—term in office. Second, the U.S. imperial project TR envisioned fell into disrepute once he left office. Policing was linked to Taft's Dollar Diplomacy and Wilson's Mexican adventure, two distasteful periods in U.S. diplomatic history in the minds of many observers. Indeed, the Hoover and Franklin Delano Roosevelt administrations explicitly disavowed the Roosevelt Corollary to mollify U.S. neighbors.

In any case, TR had left the parameters of the international police power ambiguous, perhaps for fear of tying his hands in future crises. The term suggests that a power of legislation and regulation existed in the international system as it did within sovereign states. This supervisory authority constituted a way to confront turmoil in America's backyard, and its use generally corresponded to the use of federal power within the United States. The U.S. government temporarily arrogated to itself the authority to discharge some government functions, usually relating to finances, where a foreign government was unable or unwilling to fulfill its duties. Beyond that, the prudential statesman deployed the police power on a case-by-case basis as circumstances dictated. Roosevelt hoped that, if it led by example, America could coax the other civilized powers into embracing his more humane variety of imperialism.

In Roosevelt's estimation, then, the United States was the "on the whole just power" that was best suited to lead the campaign for world order. Law-and-order was the surest means of maintaining social order, abroad as well as at home. It required armed force and efficient public administration. TR invoked the shades of great forebears to underscore his commitment to law and his revulsion for anarchy. For instance, in an April 27, 1900, speech, he made reference to President Ulysses S. Grant: "Grant, the champion whose sword was sharpest in the great fight for liberty, was no less sternly insistent upon the need of order and of obedience to law. No stouter foe of anarchy in every form ever lived within our borders."[56] Grant had brought the rebellious South, which had defied the U.S. Constitution and the laws of the land, to heel by military force.

Similarly, Roosevelt claimed to have predicated his foreign and national-security policies on securing not the peace granted by the strong to the craven and weak but the peace that came by right to "the just man armed." A well-armed but righteous United States, said TR, would be able to act in concert with the other civilized nations on behalf of world order until the international legal system matured. In his 1904 message to Congress Roosevelt observed, "it is a maxim of the law that for every wrong there is a remedy." Since international law lagged the development of municipal law by a wide margin, there was "as yet no judicial way of enforcing a right in international law." When "one nation wrongs another or wrongs many others," argued the president, "there is no tribunal before which the wrongdoer can be brought."[57] This left governments in a quandary. They could either surrender their interests, and those of their nationals, or take more forceful action.

Compounding the intrinsic defects of international law, there was no superior political authority endowed with a monopoly of force that would give it the ability to execute judgment against an offending party. It fell to the civilized powers, which boasted strong armies and navies, to supply the executive function. Roosevelt offered the following analysis and recommended a solution: "Either it is necessary supinely to acquiesce in the wrong, and thus put a premium upon brutality and aggression, or else it is necessary for the aggrieved nation valiantly to stand up for its rights. Until some method is devised by which there shall be a degree of international control over offending nations, it would be a wicked thing for the most civilized powers, for those with the most sense of international obligations and most generous appreciation of the difference between right and wrong, to disarm. If the great civilized nations of the present day should completely disarm, the result would mean an immediate recrudescence of barbarism."[58] To stave off a resurgence of barbarism, then, the great powers must maintain armed forces adequate to perform the duties that—in a more enlightened age—would fall to international police. This led inexorably to Roosevelt's conclusion that, until "international cohesion and the sense of international duties and rights are far more advanced than at present," the major powers must maintain a "sufficient armament" to "serve the purposes of international police." This was part of the "general world duty" of any country "desirous both of securing respect for itself and of doing good for others."[59]

Duty, of course, was one of the cornerstones of Theodore Roosevelt's political philosophy. But the nations endowed with the police power were often at loggerheads with one another, stymieing collaboration to promote world order. To relax the tensions that were common in the anarchic international system, Roosevelt placed a high premium on peacefully settling disputes within the community of advanced states. Otherwise the major powers would fritter away strength better used for buttressing world order in their contest for power and prestige. Pending the evolution of the international legal order, then, the civilized powers had a responsibility to promote alternatives to war, such as the 1899 Hague tribunal. "Therefore it follows that a self-respecting, just, and far-seeing nation should on the one hand endeavor by every means to aid in the development of the various movements which tend to provide substitutes for war, which tend to render nations in their actions toward one another, and indeed toward their own peoples, more responsive to the general sentiment of humane and civilized mankind"; and, on the other hand, to maintain sufficient forces to enable it, in "exceptional cases," to take actions "which in a more advanced stage of international relations would come under the head of the exercise of the international police."[60]

By assenting to arbitration in all but the most vital disputes, then, the civilized nations could both cultivate righteousness in the savage world and attend to the health of their own communal souls.[61] Complementing his effort to nudge the world toward developing international institutions, Roosevelt informally mediated disputes among the great powers, garnering the 1906 Nobel Peace Prize for his trouble. He held out the possibility of forming a true international organization through the joint patriotic action of the civilized states. "Our aim should be from time to time to take such steps as may be possible toward creating something like an organization of the civilized nations, because as the world becomes more highly organized the need for armies and navies will diminish."[62] Maintaining robust military power now, he contended, would eventually pay dividends for the peace of the world by making arms reductions possible. Hence TR managed to turn the standard wisdom on its head: far from being an obstacle to peace, the civilized world's armed might, properly used, was an instrument of law and thus a platform to enhance world order and peace.

"Chronic Wrongdoing" and "Impotence" Justify Constabulary Action

As seen earlier, combating wrongdoing and checking abuses by powerful social actors were the linchpins of Theodore Roosevelt's political philosophy. And he constantly preached that responsibility accompanies power. The cultural milieu of the nineteenth century had incubated in him romantic notions of morality and honor. From these notions flowed an aversion to wrongdoing and a resolve to deploy power in the public interest. He socialized the knightly virtues, transforming them into a collective code of conduct. Roosevelt's notion of personal and, more importantly, collective responsibility impelled him to ameliorate social wrongs at home; his conservative predilections told him that a politics of social uplift was not only morally correct but essential to preserve the institutions and freedoms bequeathed to Americans by the Founding Fathers.[63] In practice Roosevelt warred on abuses by the trusts and corporations and curbed violent labor unrest while striving to reconcile the disputants' interests. He insisted that only moderate change to the Founders' framework could conserve the ordered liberty that was the paramount aim of American government.

He assigned top priority to the Progressive project at home. Because unsettled social conditions imperiled American institutions, ordinarily "it is very much wiser and more useful for us to concern ourselves with striving for our own moral and material betterment here at home than to concern ourselves with trying to better the condition of things in other nations." Roosevelt bemoaned a litany of domestic social ills. Americans had "plenty of sins of our own to war against, and under ordinary circumstances we can do more for the general uplifting of humanity by striving with heart and soul to put a stop to civic corruption, to brutal lawlessness and violent race prejudices here at home than to concern ourselves with trying to better the conditions in other nations."[64] Nevertheless, "there are occasional crimes committed on so vast a scale and of such peculiar horror as to make us doubt whether it is not our manifest duty to endeavor at least to show our disapproval of the deed and our sympathy with those who have suffered by it."[65] Mere protests unbacked by potential or actual force went against the grain for Roosevelt. Expressions of disapproval must include assertive diplomatic, and possibly military, measures that could halt egregious humanitarian abuses.

Clearly, then, the obligations to fight wrongdoing and foster equilibrium applied equally to the international sphere, although the situations militating for forcible U.S. involvement, "as we interfered to put a stop to intolerable conditions in Cuba," were "necessarily very few." Yet there were "cases in which, while our own interests are not greatly involved, strong appeal is made to our sympathies."[66] In the Roosevelt Corollary he proposed two litmus tests for great-power (American, in the Western Hemisphere) intervention in the affairs of weaker states. First, for Roosevelt, a country committed "chronic wrongdoing" when it reneged on international commitments and failed to discharge its responsibility to safeguard foreign lives and property on its soil. Second, an "impotence which results in a general loosening of the ties of civilized society" signified an inability to maintain public order or discharge foreign obligations. Both failings stemmed from a government's failure to carry out the duties expected under the Westphalian doctrine of state sovereignty.

Roosevelt demanded an activism on the part of Latin Americans similar to what he practiced at home. A failure to act positively under the U.S. Constitution, he said, verged on governmental impotence; the Constitution to him was not simply a list of prohibitions on state activity but a mandate to act in the greater good. In the Western Hemisphere the United States would guarantee the liberty of the weaker American republics—indeed, it would attempt to adjust disputes with the European great powers when a European seizure of territory seemed probable—but it also demanded that the lesser republics accept the responsibilities that accompanied their rights under the Monroe Doctrine. That meant working toward the collective uplift of American populations by means of Roosevelt's brand of state activism.

These justifications for the exercise of international police power were strikingly similar to those he offered for the police power in the domestic context. He invoked the international police power sparingly, however, preferring diplomacy to military force. Except for the special cases of Cuba and, especially, the Philippine Islands—in which the United States had been authorized, by the treaty terms exacted from Spain, to extend the municipal police power abroad—Roosevelt was generally content to make a show of naval force, suppressing disorder in hopes that a U.S.-backed native government could then attend to the welfare of its citizens without further U.S. involvement. His devotion to a universal vision of republican self-government did not prevent TR from taking a Burkean perspective on world order. Like the great British conservative, who, pointing to India and America, had espoused diversity in political systems, Roosevelt believed that ordered liberty could flourish in varying cultures. He was generally content to impose order and allow foreign peoples to find their own paths.

Thus Roosevelt's concepts of humanitarian idealism and enlightened self-interest on the diplomatic front mirrored the Progressive politics he practiced at home. Government like that of Santo Domingo was notoriously vulnerable to revolution. The instability of the Dominican Republic and like nations not only created widespread hardship for citizens, engaging the humanitarian sentiments of the American people; it also invited great-power military action to seize their customs houses and revenues to repay European creditors. Both wrongdoing and incapacity to fulfill government obligations could indirectly trigger a great-power threat to the Western Hemisphere. Suspension of foreign debt, a common occurrence in the Caribbean Basin in Roosevelt's day, could provide a pretext for territorial aggrandizement by European powers that coveted outposts on American soil.

Since morality permeated his political philosophy, it is unsurprising that a clear humanitarian imperative underlay Roosevelt's meditations on chronic wrongdoing and governmental impotence. International anarchy militated for some sort of interventionism by industrialized nations. Theodore Roosevelt contemplated the exercise of an international police power not only by the United States but also by other civilized states. Nonetheless, he loathed the amoral strain of interventionism then practiced by the imperial powers and was happy to have the Americas quit of European imperial intrigues. On the return voyage from Cuba in 1898, Roosevelt exulted that the Spanish-American War marked the "first great triumph in what will be a world movement" against imperialism.[67] Ridding the Western Hemisphere of imperial intrigues would be an auspicious step toward world order.

A careful reading of Roosevelt's 1904 message to Congress clearly shows that the president simply intended to explain why the United States (and, he added belatedly, the great Latin American states) could rightfully exercise the police power in the New World. For him Europe's failure to police its periphery exemplified the worst in great-power diplomacy. European governments, he implied, lacked the altruistic sentiments that figured into American diplomacy. "I most severely criticized the European powers for not interfering on behalf of the Armenians" during the Turkish pogroms. Consequently, Roosevelt concluded, "in the first place our duty to humanity requires that we should interfere on behalf of the Cubans, and, in the second place, that it is obviously for the interest of our people as a whole that we should decline longer to allow this hideous welter of misery at our doorsteps, and that we should drive the Spaniard from the new world."[68] TR clearly hoped to persuade the great powers to embrace a more benevolent diplomacy that would not only serve their interests but also ease the suffering of less-advanced peoples. In the meantime he set out to exclude Europe from the Americas.

TR often pled for intervention by civilized states adjoining less-developed states in his correspondence. The police power justified the use of force to chastise miscreants. During the Boxer Rebellion, for instance, Roosevelt ardently hoped that the great powers would join to discipline those whom he regarded as little more than bandits.[69]

Giddy at the success of Japanese arms against Russia in 1904, the president told Cecil Arthur Spring Rice that Japan had a "paramount interest" in the Yellow Sea Basin, just as the United States had in the Caribbean. Consequently, he hoped the Japanese would do their part to bring China along the road to civilization that they had traveled. "I thought it for the interest of all the world," he reported telling the Japanese minister, "that each part of the world should be prosperous and well policed."[70]

Also in 1904, as he began formulating his corollary, President Roosevelt told Secretary of State Elihu Root that the United States must permit England and Germany to police the Caribbean Basin if it were unwilling to do so. And Roosevelt alluded to an exercise of the police power by major South American states such as Argentina, Brazil, and Chile in their own spheres of paramount interest. In the absence of an international authority to maintain order and promote enlightened government, the action of the advanced nations would have to suffice.

"Civilized" Status and Geographic Proximity Confer "Jurisdiction"

To President Roosevelt and his circle, the international police power was less a modified Monroe Doctrine than a legal power that all "civilized powers" could lawfully exercise. That the police power flowed from civilized status is axiomatic in Roosevelt's international-policing doctrine—more an article of faith than a matter for discussion. But what entitled nations to membership in the circle of civilized nations? Whence did America derive the right to intervene in Venezuelan, Colombian, and Dominican affairs? Theodore Roosevelt elaborated his theories of civilization bluntly enough to inspire some of his contemporaries, to alarm others, and to rub raw the sensibilities of those unfortunate enough to be saddled with the label of barbarian.

How far from their borders the nations accorded this police authority might act to discipline governments culpable for chronic wrongdoing or impotence seemed to be a function of the policing nations' national interests and ability to project force. Some American expansionists wanted to make good Richard Olney's claim of practical sovereignty over the Americas; more realistic individuals such as Alfred Thayer Mahan and Theodore Roosevelt thought better of this, largely because of constraints on military power. In practice the Roosevelt administration contented itself with policing the Caribbean Basin. Thus the parameters of great-power "jurisdiction" were necessarily ambiguous, shifting according to the facts of each case and the power that could be brought to bear.

This suited Roosevelt, whose Burkean outlook relied on prudential judgment—a mode of decision making that could not be reduced to fixed algorithms.

TR left the current composition of the civilized world somewhat vague, giving him a measure of conceptual wiggle room. On several occasions he equated civilization with Anglo-American constitutional republicanism, which he referred to somewhat cavalierly as "self-government." For all the flaws in Anglo-American society, Roosevelt maintained that the English-speaking peoples were the most reliable exponents of the civilized virtues. Asked whether his embrace of Americanism represented mindless cheerleading, TR wryly reminded onlookers that his own Germanic ancestors had been among the white savages who overwhelmed Rome.[71] Barbaric peoples could attain civilized status over time.

One thing was clear: for Roosevelt the distinction between savagery and civilization was not biologically predestined. Races were neither predestined for civilization nor doomed by inferior genes to perpetual barbarism. In no uncertain terms, he rejected the crude racism to which many Social Darwinians of his day fell prey. Rather, cultural attitudes, particularly the capacity for self-restraint, fair dealing, and fellow-feeling, were the determinants of republican self-government and the keys to expanding the realm of civilization and peace. Fellow-feeling was the lubricant by which a liberal republic could surmount the inevitable frictions among different classes and nationalities—"hyphenated Americans," as he dubbed the multitude of ethnic groups that populated the United States. Roosevelt's muscular Americanism embodied these cultural attitudes. He insisted that Americanism was equally accessible to all citizens and immigrant groups without regard to superficial characteristics such as race, ethnicity, and religion.

Included among the civilized nations were the European great powers, although TR confessed to misgivings about the Russian and German despotisms because of their lack of the ordered liberty that underpinned his conception of civilization. While Russia posed no threat to the Americas, Roosevelt genuinely feared a partition of Latin America by the great maritime powers, in particular, Britain and Germany. Washington could deter British mischief by threatening to seize Canada, but Imperial Germany was another matter. Although "Germany as a republic would very possibly be a friendly nation, . . . under the present despotism she is much more bitterly and outspokenly hostile to us than is England," TR told one English friend.[72] A British defeat in the Boer War would embolden the Germans and, in turn, compel the United States either to abandon the Monroe Doctrine or fight for it.[73] Whether Germany had truly posed a plausible threat to the New World is debatable. Roosevelt maintained, with apparent sincerity, that his combination of personal diplomacy, the Big Stick, and a preemptive use of the police power had prevented German encroachment contrary to the Monroe Doctrine—saving part of the civilized world from being either engulfed by savagery or reduced to servitude.

Of Russia Roosevelt wrote, "I see nothing of permanent good that can come to Russia, either for herself or for the rest of the world, until her people begin to tread the path of orderly freedom, of civil liberty, and of a measure of self-government. Whatever may be the theoretical advantages of a despotism, they are incompatible with the growth of intelligence and individuality in a civilized people."[74] Russia, then, was perched precariously on the dividing line between civilization and barbarity.

Where a nation stood in TR's civilizational pecking order hinged on the extent to which it displayed the manly virtues. Thus Roosevelt favored Japan, which in only fifty years had catapulted into the forefront of civilization, over Turkey, despite the ethnic ties between Turks and the English-speaking races.[75] He regularly condemned the misdeeds of the Turks against the Armenians while lauding the warrior spirit and scrupulous honesty exhibited by Japanese statesmen.[76] China was a more difficult case. TR did not—quite—banish the venerable kingdom to the ranks of the savage nations. Yet he openly despised the Middle Kingdom, historically the preeminent power in Asia. That venerable, yet at the time militarily flabby, nation had proved unable to resist European encroachment. The period of weakness and decay the Chinese were undergoing repelled Roosevelt.

With a Kantian flair, TR affirmed that the spread of civilization would diminish the frequency of armed conflict. Unlike Kant, who hoped that the spread of republican self-government would occur naturally with the spread of enlightenment, Roosevelt reasoned that the judicious use of force might be necessary to abet the growth of peace. He proclaimed that the "Golden Rule should be, and as the world grows in morality it will be, the guiding rule of conduct among nations as among individuals"; however, "the Golden Rule must not be construed, in fantastic manner, as forbidding the exercise of the police power. This mighty and free Republic should ever deal with all other states, great or small, on a basis of high honor, respecting their rights as jealously as it safeguards its own."[77]

Despite his professed loathing for violence, then, Roosevelt envisioned using military power to discipline wayward governments: "Of recent years, wars between the great civilized powers have become less and less frequent. Wars with barbarous or semi-barbarous peoples come in an entirely different category, being merely a most regrettable but necessary international police duty which must be performed for the sake of the welfare of mankind."[78] As early as 1901, then, Roosevelt had explicitly introduced the police-power concept under the rubric of pushing back the frontiers of civilization. And he had unequivocally stated his fealty to the principle of the sovereign equality of (advanced) states.

For him the advanced nations had a duty transcending realpolitik. "Every expansion of civilization makes for peace," declared Roosevelt in "Expansion and Peace." "In other words, every expansion of a great civilized power means a victory for law, order, and righteousness."[79] But "expansion" did not necessarily mean "territorial expansion" for Roosevelt. Rather, he advocated expanding the nation's overseas commitments and buttressing U.S. military power correspondingly.[80] Crucial to Roosevelt's police-power theory was his conception of civilization and the benefits its spread conferred both on civilized and barbaric peoples. Wars between civilized nations and bordering less-developed nations were a byproduct of civilization's advance. Yet, because of the ambiguities in his expansionist formula, Roosevelt envisioned deploying the police power only in the most egregious cases of wrongdoing and impotence, as well as in the cases that posed the greatest threat to American and world interests.

Elihu Root's Exposition of the Monroe Doctrine

Where President Roosevelt spoke in world-historical terms, often with scant regard for details, Elihu Root supplied a cogent legal argument for an international police power. Speaking for the president, Secretary of State Root used a December 22, 1904, address to the New England Society to lay out this legal argument. Root followed up a decade later in an address to the American Society of International Law. The former speech, recounting the history and tenets of the Monroe Doctrine, came in the immediate aftermath of Roosevelt's proclamation of an international police power and was evidently intended to mollify the president's critics at home and to soothe fears raised in Latin America. Like President Roosevelt, the secretary of state contended that the doctrine, though it did not qualify as international law per se, had "accumulated such a weight of assent upon the part of foreign nations to our rights to assert and maintain this doctrine" that it was no longer open to question.[81] If state practice was one factor contributing to the creation of international law, European acquiescence in Monroe's precepts had conferred a kind of quasi-legal status on this U.S. policy declaration.[82] This acquiescence, complemented by superior American power, made a frontal assault on the doctrine unlikely.

The Monroe Doctrine was merely a policy statement, but Root explained how the principles of 1823 derived from sovereignty and the right to self-protection, two bedrock principles of international law. Obligations went hand-in-hand with these rights. "All sovereignty in this world," he maintained, "is held upon the condition of performing the duties of sovereignty." For the weaker states, fulfilling their duties was the price of the protections from aggression that flowed from international law.[83] Under the doctrine of sovereign equality, governments were responsible for protecting foreign nationals living on their soil and obeying the strictures of international law. Consequently, "while we assert that we are entitled," consonant with the Monroe Doctrine, "to say that no foreign power shall undertake to control an American republic, that no foreign power shall take possession with or without the will of an American people their territory, that assertion is justified" only on condition that the American governments fulfill their obligations to the European great powers.[84] Contradicting Richard Olney, Elihu Root summarized the president's position thusly: Americans were arrogating "to ourselves, not sovereignty on the American continent, but only the right to protect."[85]

"We do not undertake," then, "to say that the republics of Central and South America are to be relieved from their obligations" or that "the Powers of Europe shall not enforce their rights against these members of the sisterhood of nations. It is only when the enforcement of those rights comes to the point of taking possession of the territory of any American people that we may say that is inconsistent with the peace and safety of the United States; and we cannot say it with justice unless we also say that the American republics are themselves to be just." Root pointed to Egypt and Greece, which had fallen into British and Turkish hands, respectively, as instances in which the enforcement of international obligations had led to territorial aggrandizement. If the United States was to uphold the Monroe Doctrine, which denied the great powers the right to vindicate their rights in the traditional manner, "we are bound to say that whenever the wrong cannot otherwise be redressed we ourselves will see that it is redressed."[86] This gave the police power its preemptive temper.

Here Root must have been alluding to the Roosevelt Corollary, and he might have been expected to follow up by explicating the international police power. Root's commentary on the corollary, however, was almost apologetic in tone. Gone was language referring to "chronic wrongdoing," "impotence," or even "international police power." Far from taking credit for an innovative new policy or stressing the high-minded rhetoric of uplift and civilization of which Roosevelt was so fond, Root insisted that the president's 1904 message to Congress "was not an advance, an aggression, a statement of a position beyond the purposes declared before by American statesmen." Rather, the corollary was a "definition and limitation of American purposes," an elaboration of fixed principles that had existed since James Monroe and John Quincy Adams had framed their doctrine.

Why the reticence? The most plausible explanation is that Root, possibly on instructions from TR, was backing away from language that had unwittingly alarmed many Latin American statesmen—and violated Roosevelt's own convictions about tactful statecraft. The secretary of state professed bafflement at Richard Olney's insistence, a decade before, that the United States was "practically sovereign on this continent, and its fiat [was] law." "The tremendous scope and meaning of those words for the weak little republics of Central and South America cannot be exaggerated," observed Root. Far from being a claim to a U.S. right to meddle indiscriminately in the affairs of the Latin American states, he concluded, the president's message to Congress had been "a disclaimer of all that we ought not to arrogate to ourselves in that broad and somewhat rhetorical statement of Mr. Olney, not sovereignty over the American continent, but only the right to protect."[87] Root repeatedly sounded this soothing theme during his subsequent goodwill tour of Latin America. Wary but receptive audiences greeted his charm offensive.[88]

The president himself supplied a more temperate exposition of his policy in his 1906 message to Congress. "In many parts of South America," wrote TR, with uncharacteristic use of the passive voice, "there has been much misunderstanding of the attitude and purposes of the United States toward the other American republics. An idea had become prevalent that our assertion of the Monroe Doctrine implied or carried with it an assumption of superiority and of a right to exercise some sort of a protectorate over the countries to whose territory over that doctrine applies. Nothing could be farther from the truth."[89] But Roosevelt had contemplated just that: he had explicitly used the term "protectorate" when mulling over what to do about the European blockade of Venezuela. In a bow to Latin American sentiments, the president conscripted the words of Dr. Luis Drago, the Argentine foreign minister, who he said had perfectly characterized the "true attitude" of the United States toward its American neighbors. Dr. Drago had called the doctrine "the traditional policy [by which] the United States without accentuating superiority or seeking preponderance condemned the oppression of the nations of this part of the world and the control of their destinies by the great Powers of Europe."[90]

What to make of this? Root, undoubtedly speaking on behalf of the president, had tacitly distanced the administration from the police power. He dropped the term and deemphasized the police function, denied that Roosevelt had broken new ground in enunciating his corollary, and disavowed Olney's proclamation of virtual U.S. sovereignty over the Americas (this despite the enthusiasm TR had voiced for President Cleveland's handling of the Venezuela border dispute in 1895). Furthermore, the secretary of state downplayed the Monroe Doctrine's importance even under the traditional understanding. Under international law, the United States could insist on the protection of its nationals residing abroad, and it could object to actions that might endanger its interests. Aside from protecting against new European occupation of territory in the New World, said Root, the doctrine had no "relation to the affairs of either American or European states."[91]

In effect, then, Elihu Root began to reverse Olney's expansive reading of the doctrine and restore something resembling the original understanding of the principles of 1823. He approvingly quoted John Hay, who at the time of the Venezuela blockade had informed the German government that, although the United States "regretted that European Powers should use force against Central and South American countries, [it] could not object to their taking steps to obtain redress for injuries suffered by their subjects, provided that no acquisition of territory was contemplated." Root declared that Washington could have brokered a settlement between Caracas and the European governments without recourse to the Monroe Doctrine. The United States had deployed its good offices "in the performance of no duty and the exercise of no right whatever except the duty and the right of friendship between equal sovereign states." Finally, Root denied that the doctrine imposed upon the United States any duties toward the European great powers. "It does not call upon the United States to collect debts or coerce conduct or redress wrongs or revenge injuries." He thus verged on retracting Roosevelt's claim that the United States must police the New World if it wanted to exclude the Old.[92]

In closing, Secretary of State Root emphasized the role of the national interest and power in the Monroe Doctrine. The isthmian canal sat atop the hierarchy of U.S. interests. "It is plain," he asserted, "that the building of the Panama Canal greatly accentuates the practical necessity of the Monroe Doctrine as it applies to all the territory surrounding the Caribbean or near the Bay of Panama." Sounding a Mahanian note, Root declared that history taught "that the potential command of the route to and from the Canal must rest with the United States and that the vital interests of the nation forbid that such command shall pass into other hands." Geography also played a role. "Undoubtedly as one passes to the south and the distance from the Caribbean increases, the necessity of maintaining the rule of Monroe becomes less immediate and apparent." But he was unwilling to draw a line that would interfere with prudential statecraft: "who is competent to draw the line? Who will say, 'To this point the rule of Monroe should apply; beyond this point, it should not'?"[93]

Root's temperate language made a welcome contrast with the president's rhetoric—which in all likelihood was the point. "Thoughtless people who see no difference between lawful right and physical power assume that the Monroe Doctrine is a warrant for interference in the internal affairs of all weaker nations in the New World. Against this suppositious doctrine, many protests both in the United States and in South America have been made, and justly made. To the real Monroe Doctrine these protests have no application."[94] Root's omission of the key terms from the Roosevelt Corollary may well have come at Roosevelt's instructions. The president did not himself use the police terminology again while in office, although it did appear in his postpresidential correspondence; and, as discussed earlier, his 1906 message sought to mollify Latin American governments alarmed at his rhetoric.

Still, Roosevelt's shift in tone did not necessarily signify that the president had abandoned his doctrine of international constabulary duty. For one thing, such a retrenchment would be out of character. Roosevelt held clear views on most subjects and clung to them tenaciously. The shift was probably tactical in nature. As discussed earlier, Roosevelt had developed a philosophy emphasizing tactful but forceful statecraft. Presumably he had been genuinely taken aback at negative reaction to a policy which seemed commonsensical to him. He may have backed down after realizing that he had violated the "speak softly" element of the Big Stick doctrine. Additionally, Roosevelt was generally unwilling to commit himself to any particular policy on paper for fear of inhibiting prudential statecraft. His 1904 message seemed to commit the United States in advance to international police duty that might not accord with the American national interest and might strain the nation's resources if applied consistently. In short, Theodore Roosevelt's lust for action and passion for world order had gotten the best of him, just as Cleveland and Olney had overstated the reach of U.S. sovereignty in the 1895 standoff with Great Britain.

Armed Force as an Implement of International Law

Not only forceful diplomacy but also robust military capabilities and the willingness to project these capabilities overseas were necessary to execute international police missions and implement the assertive foreign policy Theodore Roosevelt preached. The shortcomings of the international legal order, coupled with the dictates of enlightened self-interest, required the major powers to take on police duty of this kind. That Roosevelt attached tremendous significance to his correspondence with Carl Schurz, detailing these shortcomings, is abundantly clear. Much of what TR wrote seems obvious to students of international relations today. Yet the thought that the great powers could act morally to sustain world order was revolutionary in a world accustomed to austere realpolitik.

A supple diplomatic and military strategy was needed to execute the constabulary function. As chapter 9 will demonstrate, Roosevelt, his confidants, and the U.S. armed services made little distinction between the military and police functions. The "small wars" in which the army and marines engaged during the Roosevelt era required a strategy integrating direct military action, to stamp out insurgency, with civil pacification measures to improve living conditions for the occupying force and the natives and to equip the indigenous society to take on the burden of ruling itself. Since the U.S. military had no military police component until the eve of the Second World War, these tasks fell to the regular military, working in tandem with American civilian administrators and the local government.

Fittingly, Roosevelt had woven armed force into his international-policing doctrine. Any policeman needed a nightstick to carry out his duties. In practice the United States used the police power beyond its borders in two ways. First, the domestic police power was extended directly to the islands freed from Spain in 1898, although, as seen earlier in this chapter, Congress determined how completely the Constitution applied to the new possessions. The U.S. Marines and Army were the policemen of choice for suppressing postwar lawlessness, especially in the Philippines. From there it was a short intellectual leap to declare an international police power that could be used to discipline sovereign nations. Second, pursuant to the Roosevelt Corollary, the United States—and, judging from Roosevelt's explanation of the corollary, the other civilized states—might temporarily arrogate to itself the prerogatives of a political superior to countries guilty of chronic wrongdoing or impotence. This kind of transitory intervention would restore foreign governments' ability to carry out the duties expected under the doctrine of state sovereignty.

Roosevelt did not advocate the wanton use of military force in police operations any more than he had endorsed police brutality when serving as New York police commissioner. To be sure, the Filipino insurgents, who he insisted were little more than bandits resisting rightful U.S. authority, were put down ruthlessly using counterinsurgency tactics.[95] Force was necessary to police the islands seized from Spain. (Chapters 8 and 9 will describe the techniques used by the army and marines to defeat the Filipino insurgency and other uprisings.) According to Roosevelt and his cadre of expansionists, however, the operations in Cuba and the Philippines were more closely akin to domestic policing, which did not require negotiations between the government and lawbreakers. Resistance must be stamped out as a prelude to installing a republican government and returning the subject country to its inhabitants.

International constabulary missions, in which the U.S. government could not legally deploy the municipal police power, were another matter entirely. Politics intruded into such missions, in the form of international mediation and negotiation. Thus the intervention in Santo Domingo, the clearest-cut international police operation of Roosevelt's presidency, more closely resembled routine diplomacy than the workings of a police department. Since he regarded the Dominican affair as "a precedent for American action in all similar cases," his circumspect handling of the intervention should be borne in mind.[96] Roosevelt's Big Stick diplomacy, it bears repeating, required quiet, tactful diplomacy among Washington, the target country, and the aggrieved European powers that were contemplating enforcement action of their own. Roosevelt maintained that the wisest course in such sensitive matters was to seek the parties' consent to American intervention while maintaining powerful military forces nearby to lend weight to U.S. negotiating strategy.[97]

President Roosevelt used force adeptly to back up American diplomacy. Noted a recent analyst, the prudent application of national power allows the statesman "to bring moral goals into some form of approximation with the stubborn and less than hospitable realities of international politics."[98] Power improved the likelihood of peace. Flush with success at the Portsmouth Peace Conference, Roosevelt told Carl Schurz, "If I had been one of the conventional type of peace advocates I could have done nothing whatever in bringing about peace now, I would be powerless in the future to accomplish anything, and I would not have been able to help confer the boons upon Cuba, the Philippines, Porto Rico and Panama, brought about by our action therein."[99] Inaction would yield these embattled territories to great powers that were less likely to abide by enlightened moral standards.

Power worked. The deterrent effect of American force, maintained Roosevelt, had helped deter encroachment in the Western Hemisphere. Of Germany, TR's main bugaboo, the president wrote, "When I first came into the Presidency I was inclined to think that the Germans had serious designs upon South America. But I think I succeeded in impressing upon the kaiser, quietly and unofficially, and with equal courtesy and emphasis, that the violation of the Monroe Doctrine by territorial aggrandizement on his part around the Caribbean meant war, not ultimately, but immediately, and without any delay."[100] The Big Stick philosophy held true not only for the United States but for all civilized nations. "If the Japanese had not armed during the last twenty years, this would indeed be a sorrowful century for Japan," which had defeated both China and Russia in the course of a single decade.[101]

Both halves of the Big Stick philosophy—firm but tactful rhetoric and power in being—were equally critical to success in foreign policy. TR foreswore empty rhetorical gestures. Consequently, he often refused to speak out against injustice unless he could materially influence conditions. Better to stand aside altogether than to engage offenders meekly and make America a laughingstock in the bargain. This was how he justified his reluctance to act vigorously on behalf of the Armenians: the American people would never support a crusade so far from their shores and so divorced from their tangible interests, and because Europe was unable or unwilling to police its own periphery, the Turkish government never received the comeuppance TR had contemplated.

"In short," Roosevelt told Henry Cabot Lodge in reference to Germany, "I wish to see us act upon the old frontier principles 'Don't bluster, don't flourish your revolver and never draw unless you intend to shoot.'"[102] It was important, he counseled Lodge when discussing the Alaska boundary dispute with Great Britain, to stand fast on critical points but to give way on lesser issues to allow the other side to save face.[103] TR was exasperated at American politicians who inverted the precepts of the Big Stick by indulging in overbearing rhetoric while neglecting military readiness:[104] "That is to say, they talk offensively of foreign powers and yet decline to make ready for war." Referring to Japan, which he believed would be giddy after smashing the Russian fleet at Tsushima Straits, Roosevelt wrote, "I do not believe we shall ever have trouble with Japan; but my own theory is to keep our navy so strong and so efficient that we shall be able to handle Japan if ever the need arises, and at the same time to treat her with scrupulous courtesy and friendliness so that she shall have no excuse for bearing malice toward us."[105]

How were the gains in peace and justice won by American arms to be maintained? Preferably not by war—Big Stick diplomacy, as discussed earlier, was hardly a prescription for indiscriminate warfare. Rather, it was an instrument to be used sparingly for moral and pragmatic ends. For Roosevelt, world peace and world order had to be sustained by the military power of the civilized world, and especially that of the United States. "Scant attention is paid to the weakling or the coward who babbles of peace," he declared, "but due heed is given to the strong man with sword girt on thigh who preaches peace, not from ignoble motives, not from fear or distrust of his own powers, but from a deep sense of moral obligation."[106] These comments, made in the wake of the 1899 Hague conference, convey the essence of TR's thoughts on the relationship between force and law. Roosevelt maintained that vigorous U.S. diplomacy, backed by a powerful navy, would help ease the transition to a more peaceful world ruled by international law.

At the end of the day, U.S. military power would deter greatpower encroachment in violation of the Monroe Doctrine, thereby buttressing peace and justice in the Americas.[107] Vibrant forces would also give the nation the wherewithal to exercise the international police power that TR believed was vital to the civilizing mission, and thus to practice a superior brand of ethics designed to accelerate the spread of international law. And finally, only force could put teeth into the evolving international legal regime devised at The Hague. Plainly Roosevelt's foreign policy demanded a rapid buildup of naval power: "The cost of building and maintaining such a navy represents the very lightest premium for insuring peace which this Nation can possibly pay."[108] Counterintuitively, the barbarian virtues were crucial to maintaining the vigor and health of the great civilized nations. And its preparedness to fight equipped the United States for its grand mission, its share of the "great world work" in the islands and elsewhere.[109]

Roosevelt's Postpresidential Views on an International Police Power

Theodore Roosevelt's ruminations on an international police power reached perhaps their fullest expression in 1910, when he crafted an address to the Nobel Prize Committee accepting the prize awarded him for his mediation of the peace accord between Russia and Japan. Roosevelt donated the Nobel prize money to serve as "a nucleus for a foundation to forward the cause of industrial peace," which "in our complex industrial civilization of to-day [is] the only kind of peace worth having." He connected the battle against the excesses of capital and labor to the contest of the peace-loving nations against international militarism. "There is at least as much need to curb the cruel greed and arrogance of part of the world of capital, to curb the cruel greed and violence of part of the world of labor, as to check a cruel and unhealthy militarism in international relationships."[110]

How should the civilized world offset militarism and barbarity? Roosevelt struck several familiar themes. He told the Nobel Committee there were several lines of advance. For one thing, "all really civilized communities should have effective arbitration treaties among themselves," which, if comprehensive enough, "can cover almost all questions liable to arise among such nations." Crucial to such accords was a mutual pledge by each party "to respect the other's territory and its absolute sovereignty within that territory," except for the "very rare cases where the nation's honor is vitally concerned." All other controversies should be submitted to arbitration. Arbitral tribunals would effectively safeguard pacific relations among the civilized powers. But there was a catch: "There are, of course, states so backward that a civilized community ought not to enter into an arbitration treaty with them, at least until we have gone much farther than at present in securing some kind of international police action" to enforce judgments against these countries, whose compliance would presumably be uneven at best.[111]

Roosevelt also called for refining the work of the standing tribunal constituted at the first Hague conference and for implementing the Court of Arbitral Justice constituted at the second. He compared these quasi-judicial bodies with the legal systems enacted in the English-speaking world. "It has been well said that the first Hague Conference framed a Magna Charta for the nations," he told the committee. With regard to the Court of Arbitral Justice, TR urged statesmen "to study what has been done in the United States by the Supreme Court. I cannot help thinking that the Constitution of the United States, notably in the establishment of the Supreme Court and in the methods adopted for securing peace and good relations among and between the different States, offers certain valuable analogies to what should be striven for in order to secure, through The Hague courts and conferences, a species of world federation for international peace and justice." To be sure, there were "fundamental differences" between what the U.S. Constitution did and what could be achieved in the international milieu, but "the methods adopted in the American Constitution to prevent hostilities between the States, and to secure the supremacy of the Federal Court in certain classes of cases," were worth examining as nations strove to attain similar ends on a global scale.[112]

To abet peace in the less-developed world, moreover, the great powers "honestly bent on peace" should found a "League of Peace, not only to keep the peace among themselves, but to prevent, by force if necessary, its being broken by others." The main barrier to realizing the lofty aims of the Hague conferences arose from "the lack of any executive power, of any police power, to enforce the decrees of the court." Pointing to the anarchic condition of the international legal order (and alluding to his experiences in the American West), Roosevelt told the committee that, in "new and wild communities where there is violence," the man who craved security had to protect himself, "and until other means of securing his safety are devised," he should not surrender the arms on which his safety depended. And so it was with nations. Roosevelt reminded the committee that in "any community of any size" on the domestic level, "the authority of the courts rests upon actual or potential force"; that is, "on the existence of a police, or on the knowledge that the able-bodied men of the country are both ready and willing to see that the decrees of judicial and legislative bodies are put into effect." Consequently, he prescribed "the establishment of some kind of international police power," entrusted to a multinational League of Peace made up of "those great nations which sincerely desire peace," that would be "competent and willing to prevent violence as between nations" and enforce the decisions handed down by international tribunals.[113]

Roosevelt built on these themes in an essay titled "The Management of Small States Which Are Unable to Manage Themselves," which was published in *Outlook* shortly after his return from Norway. In the essay, he first affirmed the sovereign equality of states. Size was no barrier to civilized status or equality of treatment. Small states such as Switzerland and Holland, said TR, differed "only in size from the greatest of civilized nations," and thus were "absolutely competent to preserve order within [their] own bounds, to execute substantial justice, and to secure the rights of foreigners" — in short, to carry out the responsibilities that went along with the privileges of sovereignty. No meddling in their internal affairs was needed. All that was required of the great powers was to guarantee these small states against foreign aggression.[114]

At the same time Roosevelt maintained that there was "no analogy at all" between these small, well-ordered nations and "a community unable to keep elementary order, or to secure elementary justice within its own borders, and unable or unwilling to do justice to foreign nations." Indeed, the "very worst thing" that could happen to a community that could not discharge government functions "may be to guarantee it from outside aggression." Not only the civilized world but the citizens of Algeria, claimed Roosevelt, were better off under French rule than they had been before the French had arrived (and they were better off than Morocco, the site of a new great-power clash, was at the moment). The same went for English interference in the Sudan and American interference in Panama.

The former president went on to suggest how "management" of the affairs of these states by an outside party should proceed. He declared that "actual experience has shown that such interference can only come efficiently by one nation, and not by many." He was ambivalent about "multilateralism," to use the present-day term, for much the same reason he had hated administration by committee at the New York Police Department. "Untried theorists," some of Roosevelt's favorite targets, harbored "a curious fondness for trying a system of joint interference or joint control." A joint protectorate over Samoa administered by the United States, Great Britain, and Germany had been a failure; once "each power took its own sphere," however, "we have gotten along admirably." A similar arrangement in the Philippines, he contended, "would have certainly led to jealousy, bickerings, and intrigue among [the occupying powers], would have held the islands back, would have prevented any development along the lines of progress and civilization, and would have insured an endless succession of devastating little civil wars." In what may have been a backhanded swipe at the European powers, TR even maintained that it was "better for the state concerned to be under the control of a single power, even though this power has not high ideals, [than] under the control of three or four powers" that were animated by worthy motives but would be fated to squabble over administrative matters.[115]

And finally, on the eve of his departure for a goodwill tour of Brazil, Argentina, and Chile, Roosevelt laid out what he thought the Progressive Party's posture ought to be on Latin America and on foreign policy more broadly. The United States, he said, should try to open Latin American countries to U.S. business and commerce; the mounting prosperity that was sure to follow would redound to the benefit of all Americans, North and South. While material well-being was the foundation of national and international greatness, Roosevelt, like other Progressives, espoused a doctrine of "international social consciousness," which held that "in the long run it is good for each nation of mankind to see the other nations of mankind go up and not down." This was not a call for disarmament or weakness: "We no more intend to do away with the American navy and abandon the fortification of the Panama Canal, than we intend to do away with the New York police."[116] Rather, the great powers should make every effort to usher the weaker nations into the civilized world.

In the New World, because of its adherence to the Monroe Doctrine, the United States bore a special responsibility. The Caribbean states were the primary beneficiaries of U.S. supervision. Yet "as the other nations on this continent achieve political and social stability, and the economic prosperity that goes hand in hand with such stability and power, the need for treating our country as the sole and special guardian of the Monroe Doctrine" would diminish. Indeed, Roosevelt pronounced Argentina, Brazil, and Chile fit to take up this new responsibility. He declared that "the enforcement of the principle of the Monroe Doctrine as far as they are concerned can be safely left to their own initiative and interest" and called on Washington to conduct relations with these nations on an equal footing, with substantially the same attitude as it dealt with Canada in North America.[117]

John Bassett Moore's Theory of International Organization

It is intriguing to speculate about what form TR's League of Peace, his hypothetical international body equipped with the police power, would take. For clues, it profits the student of Roosevelt to consult the writings of Professor John Bassett Moore, an assistant secretary of state during the McKinley years and, during Roosevelt's presidency, a professor of international law and diplomacy at Columbia University. Strikingly, Moore, like TR's other mentors, never referred to the international police power by name. The president credited him with coauthorship of the portions of his 1903 message to Congress recounting the Panamanian revolution and aftermath. "I hope you like 'our' message in its final form. I say 'our' message advisedly, for I feel that you had about as much to do with it as I had."[118] In all likelihood, then, Moore was acquainted with—and more or less concurred with—Roosevelt's thinking about an American police power. Since President Roosevelt had invoked the police power to justify U.S. intervention on the isthmus, and since he had cited Moore on the precise interpretation of the treaty with Colombia, it is reasonable to conclude that TR took the Columbia professor's views on international law and organization seriously and to predict that he would have endorsed something similar to the organization sketched by Moore.

John Bassett Moore laid out his perspective on international law and organization in 1914, when he delivered the presidential address to the annual meeting of the American Political Science Association, held in Chicago.[119] Professor Moore reviewed the distinctions between municipal and international law exhaustively, concluding that international law differed from its domestic cousin "not in its essence or its obligation, but in the method of its declaration and administration. Within the state we have an organization for the making, declaration and enforcement of law, whereas, as between nations, we are obliged to a great extent to rely upon their voluntary concurrence or cooperation." In short, said Moore, "we lack in the international sphere that organization which gives to the administration of law within the state a certain security. This defect it is the business of nations to supply by forming among themselves an appropriate organization" endowed with "the power to legislate and the power to coerce."[120]

The international organization that Moore envisioned would be founded on three elemental principles. First, "it would set law above violence" by erecting "suitable and efficacious means and agencies for the enforcement of law" and by outlawing the use of force except in self-defense or "in support of a duly ascertained legal right." Conjuring up the shades of Chief Justice John Marshall and Swiss legal theorist Emmerich de Vattel, Moore claimed that this principle would reinforce the concept of the legal equality of sovereign states. Second, the hypothetical organization would provide "a more efficient means than now exists for the making and declaration of law." Constituting a quasi-legislative power, Moore said, would retard the capacity of a single state to thwart international law. Third, an international body would institute tribunals "possessing advisory or judicial powers, as the case might be," to investigate and adjust international disputes.[121]

Establishing a universal organization, concluded Professor Moore, would bring about striking results. "Such I conceive to be the essentials of an organization which would place international law on substantially the same footing as municipal law as regards its making, declaration and enforcement." He hoped to establish an international lawmaking authority to enact international law and an international executive to enforce the law. But, unlike Theodore Roosevelt, whose instincts had been forged in domestic law enforcement, Moore doubted the "vaulting assumption" that an international organization could bring offending nations to heel by force with the same ease "with which an individual, charged with a violation of law, can be arrested in the street and brought to justice." The Napoleonic Wars, which France had survived virtually intact after decades of bloodletting, came to mind as an example of the stubbornness nations could display. And this "example is not incapable of repetition," with the likely result being the organization's reluctance to make war on international law-breakers and, in turn, an erosion of respect for international law. Given the maddening complexity of international politics, moreover, Moore predicted that assigning blame for armed conflicts would be a colossal hurdle for jurists.[122] Yet many statesmen and theorists shared Moore's conviction that aligning international and municipal law more closely was crucial to the cause of international justice and peace.

Theodore Roosevelt certainly brought such an outlook to the Oval Office. Given the rapid pace of events during his presidency, it is scarcely surprising that Roosevelt should apply the same intellectual model to both domestic and international turbulence. The labor disturbances convulsing American society, most prominently the dispute over the anthracite coal supply, coincided with international controversies such as the European blockade of Venezuela, the Panamanian revolution, and the collapse of Dominican finances. Roosevelt's analysis of foreign turmoil bore an arresting resemblance to his meditations on capital-labor relations and social uplift at home. The supervisory power that had proved efficacious in labor disputes and strikes at home was a ready-made intellectual tool for American diplomacy. His handling of international problems was largely consistent with his handling of domestic problems.

Roosevelt and the League of Nations

President Roosevelt was not, however, an uncritical enthusiast for international organization. Some of Roosevelt's writings on the First World War may further illuminate his thinking on the international police power. Although he never abandoned his vision of a world organization capable of wielding the police power, his writings took on a sarcastic edge once the draft League of Nations Covenant was unveiled. Roosevelt condemned what he viewed as a spate of all-encompassing arbitration treaties adopted prior to the war. These too-ambitious accords, he said, had unacceptably abridged U.S. freedom to uphold its vital interests by unilateral action. He also bemoaned the downfall of the Hague movement, which he said had foundered on the Wilson administration's unwillingness to oppose Germany's breach of Belgian neutrality. These developments, not to mention the blood-letting on the western front, led a disconsolate Roosevelt to question whether the advance of international morality that he had so confi-dently predicted during his presidency was as inevitable as he had thought.[123]

Righteousness and political courage, virtues then in short sup-ply, were his solutions to the dismal state of events. "Without ques-tion," he declared in the *Metropolitan Magazine* in 1919, "there is a gen-eral desire for some kind of international agreement or union or league which will tend to prevent the recurrence, or at least to minimize the scope and the horrors of such a hideous disaster to humanity as the world war." But the simple existence of a universal accord would not bring peace. A scheme for world order would depend on "good faith among those entering into the scheme and honorable conduct in liv-ing up to the obligations incurred."[124] Roosevelt doubted that those conditions would be met in view of the fractiousness of contemporary international relations. A world body unable to achieve some unity of action would be worse than useless. Indeed, he believed it would discredit the ideal of international organization.

Characteristically, Roosevelt blamed extremists at both poles for the bleak prospects he foresaw for the League of Nations. Militarists could be faulted for obvious reasons, but "in forming the league the chief danger will come from the enthusiastic persons who in their desire to realize the millennium at once . . . play into the hands of the slippery politicians who are equally ready to make any promise when the time for keeping it is far distant, and to evade keeping it when the time at last arrives." These deluded individuals were, of course, the much-reviled "peace-at-any-price" advocates. "Nothing is easier than to be the kind of sham idealist whose idealism consists in uttering on all occasions the loftiest sentiments" and then reneging when "self-interest is dictator." Roosevelt contended that this duplicity would often be "repaid by the homage of all the foolish people who care for nothing but words." Consequently, "the idealist who tries to realize his ideals is sure to be opposed alike by the foolish people who de-mand the impossible good and by the wicked people who under cover of adherence to the impossible good oppose the good which is pos-sible."[125] In TR's view, the best remained the enemy of the good.

To TR, President Wilson was one of the worst offenders. Spe-cifically, if "the League of Nations is built on a document as high-sounding and as meaningless as the speech in which Mr. Wilson laid down his fourteen points, it will simply add one more scrap to the diplomatic waste paper basket." Most of the Fourteen Points, "like those referring to the freedom of the seas, to tariff arrangements, to the reduction of armaments, and to the treatment of colonies, could be interpreted . . . to mean anything or nothing." Compounding Wilson's sins, the administration's war aims "were absolutely true to the traditions of the bad old diplomacy, for any nation could agree to them and yet reserve the right to interpret them in diametrically opposite manner to the interpretation that others put upon them." Still worse, Wilson had indulged in secret diplomacy that made a mockery of his stated commitment to the sovereign equality of states such as Haiti, the Dominican Republic, and China.[126] Idealists estranged from the hard facts of international politics, predicted TR, would play into the hands of realpolitiker who would interpret their obligations to the league out of existence when it was expedient to do so.

Near the end of his life, and under radically altered circumstances, then, Theodore Roosevelt repeated many of the same themes that had underpinned his political philosophy since the 1880s. While the sovereign equality of states ought to be one of the overarching principles of world order, some states had not matured sufficiently to take up the responsibilities that went with the privilege of equality. Moreover, two of the civilized powers, Germany and Turkey, "ought to sit on the mourner's bench a good many years before we admit them to fellowship." And Russia's conduct since the October Revolution rendered "any international guarantee of action on her part worth precisely nothing." Roosevelt insisted, therefore, that only the wartime Allies be admitted to the league at first and that other nations be admitted on a case-by-case basis; that certain areas of national policy, such as colonial and immigration policy, be exempt from the scrutiny of the league; that as "regards impotent or disorderly nations and people outside the league," the league should refrain from issuing a guarantee to "interfere with or on behalf of them where they lie wholly outside our sphere of interest"; and "that our own sphere of special concern, in America (perhaps limited to north of somewhere near the equator), is not to be infringed on by European or Asiatic powers."[127]

So much for the principles undergirding the League of Nations. By limiting the membership of the league, TR hoped to bolster its efficacy. For the foreseeable future, the United States should "absolutely decline any disarmament proposition that would leave us helpless to defend ourselves," and U.S. citizens should remain steadfastly patriotic. On the metaphysical level, "Let us refuse to abolish nationalism;

on the contrary, let us base a wise and practical internationalism on a sound and intense nationalism." There was not the slightest chance, insisted Roosevelt, that America would become a militarist nation or pose a danger to other nations; quite the reverse. Finally, TR entreated the American people to keep good faith in their international covenants. "It will be worse than idle for us to enter any league if, when the test comes in the future, this country acts as badly as it did in refusing to make any protest when Germany violated the Hague Conventions [by breaching Belgian neutrality]." The league was no substitute for patriotism, military preparations, and a commitment to "do justice to others" while guarding "our own nation against injustice."[128] Roosevelt urged the United States to enter the league, but insisted that the international organization should not be permitted to thwart the U.S. national interest or U.S. prerogatives under the Monroe Doctrine.

President Roosevelt's final message to Congress claimed that his administration's actions had vindicated his innovative approach to international affairs. "This Nation's foreign policy is based on the theory that right must be done between nations precisely as between individuals. We have behaved, and are behaving, toward other nations, as in private life an honorable man would behave toward his fellows."[129] While the nation had pursued its self-interest, just as private individuals did, it had also taken up the mantle of international policeman on occasion for the betterment of foreign peoples. To evaluate these expansive theoretical claims, the next chapter covers the cases that shaped Theodore Roosevelt's doctrine of an international police power.

8

CASE STUDIES

"This Nation's foreign policy is based on the theory that right must be done between nations precisely as between individuals."

Theodore Roosevelt, 1908 Message to Congress

Clearly, Theodore Roosevelt and his cadre of expansionists injected an interventionist strain into American foreign relations, turning John Quincy Adams's injunction against foreign ventures on its head. It bears repeating that Roosevelt took a consistent approach to domestic and international politics. In the domestic arena he had helped inaugurate a Progressive school of thought within a Republican Party traditionally beholden to business. Reflecting his conservative inclinations, TR maintained that government intervention was a tool to mediate among competing interests such as labor and capital. It fell to wise statesmen to uphold social equilibrium and thus the essence of American institutions. He grudgingly conceded that populists, most notably William Jennings Bryan, and even the radical socialists had accurately diagnosed some of the maladies that troubled the nation. Addressing the legitimate demands of labor, insisted Roosevelt, was crucial to thwarting the appeals of demagogues and staving off social revolution. TR's first term witnessed a series of bitter labor strikes, accompanied by calls for federal intervention to restore the peace. Among the most serious of these were disputes between miners and owners in Pennsylvania, Colorado, and Arizona. His interventionism was both defensive in outlook and grounded in his Victorian morality.

TR's domestic outlook carried over into his conduct of foreign relations. To be sure, he said, the United States might help an advanced American republic such as one of the "ABC" powers—Argentina, Brazil, and Chile—repel an invasion from the Old World. But his principal worry was for the security of "the tropical states in the neighborhood of the Caribbean Sea," which had "been a prey to such continuous revolutionary misrule as to have grown impotent either to do their duties to outsiders or to enforce their rights against outsiders."[1] The Roosevelt Corollary, then, not only preempted European territorial aggrandizement but justified U.S. action to put the finances of failed governments in order and prepare native peoples for republican self-rule.

Indirectly based on the text of the U.S. Constitution, the police power was understood to empower various levels of government (a) to suppress not only routine criminal conduct but also anarchist activity, violent labor unrest, and other disturbances to allow the state to adjust disputes; (b) to oversee private contract where it impinged on the public interest but where the public lacked an advocate; and (c) to regulate labor conditions, health care, housing, and a host of conditions touching the public welfare. The judiciary often found itself called upon to decide whether these functions resided in state and local governments or belonged in the federal sphere of action. The police power, then, combined what might be thought of as routine police work—the quasi-military use of implied or real force to maintain order—with the process of devising and enforcing laws and regulations designed to better the public weal.

Military force came into the picture in extreme circumstances. If state and local police and militias were unable to control violent labor unrest, for example, U.S. Army troops could be ordered in to restore order and prepare the ground for federal mediation. Roosevelt explicitly invoked the police power in each of these areas during his terms as New York police commissioner, governor of New York state, and U.S. president. The Spanish-American War, which extended the American legal framework overseas for the first time, had imprinted on the public and elite minds the idea of maintaining order and promoting uplift among foreign peoples, including the Filipinos and Cubans. Consequently the Roosevelt Corollary, sanctifying the international police-power concept, stirred little controversy among the American people.

The Treaty of Paris and U.S. Police Power in the Islands

The Treaty of Paris bestowed the police power in the former Spanish possessions on the U.S. government, but the degree of authority conferred on Washington varied from territory to territory as Congress saw fit to extend the provisions of the U.S. Constitution. In some cases, notably the Philippines and Puerto Rico, a foreign country was annexed, and American sovereignty was extended wholesale. In the case of Cuba, the United States took on some of the authority normally allocated to the sovereign government, and through the Teller and Platt amendments, it abridged Cuban sovereignty even after American troops had withdrawn from the island.[2] A preliminary protocol concluded between the United States and Spain just after the fighting had ended obligated Spain to evacuate all of its Caribbean possessions, transfer sovereignty over Puerto Rico and the smaller islands to the United States, and "relinquish all claim of sovereignty over and title to Cuba." The protocol authorized the United States to "occupy and hold the city, bay and harbor of Manila" pending resolution of the status of the Philippine archipelago in a final peace treaty.[3] To the provision in the protocol that required Spain to give up Cuba, the Treaty of Paris added, "as the island is, upon its evacuation by Spain, to be occupied by the United States, the United States will, so long as such occupation shall last, assume and discharge the obligations that may under international law result from its occupation, for the protection of life and property." The treaty also transferred sovereignty over the Philippine Islands, Puerto Rico, Spain's other West Indies possessions, and Guam to the United States.[4]

The treaty language underlined the extension of American sovereignty to the new possessions. "The civil rights and political status of the native inhabitants of the territories hereby ceded to the United States shall be determined by the Congress," stated Article IX. (As chapter 7 showed, the U.S. Supreme Court essentially upheld this treaty provision.) Spaniards remaining in the islands and maintaining allegiance to Madrid would "be subject in matters civil as well as criminal" to the island courts, "pursuant to the ordinary laws" governing ordinary citizens. The Treaty of Paris stipulated that the United States would not assert full sovereignty over Cuba, although it would temporarily exercise the authority that went along with sovereignty. Because the island would eventually be turned over to its inhabitants, "any obligations assumed in this treaty by the United States with respect to Cuba are limited to the time of its occupancy thereof." Washington would, "upon the termination of such occupancy, advise any Government established in the island to assume the same obligations."[5]

By means of treaty law, then, the United States interjected itself into the most minute affairs of state in its new insular possessions. It would impose order in the islands by a combination of military and police action, used in conjunction with local judiciaries. It would tend to the public welfare by a range of reform measures, for instance by creating and enforcing sanitary regulations. In short, the U.S. government performed the constabulary function in the islands.

Elihu Root's Vision of American Colonial Policy

Just after the Spanish-American War, Secretary of War Elihu Root, who was charged with administering the islands wrung from Spain—and a man Theodore Roosevelt called "the brutal friend to whom I pay the most attention"[6]—laid out the principles guiding U.S. colonial policy. These principles helped lay the groundwork for Roosevelt's international police-power concept. Root found the justification for U.S. administration of the islands in the Treaty of Paris, which, as mentioned above, stated that the "civil rights and political status of the native inhabitants of the territories hereby ceded to the United States shall be determined by the Congress." In practice, however, Congress was content to entrust the day-to-day administration of the islands to the executive. What should drive the deliberations of American officials touching Puerto Rico, Cuba, and the Philippines? The secretary of war, formerly a practicing lawyer, traced the principles governing U.S. colonial policy to the legal doctrine of state sovereignty—just as he later explained that the Monroe Doctrine derived from the principles underlying sovereignty.

Clearly, the treaty with Spain conferred almost untrammeled powers on the United States where island citizens were concerned. Root declared:

> The United States has all the powers in respect of the territory it has [by treaty] acquired, and the inhabitants of that territory, which any nation in the world has in respect of territory which it has acquired; and that as between the people of the ceded islands and the United States the former are subject to the complete sovereignty of the latter, controlled by no legal limitations except those which may be found in the treaty of cession; that the people of the islands have no right to have them treated as states, or to have them treated as the territories previously held by the United States have been treated; or to assert a legal right under the provisions of the United States which [were] established for the people of the United States themselves and to meet the conditions existing upon this continent; or to assert against the United States any legal right whatever not found in the treaty.[7]

In short, Root argued that administering the islands was an entirely different matter than settling North America and that the Treaty of Paris had placed the islands under U.S. sovereignty.

This was not a call for heavy-handed treatment of the Filipinos and Cubans. With a Rooseveltian flourish, Secretary of War Root maintained that grave responsibilities accompanied the sweeping powers the U.S. government had assumed. The Progressive dogma that responsibility attended power was palpable in his correspondence. America had a duty, he proclaimed, "to make the interests of the people over whom we assert sovereignty the first and controlling consideration in all legislation and administration which concerns them, and to give them, to the greatest possible extent, individual freedom, self-government in accordance with their capacity, just and equal laws, and opportunity for education, for profitable industry, and for development in civilization." The people of Puerto Rico, Cuba, and the Philippines, continued Root, had "acquired a moral right to be treated by the United States in accordance with the underlying principles of justice and freedom which we have declared in our Constitution" and which provided a bulwark against abusive government.[8] U.S. policy flowed from moral virtue, which required generous conduct toward subject peoples, and from longstanding American traditions.

Their moral standing did not guarantee the island inhabitants a status fully equal to that of American citizens. That "provision of the Constitution prescribing uniformity of duties throughout the United States was not made for them, but was a provision of expediency solely adapted to the conditions existing in the United States upon the continent of North America"; nonetheless, island citizens were entitled to demand that they not be "deprived of life, liberty, or property without due process of law, that private property shall not be taken for public use without compensation," and that other rights should not be infringed "because our nation has declared these to be rights belonging to all men."[9] U.S. policy toward the insular territories, then, grew out of that curious blend of particularism and universalism that had underpinned the American founding.

Complicating matters, the treaty with Spain had granted the United States different degrees of sovereignty over the different territories. Puerto Rico, which was "fully and without question under the sovereignty of the United States," was the simplest case. Because the Puerto Ricans had endorsed the transfer of their island to U.S. stewardship, said Root, there was "no obstacle in the way of our providing for Porto Rico the best government which we are capable of devising for people situated as are the inhabitants of that island." For that reason, the basic principles undergirding American colonial policy are most easily discerned by examining U.S. policy toward Puerto Rico. The United States should craft a new order for the island with three questions uppermost in mind: (1) What form of government should be installed, and how should the people take part in ruling their country? (2) To what extent should the municipal laws bequeathed by Spain, which remained in force, be changed to accord with "the ideas prevalent among the people of the United States"? And (3) what economic relations should be established between Puerto Rico and the United States?[10]

Root admitted that the obstacles to this grand undertaking were monumental. Foremost was the lack of a culture of self-rule. The Puerto Ricans, said the secretary of war, had "not yet been educated in the art of self-government, or any really honest government." Simple ignorance of the intricacies of republican self-government was one problem. In Puerto Rican society, steeped in centuries of authoritarian rule, "law and freedom have been ideas which were not associated with each other, but opposed to each other." While Root professed confidence in the Puerto Ricans' ability to learn the skills of self-rule, illiteracy among the populace stood at 90 percent—making public education a matter of the utmost concern for the Roosevelt administration. Failing the emergence of a literate population, the island would eventually degenerate into an oligarchy dominated by the literate 10 percent. Even that relatively skilled minority boasted only a theoretical knowledge of the processes and methods of self-government.[11]

But the problem ran deeper than unfamiliarity with the mechanics of self-government. Not only had Puerto Ricans "never learned the fundamental and essential lesson of obedience to the decision of the majority"; they had never even embraced the more basic principle of "loyal, voluntary personal subjection to the peaceful decisions reached by lawful processes." Already plaguing the affairs of the island was the minority's habitual refusal to participate in the business of government where it could not muster a democratic majority. Puerto Rican citizens, declared Root, sounding a Burkean note, must learn self-restraint before they could be entrusted with the responsibilities of self-rule. "It would be of no use to present to the people of Porto Rico now a written constitution or frame of laws, however perfect, and tell them to live under it. They would inevitably fail without a course of tuition under a strong and guiding hand," namely that of the United States.[12] Because they could be evaded or simply ignored, then, written documents and legal arrangements were worthless unless they commanded the sincere respect of the people.

Notwithstanding his remark that the islanders had no claim to equality of treatment under the U.S. Constitution, Secretary Root then proceeded to propose that Puerto Ricans be afforded something that approximated statehood. The general U.S. laws should be extended to the island, executed by federal officers, and adjudicated by the federal courts. The indigenous government at San Juan should have the same jurisdiction over Puerto Rican citizens as that wielded by U.S. states over their citizens. Puerto Rican officials, however, would be chosen largely by the U.S. administration rather than through elections. The president should be empowered to appoint the governor, as well as officers of state such as the secretary of state and the attorney general, with the advice and consent of the U.S. Senate. The legislative function would fall to a council made up of the chief officers of state and a minority chosen by the president from among the Puerto Rican people. This legislative council could override a gubernatorial veto by a two-thirds vote. Approved legislation would be submitted to Congress for final approval.[13]

Finally, Root addressed the economic relations between Puerto Rico and the United States. Sounding a refrain similar to that of Roosevelt, William Howard Taft, and Leonard Wood, he declared, "I wish most strongly to urge that the customs duties between Porto Rico and the United States be removed." Why? For reasons closely allied to the American civilizing mission. If citizens of the island "have an abundance of the necessities of life, they will with justice be easily governed, and will with patience be easily educated." If, in contrast, "they are left in hunger and hopeless poverty, they will be discontented, intractable, and mutinous." Because Spain had enacted a tariff on Puerto Rican goods following its withdrawal from the island, and because the United States had not relaxed its own tariff barriers, the island's transfer to American jurisdiction had actually worked against its prosperity. Moral virtue—the "highest considerations of justice and good faith"—demanded immediate action to dismantle the American tariff wall.[14]

Elihu Root applied the Puerto Rican model, suitably modified to reflect the lesser authority accorded the United States by treaty, to the Philippines and, further attenuated, to Cuba. While the United States could not permanently extend the municipal police power to Cuba, "maintaining order and promoting the welfare of the people"— the two pillars of the police power—during the island's transition to independence were the U.S. military administration's duty. Thus a temporary extension of the police power was necessary to allow the Cubans to solve the social and political problems Root had foreseen for

Puerto Rico. The difficulties were much the same: a minority of "agitators who have loudly voiced their discontent over not being allowed personally to conduct the government," widespread illiteracy that enfeebled the capacity of Cubans for wise self-rule, centuries spent under "the dominion of arbitrary power" that had acculturated the Cuban people to authoritarianism, and "bitter factional feeling" from the bloody struggle that had lately convulsed the island.[15]

Root proposed a strategy for Cuba that strongly resembled his prescriptions for Puerto Rico. But the process of creating a new order on this Caribbean island had to be accelerated because of the congressional pledge to grant speedy independence. Once the Spanish citizens of Cuba decided whether to remain Spaniards or to accept Cuban citizenship, the United States would push ahead with plans for a convention "to frame a constitution and provide for a general government of the island, to which the United States will surrender the reins of government." As with Puerto Rico, it was crucial to spur Cuban agricultural exports and foreign investment on the island. Secretary Root detected a further complication for Cuba, however. Congress could grant reciprocity to Puerto Rico—and perhaps even to the British West Indies under reciprocity treaties then before the Senate— thereby placing additional impediments in the path of Cuba's economic revival. The project of erecting a liberal government on the island would be for naught if Cuban sugar producers could not sell their wares profitably in the United States, their biggest market.[16]

The great virtue of Root's style of argument lay in its lucidity, its lack of inflammatory language, and its legal precision. He was less given to brash, rhetorical speechifying than was President Roosevelt. While his calm exposition of U.S. policy reached the same conclusions as had the president's, it was less likely to incite indignation among foreign readers who might reasonably ask whether their nations would find themselves on the receiving end of an unjust American police action. Accordingly, Root was later assigned the task of explaining the Monroe Doctrine, as modified by the Roosevelt Corollary, to statesmen throughout Latin America.

◆ ◆ ◆ ◆ ◆

Why did the public greet the marked departure from American traditions in 1898 with little more than a collective yawn? Behind what principles had they thrown their support? The following case studies ferret out similarities and differences among the Roosevelt era's various police operations and discern common themes among them. Examining concrete instances of international policing will provide a way to evaluate TR's grand rhetoric on the spread of civilization and the defense of the U.S. national interest. The cases will also yield evidence as to whether Roosevelt sincerely believed in his high-minded police-power theory or had simply fabricated an elaborate excuse to meddle in the affairs of fellow American states.

The Philippines

Aside from the case of Puerto Rico, the pacification and administration of the Philippine Islands represented the fullest extension of the U.S. police power in the early twentieth century. To be sure, American activities in the islands were not carried out in accordance with the international police power Roosevelt eventually asserted in his corollary to the Monroe Doctrine; rather, the United States had annexed the islands in the wake of the Spanish-American War and extended the municipal police power to the islands pursuant to the Treaty of Paris. Roosevelt said as much in his autobiography.[17] Still, it was a short mental leap from claiming the right to police overseas territories gained by treaty to asserting a right to intervene transitorily in the affairs of sovereign states. The occupation of the Philippines served as an intellectual bridge between Roosevelt's Progressivism at home and his vision of collective uplift buoyed by the civilized powers' police activities in the wider less-developed world. And the lengthy U.S. administration of the archipelago, as opposed to the more fleeting actions in Santo Domingo and Cuba that otherwise marked TR's presidency, allowed his police-power theory to play itself out in full in the Philippines. Thus the Philippines case provides a rich fund of insights into Roosevelt's international police-power theory.

Although it antedated his presidency, Theodore Roosevelt was present at the conception of the Philippines campaign.[18] As assistant secretary of the navy, he had arranged Como. George Dewey's appointment as head of the navy's Pacific squadron, which was responsible for any actions against the Spanish Far East squadron. Roosevelt had taken advantage of a short absence by the secretary of the navy to arrange matters to his liking. While acting as secretary, TR ordered Dewey to position his fleet to engage the Spanish flotilla at Manila Bay. After demolishing the outmatched Spanish fleet, Commodore Dewey arranged the transport of Filipino rebels led by Emilio Aguinaldo to Luzon, where they immediately launched an insurrection, abetted by U.S. arms, against the Spanish administration. The Philippines' status briefly remained ambiguous once hostilities ceased.

In sharp contrast to the case of Cuba, neither Congress nor administration officials had promised to free the islands in the wake of an American victory. Even so, it seems clear that Aguinaldo believed that the rebels' labors in the American cause would be rewarded with independence. Whatever the case, the insurgents lay siege to Manila on land while the U.S. Navy blockaded the city from the sea. Together the American and native forces eventually brought about the surrender of Manila by the Spanish garrison.

After wavering, William McKinley dispelled the ambiguity about the fate of the islands, deciding to bring them under U.S. control. Why did he decide to push Congress to annex the Philippines? Largely for reasons of realpolitik: A German squadron at least equal in firepower to Dewey's squadron appeared in Manila Bay as an "observer," testifying to Germany's appetite for a stronghold in the Far East. So did a smaller British squadron, as well as a French and a Japanese warship. The United States and Britain were on fairly good terms, France lacked the wherewithal to contest U.S. control of the islands, and Japan was as yet only an emerging maritime threat. But Germany's imperial designs preoccupied the McKinley administration.

McKinley's misgivings were well founded. Berlin had instructed the German commander to monitor events in hopes that, should the United States grant the Filipinos independence, the Reich could step in, gaining partial or total control of the archipelago. In July 1898 the German foreign minister had notified the kaiser's ambassador in Washington that "His Majesty, the Emperor, deems it a principal object of German policy to leave unused no opportunity which may arise from the Spanish-American War to obtain naval fulcra in East Asia."[19] Berlin hoped to neutralize the islands pending an outright partition. Washington, then, rightly feared that allowing Germany or any other imperial power to gain a foothold in the archipelago would accelerate the drift toward a partition of China. Abandoning the Philippines to a European power would likely ruin the expansionist project espoused by Roosevelt, Lodge, and Mahan. The German admiral annoyed Dewey by opening contact with the Spanish authorities, threatening Aguinaldo's forces, and by menacing the American vessels when they shelled the city. After the surrender of Manila, however, the German flotilla steamed out of the harbor, never to return.

Subsequent events further undercut the kaiser's hopes of securing a base in the archipelago. (Frustrated in the Philippines, Germany did obtain the Carolines, the Pellews, and the Ladrones from Spain when Madrid liquidated its empire.) The armistice of August 12, 1898, authorized the United States to "occupy and hold the city, bay and harbor of Manila pending the conclusion of a treaty of peace which shall determine the control, disposition, and government of the Philippines." The Japanese government declared that it "would be willing to join with the United States, either singly or jointly with another Power having identical interests, in the endeavor to form . . . a suitable government for the territory under question under the joint or tripartite protection of the guaranteeing powers." Plainly, then, another rising maritime power, and potential U.S. rival, coveted a stake in the Philippines enterprise. Because of its proximity, Japan was far better situated geographically to exploit a base in the Philippines. But Washington politely yet firmly rebuffed the Japanese overture. This left the United States with the prospect of a long, costly occupation—especially because the administration had also rejected plans for a joint occupation of the archipelago alongside Aguinaldo's insurgents.

Gen. Wesley Merritt, the army commander, was commanded to ensure order in the Philippines once fighting had ceased. He had his hands full when Aguinaldo, realizing that his vision was at odds with that of the U.S. administration, organized an insurrection against the American occupiers. Subduing the rebels took two years, cost $400 million and seven thousand American casualties, and generated considerable ill will among the Filipino population, owing in part to the occasional excesses of the American occupation force.[20]

These costs were worthwhile for advocates of a "large" policy, such as TR, Mahan, and Lodge. Roosevelt wrote to Lodge opposing a final peace "until we get Puerto Rico, while Cuba is made independent and the Philippines at any rate taken from the Spaniards."[21] For his part, President McKinley visibly wrung his hands over whether to set the nation on a course of imperialism. Ultimately, reported McKinley, he had made the decision to annex the Philippines based on his calculation of lesser evils. The great powers clearly entertained designs on the archipelago. McKinley pointed to Germany's acquisition of Kiaochow, Russia's acquisition of Port Arthur, and other European bids for expansion as evidence that the imperial powers were determined to carve out spheres of interest in East Asia.

Great-power rivalry, he believed, thus threatened to shut out American commerce in the Far East and to damage the economic fortunes of the American people—to the detriment of whichever party held office at the time. McKinley's instructions to the American peace delegation were vague. While the delegation understood that the United States could not accept less than the island of Luzon, what to do with the rest of the archipelago was unclear. For strategic reasons it boiled down to an all-or-nothing decision. Defending the entire country, maintained military experts such as General Merritt, was easier than defending a single island or installation. President McKinley ultimately bowed to this logic. He contended that he had acted primarily in the U.S. national interest. But his decision making exhibited a strong moral tinge, as befitted an ordained minister.

In a Rooseveltian bit of analysis, McKinley concluded that moral obligations accompanied self-interest.[22]

> I am not ashamed to tell you, gentlemen, that I went down on my knees and prayed Almighty God for light and guidance more than one night. And one night late it came to me this way—I don't know how it was, but it came: (1) That we could not give [the Philippines] back to Spain— that would be cowardly and dishonorable; (2) that we could not turn them over to France or Germany—our commercial rivals in the Orient—that would be bad business and discreditable; (3) that we could not leave them to themselves—they were unfit for self-government—and they would soon have anarchy and misrule over there worse than Spain's was; and (4) that there was nothing left for us to do, but to take them all, and to educate the Filipinos, and uplift and civilize and Christianize them, and by God's grace do the very best we could by them, as our fellowmen for whom Christ also died.[23]

Emilio Aguinaldo and his cadre of Filipino nationalists took a different view of things. Although Aguinaldo and his followers had in all likelihood decided to fight it out by that time, congressional proceedings undoubtedly threw fuel on the fire. The U.S. Senate approved the peace treaty with Spain by the narrow margin of 57–27, a surplus of only two votes. In the 1898 elections McKinley had implored the electorate to return Republicans to Congress to ease the task of the peace commissioners. The voters did in fact reelect a Republican legislature, allowing the administration to assert popular approval of its wartime policies.[24]

Lodge had contended that a rejection of the pact with Spain would humiliate the president in the eyes of the civilized world. McKinley had rashly proclaimed U.S. sovereignty over the islands even before the Senate granted its consent. The vote may have turned on the actions of Roosevelt's normally anti-imperialist whipping boy, William Jennings Bryan, who urged Democratic senators to support the treaty in hopes of ending the war speedily and eliminating imperialism as an issue in the 1900 presidential election. After consenting to the treaty, the Senate rejected a resolution—with the vice president, Garret A. Hobart, casting the deciding vote—that would have promised ultimate independence to the Filipinos.

Historian Samuel Flagg Bemis called the acquisition of the Philippines "the greatest blunder of American diplomacy." It embroiled the United States in Asian politics, and, in turn, in the byzantine politics of the European great powers.[25] Although maintaining the Open Door in China had been of considerable interest to the United States before 1898, the sudden acquisition of U.S. territory in the Far East altered the picture entirely. Not only did the annexation seemingly require an extension of the Monroe Doctrine to Asia, but it also threatened to catalyze a partition of China contrary to the Open Door. Still, the advent of the United States as a major player in Asia allowed Secretary of State John Hay to secure the assent of the major powers—Russia excepted—to free and open commerce among the European "spheres of interest" in the Middle Kingdom.

The costs associated with bringing order to the Philippines were steep. Indeed, a 1929 balance sheet comparing the costs and benefits to the American and Filipino peoples from U.S. occupation of the islands had skewed sharply in favor of the Filipinos.[26] The establishment of reciprocal trade arrangements, at a time when Republicans leaned toward protectionism, was one sign of the American commitment to doing good works in Asia. Roosevelt pointed to the material benefits of the occupation for the Filipino populace as evidence of the moral worth of the enterprise. Indeed, Roosevelt, characteristically, recast an enterprise conceived as hardheaded realpolitik as a grand moral crusade. The United States, he maintained, had inherited the islands under less than optimal circumstances. Since it could not free the islands—and risk a German or Japanese incursion—America must throw its energies into collective uplift and prepare the Filipinos for self-rule. As McKinley's point man for the 1900 presidential election campaign, TR stubbornly defended the administration's imperial policies.

Why Rule the Philippines?

From his newfound bully pulpit, Roosevelt touted the administration's reasons for keeping the Philippines and devised a strategy that laid the groundwork for his doctrine of international constabulary duty. He framed perhaps the most comprehensive rationale for any intervention examined here—transposing his thoughts on the national interest and collective uplift to the international arena. Like President McKinley, TR freely conceded that realpolitik played a central role in Washington's Philippines policy. Projecting U.S. power into a region of interest and excluding U.S. great-power rivals were compelling reasons to keep the islands. U.S. policy also had a preventive tinge. To pull out would not only throw the archipelago into chaos but also invite Japan or an ambitious European power to step in, potentially shutting the United States out of the Far East.

Expansion into the Far East, claimed Roosevelt, was not a departure from but an extension of American traditions. "The history of the nation," he declared, "is in large part the history of the nation's expansion." He compared the situation in the Philippines to the pacification of the Louisiana Purchase. Thomas Jefferson had purchased Louisiana and set about imposing order in the new land. "He intended that ultimately self-government should be introduced throughout the territory, but only as the different parts became fit for it, and no sooner."[27] Consequently, Jefferson had not worried overmuch about armed occupation or oligarchy in the territories, nor had he trifled with the "consent of the governed" doctrine offered up by anti-imperialists who hoped to prevent U.S. annexation of the Philippines. Both interest and humanity, affirmed TR, had prodded the United States onto its course of expansion.[28]

American policy, Roosevelt further contended, had exemplified the best in trusteeship while remaining untainted by imperialism. "Our only justification for keeping the islands is that we intend to benefit them."[29] The Filipinos "must, of course, be governed primarily in the interests of their own citizens. Our first care must be for the people of the islands which have come under our guardianship as a result of the most righteous foreign war" in a generation.[30] Roosevelt went on to recount the further U.S. expansion across North America and overseas. "We are making no new departures," he insisted. "We are not taking a single step which in any way affects our institutions or our traditional policies. From the beginning we have given widely varying degrees of self-government to the different territories, according to their needs." It was beyond dispute, he concluded, that "there is nothing even remotely resembling 'imperialism' or 'militarism' involved in the present development of that policy of expansion which has been part of the history of America from the day when she became a nation."[31]

Why was it better for Filipinos for the United States, a foreign power, to administer their country rather than emancipating it altogether? Roosevelt distanced himself from the harsher theories of the white man's burden.[32] Rather, he professed confidence "that we can ultimately help our brethren of the Philippine Islands so far forward on the path of self-government and orderly liberty. . . . A great future lies before the Philippines, and it can only be marred if this country is so unwise as to listen to those who would let us let the islands fall back into chaos instead of cordially co-operating with the wisest and most upright among their citizens."[33] To free the Filipinos prematurely, before Burkean self-restraint had taken root among a populace that had known little besides despotism, would consign the archipelago to perpetual internecine warfare and, in the end, oligarchy. To Rudyard Kipling, TR derided "the jack fools who seriously think that any group of pirates and head-hunters needs nothing but independence in order that it may be turned forthwith into a dark-hued New England town meeting."[34]

Ultimately, the archipelago would gain its freedom from foreign rule. An indefinite period of U.S. tutelage, however, would be required for republican institutions and habits to take hold. President Roosevelt declined to fix a date for emancipation. Like Elihu Root, he vehemently rejected the anti-imperialists' notion that the U.S. Constitution could extend only where the consent of the governed had been given—a condition that emphatically had not been met in the Philippines. "I wish I could show you privately a letter from Judge Taft," he wrote Frederic Coudert in 1901, "as to the impossibility of working out the salvation of the Philippines, as we were forced to undertake the job, exactly on the terms of our government here at home; what does well here would work ruin there—trial by jury in all cases, for instance."[35] Were the anti-imperialists to gain power at home, "the result would be a frightful calamity to the Filipinos themselves, and in its larger aspect would amount to an international crime." Anarchy, the bugbear of the Rooseveltian worldview, would follow; "and the most violent anarchic forces would be directed partly against the civil government, partly against all forms of religious and educational civilization."[36] Roosevelt did, however, pledge to allow the Filipinos to decide their fate once the United States had concluded they were ready for self-rule.[37]

The Republic, declared TR, had been pursuing a sort of anti-imperial imperialism.[38] "We made a great anti-imperialistic stride when we drove the Spaniards from Porto Rico and the Philippines and thereby made ready ground in these islands for that gradually increasing measure of self-government for which their populations are severally fitted."[39] He again wove the element of self-interest into the argument. The anti-imperialists' protests notwithstanding, the only way its activities in the Philippines could lead America into militarism would be if the Republic guaranteed the islands against outside meddling and tried to prop up a central Filipino government that would inevitably have to juggle the claims of competing tribes.

That would jeopardize not only the Filipinos' well-being but also the health of American institutions. A far larger army than the one currently in the field would be required to execute such an expansive policy, and maintaining such an occupation force might overtax the U.S. government and lead to some kind of militarism. Far better, argued Roosevelt, to erect a government under U.S. auspices and "support that government until the natives gradually grow fit to sustain it themselves." For him, this was America's duty. Besides, he taunted opponents of expansion, "the question is not whether we shall expand—for we have already expanded—but whether we shall contract. The Philippines are now part of American territory. To surrender them would be to surrender American territory."[40] In Roosevelt's expansive worldview, it was impossible to disentangle enlightened self-interest from the imperative to work on behalf of the people who found themselves under U.S. stewardship.

How should the United States go about pacifying and nurturing republican institutions among a people that had never known self-rule? Roosevelt was reluctant to leave the islands to military administrators for an occupation that might last decades. Rather, he preferred to turn over the reins to civilian administrators such as William Howard Taft. Reflecting his faith in the capacities of disinterested public servants—a common thread during his career, on display most prominently during his term as U.S. Civil Service commissioner—Roosevelt insisted that the islands "must be administered in the interests of their inhabitants, and that necessarily means that any question of personal or partisan politics in their administration must be entirely eliminated. We must continue to put at the heads of affairs in the different islands such men as Gen. Wood, Governor Allen and Judge Taft."[41] Carrying the American good-government movement to the islands was the best way to cultivate the habits needed for self-rule among the Filipino populace.

The military, he told Taft, was ill-suited to the long-term administration of foreign lands. In part this was a shortcoming of army culture. "I doubt if there is a man alive who has a higher appreciation of the army than I have," he wrote in 1901. Nonetheless, "the older officers of course get ossified, and then they are very difficult to deal with in places calling for qualities which they have never exercised or had the chance to exercise; and for a flexibility for which they are not now adapted." Accordingly, "it seems to me [that] the military arm should be literally an arm directed by the civil head."[42] Roosevelt admitted indirectly that the tiny ground forces maintained by the United States were unequal to the task of administering a foreign country. Turn-of-the-century ground forces lacked the military police and civil affairs arms used to help administer Germany and Japan five decades hence. Consequently, as detailed later, the United States relied on regular troops to organize, oversee, and supplement the combat and police activities of the native constabulary.

Another problem with military occupation was the humanitarian abuses that pockmarked the bitter counterinsurgency campaign. Since civil pacification measures proceeded in parallel with the counterinsurgency effort, war crimes committed in the field could discredit the civil reform program. To avoid inflaming the Filipino population against American policy, the United States must ruthlessly punish soldiers who committed such offenses. In the islands, contended TR, his administration had "hunted down without mercy every wrongdoer in the service of the nation whom it was possible by the utmost vigilance to detect; for the public servant who betrays his trust and the private individual who debauches him stand as the worst of criminals, because their crimes are crimes against the entire community, and not only against this generation but against the generations that are to be."[43] There was no room for softheartedness toward soldiers guilty of war crimes.

Finally, Roosevelt insisted that a strong economic liberalization program accompany the U.S. occupation of the Philippine Islands. There were humanitarian reasons for bucking the protectionist orthodoxy of his own Republican Party. Economic prosperity was indispensable not only to the Filipinos' material well-being but to the stability of the government the United States was busily installing. In 1903, exasperated at the resistance to reciprocity from high-tariff proponents within his own party, TR implored Henry Cabot Lodge, "Can there not be a resolute effort made to put through the Philippine tariff bill? I think it is of the utmost importance to the islands that a large measure of tariff reduction be given them." The leaders of a party that opposed the tariff reduction, he thundered, "ought at least to be put in the position of publicly taking the responsibility for an action that may turn out to be criminal." This, he told Lodge, was a matter "not merely of propriety and expedience but of humanity."[44] The notion of helping individual Filipinos pull their own weight conformed to TR's views on the domestic police power. The state's role was to regulate living and working conditions for the working class while striving not to hamper economic prosperity.

That Roosevelt viewed the occupation of the Philippines as of a piece with U.S. diplomacy in the New World is plain from his correspondence. "The easy thing to do in international matters," he wrote to Edward Everett Hale, "is to follow those amiable but far from wise philanthropists who think we can help our brother by doing nothing whatever. . . . Unfortunately, the most difficult task is that which has been so conscientiously undertaken by Root and Taft in trying to bring the Filipinos forward in the path of orderly self-governing liberty." But "in South America it is positively difficult to know just how much it is best to leave the nations alone and how far there must be interference, and also how far we can with justice prevent interference by others; because in each case the equities vary."[45] Before long, a flare-up between Venezuela and the European great powers, seemingly posing a threat to the territorial integrity of an American republic, would impel TR to flesh out his theorizing on U.S. policing of the Americas.

William Howard Taft, the U.S. Army, and Administering the Philippines

The addresses and correspondence of William Howard Taft, a close confidant of President Roosevelt, a civil governor of the Philippines, and TR's successor in the Oval Office, shed further light on the Roosevelt administration's perspective on the respective roles of military power and of civil administrators in pacifying foreign lands. Taft's writings are worth reviewing not only because he was civil governor of the archipelago but because, from his time supervising the U.S. Army's constabulary efforts, he could offer a counterpoint to maritime enthusiasts such as Roosevelt, Lodge, and Mahan.[46] Naval victories such as Dewey's were all very well, declared Taft, and because of their dramatic nature they captured the public imagination. But to U.S. Army troops fell four years worth of "arduous and delicate work" following the defeat of Aguinaldo's insurrection. Indeed, the army was the primary instrument by which "the benevolent policy of McKinley" had been carried out in the Philippines.[47]

According to Taft, not traditional military valor but "accomplishment by patient effort," characterized by "close attention, tenacious courage and self-restraint," was the touchstone of U.S. ground operations in the Philippines. Carrying out the occupation was a far different matter than fighting a conventional army. Indeed, the army's "work has been not only that of attack but more often and for longer that of police administration and pacification." Like Theodore Roosevelt, Taft mingled the domestic and foreign policy arenas, pointing to the army's role in maintaining order in the aftermath of the disastrous 1906 San Francisco earthquake. Army commanders had taken control of the stricken city, after which "theft and rapine and violence were banished by the long faithful hours of the regular soldiers on guard."

Likewise, in Cuba "the formidable naval fleet came first and gave to the hands of those seeking peace the effective power to command" the island's destiny. Within two weeks, however, "to the Army fell the task of garrisoning the island in such a way as to discourage lawlessness and encourage the friends of order."[48] Naval power was the enabling force, then, but nautical triumphs swiftly gave way to the ground forces' less glamorous but even more crucial pacification efforts. Respect and sensitivity, unwonted virtues for military men, came to the fore during these police operations. "I ask you," exulted Taft, "has anything been finer in the history of the Army than the way in which our 5,000 men have settled down in an alien country like Cuba, have secured the maintenance of peace and order without the slightest complaint that any officer or soldier has exhibited any lack of respect for the feelings of Cubans under the trying circumstances of our occupation, or any lack of tact in carrying out the difficult task assigned to them?"[49]

This observation led William Howard Taft to propose that the United States needed an army for three elemental reasons. First, and most obviously, an army was "essential to any satisfactory system of national defense." Second, it was "an indispensable instrument in carrying out our established international policy." And third, the army was Washington's chief instrument for "the suppression of insurrection and civil strife" when state and local police and militias fell short. Taft tied the army's second purpose to the Monroe Doctrine. "How could we maintain such a doctrine"—especially if, as he insisted, the doctrine extended as far as Tierra del Fuego—"if it should ever be questioned in the strenuous race for trade and for colonization that now is rife among the European powers?" While America's powerful new navy could perform a useful function by blunting an outright invasion of Latin America, "it would make but little headway against hostile forces landed therein." After that, the United States would ineluctably be forced to rely on "an expeditionary force to the country invaded for the purpose of assisting the local forces in repelling the invader."

With the extension of the domestic U.S. police power to the nation's island possessions, the second purpose of the army shaded into the third. At home, should "the forces of anarchy and socialism and revolt against organized government manifest themselves, a well-organized militia would be most necessary." While the "suppression of local disturbances is to the regular army a very unpleasant duty," and one to which "the President would summon regular troops with great reluctance," the "moral effect of a regular army . . . to discourage lawlessness is valuable."[50] Like Roosevelt, Taft viewed military force as a last line of defense against anarchy. Troops furnished the security that underpinned pacification and social uplift.

Judge Taft gently rebuked Congress and the administration for maintaining expeditionary forces unequal to the vast foreign commitments the Republic had undertaken. The legislature had authorized a total U.S. Army end strength of one hundred thousand men. Of these the president had ordered a force raised that numbered approximately seventy-six thousand. The "mobile" army—as opposed to the "immobile" force that manned the nation's coastal fortifications—totaled around fifty-five thousand troops, whereas the law permitted its expansion to eighty thousand. Since the United States had deployed five thousand soldiers to Cuba and an additional twelve thousand to the Philippines, Taft concluded that the army was dramatically overburdened.[51] He implied, then, that the nation had adopted expansive foreign-policy ends without generating the military means to achieve them.

As discussed earlier, twin elements comprised the police power. Paired with routine law enforcement were the labors of civil servants who were charged with improving the health and welfare of Filipinos through judicious administration. Taft spoke at length about civil administration in the archipelago on two occasions: first, in his inaugural address as civil governor of the islands in 1901 and, second, to commemorate the inauguration of the Philippine Assembly in 1907. As the army and marines pacified the various provinces, the legislative and executive powers were gradually transferred to civil provincial governors, who in turn reported to the American governor of the country and a joint U.S.-Filipino commission.

Once the insurgents had been subdued in a province, U.S.-supervised governments were installed in fairly short order. Twenty-seven provincial governments had been organized by mid-1901, sixteen provinces awaited organization, and the Municipal Code had been extended to many of the towns in those provinces—conferring autonomy on the adult male citizens of these localities (with the exception of Manila, which was administered by the central government). The U.S. secretary of war was assigned overall responsibility for making "the territory of these Islands ripe for permanent civil government on a more or less permanent basis."[52] This was a stiff challenge after a debilitating war that had robbed many Filipinos of the "habits of industry" and had given rise to famine and disease. Shortly after Taft took office, the secretary of war ordered the creation of executive departments of the interior, commerce and police, justice and finance, and public instruction.

The army's role in "punishing and repressing crime" diminished with the advent of civil government in the islands. The civil government, said Taft, "must prepare to stand alone and not depend on the army to police the provinces and towns."[53] The occupation forces would withdraw to "larger garrisons where, in cases of emergency only, they can be called on to assist the local police . . . but the people must be enabled by organization of native police under proper and reliable commanders to defend themselves against the turbulent and vicious of their own communities." As the military gradually relinquished these "quasi-civil duties of police," it would also turn over the "jurisdiction of military commissions to try ordinary criminal cases" to appointed judges acting under a recently passed judiciary law.[54]

Under the watchful gaze of the indigenous Philippine Constabulary, a body of Filipino paramilitary troops officered by U.S. soldiers, provincial officials took up the full panoply of chores entrusted to government.[55] In the Philippines, an archipelago made up of thousands of islands, a fleet of steamers was needed to facilitate ordinary communications and postal deliveries; a public-school system was established around a core of a thousand American teachers to teach the rudiments of republican self-rule and, on a more basic level, a common language; and so forth. Like Roosevelt, Taft viewed the staffing of the civil administrations, not to mention the joint Filipino-American judiciary, as an extension of the good-government movement that was then in full swing in the United States and in which TR, as U.S. Civil Service commissioner, had played a leading role. Forestalling a spoils system similar to the one that had debased American politics was one of the Roosevelt administration's chief worries in the area of civil pacification.[56] Corrupt practices would sow distrust among Filipinos, potentially discrediting republican government.

Why was uprightness among civil servants so important? Because, said William Howard Taft, a U.S. official dispatched to the islands was "the representative of the great Republic among a people untutored in the methods of free and honest government, and in so far as he fails in his duty, he vindicates the objection of those who have forcibly resisted our taking control of these Islands and weakens the claim we make that we are here to secure good government for the Philippines."[57] To that end, Congress had enacted appropriate civil-service legislation. The pacification strategy, then, was fourfold. The army, in cooperation with the native constabulary, defeated the insurgents and then undertook routine law enforcement activities. Civil servants supplied the vital services needed by the populace. Americans, both by education and by example, inculcated the habits of republican self-government. And Congress—in theory at least—slashed tariffs, promoting trade between the archipelago and the United States and jumpstarting an economy ravaged by guerrilla warfare.[58]

What of the Filipinos' ultimate fate? Like President Roosevelt, Taft was forthright about this touchy subject. In his 1907 address to the Philippine Assembly, he seized on rumors that Washington was contemplating selling the islands to another great power to draw a stark contrast between American and European imperialism. "Those who credit such a report little understand the motives which actuated the American people in accepting the burden of this Government. The majority of the American people are still in favor of carrying out our Philippine policy as a great altruistic work. They have no selfish object to secure." He professed satisfaction at the dismay the prospect of a sale provoked in critics of the Roosevelt administration's "alleged lack of liberality toward the Filipino people and of sympathy with their aspirations." This, said Judge Taft, threw into sharp relief "the rigid governmental control which would be exercised over the people of the Islands under the colonial policy of any one of the powers to whom it is suggested we are about to sell them."[59]

Taft thus echoed McKinley's thesis comparing American altruism favorably with exploitative European imperialism. While the United States intended to gradually shift government responsibilities to the Filipinos—indeed, Taft credited the empowerment of the Filipinos with quieting objections to a period of U.S. military occupation—it could not fix a date for the transfer of sovereignty. Progress was halting and uncertain. The fear entertained by American statesmen such as TR was that prematurely announcing Washington's intentions regarding emancipation would encourage the insurgents to renew the fight and otherwise disrupt Filipino politics.[60] No one could say how long it would take for the "great experiment" in self-government to take root.[61]

Taft forecast that preparing the Philippines for self-rule would consume a generation. In 1907 he reminded the newly inaugurated Philippine Assembly that the U.S. Congress had the final say on the sovereignty question, notwithstanding the "wide discretion [that] has been vested in the President to shape affairs in the Islands." Nonetheless, the McKinley and Roosevelt administrations' avowed policy, observed Taft, had been "to govern the Islands, having regard to the interest and welfare of the Filipino people. . . . As this policy of extending control continues, it must logically reduce and finally end the sovereignty of the United States" in the archipelago, unless the Filipinos themselves freely opted for some form of confederation.[62] For his part,

President Roosevelt in 1908 commended the Filipinos for clear progress toward self-government. "Hitherto the Philippine legislature has acted with moderation and self-restraint," evidently recognizing that "the only way in which any body of individuals can escape the necessity of being governed by outsiders is to show that they are able to restrain themselves, to keep down wrongdoing and disorder."[63]

The U.S. Army and Pacification Strategy: Military Measures

Now consider the operational aspects of the Philippine campaign. Military and civil pacification strategies ended up being pursued in tandem, but the emphasis on either strategy fluctuated over time.[64] Pacification was "more alchemy than science," concludes a contemporary analyst.[65] The U.S. Army tried out various schemes, focusing at first on civil pacification and later, seeing that benevolence alone could not pacify the Philippine Islands, on the military dimensions of counterinsurgency strategy.[66] In the end, this experimentation process demonstrated that civil pacification was crucial but that military victory was the enabling factor that allowed civil pacification to go forward.[67] In December 1898, after the treaty with Spain had been signed, President McKinley maintained that high motives had animated his decision to seek annexation of the archipelago. The president asserted that the "mission of the United States is one of benevolent assimilation" that would rest on the occupation force's efforts to "win the confidence, respect, and affection of the inhabitants of the Philippines." To give effect to his statement, McKinley directed the American military government, at that point still confined to Manila, to "be extended with all possible dispatch to the whole of the ceded territory." The president hoped the islands would be brought under American sway nonviolently. "Am most desirous that conflict be avoided," he told Maj. Gen. Elwell S. Otis, the American commander until mid-1900. "Time given the insurgents can not hurt us and must weaken and discourage them. They will come to see our benevolent purpose and recognize that before we can give their people good government our sovereignty must be complete and unquestioned. Tact and kindness most essential just now."[68]

So it went—for a time. Kind intentions or not, the United States could not pacify the Philippines without defeating the revolutionaries. The U.S. Army overcame Emilio Aguinaldo's Republican Army in fairly short order, inducing Aguinaldo to abandon his conventional military strategy in favor of guerrilla warfare. The guerrillas sought to protract the war in hopes that disease would ravage the U.S. occupation force and in hopes of influencing the 1900 U.S. presidential election, in which they expected the Democratic nominee, William Jennings Bryan, to run on an anti-imperialist platform.[69] In most areas, guerrilla forces were loosely divided into partisans and militia. The former, led by officers recruited from provincial elites, made it their job to ambush U.S. Army convoys, cut telegraph lines, and attack towns that had embraced American civil government. The latter, known as "amigos," freely shifted between civilian and military identities, grew food for the partisans, monitored U.S. military activities, and terrorized villagers into cooperating with the insurgency—the civilian populace being their chief source of recruits and supplies. William Howard Taft asserted that guerrilla warfare could not have lasted as long as it did without intimidating ordinary Filipinos.[70] The guerillas made "cruelty deliberately part of their policy," claimed Taft, and "without that system of terrorism the guerrilla campaign would have ended very quickly, because the people wanted peace."[71]

The army thus had to develop counterinsurgency policies combining efforts at civil administration with military pursuit of the enemy.[72] Commanders dispatched to the archipelago, accordingly, were admonished that American forces had not only a military but a civilizing mission.[73] General Otis ordered U.S. garrisons to be stationed in as many villages as possible to demonstrate to the Filipinos their ability to bring peace and order, to win their support for the U.S. pacification strategy, and to deny the insurgents their primary source of supplies.[74] Local army commanders made up manpower shortfalls in the garrisons by recruiting local scouts, or "constabularies." This gave them the capacity to maintain preponderant force in the villages while waging counterinsurgency campaigns in the brush.[75] Underlining the civil character of the U.S. occupation, GO (General Orders) 43 (1899) and GO 40 (1900) directed army officers to establish municipal governments, each consisting of a local mayor or *presidente*, a town council, and a police force.[76] While instituting civil government, the army enacted sanitary regulations, cleared roads, and built schools.[77]

The army's labors in social reform improved ordinary citizens' quality of life. An aggressive guerrilla offensive in the fall of 1900, however, showed American leaders that they had woefully underestimated the insurgents and prompted them to enact sterner policies. A more balanced pacification effort resulted. Secretary of War Elihu Root announced that the United States would resort to some of the "methods which have proved successful in our Indian campaigns in the West." In this Root's thinking paralleled that of Roosevelt, who, as seen earlier, often likened the pacification of the Philippine Islands to that of the American West.[78] In keeping with this more forceful approach, Gen. Arthur MacArthur, who relieved Otis in mid-1900 and served until Taft had him replaced in mid-1901,[79] placed the islands under martial law under GO 100. This "new and more stringent policy" abandoned previous efforts to court Filipino elites, one of the main-stays of the insurrection, called for more drastic uses of force, and instructed U.S. forces to focus their attentions on disrupting the flow of supplies to the guerrillas. The new policy also contemplated "ex-emplary punishment" for breaches of the laws of war.[80] MacArthur announced that amigos found conducting military activities in civil-ian garb would henceforth be punished as "war rebels, or war trai-tors" and that insurgents who resorted to terrorist tactics would be punished as such. Military commissions tried and occasionally ex-ecuted such individuals; army provost courts operating in areas un-der martial law struck at the guerrillas by issuing stiff sentences to Filipinos found to have paid taxes to the insurgents, provided them with supplies, or rendered other forms of assistance.[81]

The pendulum swung from military toward civil government with the waxing success of American arms. The arrest of Aguinaldo, who issued a proclamation acknowledging U.S. sovereignty, helped deflate the revolutionary movement; so did the U.S. practice of quickly erecting civil government, complete with a measure of local autonomy, in pacified areas.[82] So, too, did aggressive combat patrolling, instituted at General MacArthur's behest. Small units sought to maintain con-tinuous contact with and to defeat the guerrillas rather than content-ing themselves with the rather static, defensively minded approach that had dominated U.S. strategy in the early going. Perpetual harass-ment and pursuit of the insurgents, compounded by the destruction of their supplies and equipment in the countryside, rather than the vil-lages, were the keystones of American success.[83] Some local command-ers, notably Brig. Gen. Jacob H. ("Hell-Raising Jake") Smith, adopted tactics, such as reconcentration and mass slaughter, that led to war-crimes trials and ultimately helped bring the U.S. war effort into disre-pute.[84] Yet there was no disputing the effectiveness of these tactics.[85] Despite orders from Manila forbidding harm to noncombatants, some senior officers had concluded that, to quote one, "the judicious appli-cation of the torch is the most humane way of waging such a war." Some decided to "burn the place."[86]

By mid-1901, as mentioned earlier, Taft was appointed civil governor of the islands, assuming control of regions in which guer-rilla resistance had been effectively quelled. Victory had been sub-stantially achieved in Luzon by 1902, although the Moros continued to wage guerrilla warfare in some of the outlying southern islands for several more years. A contemporary analyst credits the "U.S. Army's growing willingness and ability to inflict social, economic, and physical pressure" with compelling Filipino elites, and thus ordinary citizens, "to accommodate themselves to American rule or risk destruction."[87] The relatively mild treatment accorded those who accepted U.S. military and civil government provided a better alternative than destruction at the hands of Hell-Raising Jake Smith and his ilk.

A final measure that helped impose order in the archipelago straddled the line between military and civil pacification strategies. In July 1901, coinciding with Taft's appointment as the civil governor of the islands, the civilian Philippine Commission formally established a Philippine Constabulary. Composed of 150-man units, the constabulary served as a combination of police and scouts, tracking down criminals and sometimes insurgents and, above all, providing invaluable intelligence to the American government.[88] While the Philippine Constabulary was an arm of the civil government, the U.S. Army provided almost all of its officer corps. American officers routinely returned to the regular army after a spell of police duty.[89] Both the military and the constabulary functions were gradually transferred to this indigenous organization as pacification proceeded.[90] In 1906, at the direction of Philippine Constabulary commander, Brig. Gen. Henry T. Allen, a *Manual for the Philippine Constabulary* was published. While the manual prescribed tactics for counterinsurgency warfare, it placed great weight on the police functions, describing, for instance, arrest procedures and methods for collecting evidence. It emphasized that the constabulary members were more than mere police or military men: they were civilizing agents whose mission was to win Filipinos' allegiance with minimal violence.[91]

The U.S. Army and Pacification Strategy: Civil Measures

Paired with a forceful military campaign, civil pacification measures ultimately worked to bring the Philippine Islands under full American sovereignty. One veteran army officer testified to the shift in emphasis from the days of the Indian wars: The occupation force was entrusted with the "formation of local governments including the establishment of educational, sanitary, fiscal and welfare systems. . . . Reversing the policy [of] extermination applied to our American Indians, we were determined to preserve the Filipino [by] raising his standards and cultivating his friendship."[92] The army's counterinsurgency actions, once suitably refined and adapted to conditions in each region, gave the Filipino elites whose support buoyed the insurgency a stark choice between U.S. rule and destruction; civil government and social reform showed archipelago inhabitants that accepting U.S. sovereignty was much to be preferred.[93] The blend of carrots and sticks ultimately worked to U.S. advantage.

Normalizing living conditions for the populace, in Manila and subsequently in outlying provinces, was the first hurdle for the occupying army. Sanitation measures were implemented in the capital city to combat disease, which had run rampant during the American siege of Manila. Medical facilities sought to stem the spread of disease. The army secularized education and opened new schools, serving the dual purposes of educating Filipino young—crucial to fending off oligarchy over the long haul—and keeping disenchanted youth off the streets.[94] The army designated the capital city a free-trade port, admitting vessels from all nations on an equal basis in a bid to stimulate the local economy. As an additional boost to the economy, the army undertook a variety of public-works projects, such as constructing the roads, bridges, and marketplaces needed to revive internal trade in the archipelago.[95]

After the Republican Army was vanquished and Aguinaldo's followers turned to guerrilla warfare, the U.S. Army initially busied itself with trying to extend civil reforms to the provinces, much as it had done in Manila. Army leaders failed to make the connection between military victory—the fact that the United States had imposed peace in the capital by force of arms—and the successes achieved with improving living standards there. General Otis did not trouble himself overmuch with efforts to combat the insurgency militarily. Rather, the army built hospitals, schools, roads, and other civilian infrastructure.

One innovation launched in the wake of the fall 1900 guerrilla offensive was martial law: the suspension of civil judicial rights. American military officials were given summary court powers and authorized to suspend local due process rights, including the right to a trial. Travel restrictions and curfews were imposed, helping the occupation force track the movements of Filipino citizens; identity papers were issued and scrutinized; and town *presidentes* were directed to record the comings and goings of all residents. Martial law also allowed U.S. commanders to strike directly at the elites who formed the insurgency's social and economic backbone. Local patricians who supported Aguinaldo could be summarily imprisoned or exiled, their property forfeit at the order of army tribunals.[96]

Cuba

Like the Philippine Islands, Cuba fell to U.S. administration under the terms of the treaty with Spain; and, also like the Philippines, the Cuba case does not fall under the 1904 international police-power concept. Rather, the island was governed under a modified version of the municipal U.S. police power, its contours laid out in the Platt and Teller amendments.[97] One British observer of the day noted that the "Spanish-American war did not conspicuously break down the old tradition of the fathers of the republic. . . . Cuba lay at your back door, and even the Philippines came in as a corollary to an operation of domestic police."[98] Yet American stewardship over Cuba bears examination because it helped to bridge the gap between the domestic and international missions Theodore Roosevelt thrust upon the United States. And the president cited its salutary effects as justification for further international police work.[99]

"The purpose of our military government," declared Gen. Leonard Wood, the second U.S. governor of the island,[100] "was to prepare the Cubans for self-government and to establish conditions which would render the establishment of a Cuban republic possible and its orderly and successful maintenance probable."[101] The military occupation had a precedent-setting effect for Roosevelt, who often boasted that the withdrawal of American forces from the island in 1902 had been a signal event in world history: a display of moral virtue by a great power at the expense of its pragmatic self-interest. The pullout was, he declared, the first instance in which a great power had voluntarily handed back territory it had won by force of arms.[102] The brief occupation in 1898–1902 and the subsequent intervention in 1906–9, he said, constituted proof of U.S. worthiness to take on the role of a benevolent, disinterested guardian of the Western Hemisphere. U.S. efforts to restore order and tend to the island's prosperity, declared TR, had prepared the Cubans for republican self-government. One historian agreed, noting that, while many of the reforms superintended by the United States proved fleeting once the occupation ended, "American military administration under the direction of Gen. Leonard Wood gave the island the best government it had ever known."[103]

Alongside the multitude of similarities were important differences between the U.S. operations in Cuba and the Philippines. The Teller Amendment, issued at the start of the Spanish-American War, had pledged to restore Cuba to the Cubans — while Congress had narrowly voted down a similar pledge to the Filipinos and Roosevelt stubbornly refused to set a deadline for Filipino independence. Why so vast a difference in U.S. policy toward an island critical to the defense of an isthmian canal and an archipelago that projected U.S. power into an important, but hardly vital, region of the world? Roosevelt reconciled the disparity in his habitual manner: by invoking his concepts of civilization and progress. The Cubans, vouchsafed TR, had trodden farther along the path to civilization and thus were ready for self-rule at an early date. The Filipinos, by contrast, were an unruly assortment of tribes and factions who lacked even the rudiments of republican self-government. In order to damp down Filipino demands that could lead to premature emancipation, it was essential not to make promises that might not be fulfilled for decades. Erecting the infrastructure and traditions of self-government in the archipelago promised to be a long and agonizingly drawn-out, if ultimately beneficial, process.

As secretary of war, entrusted to oversee the administration of the islands, Elihu Root shaped the U.S.-Cuban relationship. Root insisted that the United States be left no worse off with respect to its vital interests on the island than it had been when Cuba was governed by Spain. Thus no foreign power should be permitted to interfere with the island's destiny. Root's reasoning led implacably to the conclusion that the United States must erect some kind of protectorate. His proposals, submitted to the Cuban constitutional convention, were later enshrined in the Platt Amendment, which laid down the following terms:[104]

1. Cuba was not to enter into any pact with a foreign power that would impair its independence. Nor would the island permit colonization that would bring it under foreign naval or military control.

2. Cuba was not to contract any public debt beyond its resources, reasonably estimated.

3. The United States had the right to intervene "for the preservation of Cuban independence, the maintenance of a government adequate for the protection of life, property, and individual liberty" and to discharge the obligations set forth in the Treaty of Paris.

4. Cuba was to ratify all acts taken by the United States during the military occupation.

5. Cuba was to execute all the sanitary arrangements already begun by the United States, to ward off infectious disease both on the island and in the southern U.S. ports.

6. The title to the Isle of Pines, off Cuba's southern coast, was left to future negotiations.

7. The United States was to have the right to purchase or lease two naval stations.

The Platt Amendment provisions were embodied in a treaty concluded between the two countries on May 22, 1903, and they were built into the Cuban constitution.[105] Speaking for the president, Root managed to surmount the Cubans' initial resistance to his proposals—the right of intervention and the U.S. acquisition of naval stations on their soil were particularly nettlesome—by explaining that the amendment was "not synonymous with intermeddling or interference with the affairs of the Cuban Government, but the formal action of the Government of the United States, based upon just and substantial grounds, for the preservation of Cuban independence and the maintenance of a government adequate for the protection of life, property, and individual liberty, and adequate for discharging the obligations with respect to Cuba imposed by the treaty of Paris on the United States."[106]

General Wood, a leading expansionist in 1898, a close friend of Roosevelt, and as he was aptly dubbed, an "Armed Progressive," was installed as military governor of the island.[107] Wood confided to President Roosevelt that the Platt Amendment would in effect annex Cuba, as many inhabitants of the island feared.[108] American public opinion, however, endorsed—or, at any rate, did not oppose, which was just as good from the vantage point of the White House—U.S. trusteeship over Cuban independence, consistent with U.S. strategic interests. The reasons for this popular acquiescence were straightforward. Despite occasional intrigues by Cuban political parties during times of political disorder—Cuban factions were prone to appeal to Washington, an external power broker, to back their claims—the island remained placid compared to the upheaval of the 1890s.

The twin prongs of U.S. strategy on the island were (1) providing a stable government that could maintain order and improve living conditions for the populace and (2) establishing commercial arrangements that would rejuvenate Cuban sugar exports devastated during the fighting with Spain. Roosevelt later noted with satisfaction his success at pushing reciprocal trade arrangements through a Congress that was both inclined to protectionism and responsive to the outcry from American sugar growers. He wondered rhetorically whether his domestic political opponents objected "to the fact that after freeing Cuba we gave her reciprocal trade advantages with the United States, while at the same time keeping naval stations in the island and providing against its sinking into chaos, or being conquered by any foreign power?"[109]

Maintaining political stability on the island with a minimum of U.S. intervention was trickier than devising a trade regime favorable to the Cubans. When the results of the 1906 national election paralyzed the Cuban government, and anarchy loomed, the United States reluctantly stepped in to set up a provisional government. The intervention, which lasted until 1909, restored a modicum of stability to Havana. The Cuban people, attesting to the necessity of U.S. interference, offered no resistance—allowing Roosevelt to tout the operation as an act of benevolence unexampled in history.

Leonard Wood on Administering Cuba

Leonard Wood, who governed the island from December 1899 until the U.S. withdrawal, echoed many of the same themes sounded by William Howard Taft in the Philippine Islands. Because his views were in substantial accord with those of Taft, much of Wood's commentary need not be repeated here. The striking point about General Wood's account of the pacification of Cuba, like Taft's recollections on the Philippines, is that the bulk of the task that fell to the military government was nonmilitary in nature. That was doubly true in Cuba, where troublesome guerrilla warfare did not impede U.S. efforts to impose the police power. U.S. Army forces, operating in concert with a hastily organized Cuban constabulary, suppressed anarchy in the countryside and the cities while concurrently fighting disease, restoring vital services, and laying the groundwork for republican self-rule. In short, the Cuban occupation reinforced the legal conception of the police power as having a dual nature: law enforcement combined with a variety of activities connected to self-rule and the public welfare.

The plight of war-torn Cuba represented a challenge of considerable magnitude for the United States. The island had been a Spanish military colony for centuries, some 70 percent of the population was illiterate, democratic elections were unknown, and the nation, riddled with poor sanitary conditions, was racked by disease. Claimed Wood, in Santiago, capital of the first province transferred to American jurisdiction, conditions were "as unfavorable as can be imagined. Yellow fever, pernicious malaria and intestinal fevers were all prevalent to an alarming extent. The city and surrounding country were full of sick Spanish soldiers, starving Cubans and the sick of their own army. The sanitary conditions were indescribably bad. There was little or no water available and the conditions were such as can be imagined to exist in a tropical city following siege and capture in the most unhealthy season of the year."[110]

How did General Wood and his staff come to grips with this dispiriting situation? By following the formula that was becoming more or less standard in the aftermath of the war with Spain. A regiment of army regulars and several regiments of U.S. Volunteers were stationed in the province to maintain order and to perform the multitude of tasks catalogued by Wood. In Santiago "the first work undertaken" by these troops "was feeding the starving, taking care of the sick, cleaning up and removing the dangerous material in the city. In addition to correcting these local conditions, it was necessary to send food and medicine throughout the province, maintain order, re-establish municipal government, reorganize the courts, and do the thousand and one things incident to re-establishing the semblance of government in a stricken and demoralized community." Compounding these difficulties were the language barrier and a high rate of illness among the occupation force.

Once the military government had fended off the immediate threats of starvation and disease, it set about installing local governments—largely by edict of the U.S. governor.[111] "There was no time to write an electoral law and put it in force," contended Wood. Rather, the "method adopted was to go to a town, assemble from sixty to one hundred men representing all classes of the people and ask them to name municipal officers and to present their list as soon as completed." The new governments enacted temporary regulations on local taxation. Aided by the newly formed "rural guard" or native constabulary, consonant with the procedures elaborated in the U.S. Marines' *Small Wars Manual* (covered in chapter 9), U.S. troops established customs houses to provide revenues for the array of public works needed to resuscitate Cuban society. For obvious reasons, schools and hospitals were foremost among these.[112]

The United States set about erecting the legal edifice for the qualified form of independence Congress envisioned for the island. Progress was swift, said Wood. By the end of 1898, municipal courts and a provincial supreme court were in place in Santiago. Customs houses were functioning. A proclamation by the military government "embodying the general principles of a Bill of Rights had been published, giving the people the right to carry arms, to hold public meetings, and, in fact, to do all things which people do under free governments." By December 1899, when Wood was formally appointed military governor, a rudimentary school law was in force, and the military government had begun to overhaul "the law of public works, beneficence, education, municipal administration, [and] prison administration," as well as the island's electoral machinery. Habeas corpus and Cuban-staffed police courts followed the reform of Cuban administrative law.[113] A census was held to support the local elections, a constitutional convention was convened in 1900, and a preliminary draft constitution was complete by early 1901.

William Howard Taft (left) and Elihu Root were two of TR's closest confidants, serving in various posts in the Roosevelt administration. Taft, who succeeded TR to the Oval Office, served as the first civil governor of the Philippines and later as secretary of war. Root served as secretary of war and secretary of state. In the latter capacity, Root, "the brutal friend to whom I pay the most attention," helped shape the Roosevelt Corollary to the Monroe Doctrine and attempted to explain the corollary to wary Latin American officials. *Library of Congress*

Montauk Point
Rough Riders - Col. Roosevelt

61368

Theodore Roosevelt and his friend Leonard Wood hastily organized the First U.S. Volunteers, or "Rough Riders," in 1898 to join the war against Spain. TR served as lieutenant colonel, and later colonel, of the unit. President William J. Clinton posthumously awarded him the Medal of Honor for gallantry in combat. *Library of Congress*

"It is no child's play going after lion, elephant, rhino, and buffalo."
After leaving office in 1909, TR embarked on an extended safari
in British East Africa and Egypt. *Library of Congress*

Populist William Jennings Bryan was a perennial Democratic contender for the White House in turn-of-the-century America. TR railed against what he viewed as Bryan's extreme partiality to labor, while conceding that the Democrat had correctly appraised many of the social problems that accompanied industrialization. *Library of Congress*

Henry Cabot Lodge, pictured here circa 1898, was an influential Republican senator from Massachusetts and perhaps TR's closest friend and confidant. *Library of Congress*

In the 1890s, naval strategist and historian Alfred Thayer Mahan joined with TR to urge America to become a great maritime power. Mahan prescribed a form of sea power founded on a potent battle fleet, overseas colonies, international commerce, and merchant shipping. *Library of Congress*

This 1902 portrait shows Roosevelt during his first full year as president. *Library of Congress*

Engraved for the Universal Magazine.

EDMUND BURKE Esq.

Printed for J. Hinton at the Kings Arms in Paternoster Row.

Edmund Burke was an eighteenth-century British parliamentarian and political philosopher. TR admired Burke's theory of prudential statecraft, exemplified by his doctrine of the "Golden Mean" between political extremes. Roosevelt twice quoted Burke in his annual messages to Congress—the only philosopher thus honored. *Library of Congress*

Roosevelt viewed naval power as the military sustenance for his Big Stick doctrine, which emphasized quiet, circumspect diplomacy backed by physical force. This 1905 illustration from *Puck*, entitled *Peace*, shows Columbia dressed in armor riding a battleship with TR's face on the bow. In 1907 Roosevelt ordered the U.S. Navy's battle fleet on a world cruise—in part to convey American power and steadfastness to Japan. *Library of Congress*

TR brokered an end to the Russo-Japanese War at the Portsmouth Peace Conference, earning the Nobel Peace Prize for his effort—the first American president so honored. By mediating an equitable settlement, he hoped to preserve great-power equilibrium in East Asia. This postcard bears pictures of Tsar Nicholas II (upper left) of Russia, Roosevelt, Japanese Emperor Mutsuhito, their negotiators, and the marine arsenal in Portsmouth, New Hampshire. *Library of Congress*

The economic dimension was equally critical to the success of American stewardship over Cuba. The United States had borne the expense of organizing and outfitting the Cuban government. But, like Taft and Roosevelt, Leonard Wood insisted that reciprocal trade arrangements between the United States and the Republic's new possessions were the fulcrum for an economic renaissance. In 1920 he estimated Cuban exports to the United States at $68 million annually but predicted that, under reciprocity, this total would triple within eight years. Bolstering the island's export trade, insisted General Wood, would help generate the domestic prosperity that was crucial to its ability to maintain its independence—and to resist the blandishments of great powers that might have entertained hopes of replacing Spain as an imperial power in the Caribbean.[114]

In stark contrast to the Philippines, where American statesmen doubted the inhabitants' capacity for republican self-government, Wood believed his chief function was to swiftly hand over the reins of government to the Cubans. Consequently, he chortled, "The government of Cuba was 'military' in name only." After little more than three years of American occupation, Cuban officials held nearly all public offices, the natives could appeal the military governor's decisions to their own supreme court, and the Cuban treasury was in surplus. That the United States had abridged Cuban sovereignty, claimed General Wood, detracted not one whit from the achievement of transmuting a "Latin military colony, in one of the most unhealthy countries of the world" into "a republic modeled closely upon the lines of our own great Anglo-Saxon republic."[115] In Wood's mind, as in Roosevelt's, the Cubans' relatively civilized status entitled them to speedy admission into the fraternity of liberal republics.[116] Secretary Root pointed to the "universal expressions of gratitude, esteem, and affection" with which Cubans greeted the American withdrawal, while General Wood claimed that it would have been "impossible for any people to have shown more friendship and cordiality to the representatives of another nation than was shown by the people of Havana . . . to the representatives of the late military government. . . . It is safe to say that at least 100,000, probably 150,000, people were assembled along the water front . . . to see the troops off."[117]

Renewed Intervention in Cuba, 1906

President Roosevelt did, albeit with palpable reluctance, exercise his prerogatives under the Platt Amendment during his second term.[118] In 1906 an insurrection flared up on the island, "which it speedily grew evident that the existing Cuban Government was powerless to quell." Cuban president Tomas Estrada Palma appealed to Washington for help, finally resigning because, in Roosevelt's words, "he was powerless to maintain order" and "chaos was impending."[119] No one in the Cuban cabinet would accept responsibility for restoring order. This raised the possibility that "the representatives of various European nations in the island would apply to their respective governments for armed intervention in order to protect the lives and property of their citizens." Roosevelt speedily dispatched navy warships to put down the insurgents; ordered army troops in to relieve the navy personnel; and pursuant to "the so-called Platt amendment, which was embodied in the constitution of Cuba, I thereupon proclaimed a provisional government for the island," initially under the leadership of William Howard Taft, now serving as secretary of war. "I most earnestly adjure [the Cubans] solemnly to weigh their responsibility and to see that when their new government is started it shall run smoothly, and with freedom from flagrant denial of right on the one hand, and from insurrectionary disturbances on the other."[120]

The president was wary about perceptions that he was creating a client state on the island. "There can be no talk of a protectorate by us," he told Taft. "Our business is to establish peace and order on a satisfactory basis, start the new government, and then leave the Island, the Cuban government taking the reins into its own hands; tho of course it might be advisable for some little time that some of our troops should stay in the Islands to steady things."[121] This was quite a change from the days of the Venezuela blockade, when Roosevelt had pondered declaring just that—a protectorate over Latin America.[122] The president peremptorily ruled out any "plan for a protectorate, or any plan which would imply our breaking our explicit promise because of which we were able to prevent a war of devastation last fall. The good faith of the United States is a mighty valuable asset and must not be impaired."[123] Even the Platt Amendment, founded on explicit provisions of treaty law, was not to be invoked lightly. Here again, Theodore Roosevelt had established principles of impressive sweep, yet implemented them sparingly, with an eye on the likely repercussions should the United States throw its weight around too promiscuously.[124]

Fortune favored him. Upon the arrival of American forces, the "insurgent chiefs immediately agreed that their troops should lay down their arms and disband," allowing the U.S.-backed government to "administer the island for a few months until tranquillity can be restored, a new election properly held, and a new government inaugurated."[125] Once this was accomplished, Roosevelt pledged to withdraw U.S. forces from Cuban soil; but he warned that, if "the insurrectionary habit becomes confirmed in the Island, it is absolutely out of the question that the Island shall continue independent; and the United States, which has assumed the sponsorship before the civilized world for Cuba's career as a nation, would again have to intervene and to see that the government was managed in such orderly fashion as to secure the safety of life and property."[126] As will be seen, TR's final foray into policing Cuba bore a sharp resemblance to the doctrine laid out in the Roosevelt Corollary, despite the unique prerogatives the United States enjoyed in Cuba.

Venezuela

A blockade of Venezuela by European warships, which came in 1902–3, while memories of the Cuban occupation and the Philippine War were still fresh, set Theodore Roosevelt to thinking about a U.S. protectorate over the Western Hemisphere. Although he did not refer to an international police power by name—the Roosevelt Corollary was still two years in the future—TR clearly regarded his actions as a precedent for American police action in the nation's geographic environs. Nor was Roosevelt the only one to make the connection between Venezuela and subsequent police actions. William Howard Taft stated that Roosevelt had improved on James Monroe's purely reactive formula. If a controversy seemed likely to engender armed confrontation and was in proximity to American shores or vital interests, then Washington might legitimately mediate a peaceful settlement—heading off a breach of the Monroe Doctrine. "This," said Taft, "is what Mr. Roosevelt did in Venezuela and in Santo Domingo."[127]

The element of national interest was the crux of any U.S. decision to uphold the doctrine. Roosevelt did not regard his corollary as automatically triggering American diplomatic and military action. Because of its apparent designs on South America and its waxing military power, Wilhelmine Germany was the European power that most aroused Roosevelt's suspicions.[128] The Germans were latecomers to the competition for colonial territories and the beneficiaries of burgeoning naval power. Inspired by Alfred Thayer Mahan's ideas, and at the urging of Adm. Alfred von Tirpitz, Kaiser Wilhelm II had scarcely bothered to conceal his desire for bases athwart the Caribbean sea-lanes. Wilhelm and Tirpitz dreamt of building a ring of coaling stations spanning the globe. Warships operating from outposts in the Caribbean Sea could menace the approaches to the proposed isthmian canal, one of Roosevelt's fondest ambitions.

President Roosevelt believed, not unreasonably, that the Germans were searching for a pretext for territorial aggrandizement in the New World. Berlin seemed to have found such a pretext in 1902. Like most Caribbean countries, Venezuela was heavily in debt, its government and citizens having taken on heavy financial obligations to wage war, to build railroads and other infrastructure, and to develop natural resources. Caracas had also indulged in a variety of wasteful and unsavory endeavors. "Loot, pillage, and exploitation in the worst sense of the term," declared one historian, "had characterized many of the self-seeking governments."[129] Writing anonymously, one "American Business Man" declared, "Occasionally a newspaper correspondent, some disciple of Mark Twain, as a huge joke writes about an election in Venezuela or Colombia, the same as he might about a sea serpent, but not within the memory of any living man has there been a real election in these countries."[130] Faction and corruption were rife in Venezuela. Once in power, a faction generally conducted business on the principle against which TR had railed during his forays into public administration—that to the victor go the spoils—parceling out government offices and public revenues to its supporters.[131]

After Venezuelan president Cipriano Castro suspended repayment of the country's foreign debt, the great powers organized a naval blockade along the Venezuelan coastline.[132] While TR did not object to a transitory European police action—"If any South American State misbehaves toward any European country," he said, "let the European country spank it"[133]—the bombardment of shore positions by the German flotilla convinced him that the blockade was a prelude to the occupation of Venezuelan customs houses. The paternalistic connotations associated with allowing civilized European powers to "spank" their less-advanced brethren in South America perhaps betrayed the immature state of Roosevelt's thinking about the police power.[134] Further thought led the president to conclude that the great powers should act not as fathers disciplining wayward children but as policemen upholding the rule of law and discharging other constabulary duties.[135] In any case, even a legitimate punitive action against Venezuela might, if it involved a seizure of customs houses, give Germany a permanent foothold on American soil, breaching the Monroe Doctrine. "I do not wish the United States or any other country to get additional territory in South America," he exclaimed to Hermann Speck von Sternburg. "It would be a misfortune all around."[136]

Only a show of force, decided Roosevelt, could stave off this misfortune. To check Berlin's ambitions, the president ordered a powerful naval squadron under Adm. George Dewey to shadow the European warships, deterring any occupation of Venezuelan territory. Whether Germany really planned to acquire a base at the expense of

Caracas is doubtful. Nonetheless, TR genuinely seemed to fear that the great powers would attempt to partition the New World, much as they had large swathes of Africa and Asia.[137] The equivocal language Kaiser Wilhelm's representatives used to reassure Washington only inflamed the president's suspicions. In 1901 Berlin had declared that negotiation with Venezuela was hopeless and insisted that "under no circumstances do we consider in our proceedings the acquisition or permanent occupation of Venezuelan territory." If a blockade could not compel Castro to comply, however, "we would have to consider the temporary occupation on our part of different Venezuelan harbor places and the levying of duties in those places."[138]

The affair convinced Roosevelt both that the Americas faced an immediate threat and that the Monroe Doctrine conferred the responsibility to act preemptively to avert European encroachment.[139] In 1916 he told one of his biographers, William Roscoe Thayer, that he had become "convinced that Germany intended to seize some Venezuelan harbor and turn it into a strongly fortified place of arms, on the model of [Kiaochow], with a view to exercising some degree of control over the future Isthmian Canal, and over South American affairs generally." Germany, the ringleader (or so TR thought), had counted on "our well established jellyfish squashiness and felt sure they had a free hand." The president recounted asking the German ambassador "to look at the map, as a glance would show him there was no spot in the world where Germany in the event of a conflict with the United States would be at a greater disadvantage than in the Caribbean Sea."[140] Its local naval supremacy gave the United States a say in the Euro-Venezuelan dispute.

In the end, after a series of proposals and counterproposals for U.S. arbitration—Roosevelt reluctantly declined to adjudicate the controversy, pointing out that the United States had also lodged claims against Venezuela[141]—the powers submitted their dispute to the Hague tribunal for arbitration. After the blockade ended, the Wilhelmstrasse suggested that the great powers jointly administer Venezuela's finances to assure repayment of foreign creditors. When Sternburg broached the subject with Roosevelt, the president intimated, "A control of the finances of Venezuela through American and European financial institutions would be condemned by public opinion here. These wretched republics cause me a great deal of trouble. A second attempt of foreign powers to collect their debts by force would simply not be tolerated here. I often think that a sort of protectorate over South and Central America is the only way out."[142] Later, in the Santo Domingo case, President Roosevelt rejected similar proposals for joint U.S.-European administration of Dominican finances.

His correspondence with Secretary of State John Hay betrayed the scope of his misgivings: "Speck was in today, evidently inspired from Berlin," he told Hay, "to propose for our consideration in the future the advisability of having the great Powers collectively stand back of some syndicate which should take possession of the finances of Venezuela" in an effort to "put a stop to the motive for revolution," stimulate prosperity in the country, and ultimately "do away with the chance for a repetition of punitive expeditions by European powers to collect debts." Roosevelt demurred, telling his friend "that our people would view with the utmost displeasure any such proposal," because it could "pave the way for reducing Venezuela to a condition like that of Egypt, and [because] the American people interpreted the Monroe Doctrine as meaning of course that no European power should gain *control* of any American republic" (emphasis in original).[143] The president subsequently confided his belief that the Danish West Indies and other Caribbean holdings of the weaker European states would be a permanent temptation to ambitious great powers such as Wilhelmine Germany should he fail to craft some policy to discourage encroachment.[144] Deflecting the immediate threat of European naval action clearly did not alleviate Roosevelt's qualms about the long-term great-power threat to the Americas.[145]

In the early going, then, Roosevelt envisioned the international police power as something more sweeping than its ultimate form: a kind of wide-ranging license for U.S. diplomatic and military intervention, a Platt Amendment writ large that would abridge the sovereignty of the Latin American republics. Although Roosevelt disavowed his philosophizing about an American protectorate almost instantly, his words revealed the drift of his thinking about international police duty in the wake of the Venezuelan affair. The United States, overseeing a benevolent protectorate and mindful of its own interests in the Caribbean Sea, could take preemptive action to deter European territorial aggrandizement. President Roosevelt prescribed discreet diplomacy backed up by U.S. naval power to deter German encroachment. With any luck, European claims could be settled without resort to arms. Over the long term, a combination of measures involving diplomacy and public administration would help fortify the Caribbean republics to stand on their own.[146] Like the Philippines and Cuba before, the Venezuela incident acted as a catalyst for the concept, as yet ill formed, of an international police power.

Panama

In 1903 a revolution detached Panama from Colombian rule, and an American military response kept sovereign Colombia from intervening. The Panama affair thrust the international police-power theory bodily into Roosevelt's Caribbean diplomacy. "Nothing in his public career seems to have given Roosevelt more gratification or have been regarded by him as of greater importance than the construction of the Panama Canal," observes one historian.[147] Years later Roosevelt made a categorical claim about the propriety of his actions in the affair. "Every action taken," he wrote, "was not merely proper, but was carried out with the highest, finest, and nicest standards of public and governmental ethics. . . . The United States has many honorable chapters in its history, but no more honorable chapter than that which tells of the way in which our right to dig the Panama Canal was secured."[148] Historians have generally treated that claim with disdain, not without reason.[149]

An isthmian canal had long been among the most cherished desires of expansionists such as Mahan and Roosevelt. Arising as it did from immutable facts of geography, this desire well antedated the 1903 crisis. A canal would spare merchant shipping the arduous journey around South America while enabling the U.S. Navy to concentrate force far more readily. Says historian Howard C. Hill, the "long, doubtful voyage" of the battleship *Oregon* around Cape Horn on the eve of war with Spain had "impressed [TR], as it did other thoughtful Americans, with the need of an interoceanic canal which would not only be of notable value to commerce but which would also virtually double the strength of American naval forces."[150] The Asia trade beckoned, to be sure. But did even an overriding national interest warrant U.S. meddling in the affairs of the American republics?

In 1901, as recounted in the Philippines case, Roosevelt had agonized over "just how far it is best to leave the [Latin American] nations alone and how far there must be interference."[151] Interference won the day in the case of Panama. After debating the merits of canal routes through Panama and Nicaragua from an engineering standpoint and sparring with a French engineering firm over the price of the concession, the Roosevelt administration had finally persuaded the Colombian government to assent to a draft canal treaty. After prolonged dickering, the U.S. House and Senate agreed to fund the Panama concession while authorizing the president to proceed with the Nicaraguan canal should Bogotá refuse the latest U.S. offer. The secretary of state and the Colombian minister signed the accord, dubbed the Hay-Herrán Treaty, on January 22, 1903. The Colombian province, it appeared, would after all be the site for an isthmian canal.

Trouble arose when the Colombian Senate opened deliberations on the treaty.[152] Under the treaty terms the United States pledged to pay Bogotá $10 million immediately and an annuity of $250,000 in gold beginning nine years after the exchange of instruments of ratification. Beyond the monetary value of the deal, the canal promised to be a colossal boon for a country that would now play host to one of the crossroads of world shipping. However, the Colombian Senate refused to approve the Hay-Herrán Treaty, evidently convinced that it could exact additional money from the U.S. government and the French-owned New Panama Canal Company.[153] Because Colombian president José Marroquin wielded immense power over the legislature, which had not convened for five years, President Roosevelt concluded that Marroquin had intervened in the ratification process and blamed him in large part for the ensuing debacle.[154] Roosevelt was unsure what to do next. Should he opt for a Nicaraguan route or "in some shape or way . . . interfere when it becomes necessary so as to secure the Panama route without further dealing with the foolish and homicidal corruptionists of Bogotá"?[155] One thing was certain: "I am not inclined to have any further dealings whatever with those Bogotá people."[156]

Ultimately TR refused to allow a matter he regarded as of surpassing importance to languish—especially when only the diplomatic niceties accorded "those Bogotá people," a sorry and uncivilized lot in his view, were holding up the wheels of progress. He leapt at a confidential memorandum prepared by John Bassett Moore, an eminent international lawyer, Columbia University professor, and former assistant secretary of state, in which Moore maintained that the 1846 Treaty of Amity, Commerce, and Navigation between the United States and New Granada, the predecessor of Colombia, could be interpreted so as to allow the U.S. government to press ahead with construction even in the absence of a canal treaty.[157] This was enough for Roosevelt. "If under the treaty of 1846 we have a color of right to start in and build the canal," he wrote Secretary of State John Hay, "my off-hand judgment would favor such proceeding."[158] The first draft of the president's 1903 message to Congress recommended carrying on with the project even over Colombian objections.[159] Moore contended that the treaty empowered the United States to safeguard transit rights across the isthmus against domestic disturbances—even to the point of using armed force to prevent Colombia from suppressing an insurrection.[160]

Since 1846 the United States had deployed the police power repeatedly at Bogotá's request to put down revolution; thus it could, asserted Professor Moore, turn that power against Colombia at its discretion. The logic of this claim is dubious at best.[161] Nonetheless, Roosevelt recited Moore's argument almost verbatim in both his private correspondence and his 1903 message to Congress, saluting the professor for virtually coauthoring the part of his message that described events in Panama.[162] "For half a century," he informed his son Kermit just after the revolution, "we have policed that Isthmus in the interest of the little wildcat republic of Colombia. Colombia has behaved infamously about the treaty for the building of the Panama Canal; and I do not intend in the police work that I will have to do in connection with the new insurrection any longer to do for her work which is not merely profitless but brings no gratitude. Any interference I undertake now will be in the interest of the United States and of the people of the Panama Isthmus themselves."[163]

The legal case was compelling to a president who was itching for a reason to act. Moore began by approvingly quoting Secretary of State Lewis Cass, who in 1858 had assessed the situation through the prism of national sovereignty. "Sovereignty has its duties as well as its rights, and none of these local Governments . . . would be permitted in a spirit of Eastern isolation to close these gates of intercourse on the great highways of the world, and justify the act by the pretension that these avenues of trade and travel belong to them."[164] This conveyed the essence of Moore's memorandum. He maintained that sovereignty did not confer carte blanche to deprive the advanced maritime nations of a useful shortcut between Atlantic and Pacific. Such a stubborn attitude represented an affront to the civilized world.

Consider Moore's chain of reasoning. He pointed to Article XXXV of the 1846 treaty, under which New Granada had granted the United States transit rights on the isthmus, using whatever mode of conveyance was then in use or might be built in the future, and the United States had reciprocated by guaranteeing "the rights of sovereignty and property which New Granada has and possesses" over the restive province.[165] Observed Moore, Article XXXV had in effect "created on the part of the United States an offensive and defensive alliance with Colombia and constituted a sort of supportant partnership in sovereignty, and that the object in assuming this burden was to secure primarily a canal."[166]

For decades Bogotá had taken a broader view of U.S. prerogatives on the isthmus than had American statesmen themselves. First, and most obviously, the Colombians expected the United States to shield the isthmus from foreign attack. Moore noted that Colombia and Italy had nearly come to blows during a controversy in 1886. An armed clash on the isthmus involving a European power would have humiliated the United States, which was bound by treaty to maintain order. Second, "Colombia has again and again claimed that it was our *duty* to protect the route against domestic interruption or attack" (emphasis in original), in contrast to the American view that the treaty had simply conferred a *right* to intervene. Moore concluded that Bogotá's novel "claim has in reality approached the point of making us responsible sovereign on the Isthmus." Under Secretary of State William Seward, he remarked, the U.S. government had taken the stance that the United States would remain neutral during domestic disturbances on the isthmus but would intervene to restore order when foreign attack or domestic turmoil imperiled its transit rights.[167]

From this analysis John Bassett Moore concluded that "*the Panama Canal, so far as built, has actually been constructed under the protection of this very guarantee*" extended by the treaty of amity and commerce (emphasis in original). "The persons that undertook it failed to finish it. The United States would be justified in asserting and maintaining a right to finish it."[168] Taken together, the virtual joint sovereignty over the isthmus, buttressed by force of American arms amid repeated revolutions, wording that seemed to envision canal or railroad construction at some future date, and the 1879 protocol granting the right to land U.S. troops, made a convincing case for proceeding with construction of a canal. Moore's meditations found a receptive audience in the Oval Office.

These arguments nonetheless had a strong whiff of sophistry about them. The treaty between the United States and New Granada had simply guaranteed transit rights for American citizens using whatever mode of transportation might be in use at the time. Its terms contemplated canal or railroad construction by Colombia or by permission of the Colombian government. There was no mention of a foreign government's or a private concern's undertaking the project independently. And the treaty certainly did not envision forcible action by one of the parties to install a new mode of transportation on the isthmus. The relationship of Professor Moore's analysis to the letter of the 1846 treaty was tenuous, and his reasoning certainly violated the spirit of the treaty. His memorandum made shaky ground on which to found a legal case for military action. Yet the president latched onto it. One of Roosevelt's least appealing traits, his willingness to disregard "technicalities" for a higher purpose, was in full view during the Panama affair.

The revolution originated within the New Panama Canal Company when Philippe Bunau-Varilla, a Frenchman and former chief engineer for the company, organized an uprising with the help of a New York lawyer. Bunau-Varilla visited the United States in the weeks leading up to the revolution, meeting with Professor Moore, Secretary of State Hay, and President Roosevelt. His visit gave rise to decades of historical controversy. Although no evidence suggests that the U.S. officials conspired with the plotters, they were clearly aware that something was afoot.[169] The president acted opportunistically, directing the navy to position warships in easy striking range of the transit route.[170] On November 2 he ordered the captains of these vessels to maintain unimpeded transit on the isthmus and authorized them to use force to occupy the route and prevent Colombian troops from landing.[171]

A brief and bloodless affair, the revolution took place on November 3, 1903.[172] As the revolutionaries had anticipated, American forces landed to prevent Colombia from attempting to restore its sovereignty on the isthmus. On November 6 the United States recognized the de facto government of Panama, on November 11 Washington formally notified Bogotá that it would use force to prevent a Colombian expedition from suppressing the insurrection, and on November 18 representatives of Panama and the United States concluded a canal treaty essentially making Panama an American protectorate. The European powers quickly recognized the new country, and by March 1904 all of the Latin American republics save Colombia had followed suit—in effect ratifying TR's inventive interpretation of the 1846 treaty and U.S. conduct in the matter.

Mindful of the uproar his actions had touched off, Roosevelt stoutly defended himself. The president pointed out, first, that Colombia's ability to maintain sovereignty over Panama had always been tenuous for geographic and military reasons. "Only the active interference of the United States," proclaimed his 1903 message to Congress, "has enabled her to preserve so much as a semblance of sovereignty. Had it not been for the exercise by the United States of the police power in her interest, her connection with the Isthmus would have been sundered long ago."[173] Second, the president offered a novel legal assessment, hinting, implausibly, that Colombia was not the rightful state successor to New Granada on the isthmus. Thus Bogotá had no claim to sovereignty on the isthmus, while the United States maintained its police authority under the 1846 treaty. Third, he declared that the revolution had commanded virtually unanimous support among Panamanians, giving it the stamp of popular approval. Fourth, U.S. military action had actually saved the Colombian expeditionary force from annihilation by a much larger Panamanian force.[174]

TR's arguments were unwontedly evasive. At best he demonstrated that the Panamanian revolutionaries had acted legitimately. Whether the U.S. role was aboveboard was another question entirely. For one thing, Roosevelt's view of state succession was outlandish.

His sudden discovery—after fifty-seven years of U.S. action to uphold Colombia's control of the isthmus—that the treaty with New Granada was invalid persuaded few. The Roosevelt administration might reasonably have stood aside in 1903 and let the revolution take its course, but it clearly could not use force to thwart Bogotá's efforts to restore sovereignty over the isthmus. Its haste in recognizing the de facto government and its use of force to prevent the parties from settling the question in the traditional manner—on the battlefield—were beyond the pale. Yet TR breezily announced that, having previously used the police power to sustain Colombian sovereignty, the United States would now use it to support the insurgents.

Whether by deliberation or by indifference, American public opinion sustained his decision. But the president had done violence both to international law and to the U.S. Constitution. The intent of the framers of the 1846 treaty with New Granada clearly was not to grant to the U.S. a generalized police power that American presidents could wield on the isthmus as they saw fit. Roosevelt willfully ignored that fact, turning the treaty against one of the parties. With respect to U.S. constitutional law, TR insisted, "Neither in this nor in any other matter has there been the slightest failure to live up to the Constitution in letter and in spirit." But then, executing a logical two-step, he declared, "the Constitution must be observed positively as well as negatively. The President's duty is to serve the country in accordance with the Constitution; and I should be derelict in my duty if I used a false construction of the Constitution as a shield for weakness and timidity or an excuse for governmental timidity."[175]

Not only *could* he intervene in Panama, said the president, but his reading of the Constitution, as well as his Lincoln-Jackson perspective on executive power, *compelled* him to act as he did. His defense of his actions was of a piece with his insistence, at the time of the anthracite coal strike, that the president could take any action not specifically prohibited by the Constitution or federal law. This troubling inversion of the traditional understanding of the U.S. Constitution warrants extreme caution in accepting Roosevelt's depiction of the Panamanian revolution as a justified use of police powers. Theodore Roosevelt's least endearing traits were in view during the Panama affair.[176]

Treaty Law and Shared Police Powers in the Canal Zone

Once the Panamanian government was on its feet, the Roosevelt administration acted swiftly to consolidate its gains, negotiating a treaty with Panama that provided both for canal construction and for

U.S. legal prerogatives in the lands adjacent to the proposed watercourse. The resulting Isthmian Canal Convention envisioned a kind of shared authority over the territory adjoining the canal. The convention authorized "the President of the United States . . . to acquire within a reasonable time the control of the necessary territory of the Republic of Colombia," while also noting that "the sovereignty of such territory [was] actually vested in the Republic of Panama." Panama granted to the United States the "use, occupation and control" of a ten-mile-wide strip of land, five miles on either side of the watercourse.[177] While Panama maintained ultimate sovereignty over this Canal Zone, it allocated "to the United States all the rights, power and authority within the zone mentioned . . . which the United States would possess and exercise as if it were the sovereign of the territory within which said lands and waters are located to the entire exclusion of the exercise by the Republic of Panama of any such sovereign rights, power or authority." The document also gave the United States a monopoly over the construction of a railroad or canal across Panamanian territory.[178]

Because of what was in effect an overlapping sovereignty, the possibility of a conflict of police powers arose. In an effort to head off disputes, the Isthmian Canal Convention stipulated that the property rights of Panamanian residents of the Canal Zone would be upheld, and that a joint U.S.-Panamanian commission would fix compensation for property damage arising from the construction of the canal. Damages would be assessed based on the value of the property before the convention was concluded.[179] The police powers bestowed on the United States were extensive. Washington was authorized to exercise the right of eminent domain in the Canal Zone in order to obtain "any lands, buildings, water rights or other properties necessary and convenient for the construction, maintenance, operation and protection of the Canal," and to engage in public works such as "sanitation, . . . the collection and disposal of sewage and the disposition of sewage and the distribution of water in the . . . cities of Panama and Colon."[180]

The U.S. government could also take on law-enforcement duties if it saw fit. "The same right and authority are granted to the United States for the maintenance of public order in the cities of Panama and Colon and the territories and harbors adjacent thereto in case the Republic of Panama should not be, in the judgment of the United States, able to maintain such order." The two parties to the convention pledged to work out a procedure for extraditing civil or criminal lawbreakers within the jurisdiction of one of the parties before fleeing to points within the jurisdiction of the other.[181] Finally, Panama entrusted the security of the Canal Zone to Washington. "[I]f it should become necessary at any time to employ armed forces for the safety or protection of the Canal," stated the document, "the United States shall have the right, at all times and in its discretion, to use its police and its land or naval forces or to establish fortifications for these purposes." To bolster U.S. naval protection, Panama agreed to lease "naval or coaling stations" on its Pacific and Caribbean coasts for the U.S. Navy's use. Evidently neither party saw the need to differentiate police from military functions where the security of the Canal Zone was at stake.[182]

Santo Domingo

Coming as it did on the heels of the post-1898 extension of the municipal police power to Cuba, Puerto Rico, and the Philippines, the European maritime blockade of Venezuela, and the Panamanian revolution, persistent turbulence in the Dominican Republic prodded Roosevelt to formally state a new policy embodying his notion of an international police power. As seen earlier in this chapter, the campaigns in the Philippines and Cuba set a precedent for the extension of police powers abroad. Venezuela had encouraged Roosevelt to contemplate an American protectorate over Latin America. Panama had done the same by seeming to legitimize the use of force in the service of the interests of the United States and civilization. The Santo Domingo episode, which precipitated the Roosevelt Corollary, rounded out the conceptual development of the international police power and gave the police power its self-limiting character.[183] Observes one historian, "'Watchful vigilance,' as President Roosevelt styled his attitude in the Venezuelan crisis, was succeeded by a policy that might be called 'preventive action.'" Convinced that the policy of "negation and mediation" he had deployed in Venezuela held real dangers, Roosevelt now embarked on "a course of positive action, a course more in harmony with his own character and better designed, so he believed, to prevent the recurrence of crises such as the one just surmounted."[184]

Politics on Santo Domingo was fluid at the best of times. Repeated revolutions had wrecked Dominican finances, trying the patience of foreign creditors and their protectors in government. In 1898 Ulysses Heureaux, the only president in the republic's history to maintain any semblance of order, was assassinated. Revolution followed, and by 1902 the country had descended into civil war.[185] The short-lived governments of this period, observes Hill, "lived a hand-to-mouth existence on funds secured by confiscations, by short-term loans at high rates of interest, and by deals permitting the importation of goods at less than the legal rates." Every town, city, and province suffered bloodshed, pillaging, and destruction of property. Interest on the public debt went unpaid. A conference held on board the American cruiser *Detroit* brought Carlos F. Morales to power and, for a time, brought a modicum of peace to the island. Still, the Dominican Republic faced massive debt, accumulated over the years by leaders who had accepted loans on exorbitant terms to exploit the country's resources, build railroads, and wage war.[186]

Since 1893 an American corporation known as the Santo Domingo Improvement Company had administered Dominican customs. In 1901 the then-existing government nullified this arrangement, prompting the company to appeal to the U.S. State Department. The State Department negotiated compensation for the Improvement Company in the amount of $4.5 million, the manner of payment to be determined by an arbitral commission.[187] The protocol was never submitted to the Senate and in fact may have been unknown to the White House. In any event, the European governments responded sharply when the Morales government could not make its payments to the Improvement Company and, under the agreement, was compelled to turn over Puerto Plata. The American minister to the island subsequently reported a scheme by the Dominican foreign minister to establish free ports in Samaná and Manzanillo in the interest of Germany. On behalf of its citizens who held Dominican securities, the Belgian government next proposed joint action with the United States to take control of the Dominican customs houses. Under the Belgian proposal, Dominican finances would be administered by a commission appointed by France, Belgium, and the United States.[188]

Taken together, these events seemed to the Roosevelt administration to endanger the territorial integrity of an American republic and to threaten a repetition of the Venezuelan crisis, with all the latent danger that crisis had entailed.[189] Chaos had engulfed the Morales government, imperiling the well-being of American lives and property and straining the patience of the island's European creditors. In February insurgents had fired on the American cruiser *Yankee* and menaced American property on the island, prompting the president to order the commander at Guantanamo Bay to take "immediate steps for protection of United States citizens and property."[190] Worse might have been in store. Since the great powers often used force to collect debts owed their citizens, and since seizing customs houses was a favorite tactic, reasoned President Roosevelt, the Monroe Doctrine was in jeopardy.

As conditions continued to worsen, the president mulled declaring a protectorate over the island. Alarmed at the danger of domestic insurrection and European intervention, General Morales solicited U.S.

help. In early 1904 the Dominican foreign minister traveled to Washington, where he invoked the Monroe Doctrine and appealed for assistance. At first the administration demurred. On February 23, 1904, President Roosevelt confided to Joseph Bucklin Bishop that the Dominican government had been "bedeviling us to establish some kind of protectorate over the islands, and take care of their finances. We have been answering them that we could not possibly go into the subject now at all." Added Roosevelt, "If I possibly can, I want to do nothing to them. If it is absolutely necessary to do something, then I want to do as little as possible."[191] The Hague Court inadvertently spurred U.S. action when it ruled unanimously that the powers that had blockaded Venezuela were entitled to preferential treatment in the collection of their claims against Caracas. One startled State Department official exclaimed that the court's ruling placed a "premium on violence" against American states that defaulted on loans.[192]

In consequence of the Hague tribunal's decision, it seemed imperative for the United States to head off a similar European use of force against the Dominican Republic. The Roosevelt administration began to drift toward intervention. At a banquet on May 20, 1904, commemorating the second anniversary of Cuban independence, Secretary of State Elihu Root read a letter from the chief executive. President Roosevelt protested that the sole U.S. desire was "to see all neighboring countries stable, orderly, and prosperous." Provided a nation "knows how to act with decency in industrial and political matters, if it keeps order and pays its obligations, then it need fear no interference from the United States. Brutal wrongdoing, or an impotence which results in a general loosening of the ties of civilized society, may finally require intervention by some civilized nation, and in the Western Hemisphere the United States cannot ignore this duty."[193]

TR had skillfully cleared the decks for action in Santo Domingo and for a formal declaration of U.S. policy—prefiguring his 1904 message enunciating the international police power. "Of course, what I wrote is the simplest common sense," he remarked wryly after the Root address, "and only the fool or the coward can treat it as aught else. If we are willing to let Germany or England act as the policeman of the Caribbean, then we can afford not to interfere when gross wrongdoing occurs. But if we intend to say 'Hands Off' to the powers of Europe, then sooner or later we must keep order ourselves."[194]

In July the arbitral commission designated to determine the manner of repayment for the Santo Domingo Improvement Company issued its decision. The commission decided that, in the event of a default, the United States would assume control of the customs house at Puerto Plata and would, if necessary, take over several additional facilities.[195] When the default took place two months later and an American official was installed as receiver, the European powers began voicing their displeasure at losing the receipts from Puerto Plata. The French government was particularly insistent, telling Washington bluntly that its patience was nearing an end. The European protests induced President Morales to clamor anew for American assistance.

Roosevelt's triumph in the 1904 election emboldened him to make a sweeping policy statement. The Roosevelt Corollary, issued as part of his December 1904 message to Congress, reprised the language read by Root in May. However, Roosevelt's annual message justified an international police power by reference to the Monroe Doctrine for the first time. Secretary Root amplified TR's themes in an address at the New England Society on December 22. Shortly afterward the administration instructed the minister to Santo Domingo to inquire "whether the Government of Santo Domingo would be disposed to request the United States to take charge of the collection of duties and effect an equitable distribution of the assigned quotas among the Dominican Government and the several claimants."[196] In early January 1905 a special commissioner was appointed to supervise the negotiations, and two U.S. warships anchored in Santo Domingo harbor to signal American resolve in the matter.

By February 7 the countries had agreed to a protocol authorizing the United States to administer Dominican customs. The treaty's preamble justified U.S. involvement in Dominican finances on grounds that "any attempt on the part of the governments outside of this hemisphere to oppress or control the destiny of the Dominican Republic [was] a manifestation of an unfriendly disposition toward the United States." When the president transmitted the document to the Senate on February 15, he again cited the principles of 1823, declaring that his actions represented not change but continuity. "Either we must submit to the likelihood of infringement of the Monroe Doctrine or we must ourselves agree to some such arrangement as that herewith submitted." Roosevelt further noted that the United States was "simply performing a in peaceful manner, not only with the cordial acquiescence, but in accordance with the earnest request of the government concerned, part of that international duty involved in the assertion of the Monroe Doctrine."[197]

TR's protestations notwithstanding, U.S. involvement in Dominican affairs as contemplated in the protocol clearly represented a break with tradition. When the U.S. Senate balked at approving the treaty, rumors of revolution swirled throughout the Dominican capital, threatening to vitiate the whole arrangement. Roosevelt directed the State Department to negotiate a modus vivendi with the Morales government pending ratification.[198] Under the formula devised by the U.S. minister, the Dominican government received 45 percent of receipts, with the remainder deposited in a New York account for distribution among the foreign creditors.[199] The European governments agreed to refrain from further provocative actions; an American citizen, Col. Charles R. Colton, was designated as receiver;[200] and the arrival of an Italian cruiser in Dominican waters on March 14 gave the beleaguered Morales the necessary push to acquiesce in this arrangement.[201]

It became clear that TR would brook no opposition to the new scheme by aspiring Dominican revolutionaries.[202] "American citizens in the customs houses," he told William Howard Taft, "are there to stay until we ourselves take them out, and no revolutionists will be permitted to interfere with them."[203] In practice this meant that U.S. Navy warships would thwart any new revolution on the island. When the Morales government appeared to be teetering in the fall of 1905, Roosevelt instructed Secretary of the Navy Charles J. Bonaparte to "tell Admiral Bradford to stop any revolution. I intend to keep the island in status quo until the Senate has had time to act on the treaty. I shall treat any revolutionary movement as an effort to upset the modus vivendi. That this is ethically right I am dead sure, even though there may be some technical or red tape difficulty."[204] Having reached a modus vivendi, TR was prepared to uphold it by force until Congress, which he described with typical restraint as an assemblage of "prize idiots,"[205] finally approved the protocol (in 1907).[206] As befitted a man immortalized by Henry Adams as "pure act,"[207] Theodore Roosevelt acted first and let the legal niceties sort themselves out later.[208]

Treaty Law and U.S. Administration of Dominican Finances

When the proposed treaty with Santo Domingo bogged down in the U.S. Senate, the Dominican Republic and the Roosevelt administration concluded a modus vivendi that in effect executed the treaty terms without legislative consent.[209] The agreement authorized the U.S. president to designate an official to serve as "General Receiver of Dominican Customs." Forty-five percent of receipts were to go to the government to defray administrative expenses and pay the customs officials' salaries; the remainder was to be deposited in a New York bank pending Senate approval of the convention. Once the Senate acted, "the sums so deposited [would be] distributed among the creditors in proportion to the just claims in accordance with said convention."[210] Alongside the U.S.-supervised adjustment of Dominican finances, the declared U.S. purpose was to provide the Morales government with "such other assistance as [it] may deem proper to restore the credit, preserve the order, increase the efficiency of the civil administration and advance the material progress and welfare of the Dominican Republic." In essence, then, the modus vivendi committed the Roosevelt administration (1) to adjust the republic's foreign and domestic debt, and to gauge the validity of all pending claims; (2) to administer its customs facilities, delivering the agreed share of the receipts to the government and using the balance to retire the public debt and the claims of creditors; and (3) to afford President Morales such additional assistance as he might require to attain orderly and efficient government.[211]

By the time the U.S. Senate fulfilled its advise-and-consent duty, observed the final text of the U.S.-Dominican convention, some $17 million in claims against the Dominican government remained. The convention stipulated that the revenues collected at the nation's customs houses would be "applied first to the payment of said debts and claims as adjusted and second . . . to the retirement and extinction of certain concessions and harbor monopolies which are a burden and hindrance to the commerce of the country and third the entire balance still remaining to the construction of certain railroads and bridges and other public improvements necessary to the industrial development of the country."[212] The convention obliged the Dominican government to "provide by law for the payment of all customs duties to the General Receiver and his assistants, and [to] give to them all needful aid and assistance and full protection to the extent of its powers." Similarly, the U.S. government pledged to afford the receiver and his staff "such protection as it may find to be requisite for the performance of their duties." To assure that Dominican finances were placed on a sound footing, finally, Santo Domingo agreed not to increase its public debt "except by previous agreement" with the American administration. Both the U.S. State Department and the Contaduria General of the Dominican Republic would scrutinize the receiver's accounts on a monthly basis.[213]

The Dominican episode demonstrated President Roosevelt's preferred methods for exercising an international police power. First, the United States would attempt to negotiate an agreement with a country afflicted by chronic wrongdoing or impotence that authorized the U.S. administration to undertake certain duties that normally fell to the sovereign government. Overseeing a weak government's finances was the best method to allow the country to get its financial house in order while staving off the threat of foreign military intervention and potentially territorial aggrandizement. Second, the burden of internal police was best left with the indigenous government to the maximum extent possible, allowing local authorities to tend to their own affairs. Third, while a show of force usually had salutary effects, the United States would refrain from actually using force unless revolutionary unrest seemed to imperil the arrangement. For Roosevelt the decision when and how to carry out international police actions was presumably a matter of political prudence, to be decided on a case-by-case basis.

Selling the Treaty with Santo Domingo

Roosevelt's advocacy of an international police power peaked in his 1905 message transmitting the accord with Santo Domingo to Congress. Although the document of course bore the president's signature, one detects Secretary of State Root's hand in its dispassionate, scrupulously legalistic tone and terminology, which closely resemble Root's own discourses on the Monroe Doctrine. Because "conditions in the Republic of Santo Domingo have been growing steadily worse for many years," declared TR, many foreign governments "feel themselves aggrieved because of the non-payment of debts due their citizens." Indeed, the only way for foreign governments to assure repayment of their creditors was "either by the acquisition of territory outright or temporarily, or else by taking possession of the custom-houses, which would of course in itself, in effect, be taking possession of a certain amount of territory."[214]

President Roosevelt bemoaned the clash between the Monroe Doctrine and the rigorous demands of international equity, which together had thrust the United States onto the horns of a dilemma. "It has for some time been obvious that those who profit by the Monroe Doctrine must accept certain responsibilities along with the rights which it confers." While the United States "has not the slightest desire for territorial aggrandizement at the expense of any of its southern neighbors," it would nonetheless exercise the measure of control necessary to rehabilitate Dominican finances, namely "in connection with the collection of revenue, part of which will be turned over to the Government to meet the necessary expense of running it, and part of which will be distributed pro rata among the creditors of the Republic upon a basis of absolute equity." While the doctrine was not international law, as Roosevelt and Root again reminded Americans, legal rights and obligations did flow from U.S. adherence to the principles of 1823, giving the doctrine a sort of quasi-legal status.[215]

How did the president square the doctrine, a unilateral policy statement, with the requirements of international law? "Under the accepted law of nations," proclaimed Roosevelt, "foreign Governments are within their right, if they choose to exercise it, when they actively intervene in support of the contractual claims of their subjects."[216] A great power thus could rightfully "take what action it sees fit in the adjustment of its disputes with American States, provided that action does not take the shape of interference with their form of government or of the despoilment of their territory under any disguise." Even the full-fledged Roosevelt Corollary, then, did not seek to prevent Europeans from administering a "spanking" to wayward American republics so long as punitive action contained no hint of an extension of the European political system to the New World. As in the Venezuela incident of 1902, Washington would construe even a naval bombardment or seizure of customs facilities as a seizure of territory. That left the European governments few options to collect debts. "The justification for the United States taking this burden and incurring this responsibility is to be found in the fact that it is incompatible with international equity for the United States to refuse to allow other powers to take the only means at their disposal of satisfying the demands of their creditors and yet to refuse, itself, to take any such steps."[217]

Consequently, American commercial interests—and thus the political fortunes of the Republican Party, a not-inconsequential factor for the president and the majority in Congress—hinged on an equitable settlement of the Santo Domingo dispute. While the United States was normally content to "go no further than the mere use of its good offices" to adjust disputes between Caribbean and European powers, this approach "frequently proves ineffective." When European governments intervened forcefully to enforce contractual claims, "American concessionaries, supported by powerful influences, make loud appeal to the United States Government in similar cases for similar action." Were the U.S. administration to turn down the pleas of its own citizens,[218] they would complain "that in the actual posture of affairs their valuable properties are practically confiscated, that American enterprise is paralyzed, and that unless they are fully protected even by the enforcement of their merely contractual rights, it means the abandonment to the subjects of other Governments of the interests of American trade and commerce."[219]

In short, domestic politics would come into play, for Washington's "attempted solution of the complex problem by the ordinary methods of diplomacy reacts injuriously upon the United States Government itself, and in a measure paralyzes the action of the Executive in the direction of a sound and consistent policy." This would leave the U.S. government with few good alternatives. "In view of the dilemma in which the Government of the United States is thus placed, it must either adhere to its usual attitude of non-intervention in such cases—an attitude proper under normal conditions, but one which in this particular kind of case results to the disadvantage of its citizens in comparison with those of other States—or else it must, in order to be consistent in its policy, actively intervene to protect the contracts and concessions of its citizens . . . in competition with the subjects and citizens of other States."[220] Complementing his other arguments, the president offered up the traditional rationale for intervention: to protect the interests of U.S. citizens clamoring for protection against a crooked or incompetent government.

Roosevelt also described the impotence of the Dominican government in his address to Congress. As of September 1904 Santo Domingo's public debt had totaled some $32.3 million, while the ill-managed customs service had taken in only $1.85 million in revenues—leaving a paltry $550,000 to retire the nation's foreign debt after the government's budget was subtracted. "It is therefore impossible under existing circumstances, which are chronic," declared TR, "to defray the ordinary expenses of the Government and to meet its obligations."[221] Worse yet, strenuous efforts by the European governments to obtain repayment of their "just claims" would, under the decision of the Hague tribunal in the 1902 Venezuela case, entitle European claimants to preferential treatment—that is, to have their contracts fulfilled first, to the detriment of American creditors. If Washington declined to act, its great-power rivals would be "forced to resort to more effective measures of compulsion to secure the satisfaction of their claims." For the United States to declare in essence that "it will protect its own citizens and interests, on the one hand, and yet on the other hand refuse to allow other Governments to protect their citizens and interests" would represent an "unfortunate attitude."[222]

In sum, because "the ordinary resources of diplomacy and international arbitration are absolutely impotent to deal wisely and effectively with the situation in the Dominican Republic," the Roosevelt administration was left with the unpalatable choice between abandoning America's "duty under our traditional policy toward the Dominican people, who aspire to a republican form of government while they are actually drifting into a condition of permanent anarchy," and adopting a more forceful policy. The Dominican government had repeatedly requested American help. Cuba, under the Platt Amendment regime, supplied a model for U.S. policy toward the island. If the United States asserted a similar power of supervision over Dominican finances—essentially claiming a say-so over the issuance of government bonds that allowed it to mandate that "no larger debt would be incurred than could honestly be paid"—then anyone who purchased bonds not so authorized would be relegated to the "category of speculators and gamblers" who "deserved no consideration and who would be permitted to receive none."[223] Honest creditors, then, would be repaid, removing any excuse for European encroachment in the Western Hemisphere.

Lastly, Roosevelt restated several themes underlying his international police-power doctrine. First, the United States was taking up the responsibilities prescribed by the president with the "cordial acquiescence" of the nation slated for intervention. Second, Americans "are bound to show that we perform this duty in good faith and without any intention of aggrandizing ourselves at the expense of our weaker neighbors or of conducting ourselves otherwise than so as to benefit both these weaker neighbors and those European Powers which may be brought into contact with them." Third, it was pivotal that "we should prove by our action that the world may trust in our good faith and may understand that this international duty will be performed by us within our own sphere, in the interest not merely of ourselves, but of all other nations, and with strict justice toward all." If Congress approved the treaty and the United States adhered scrupulously to its terms, "a general acceptance of the Monroe Doctrine will surely follow," and helping the cause of civilization, America would arrest the spread of anarchy in the Caribbean and expand "the sphere in which peaceful measures for the settlement of international difficulties gradually displace those of a warlike character."[224] The United States, affirmed President Roosevelt, could harvest immense benefits from undertaking a minor police action that set a good example for the rest of mankind.

Lessons of the Santo Domingo Police Action

The international police-power doctrine reached its summit in Santo Domingo, sparked protest, and then, surprisingly, faded rapidly into obscurity. Both Roosevelt's public pronouncements and his private correspondence on the affair referred frequently to the police power—testifying that the concept was uppermost in his mind. What were the tenets of the police power? First and foremost, the Dominican crisis had engaged U.S. national interests. The insurgents had directly assailed American servicemen and property. From a broader perspective, intelligent self-interest required the United States to underwrite its commitment to the Monroe Doctrine with vigorous diplomacy. Since he had come to believe that the doctrine conferred responsibility as well as privileges, Roosevelt was willing to deploy the police power, backed by the U.S. Navy. After all, he noted, if the United States was unwilling to permit England and Germany to exercise the police power in the Caribbean littoral, it must do so itself. To do otherwise would earn America the enduring enmity of the civilized world. The international police power was at once defensive and preemptive in nature.

Second, Roosevelt insisted that the intervention had promoted lofty ideals. During the run-up to the intervention, he had claimed that his attitude toward "the weak and chaotic governments and people south of us is conditioned not in the least upon the desire for aggrandizement on the part of this Nation, but solely on the theory that it is our duty, when it becomes absolutely inevitable, to police these countries in the interest of order and civilization."[225] Not only had America benefited from the Santo Domingo operation, he declared, but the interests of the Dominican people, the Latin American states, and international order writ large had been advanced. Since the existing regime had proved itself "utterly incompetent for government work," a period of limited supervision was necessary to allow the Dominicans a respite from European intimidation.[226]

The ties of civilized society, Roosevelt asserted credibly, were restored by the low-key American intervention. Afterward the president noted with satisfaction that the Dominican government, under American tutelage, now received a greater share of its own customs revenues than ever before. By placing Dominican finances on a sound footing, he believed the United States had interrupted the cycle of revolution and foreign intervention that had impoverished the island. American preemptive action bolstered the security of the Latin American republics in the face of European intrigues. TR later professed, with considerable exaggeration, that U.S. actions in Santo Domingo had been purely selfless.[227] Even so, altruism was a welcome addition to great-power diplomacy.

Third, Roosevelt exhibited a genuine reluctance to interfere in the Dominican crisis, and indeed in the affairs of Latin America at large. In 1901 he had complained, "in South America it is positively difficult to know just how far it is best to leave the nations alone and how far there must be interference, and also how far we can with justice prevent interference by others; because in each case the equities vary."[228] Fluid conditions demanded a prudential approach predicated on minimizing U.S. intervention. "I have been hoping and praying for three months that the Santo Domingans would behave so that I would not have to act in any way," he confessed to his friend and biographer Joseph Bucklin Bishop in late February 1904.[229]

Nonetheless, the course of events and President Morales's urgent pleas militated for decisive action. TR told his eldest son Ted, "it seems to me inevitable that the United States should assume an attitude of protection and regulation in regard to all these little states in the neighborhood of the Caribbean. I hope it will be deferred as long as possible, but I fear it is inevitable."[230] In the end he maintained, "We have taken the necessary step; but it was one of those cases where trouble was sure to come, whether from action or from inaction. I felt that much less trouble would come from action."[231] Luckily for the president's political fortunes, he concluded, "Apparently every body has acquiesced in what I have done in Santo Domingo." He foresaw the deadlock over the Santo Domingo treaty, predicting that "of course there will be a storm over it when Congress meets."[232] This domestic political unpleasantness notwithstanding, and from the doctrine of lesser evils, Roosevelt resigned himself to prolonged entanglement in Dominican affairs.

Fourth, the American action was transitory and self-denying in nature. Roosevelt disavowed territorial ambitions in emphatic terms. "I want to do nothing but what a policeman has to do in Santo Domingo," he informed Bishop, who had questioned his motives. In this case the constabulary function involved not law enforcement, but public administration—testifying to the breadth of the police power and the flexibility with which Roosevelt was prepared to apply it. "As for annexing the island, I have about the same desire to annex it as a gorged boa constrictor might have to swallow a porcupine wrong-end-to." The president also disclaimed any sweeping plans to reform the island. "If I possibly can I want to do nothing to them. If it is absolutely necessary to do something, then I want to do as little as possible."[233] Like a policeman, he planned to restore order, avert a violent escalation, stabilize the island's government, and trust that, left to their own devices, the Dominicans would mend their affairs.

Fifth, despite his circumspection, Roosevelt acted boldly once he had decided to intervene. An accomplished practitioner of diplomacy, he knew that force underlay successful international negotiation. A firm stance buoyed by strength not only was wise but embodied elementary decency. Despite his frequently bombastic rhetoric, then, Theodore Roosevelt was not the bloodthirsty firebrand of popular (and academic) lore. As implied by the West African maxim of the Big Stick, Roosevelt's guide to negotiation, his approach to international policing emphasized tact and forbearance punctuated by force in being.[234]

TR chose to interpret the political quietude of the American people, and indeed of the Dominicans themselves, as an endorsement of both the Roosevelt Corollary in general and of his handling of the Dominican controversy in particular.[235] Emboldened, he envisioned pressing this model of statecraft into service again in the future should the need arise. Roosevelt fantasized about chastising Venezuela for its intransigence when a new conflict between Paris and Caracas loomed in 1905. He branded President Castro "an unspeakably villainous little monkey" and wished "on ethical grounds, as well as to give exercise to the United States Army, . . . to send an expedition against him." Because of the vagaries of national and international politics, however, the president concluded, "there is nothing to do but keep our temper."[236] Political prudence dictated restraint in all but the most egregious cases of chronic wrongdoing and governmental impotence.

Finally, Roosevelt's was not a doctrinaire adherence to the principles of the Roosevelt Corollary. He did not object, for instance, when in 1905 the French government notified Washington that it was considering a punitive action against Venezuela that might extend to temporary occupation of customs facilities. Most likely the difference between his attitudes in Santo Domingo and Venezuela may be explained by the lack of German involvement in the latter. Because of its relatively meager ability to project power, France presented little threat to the territorial integrity of the American republics, and thus to the U.S. national interest, whereas the German threat transfixed him because of the Reich's growing naval power and design on Caribbean bases. Thus the United States had no pressing need to deter French intervention. TR refused to let even his own policy statements interfere with the exercise of prudence.

Reassuring the Latin American Republics

Yet President Roosevelt had transgressed—or was perceived to have transgressed—against the Big Stick doctrine. Appalled at the negative reception accorded his 1904 message to Congress in some Latin American capitals, Roosevelt and Secretary Root set out to allay fears of indiscriminate U.S. meddling. Root embarked on a goodwill tour of the region that culminated in an address to the Third Pan-American Conference at Rio de Janeiro. "In many parts of South America," recounted the president in his 1906 message to Congress, "there has been much misunderstanding of the attitude and purposes of the United States toward the other American republics. An idea had become prevalent that our assertion of the Monroe Doctrine implied, or carried with it, an assumption of superiority, and of a right to exercise some kind of protectorate over the countries to whose territory that doctrine applies. Nothing could be farther from the truth." Having tacitly dropped his own ideas about erecting just such a protectorate, Roosevelt now went out of his way to reassure Latin Americans of his munificent intentions. In the process it became clear that he envisioned an exercise of the international police power not only by the United States but also by the other advanced nations.

His energetic campaign to alleviate South American suspicions, then, is instructive. First and foremost, Roosevelt assured the southern republics that he regarded them as equal members of the community of civilized states, entitled to the same respect he afforded the European powers. "We must recognize the fact that in some South American countries there has been much suspicion lest we should interpret the Monroe Doctrine as in some way inimical to their interests, and we must try to convince all the other nations of this continent once and for all that no just and orderly government has anything to fear from us. There are certain republics to the south of us which have already reached such a point of stability, order, and prosperity that they themselves, though as yet hardly consciously, are among the guarantors of this Doctrine."[237] The United States regarded these advanced republics as equals and friends worthy of jointly guaranteeing world order. To provide tangible proof of his goodwill, TR arranged for them to be invited to the second Hague conference, signifying their admission into the community of civilized states.

Second, TR proclaimed that the Monroe Doctrine was in the common interest of the American states, which valued their independence from European rule, and he implicitly proffered the police power to the Latin American nations. "If all of the republics to the south of us will only grow as those to which I allude have already grown, all need for us to be the especial champions of the Doctrine will disappear, for no stable and growing American Republic wishes to see some great non-American military power acquire territory in its neighborhood." Maintaining internal order and behaving with a "just regard" for the rights of foreigners were the keys to civilized status, while deterring European territorial aggrandizement was in the interest of all American states.[238] Great civilized nations such as Brazil and Argentina, declared Roosevelt on another occasion, were themselves endowed with the police power and could maintain order in their own backyards, just as the United States claimed the prerogative to act in the Caribbean Basin. He even hinted at joint exercise of the police power by the United States and Latin American governments where unrest threatened their common interests.[239]

Third, TR circumscribed the "jurisdiction" within which the United States asserted an international police power. Aligning his vision with that of Alfred Thayer Mahan, he implied that the United States would exercise the police power only in the Caribbean Sea, where instability plagued many governments and placed the U.S. interest in the isthmian canal at risk. Indeed, he had weighed explicitly limiting the Monroe Doctrine to the Caribbean but decided to leave matters ambiguous for fear of encouraging European encroachment in South America. Roosevelt also insisted that the United States had no territorial ambitions in the Western Hemisphere. "It must be understood that under no circumstances will the United States use the Monroe Doctrine as a cloak for territorial aggression." While it might be compelled to exercise the police power, "such action will not be taken with a view to territorial aggression, and it will be taken at all only with extreme reluctance and when it has become evident that every other resource has been exhausted."[240]

Fourth, the president reminded Latin American onlookers that the United States did not seek to recover debts by force. While it would not resist European military actions designed to recover just debts—provided, of course, that no territorial expansion, including the seizure of customs houses, was involved—the U.S. government had "always refused to enforce such contractual obligations on behalf of its citizens by an appeal to arms."[241] Indeed, at the second Hague conference, Roosevelt instructed the U.S. delegation to back a proposal by Argentina's Dr. Luis Drago under which the great powers formally renounced forcible debt collection.[242] In short, said Roosevelt, his corollary was a proclamation designed to exclude the great powers from the New World and stave off imperialism—not to substitute an American imperialism. It buttressed the civilized powers' parochial interests and served as an instrument of benevolence that furthered the interests of mankind.

Fifth, in 1906 Roosevelt dispatched Root on a goodwill tour of South America. While he did not mention the international police power by name, the secretary of state did allude to it, denying that the United States had claimed a license to subjugate fellow American republics or indulge in military intimidation. The impression that Washington had sinister motives, wrote Roosevelt in December 1906, "continued to be a serious barrier to good understanding, to friendly intercourse, to the introduction of American capital and the extension of American trade. The impression was so widespread that apparently it could not be reached by any ordinary means." Combating these perceptions thus became a matter of some importance to the national interest.

Consequently, said the president, "It was part of Secretary Root's mission to dispel this unfounded impression" during his visits to Latin American capitals. At the Rio conference (July 31, 1906), Root explicitly disavowed Richard Olney's assertion of practical sovereignty over the Americas. Olney had overreached. The president quoted Root approvingly in his 1906 message to Congress: "We wish for no victories but those of peace; for no territory except our own; for no sovereignty except the sovereignty over ourselves." The United States, furthermore, affirmed that "the independence and equal rights of the smallest and weakest member of the family of nations [were] entitled to as much respect as those of the greatest empire, and we deem the observance of that respect the chief guaranty of the weak against the oppression of the strong. We neither claim nor desire any rights or privileges or powers that we do not freely concede to every American republic." Root's Rio address echoed the president's stance on international policing—that is, that the great Latin American republics could wield the police power in their own neighborhoods.[243]

The U.S. diplomatic offensive seemed to work. Indeed, the editor of the *American Journal of International Law* was moved to forecast that, "while it is impossible to estimate accurately at this moment its effect upon the relation of the North to the South, it is little less than a moral certainty that [Root's] visit in itself and the friendliness everywhere evidenced will draw the republics into closer relations."[244] Secretary Root's effectiveness, however, should not obscure the fact that his Latin American tour was an exercise in political damage control.

Morocco

The 1905–6 Morocco affair differed sharply from the other interventions examined here. First, Theodore Roosevelt's effort to mollify France and Germany was premised entirely on preventing a war that would not directly menace the New World. Rather, TR argued that, should a single great power dominate the European continent, it would eventually come to pose a threat to the United States and the other American republics. Second, this U.S. diplomatic intervention was circumspect compared to the other cases examined here. The Moroccan incident is included here because Paris and Berlin were wrangling in part over who should control the Moroccan constabulary—that is, over partial control of the police power in a North African state. The Moroccan crisis involved not an exercise of an international police power in the Rooseveltian mold but an exercise of something resembling it by the great powers. The standoff over Morocco and the Roosevelt administration's diplomatic intervention warrant attention because this dissimilar case offers a glimpse into Roosevelt's thoughts on a wider implementation of international policing and consequently may provide additional evidence on the hows and wherefores of international constabulary duty. TR's comments add texture to his theorizing on the purely American brand of international policing.

Now the facts in brief.[245] Over the preceding decades, misgovernment of Morocco, and the resulting threat to the well-being of foreigners in the sultanate, had precipitated great-power intervention on behalf of European citizens residing there. However, the right to extraterritorial protection of citizens, which has a long pedigree under international law, gradually mutated into an excuse for infringing Moroccan sovereignty. The major powers' representatives, the American consul included, increasingly made a habit of taking Moroccan citizens under their protection, setting a pattern for outside meddling. The removal of a substantial portion of the population from the government's jurisdiction constituted a clear threat to the integrity of Morocco; and in 1880 Britain and Spain, which favored the integrity of the Sharifian Empire for their own reasons, called an international conference at Madrid to address the situation.

At the Madrid conference, the French delegation refused to permit modifications to the treaty framework sufficient to end the abuse of extraterritorial jurisdiction. Anxious to divert France, which was still smarting from its humiliation in the Franco-Prussian War, from the issue of Alsace-Lorraine, Berlin supported the French position. Unsurprisingly, in view of the deadlock, the resulting Madrid Convention failed to stem the problem of extraterritorial protection. Indeed, the French eventually took a pretender to the Moroccan throne under their protection. The Morocco question thus found its way into the affairs of the European concert. More important for present purposes, the United States had participated in the Madrid Conference and ratified the convention—giving Washington a voice in Moroccan affairs and entangling the United States to a minor degree in European politics.

How did the status of a minor North African principality escalate into a clash between France and Germany? By the vagaries of realpolitik. By the early 1900s the provocative diplomacy of Otto von Bismarck's successors, not to mention the rapid construction of a powerful German navy, had begun to bring about the *umkreisung*, or geographical encirclement, that so vexed German geostrategists. Exploiting the agonies of Russia, which in March 1905 had suffered a defeat at Japanese hands at Mukden, Berlin decided to use Morocco to drive a wedge into the emerging Anglo-French entente cordiale. Additionally, Kaiser Wilhelm II's government hoped to split the Franco-Russian alliance and attach Russia, once it recovered from its humiliation in Asia, to the Reich in a defensive pact.

Easing the long-festering colonial rivalry that had pitted Great Britain against France throughout the latter half of the nineteenth century was the key to sustaining the entente. To help defuse the tension, Britain had offered France a free hand in Morocco in turn for a French promise to stop meddling in British affairs in Egypt. By the terms of a secret treaty, Great Britain assented to a partition of Morocco between France and Spain. Spain and France, in turn, agreed that Spain would keep the Rif strip of territory, directly opposite Gibraltar, in any future partition. Most of the remainder of the country would fall to France. In 1902 France enlisted Italian support for the new arrangement by ceding control of Tripoli to Rome.

The United States and Denmark, which held major commercial interests in Morocco, did not object when the Anglo-French bargain came to light. Germany did. For Berlin the affair had become a *machtfrage*, a question of power politics. Why did the partition concern the Reich, which had little interest in becoming a Mediterranean power? For one thing, Germany had built up a substantial commercial interest of its own in Morocco and thus, under the model of great-power relations of the day, deserved to be consulted about such a sweeping change in the treaty framework governing the sultanate. The secret doings among Britain, France, Spain, and Italy thus affronted German power and prestige.

The Germans were also fearful of appearing to acquiesce in French intrigues. Buckling under, they believed, might encourage further mischief at the Reich's expense. In early March 1905, Ambassador Hermann Speck von Sternburg told President Roosevelt that Berlin could not idly tolerate the infringement of its overseas commercial interests. Moreover, "she is bound to think of her national dignity. . . . As soon as France discovers that Germany meekly submits to her bullying, we feel sure that she will become more aggressive in other quarters and we do not consider a demand for a revision of [the treaty settling the Franco-Prussian War] to be far off."[246]

Both France and Germany pled privately with Roosevelt to intercede with the other. Citing the "political unity" of France and Spain, which supposedly intended to debar Moroccan markets from the rest of the world, Wilhelm II appealed to Roosevelt to urge Paris to accept his proposal for a conference of the Madrid signatories and to discourage London from providing military support to the French. America, believed German officials, could dissuade Great Britain from taking rash action on behalf of its new partner. Ever so gently, the president held Berlin at arm's length. He sized up the Morocco affair in a letter to Whitelaw Reid. Despite Wilhelm's claim that he was championing the interests of the civilized world, including the United States, TR denied that the United States had much of a stake in the dispute. "I do not feel," he wrote, "that as a Government we should interfere in the Morocco matter. We have other fish to fry and we have no real interest in Morocco. I do not care to take sides between France and Germany in the matter."[247] These "fish" included Panama, Venezuela, and Santo Domingo, which were closer to home and of more immediate concern. His attention fixed on events in the Americas, the president had misgivings about taking a stance on a European dispute.

Still, the fraying of great-power relations was worrisome. The president hoped to appease Berlin insofar as possible and to relax the growing tension between the Germans and British. Roosevelt summed up the situation with a bit of Thucydidean analysis: "Each nation is working itself up to a condition of desperate hatred of the other; each from sheer fear of the other." Finally, the president professed a desire "to do anything I legitimately could for France; because I like France," and because the French would bear the brunt of the land war that seemed to be looming.[248] While he was unwilling to line up with either side, then, TR hoped that unobtrusive U.S. involvement could help alleviate the tensions mounting between Germany and the entente.

In the end Prince Bernard von Bülow, the German chancellor, and his adviser, Baron Friedrich von Holstein, resolved to use Morocco as a pretext for a display of German power on the Continent, to deter French maneuvering that might jeopardize German interests, to deflect the ridicule then being heaped on the government by its liberal antagonists in the Reichstag, and with any luck, to expose the Anglo-French entente as a hollow shell and thus thwart the encirclement of Germany. Berlin forced the issue. Bülow and Holstein persuaded the volatile Kaiser Wilhelm to undertake a sea voyage to Morocco and disembark at Tangier for an official, and well-publicized, call on the sultan. On debarking the imperial yacht, alluding to the Open Door, Wilhelm declared, "I hope that under the sovereignty of the Sultan a free Morocco will remain open to the peaceful rivalry of all nations without monopoly or annexation. . . . I am determined to do all in my power to safeguard efficaciously the interests of Germany in Morocco, for I look upon the Sultan as an absolutely independent sovereign."

The kaiser's public vow to oppose French designs thrust the Reich bodily into the diplomatic brawl over Morocco. Among the

French demands on the sultan were a reorganization of the army and police under French tutelage, French control of Moroccan finances, and a treaty excluding the political influence of all nations other than France from the sultanate's affairs. Rather than yield to the further erosion of his authority, the sultan threw his support behind German calls for a conference to discuss how to reform the Moroccan government. When the French foreign minister, Théophile Delcassé, resisted the German call for a conference, the French government, unwilling to risk a military showdown, quietly removed him from office and agreed to a compromise formula for the international gathering. Though he had demurred from weighing in overtly on Germany's behalf, TR did advise the French government to agree to a conference — and intimated that he would stand behind Paris during the negotiations.[249] Paris grudgingly agreed to the president's overtures, and the Madrid signatories convened at Algeciras, Spain, on January 16, 1906.

France's humiliation, duly gloated over in the German press, further ratcheted up the tension and encouraged the kaiser to pursue an even greater diplomatic victory. Intricate bargaining ensued at Algeciras. In keeping with its original demands on the sultan, Paris hoped to secure a mandate south of the Rif, giving Morocco to France outright (together with an empire that would at last be contiguous). Failing that, it wanted the authority to staff the police and army with French, or perhaps French and Spanish officers, as well as control of an international bank to shore up Morocco's finances. At a minimum the sultanate would become a French sphere of influence.

For its part, Berlin wanted to prepare the ground for an eventual partition of the sultanate. Germany hoped to gain control of the police in some of the Moroccan ports, implying a partition. Failing that, it hoped either to preserve the sultan's freedom to choose such foreign officers for the police and army as he saw fit—in hopes that German officers would be chosen—or to arrange for some minor power such as Denmark to provide the officers for the Moroccan security services. Either by obtaining a foothold in the sultanate or by keeping Morocco out of French hands, Berlin would have dealt Paris a diplomatic defeat and created favorable conditions for future German intrigues in North Africa.

The European powers split fairly evenly between advocates of the French and German positions. While Great Britain hesitated to pledge military support in case of war, Sir Edward Grey, the foreign secretary, informed the German ambassador that public sentiment would compel the British government to act should Germany attack France. Italy, recipient of a free hand in Tripoli by means of a secret treaty with the French, lined up with Paris, as did Spain. Austria-Hungary supported Germany, as did Russia, although the tsar, his nation weakened by the war with Japan, could provide no tangible support.

Henry White, the American representative at Algeciras, followed President Roosevelt's instructions to remain on friendly terms with all of the parties but to "help France get what she ought to have." When the two sides came to loggerheads, Roosevelt devised a compromise formula that ended up being adopted in all its essentials. Secretary of State Root proposed "to entrust the Sultan of Morocco with the organization of the police forces within his domains and to allow him certain funds, and to establish an international control with regard to the management of these funds, and the carrying out of the whole plan." The police power would fall neither to Germany nor (exclusively) to France. Roosevelt, Root told Speck, would propose:

1. That the organization and maintenance of police forces in all the ports be entrusted to the Sultan, the men and officers to be Moors.

2. That the money to maintain the force be furnished by the proposed international bank, the stock of which shall be allotted to all the powers in equal shares (except for some small preference claimed by France, which he considers immaterial).

3. That duties of instruction, discipline, pay, and assisting in management and control be entrusted to French and Spanish officers and non-commissioned officers, to be appointed by the Sultan on presentation of their names by their Legations . . .

4. That full assurances be given by France and Spain, and made obligatory upon all their officers who shall be appointed by the Sultan, for the open door, both as to trade, equal treatment and opportunity in competition for public works and concessions.[250]

Some aspects of Roosevelt's proposal met with German opposition. The kaiser complained that the American program "would place the police forces entirely into [French and Spanish] hands" because Paris and Madrid would name the officers. Consequently, maintained Berlin, "the police organization would be tantamount to a Franco-Spanish double mandate and mean a monopoly of these two countries, which would heavily curtail the political and the economic positions of the other nations." To prevent an effective transfer of Morocco to France, the sultan might be empowered to select the officers from among the members of the new bank, or from at least four specific nations. Finally, Germany would agree to French control of the police in Tangiers, and perhaps one other port, with the other ports falling to the jurisdiction of the Madrid signatories.[251]

Roosevelt politely rebuffed the kaiser's entreaty. In a diplomatic note from Root, the president told Wilhelm, "I cannot bring myself to feel that I ought to ask France to make further concessions than the arrangement suggested in [Root's note proposing the compromise] would require." Now a veiled threat to scuttle the conference: "This being so, I would gladly drop the subject, in which our traditional policy of abstention from the political affairs of Europe forbids the United States to take sides." TR also reminded Wilhelm that he had agreed to abide by Roosevelt's advice should the negotiations grind to a halt, and he forecast that the Reich would be blamed for whatever evils followed a breakdown at Algeciras.[252]

Washington's adherence to the Open Door accorded with its view of the police issue. When at the last moment Wilhelm II hedged on international control of the Moroccan police, Root reminded him tartly of the principle guiding the American mediation effort, namely "that all commercial nations are entitled to have the door of equal commercial opportunity in Morocco kept open, and the corollary to that principle that no one power ought to acquire such a control over the territory of Morocco as to justify the belief that she might ultimately come to regard and treat that territory as her own, to the exclusion of others." Roosevelt's compromise arrangement, contended the secretary of state, satisfied the special claims of France while deterring outright annexation of the sultanate.[253]

Faced with this judicious arm-twisting by President Roosevelt— amplified by a threat to publish all of the correspondence between Washington and Berlin on the Moroccan question—the German government hastily assented to a pact closely resembling the U.S. compromise proposal. Wilhelm claimed to have been won over by the internationalist hue of the American proposal, which was not the product of Anglo-French collusion.[254] Signed on April 7, 1906, the Algeciras Convention certified the sovereignty and independence of the sultan, the integrity of his domains, and the absolute equality of the foreign powers holding commercial interests in Morocco. The parties also created a state bank in which France held the dominant, though not majority, interest. Of more immediate interest, the document provided for a reorganization of the police under French and Spanish officers, essentially as Roosevelt and Root had envisioned.

In effect, then, both sides got the bulk of what they had wanted from the Morocco episode. Germany demonstrated its diplomatic and military clout by forcing France to agree to a conference in the first place. It also secured a guarantee, on paper at least, that the Open Door would remain the principle governing great-power relations in Morocco. At the negotiating table, however, Paris gained most of its objectives short of actual sovereignty over the sultanate. All of the great powers benefited by postponing a confrontation—even though the pacific outcome at Algeciras did little to arrest the downward spiral into further backbiting and, ultimately, world war.

Henry White congratulated President Roosevelt on having helped broker a "solution . . . satisfactory to both sides," a solution that was, "with the exception of a Swiss instead of an Italian inspector, exactly the proposal you made." White further congratulated TR for having compelled those in the U.S. Senate who had objected to his involvement in a purely European affair to "admit that it is possible for us to take an important part in a European assemblage . . . and to fully assert our right to equality of rights commercial and economical . . . and yet in nowise to take sides in any of the political questions." White wrote Henry Cabot Lodge that the "conclusion reached . . . has afforded great relief in circles susceptible to the effects of war scares." By helping defuse a war that in June 1905 he had believed to be "imminent," Roosevelt had successfully wielded his "second Corollary."[255]

The Algeciras Convention and Police and Financial Reform in Morocco

The two main issues addressed in the Algeciras Convention were police regulation and financial reform. Under the terms of the convention, the police remained under the sultan's sovereignty and were stationed in the eight ports open to foreign commerce. (The treaty stipulated that the police would be organized into bodies ranging from 150 to 600 men in size, "according to the importance of the ports.") Police commanders and officers were recruited from the indigenous population. The Spanish and French governments supplied officers and noncommissioned officers to the police force to serve as instructors.[256] During their five-year tour of duty, declared the treaty, the European instructors were to "assure instruction and discipline in conformity with the regulations to be drawn up" to govern the police and assure that recruits were "fit for military service." The aforementioned regulations "to assure the recruital, discipline, instruction, and administration of the bodies of police," whose total manpower was pegged at between two thousand and twenty-five hundred, were devised through consultations between the Moroccan minister of war, top-ranking Spanish and French advisers, and an inspector general appointed by the

Swiss government.[257] As a compromise measure, control of the police in the various Moroccan ports was divided between France and Spain. "The staff of instructors of the Shareefian police," said the Algeciras Convention, "shall be Spanish at Tetuan, mixed at Tangier, Spanish at Larache, French at Rabat, mixed at Casablanca, and French in the other three ports."[258]

To restore the sultanate's financial health, the Algeciras Convention also organized a state bank of Morocco under French law to "discharge the duty of disbursing treasurer of the Empire." The sultan's government agreed to deposit its customs revenues, along with assorted other revenues, in the national bank. In turn, the bank was to open a credit account for the government, to be "employed primarily for the expenses of establishing and maintaining the bodies of police," and secondarily for public works projects.[259] The great powers acquired a considerable say in Moroccan financial affairs. The convention empowered each of the national banks of Germany, England, Spain, and France to appoint "a Censor for the State Bank of Morocco," subject to their home government's approval, for a four-year term. The censors were authorized to inspect the Moroccan bank accounts at any time in an effort to "see that the Bank is efficiently operated and insure the strict observance of the clauses of the concession and of the statutes." The convention, however, enjoined the great-power representatives from meddling in the day-to-day administration of the bank.[260]

Finally, the Algeciras Convention obligated the sultan not to award concessions for public works and services preferentially. The competition for concessions for "roads, railways, ports, telegraphs, and other public works" was to be based on the "principle of public awards on proposals, without preference of nationality." Morocco agreed to notify the signatory powers about public projects it was contemplating, so that their firms could compete on an equal basis.[261] Clearly, the Algeciras Convention apportioned among the great powers much of the authority that went with state sovereignty.

Final Thoughts on Algeciras

What are the lessons of Algeciras as regards the international police power? None that are explicit: Roosevelt was silent on whether his Corollary to the Monroe Doctrine had any bearing on the Morocco controversy. He did allude to the matter as an instance of preserving the Open Door, much as he discussed Latin America and China in these terms. This suggests that he applied a common template to different regions. And he told a group of German war veterans, invited to the White House so that the president could praise the statesmanship of Wilhelm II, that the conference had "added to the likelihood of the betterment of conditions in Morocco itself, has secured equitable dealing as among the foreign powers who have commercial relations with Morocco, and has diminished the chance of friction between those powers."[262] From the standpoints of self-defense and free commerce, then, Algeciras represented a highly favorable outcome for the United States.

Some insights accrue from reading between the lines, both in TR's address and in his correspondence. First, Roosevelt welcomed a European exercise of the police power in Morocco, much as he urged Japan and the major Latin American powers to take on the same burden in their geographic vicinities. TR's writings show that he hoped the European great powers would act as the guardians of order within their extensive spheres of influence. U.S. commercial interests benefited from sound finances and law and order. Presumably, then, either French or German stewardship over Morocco was preferable to the disorder that threatened to engulf the sultanate. The president did not object in principle to France's or Germany's exercise of the police power, on whatever terms may have been agreeable to both sides. His swing toward France during the negotiations was largely tactical in nature.

Second, the police power was not the uppermost concern in Roosevelt's mind; rather the well-being of the United States was. He had no intention of pressing his vision of international constabulary duty on the Europeans when more important matters, such as the great-power equilibrium, hung in the balance. The standoff over Morocco had seemed, momentarily at least, to portend a general European war that would have been ruinous for both Europe and America. While important, police activities in the less-developed world had to give way to transcendent concerns such as lubricating Franco-German relations and defusing the Anglo-German naval rivalry. Staving off a conflagration was the key to preventing a European threat to the New World's well-being.[263]

Third, it was desirable not to assent to European stewardship over a targeted country if it smacked too loudly of imperialism. In essence Roosevelt went along with Wilhelm II's self-serving if plausible claim that control of a nation's police, military, and financial institutions equated to control of the nation itself; and he had loudly proclaimed his disgust for territorial aggrandizement. (Of course, the kaiser had nimbly reversed his fealty to international control and sought partial control of the Moroccan police.) Endorsing the principle of international control helped Roosevelt to reconcile his enmity toward European imperialism with the undeniable—for him—need for the great powers to provide some form of supervision in the developing world.

Fourth, and closely related, great-power stewardship over a targeted country should be geared toward preparing that country for republican self-rule—not for serving as a political appendage of the great power wielding the police power. By that standard, the Algeciras Convention was undoubtedly too intrusive for Roosevelt's taste, but as noted above, for him the security of the civilized world outweighed any infringements on the sultan's prerogatives. The parties at Algeciras did sanctify Moroccan sovereignty, however flimsy and ephemeral the pact turned out to be. President Roosevelt's effort to keep France and Spain from carving up Morocco at least avoided throwing U.S. prestige behind the continuing French effort to gain control of the sultanate and spared Roosevelt the domestic political fallout associated with throwing in with one or more of the imperial powers.

9

STRATEGIES FOR

CONSTABULARY ACTION

C. E. Callwell, "Small Wars," and European Police Action

As seen earlier, Theodore Roosevelt took a jaundiced view of European imperialism and sought desperately to differentiate his own brand of interventionism from that practiced by the European great powers. The strategies associated with imperial rule accounted in large part for his revulsion. Roosevelt maintained that, on balance, great-power expansion—in particular British imperialism—had been a boon to the less-developed world. Why? Because it forcibly transplanted the institutions and habits of constitutional republicanism to backward nations. At the same time TR pointed out that imperialism's benefits had come at a steep cost to native populations. This was especially true in the case of Russian and French expansion. The more dispirit-ing facets of the European imperial enterprise left TR cold and, in-deed, inspired him to attempt to craft a superior, American form of the international police power. A British analyst (and veteran of colo-nial warfare) of the day, Col. Charles E. Callwell, shows why Roosevelt had misgivings about the great powers' police efforts. Callwell's *Small Wars: Their Principles and Practice*, a minor classic in the field of strate-gic theory, is at once a chronicle of great-power expansion and a com-prehensive analysis of imperial policing in the nineteenth century.[1]

Whether Roosevelt was familiar with Callwell's work is unknown, and probably unknowable: he did not list the British colonel's writings among the "books one ought to read,"[2] but that list, extensive as it was, was scarcely comprehensive given the voracity of TR's reading. (He reported devouring two to three books a day.) TR was keenly inter-ested in Callwell's subject matter and followed British affairs closely.[3]

It stands to reason that Roosevelt was acquainted with unconventional-warfare theory and, thus, in all likelihood, with *Small Wars*, the best-known work of its kind. The book may well have spurred Roosevelt to ponder the mechanics of international policing, and its relative indifference to politics, the overriding factor in any armed conflict, must have startled him. Some of the book's observations must have stung his pride, especially its use of the Indian wars in the American West and the Philippine War as evidence.[4] To Roosevelt's credit, his own conduct of this kind of operation was acutely sensitive to politics—as the U.S. Marine Corps's *Small Wars Manual*, the American counterpart to Callwell's book, attests.[5]

Small Wars purported to be a how-to manual for combating insurgencies, people's wars, and other unconventional military campaigns. Of Callwell, a present-day observer declares, "no author in his century commanded a more sweeping knowledge of that subject, or was more able to distill and compress information from such a staggering variety of campaigns." Indeed, he could rightly be called "the Clausewitz of colonial warfare."[6] And, to be sure, his work lives up to its billing in many respects, abounding with intricate details about the strategy, tactics, logistics, and intelligence needed to defeat popular uprisings in the non-Western world.[7] Yet the book's strength in the nuts-and-bolts of unconventional military operations accentuates its severe myopia in the realm of politics—the realm in which, following from Carl von Clausewitz, the nation that asserted the international police power ultimately had to prevail. This is a striking shortfall, since *Small Wars* was published in the heyday of imperialism, when European statesmen and soldiers should have mastered the art of fusing armed force with the other implements of national power for political ends.

Callwell can certainly be faulted for lacking guile. "Inferior races," he said, should be smashed. He evinced little sensitivity to the notion that indigenous societies were complex organisms, made up of various groups, with some of which British commanders could make common cause. It ill befitted the "Clausewitz of colonial warfare" to ignore Clausewitz's injunction to understand the enemy and the nature of the war, or to overlook the subtlety with which clever British commanders, like Wellesley in India, had been able to turn indigenous politics to their advantage. *Small Wars* relies excessively on operational remedies for political afflictions. Because of the diffuse nature of their enemy, colonial commanders were often compelled to wreak "havoc which the laws of regular warfare do not sanction," adopting tactics that "may shock the humanitarian." For instance, acknowledging that decisive victories were elusive, especially given the great-power pre-dilection for attrition warfare, he counseled commanders to attack the indigenous economic base. Forbearance was an empty gesture, largely wasted on "uncivilized races" that "attribute leniency to timidity. Fa-natics and savages must be thoroughly brought to book or cowed or they will rise again."[8]

Callwell likewise paid little attention to the complex dynamics involved in using native troops to perform police and military func-tions. To him, indigenous soldiers were interchangeable with Euro-pean regulars or with members of cadres that specialized in colonial wars, such as the Foreign Legion. This shortfall in his analysis was consistent with his inability to differentiate among various native fac-tions or grasp that indigenous populations had complex societies of their own. For the United States under Theodore Roosevelt and his successors, insight into indigenous complexities would have been use-ful. American police operations generally aimed to restore native gov-ernment, complete with police functions, at the earliest possible op-portunity; recognizing that native soldiers had their own interests and loyalties was an important part of U.S. colonial war strategy.

By drawing together an immense amount of historical material and identifying common themes in the European colonial experience, then, Charles Callwell provided a useful foundation for American strat-egy in police operations. Overall, however, the immorality of many of the tactics he prescribed and his obtuse indifference to political con-siderations represented an indictment of European imperialism. This must have repelled Theodore Roosevelt, who set out to correct the deficiencies of European imperialism.

Merits of U.S. Cooperation with Europeans

Even so, at times the interests of the United States and Europe converged enough to justify joint action. Hard on the heels of the Boer War, which worried TR for several reasons, came a flare-up of antifor-eign sentiment in China that spurred the great powers to intervene forcibly in Chinese affairs.[9] What justified such an infringement of Chi-nese sovereignty? The rebellion by the Boxers, or the "Righteous and Harmonious Fists," as they called themselves, arose in large part out of a clash of cultures, as modernity, backed by Western arms, increas-ingly impinged on traditional ways of life. The Boxer Rebellion was more a spontaneous uprising than an organized political movement. When violence erupted in the spring of 1900, egged on by xenophobic elements at court, the Boxers advanced on Peking and lay siege to the foreign embassies in Legation Quarter. "Situation extremely grave," read a June 9 cable from British minister Sir Claude McDonald to Vice Adm. Sir Edward Seymour, stationed in Tientsin. "Unless arrangements are made for immediate advance to Pekin, it will be too late."[10]

The Western powers and Japan hastily organized a force to lift the siege and succor the embattled legations. After hedging, William McKinley, amid a presidential campaign in which imperialism was a major issue, agreed to allow U.S. forces to join the multinational force. After bitter infighting among the Chinese over the proper official response to the turmoil—one faction wanted to suppress the Boxers and rescue the legations, the other to wipe out the "foreign devils"—Empress Dowager Tz'u-hsi decided to declare war on the foreigners.[11] After a bloody battle at Tientsin, the allied force advanced on Peking. Once they had conquered the capital, however, they faced a dilemma: what should be done with the empress? If she were deposed, China would have no government with which to conclude peace; if the allies violated the Forbidden City, her private domain, she might lose face irreparably with the populace. Both sides concluded it was best to ignore reality. Tz'u-hsi slipped out of the capital in disguise. The imperial court absented itself from the capital, commencing a grand tour of the Chinese countryside and pretending that outsiders did not occupy Peking. For their part, the allies chose to ignore the Chinese declaration of war, adopting instead the polite fiction that the great-power intervention had sought only to quash a Boxer "rebellion."

The allies divided up the capital city into administrative districts. Gen. Adna R. Chaffee, the U.S. commander (and future military commander in the Philippine Islands), and his second in command, Brig. Gen. James H. Wilson, were well prepared for civil administration in China. General Chaffee had served as an Indian agent; General Wilson had served in military government during Reconstruction; and both men were fresh from helping administer Cuba. Having won the military conflict in China, they set out on an ambitious civil pacification scheme, familiar from the army's experiences in Cuba, Puerto Rico, and the Philippines. The army restored law and order, first by using military courts, later by reestablishing the Chinese police and judiciary. Rigorous health and sanitation measures were put in place, and infrastructure was rebuilt. General Chaffee ruled as mildly as possible, striving to respect Chinese customs and mores.[12] Indeed, the American zone was so well administered that people flocked to it from other quarters. While misconduct was not unknown among the U.S. occupation force, its overall performance during the Boxer Rebellion burnished the U.S. Army's reputation.[13] The multinational force began evacuating Peking in September 1901 after wringing from the imperial government a protocol requiring China to pay a $335 million indemnity for its failure to suppress the Boxers.[14]

With no direct hand in national policy, Roosevelt played no role in the Boxer intervention, but he did comment on it and his thoughts are suggestive. He applauded the news that President McKinley had approved a July 3 circular by Secretary of State John Hay, committing the United States to maintaining the administrative and territorial integrity of China despite the Boxers' transgressions. Since 1857, declared the circular, U.S. policy toward China had rested on "furtherance of lawful commerce, and [on] protection of lives and property of our citizens by all means guaranteed under extraterritorial treaty rights and by the law of nations." The McKinley administration viewed "the condition at Pekin as one of virtual anarchy, whereby power and responsibility are practically devolved upon the local provincial authorities." The United States regarded the provincial governments as the lawful representatives of the Chinese people, except where they were found to be colluding with the Boxers. The overall "policy of the Government of the United States is to seek a solution which may bring about permanent safety and peace to China, preserve Chinese territorial and administrative entity, protect all rights guaranteed to friendly powers by treaty and international law, and safeguard for the world the principle of equal and impartial trade with all parts of the Chinese Empire." Lifting the siege of the legations was the immediate priority. "The President," opined Roosevelt to Henry White, "has I think done well in the Chinese matter," which marked "one of the turning points of our history."[15]

The Boxer Rebellion, then, prodded Theodore Roosevelt to continue his ruminations about great-power policing and especially about a joint Anglo-American exercise of the police power. "The stupendous revolution now going on in China is an additional reason why we should work together" as a bulwark against savagery, he told Arthur Lee during an exchange of letters on foreign-policy matters.[16] TR later admitted that the "trouble with China was, as with most great questions, that the problem was infinitely complicated." He owned up to "the smallness of my knowledge" about the events that had triggered the siege of the Peking legations. Yet the "Chinese outrages *had* to be stopped and the Chinese bandits punished" (emphasis in original).[17] ("Bandits," of course, was the term TR routinely applied to Emilio Aguinaldo's insurgents in the Philippines.) If China's imperial regime was unable to protect foreigners, then outsiders were entitled to do it in Peking's stead.

Not only were the Boxers culpable for outrages against foreign diplomats, justifying great-power intervention in Chinese affairs, they were also, implied Roosevelt, bent on overthrowing the imperial government and installing an oligarchy or other form of despotism. TR compared the situation in China to that in the Philippines. The McKinley administration had vowed to provide the archipelago with "a stable form of government." The problem with emancipating the Filipinos prematurely was that, if "they are now entitled to independence, they are also entitled to decide for themselves whether their government shall be stable or unstable, civilized or savage, or whether they shall have any government at all." Under these circumstances the United States could scarcely guarantee the islands against outside interference, for Washington would lack the authority over Manila to assure that the Filipinos discharged their duties to foreigners and their own citizens. Likewise, he despaired of rehabilitating the Boxers, "who are merely the Chinese analogues of Aguinaldo's followers." However farfetched the likeness between the xenophobic Boxers and Aguinaldo's insurgents, who had tried to form a legitimate government, the idea had been implanted in Roosevelt's mind that the responsibility of safeguarding a foreign people from great-power meddling must be accompanied by the power to assure their good behavior. "If we have a right to establish a stable government in the islands it necessarily follows that it is not only our right but duty to support that government until the natives gradually grow fit to sustain it themselves."[18]

Finally, the Boxer Rebellion provided ample opportunity to weigh the merits of combined police actions. Roosevelt compared the performance of the national contingents during the battles at Tientsin and Peking. The French and Russian forces acquitted themselves poorly—confirming his low opinion of French and Russian imperialism. American observers in China "were all in a unit in condemning the French as inefficient and as inconceivably and wantonly cruel toward the Chinese. In point of efficiency they rank them the lowest of all." The Russians were "good troops but not intelligent and very brutal toward noncombatants—brutal rather than cruel, showing themselves to be heavy animals rather than fiends." The German expeditionary force exhibited great "drill and discipline," while the American, German, and English troops were "the only ones that have not committed cruel and wanton outrages on women and children." Regrettably, the observers seemed "inclined to put the organization and general equipment of our army below that of any army there." They reserved their highest praise for the Japanese soldiers, who were "most efficient of all, and though very callous in their cruelty, yet [said] that their commanders took more pains to stop the cruelty than was the case with any other nation."[19]

From his admittedly meager knowledge of the Boxer Rebellion, then, Theodore Roosevelt drew several lessons. First, the West (and Japan) sometimes had to intervene in the affairs of foreign states to safeguard their citizens. The imperative in many cases was to restore a native government able to conduct foreign relations, safeguard commerce and foreign nationals, and maintain order within its own territory—in short, to restore a sovereign government. In extreme cases, the great powers might rightfully step in to exercise a kind of temporary stewardship.

Second, if the United States were to accept responsibility for protecting a foreign people, it had to prepare the indigenous society to take up government responsibilities itself. Depending on the case, this schooling process could require anything from a transitory show of force to back up U.S. mediation to the indefinite occupation and U.S. administration of the country.

Third, joint action by the great powers was sometimes a useful way to carry out police actions. Because of divergent interests in the Far East, however, orchestrating a coherent joint policy among the great powers was difficult. Although Roosevelt did not point directly to the Boxer Rebellion as evidence, he did ultimately conclude that a single civilized power was best able to administer less-developed countries.[20] In his mind the performance of the Japanese expeditionary force confirmed the worthiness of Japan to serve as the principal police authority in East Asia, although he also alluded to joint U.S.-British and U.S.-German action.[21] Furthermore, TR did not object to placing U.S. troops under competent foreign officers during multinational military operations, provided their units were kept intact within the expeditionary force and the United States was represented on the commander's staff.

Fourth, notwithstanding the merits of international cooperation, the upheaval in China raised the possibility of an outright partition of Chinese territory among the great powers. His fears were well founded, even though they were never realized. The series of treaties concluded between European governments and Peking during the late nineteenth century in effect transferred Kiaochow, Weihaiwei, and Port Arthur, and to a lesser extent the adjoining territories, to great-power sovereignty.[22] The same might be in store for Latin America if the United States did not extend some limited form of protectorate over its southern neighbors.[23] While President Roosevelt was intrigued by the merits of joint police action, and later spoke out in favor of entrusting the police power to an international League of Peace, there were clearly limits to international cooperation at the present stage of human civilization.

Army Small-Wars Doctrine Remains Sparse to Nonexistent

In Roosevelt's day there was no dearth of thinking about U.S. foreign policy at the level of high politics. The outward focus of U.S. foreign policy after 1898 was, however, slow to manifest itself in military doctrine. Despite its experiences with constabulary duty on the American frontier and in the former Spanish possessions, the U.S. Army was slow to develop a doctrine that told its officers how to mesh the various measures tested in the Philippines—military and civil administration, counterinsurgency warfare, and law enforcement—to form a coherent pacification effort. Officers passed after-action reports on to their superiors; senior commanders, including Gen. Arthur MacArthur, occasionally wrote explicit instructions synthesizing the operation's key themes; and knowledge diffused through the officer corps through informal social contacts, official reports, and articles in professional journals. Yet reports and articles were few and far between. The army did not launch a systematic effort to learn the lessons of the small wars, such as the Philippine War and the 1906 Cuban insurgency, until 1911. The conventional-war mindset continued to dominate strategic thought among the army's elites, despite army officers' acknowledgement that irregular warfare was likely in stricken Latin American countries.[24]

Of six U.S. Army doctrinal manuals issued between 1898 and 1915, for instance, only two contained more than a cursory review of the lessons from the Philippine and Cuban campaigns—and these were published after the Roosevelt presidency. The 1905 edition of *Field Service Regulations*, published under a new army educational system instituted by Elihu Root, was the first manual to discuss insurrections. The manual instructed commanders that their two primary concerns were to protect the loyal indigenous population and place the burden of war on enemy insurgents. Some of the general observations presented in *Field Service Regulations* were sound: the notion that it was "victory in the field that ends the strife and settles the future relations between the contending parties" and a statement that commanders would be granted broad powers to "expel, transfer, imprison, or fine revolted citizens." The manual, however, discouraged combat patrolling, directly contravening the lessons of the Luzon campaign, made no mention of garrisons, and on the all-important subject of intelligence, offered nothing more than a banal statement that "the search for information acquires special importance" when the "enemy has adopted special warfare." Later editions of *Field Service Regulations* omitted even this sparse coverage of guerrilla warfare. The predicament was similarly bleak in other doctrinal publications such as *Cavalry Drill Regulations* and *Infantry Drill Regulations*, which acknowledged "minor warfare" as a distinct war genre but completely neglected civic measures, garrisoning, intelligence, and search-and-destroy tactics.[25] To the U.S. Marine Corps fell the chore of analyzing small wars beyond this rudimentary phase.

U.S. Army Doctrine: Learning from Experience and History

A striking facet of the Roosevelt era experience with international policing is no clear distinction was drawn between the military and police functions.[26] In its quest to erect stable governments in countries afflicted by corruption or impotence, the United States undertook not only counterinsurgency campaigns but also occupation duties that placed heavy emphasis on civilian administration and policing. In the polar case, the pacification of the Philippines, a full-fledged U.S. military government boasting a version of the police power was installed in Manila. Even after civil government was instituted, military officers continued to perform these functions in regions where the insurgents continued to contest U.S. control. Not only did the army work to quell the Aguinaldo insurgency, but it also trained a native Philippine Constabulary, (eventually) oversaw elections to a Philippine Assembly, and performed a host of other duties not obviously derived from the military function. In short, until the U.S. civil administration was in place and ready to take responsibility for law enforcement and the public welfare, the army carried out tasks normally entrusted to civilian administrators. Yet it took the Second World War and the military occupation of Germany and Japan to spur the army to codify the lessons it had learned during the Roosevelt presidency and ensuing decades.

As it matured, army doctrine clearly envisioned making the laws of war and the laws of countries administered by the United States, whether by right of military occupation or by consent of the host government, the basis of military jurisdiction. U.S. Army Field Manual 27-5, *Military Government* (1940), which drew on the Lieber Code, GO

100, and other documents examined previously, made this clear in its discussion of military tribunals. A subsequent doctrine statement, U.S. Army Field Manual 27-10, *The Law of Land Warfare* (1956), defined military government as "the form of administration which may be established and maintained for the government of areas" such as enemy territory, allied territory recovered from enemy occupation, neutral territory unlawfully annexed by the enemy, and domestic territory recovered from "rebels treated as belligerents." Field Manual 27-10 was careful to distinguish this mode of governance from martial law, which was "the temporary government of the civil population of [U.S.] territory through the military forces, without the authority of written law, as necessity may require." Unlike military government, martial law was "governed solely by the domestic law of the United States."[27]

Military government did not involve a transfer of sovereignty—the *Law of Land Warfare* did not even contemplate American wars aiming at permanent conquest—but rather a transitory "authority or power to exercise some of the rights of sovereignty," wrested away from the indigenous government. Belligerent occupation, which conferred this authority to exercise police powers in the wake of an armed conflict, must be "actual and effective," meaning that "the organized resistance must have been overcome and the force in possession must have taken measures to establish its authority." The United States could substitute its own authority for that of the indigenous government and thus arrogate to itself the prerogative to exercise some of the rights that went with state sovereignty, only through battlefield victory. Field Manual 27-10 envisioned the use of "fixed garrisons or flying columns" appropriately sized to impose order, but from a legal standpoint the configuration of the occupying force mattered little "so long as the occupation is effective." Legal responsibility accompanied the pacification process. The "authority of the legitimate power having in fact passed into the hands of the occupant, the latter shall take all the measures in his power to restore, and ensure, as far as possible, public order and safety, while respecting, unless absolutely prevented, the laws in force in the country."[28]

Military government, then, lay at the nexus among politics, warfare, and law. "Subject to the restrictions imposed by international law," declared the *Law of Land Warfare*, "the occupant can demand and enforce from the inhabitants of occupied territory such obedience as may be necessary for the security of its forces, for the maintenance of law and order, and for the proper administration of the country." Indigenous laws "will be administered by the local officials as far as practicable. Crimes not of a military nature and not affecting the occupant's security are normally left to the jurisdiction of the local courts." Breaches of criminal law would be adjudicated by "properly constituted, non-political military courts" instituted by the occupying power, preferably in the occupied country, while courts of appeal should also "preferably sit in the occupied country."[29]

Civil affairs administration, a final form of military administration, was not imposed by right of conquest but was "that form of administration established in friendly territory whereby a foreign government pursuant to an agreement, expressed or implied, with the government of the area concerned, may exercise certain authority normally the function of the local government." The United States was normally required to undertake this kind of administration "when the government of the area concerned is unable or unwilling to assume full responsibility for its administration." Territory "subject to civil affairs administration is not considered to be occupied." Civil affairs administration, then, was a stopgap measure designed to help enfeebled governments get back on their feet—much as the Roosevelt administration did when it temporarily assumed stewardship of the Dominican Republic's finances. Full-blown military government was an acceptable "provisional and interim measure" if circumstances had "precluded the conclusion of a civil affairs agreement with the lawful government of allied territory recovered from enemy occupation or of other territory liberated from the enemy," but the *Law of Land Warfare* instructed commanders to conclude a civil affairs agreement "with the lawful government at the earliest possible opportunity."[30]

The U.S. Marines Develop a Doctrine for International Police Duty

Like the U.S. Army, the U.S. Marine Corps bore a strong conventional-war outlook during the Roosevelt presidency. Yet the barriers to devising small-wars doctrine were not so formidable in the Marine Corps as in the army. Steeped in nontraditional military missions, the marines boasted a culture that prized flexibility and thus lent itself to the conduct of small wars—wars in which victory relied as much on law enforcement, public administration, and social reform as on defeating the enemy in battle. In the days of the American Revolution, marines had been assigned to sail-driven warships to provide security for the captain and officers; in naval engagements they typically carried their muskets aloft into the rigging, raking enemy decks from above. One analyst has described them as "police at sea."[31] That the military and constabulary functions were compatible was axiomatic for the marines. During the wars of the early Republic, they had performed various tasks such as providing troops for landing parties and guarding navy yards. During the Civil War era the Marine Corps returned to its police roots, suppressing the New York draft riots (1863), preventing Cuban filibusters from marching on New York City (1869), putting down election riots in Philadelphia (1870), and combating the illicit liquor trade in Brooklyn (1867–70). In short, these seafaring soldier-policemen took on whatever mission they could find.

In the aftermath of the war with Spain, the influential Navy General Board, headed by Adm. George Dewey, formally assigned the Marine Corps the mission of seizing and defending advanced bases in the Caribbean Sea, and possibly off the Chinese mainland. While this assured the survival of the corps in the face of powerful opposition (President Roosevelt considered merging the marines into the army), the advanced base mission, backed by a new School of Application in Washington, instilled the art of warfare, as opposed to police operations, among newly commissioned Marine Corps officers.[32] Nonetheless, political developments in the Roosevelt administration, especially in the Caribbean, "slowly forced the Corps toward small war operations as its primary mission."[33]

Between 1898 and 1934, U.S. Marine Corps forces, assisted on occasion by shipboard navy personnel, landed in the Philippines, Cuba, Honduras, Mexico, Puerto Rico, Guam, Samoa, China, Nicaragua, and Santo Domingo. That TR's police operations ended up being peaceful evidently reinforced small-wars doctrine advocates in their running debate with partisans of the advanced base mission. In any event, the marines set about building on the rudimentary doctrine handed down by the U.S. Army. (In 1918 the army produced a monograph titled *Studies in Minor Tactics* that may have fed into the marines' meditations on small wars.) Because of the shortcomings of army doctrine, however, the marines had to learn for themselves about garrisoning, native constabularies, intelligence gathering, and search-and-destroy tactics. During their Haitian campaigns, marine officers gradually began to transmit their knowledge and experiences to fellow officers, both by informal mechanisms and, increasingly, by formal channels that created a body of lessons learned about unconventional warfare.[34]

Alone among the U.S. armed forces, then, the U.S. Marine Corps made a concerted effort to learn the lessons of the Philippines insurrection and subsequent police operations and to transcribe these lessons into doctrine.[35] From their analysis marine officers compiled the *Small Wars Manual*, in effect a handbook on counterinsurgency operations theory and practice, as well as on techniques for preparing subject populations for self-rule. In most respects the corps adhered to the progression of military and civil operations outlined by William Howard Taft and other veterans of the Philippines and other foreign enterprises. The manual, which focuses predominantly on the nuts-and-bolts of international police strategy, is a useful adjunct to Taft's ruminations on matters of high policy. It is a trove of information that is worth consulting whenever the United States contemplates intervening in regions such as the Balkans, West Africa, or the Middle East.

The *Small Wars Manual* had its origins in the schoolhouse. At first the Field Officers School at Quantico, Virginia, offered nine hours of instruction on the theory and techniques of small wars. By 1932 the curriculum had expanded to nineteen hours under the direction of Maj. Harold H. Utley, who had commanded marines in eastern Nicaragua.[36] First published in 1935, the *Small Wars Manual* was a systematic analysis of the "banana wars," distilled into book form by veterans of Caribbean deployments. It is the best—indeed, the only contemporary— compilation of the principles undergirding U.S. international police activities in the Roosevelt era. The manual's authors devoted considerable energy to assessing the dynamics of revolutionary activity, the impassioned political climate in which they ordinarily had to operate. The manual is a remarkable book, as much for its political sensitivity as for its advice on military strategy.

First, the authors emphasized that small wars differed dramatically from conventional wars and, consequently, that a far different strategic approach was necessary for such operations. In conventional wars, force was a last resort, typically brought to bear to compel a government to do America's bidding after diplomacy failed. In stark contrast, by intervening in the *internal* affairs of a foreign state, the United States might hope to effect a restoration of order, "to sustain governmental authority, to obtain redress, or to enforce the fulfillment of obligations between the two states."[37] In small wars U.S. political leaders could be expected to maintain unusually tight control of operations, even after they had authorized the use of violence. The pervasiveness of political considerations, it followed, would strongly influence the strategies and even the tactics available to the field commander. Thus, observed the manual wryly, U.S. marines were often dubbed "State Department Troops."[38]

Second, the authors argued that violence alone could not achieve American objectives in small wars. Commanders had to address the nonmilitary causes of insurgencies and avoid embittering the local population against the United States. While guerrilla fighters could be expected to "disregard, in part or entirely,

International Law and the Rules of Land Warfare in their conduct of hostilities," American military commanders would alienate the native populace should they follow suit. The occupying force had to weigh the reaction of the American public and foreign powers to its actions. Heavy-handed tactics could undercut political support for the president among the American electorate, while diplomatic fallout could threaten U.S. diplomatic and economic relations abroad. Thus, small wars required a different psychology from conventional wars, in which hatred of the enemy was commonplace—indeed, often indispensable.[39]

In small wars it was necessary to be firm, even occasionally ruthless. Yet, since the goodwill of the native citizenry was crucial to success, the marines generally had to be tolerant and sympathetic in their treatment of ordinary people, not to mention knowledgeable about local customs and culture. Above all, nothing "should be said or done which implies inferiority of the status or of the sovereignty of the native people. They should never be treated as a conquered people." Only by mild treatment could American forces instill respect for law and order, justify U.S. military intervention to civilians who would be suspicious of their motives, and counter the propaganda of the insurgents. "The purpose should always be to restore normal government or to give the people a better government than they had before, and to establish peace, order, and security on as permanent a basis as practicable." Above all, declared the manual, "there must be instilled in the inhabitants' minds the leading ideas of civilization, the security and sanctity of life and property, and individual liberty."[40] Nurturing this cultural transformation would be a gradual process, reliant on the patience and example of Americans stationed in a country.

There were five phases to a naval police deployment. First, because of the tempestuous political conditions that characterized occupied countries, the marines would deploy incrementally—"dribble in," in the authors' evocative formulation—without a congressional declaration of war that might rouse local sentiments against the United States. The on-scene commander might not have clear orders, since small wars were "conceived in uncertainty, . . . conducted often with precarious responsibility, under indeterminate orders lacking specific instructions."[41] These nebulous conditions, noted the authors, were "quite natural," since the U.S. government was not at war with the host country and had no aggressive intentions or designs on its territory. Indeed, Washington hoped the locals would perceive it as "endeavoring to accomplish its end with the minimum of troops"—and violence—feasible. Above all, the marines were to secure U.S. objectives with "as little military display as possible with a view toward gaining the lasting friendship of the inhabitants." The manual thus sets forth a daunting task for the marine commander: to refrain from military intimidation and respect local customs, even while stamping out bands of guerrillas and instilling the Western tradition of republican self-rule.[42] Consolidating defensive strongholds in the country was a first step toward reestablishing law-and-order and thus guaranteeing the rights to life and property for ordinary citizens.

During the initial phase a "vanguard" composed of small marine units or mixed units of sailors and marines would be landed at key points such as seaports and the capital. The vanguard's task was to prepare the way for the second, offensive phase of operations. Suitably reinforced, the marines would commence field operations. In a typical pattern, the landing force occupied a coastal area and then moved inland, occupying principal cities and economically vital areas and stationing garrisons in fortified outposts, from which combat patrols would range across the countryside "in all directions" to engage guerrilla units. To insulate the marines from native resentments, the occupying force was to leave native officials in charge of the government to the maximum extent possible, except for the customs houses, a vital source of revenue to fund government activities. In theory, entrusting the judicial and police functions to the indigenous government would spare the marines the public hostility that would be likely if American troops disarmed civilians and punished lawbreakers.

An initial, conventional battle with the enemy force was probable, after which the (presumably defeated) enemy would most likely dissolve into armed bands of guerrillas, much as Aguinaldo's army had, resorting to an unconventional strategy in the wake of its misfortune on the battlefield. Marine commanders must then be prepared to dispatch lightly armed patrols equipped for rapid movement. The second, counterinsurgent phase, noted the manual, was "the most arduous of all operations," since the idea was "to combat the native [guerrilla] at his own game on his own ground." It also allowed natives to protract the war in an effort to sap U.S. will—an effort at which the Filipinos had failed, largely because the insurgents never managed to rally the populace to a true "people's war." Recognizing that the insurgents would blend in with the local population, both for concealment and in an attempt to provoke American atrocities, the manual's authors frankly conceded that the marines would alienate the natives to some degree. They could not avoid this dynamic of counterinsurgency warfare. The authors settled for warning that reprisals and other drastic actions would "create sympathy for the revolutionists, . . . destroy lives and property of innocent people, and . . . have adverse effect on the discipline of our own troops."[43]

Meanwhile, as pacification efforts progressed during the second phase, the marines would begin to organize a local constabulary, composed of "the best types of natives," that would ultimately assume responsibility for internal and external defense, as well as the police functions and a host of civil responsibilities.[44] Not only would this begin to equip the native government to resume control of its own affairs, but it would allow U.S. Navy personnel from the vanguard to return to their duties aboard ship.[45] Although the manual envisioned organizing the constabulary along U.S. military lines and schooling its members in U.S. tactics, it also allowed considerable latitude for employing native methods of organization, particularly under emergency conditions that ruled out a more leisurely approach. Because the manual instructed marine commanders to learn the natives' traditions and mores, it also recognized that its prescriptions must be adapted to local conditions.[46] In general, American troops would not directly carry out police activities. "United States forces . . . will not, as a rule, participate in matters concerning police and other civil functions. The military forces usually constitute a reserve which is to be made available only in extreme emergencies to assist the native constabulary in the performance of its purely police mission."[47]

"The mission of our forces," rather, "usually involves the training of native officers and men in the art of war, assisting in offensive operations against organized banditry and in such defensive measures . . . as are essential to the protection of lives and property." Since the civil police functions were usually "vested in the native military forces of the country," local soldiers had both to combat insurrection and to carry out "a police task involving in general the enforcement of the civil and criminal laws." Among these enforcement activities were controlling the flow of arms and ammunition, monitoring compliance with "police, traffic, and sanitary regulations," administering prisons, and performing "numerous other duties that, by their nature, may obviously, directly or indirectly, play an important part in the accomplishment of the military mission."[48]

To be sure, American officers and enlisted men would be—temporarily—assigned to influential posts in the native constabulary. Adherence "on the part of our personnel, to the dictates of the local laws and regulations, and a thorough knowledge of the scope of authority vested in the native police force" were essential to effective law enforcement and to "maintain[ing] the respect and confidence of the community as a whole." The authors of the manual hoped that

U.S. military personnel, steeped in local laws and traditions, would be able to maintain cordial relations with the judiciary, which would remain largely under native control and whose judges would be well-positioned to hamper American counterinsurgency and law-enforcement activities if a spirit of cooperation did not prevail.[49]

Led by marine officers, the native constabulary would also be assigned tasks such as flood and earthquake relief, which the marines believed would help them to secure the trust and friendship of the citizenry. Additionally, constabulary troops would accompany marines on combat patrols so that "the constabulary, as well as the native popu-lation[, would] feel that the local situation [was] being handled by their own government agency and not a foreign power." By helping reduce impressions that foreigners were subjugating the country, the manual's architects hoped to enlist the support of the natives, or at least to mute their discontent with U.S. policy.[50]

Third, U.S. forces would assume control of the native government's executive agencies, leaving the judicial and legislative powers in native hands. Depending on how the combat forces fared, this could involve "the establishment of military government or mar-tial law in varying degree from minor authority to complete control of the principal agencies." Further U.S. reinforcements would arrive in the meantime, allowing the marines to "carry the burden of most of the patrolling." The burden of combat patrols would be incrementally transferred to native troops as they were recruited and trained.[51] The third phase would continue until the insurgents, or "lawless elements," were subdued, and would wind down as the military operation neared success. The marines would begin gradually relinquishing command of the constabulary to native officers, while native officials would be-gin to resume control of government executive organs. The American troops, meanwhile, would withdraw to large outposts where they would act as a potent reserve, largely out of sight but available should hostilities flare up again.[52]

Fourth, during the phase dubbed "routine police operations," the occupying force would continue discharging the executive functions while commencing preparations for "free and fair" elec-tions. The *Small Wars Manual* enjoined American commanders to refrain scrupulously from taking on "any judicial responsibilities over local inhabitants beyond that expressly provided by proper authority," namely authority flowing from "law and our treaty rights" that had authorized American intervention in the first place. Any judicial powers wielded by U.S. military officials, then, must be clearly spelled out in "orders from superior authority" to avoid conveying the impression that America was a conqueror, and not a benefactor, of the stricken nation. The amount of U.S. involvement in the judicial function would vary from operation to operation, depending on the extent of disarray in the indigenous government.[53]

The main point was to preserve the appearance of American commitment to the rule of law, and thus, by example, to nourish respect for law-and-order among the populace. Accordingly, the manual laid down precise instructions for conducting and supervising elections. A National Board of Elections, staffed mainly by native officials, would nominally direct the electoral machinery, while an American Electoral Mission made up of U.S. military and civilian personnel would exercise real control of the process. Military forces would be positioned to prevent armed revolutionaries or anyone else from disrupting the balloting process and thus thwarting lawful elections.[54] Fifth, and finally, the natives would resume full control of their affairs. The marines would withdraw from the interior and eventually leave the country altogether.

To be sure, many ambiguities mar the *Small Wars Manual*. The authors could be faulted for instructing marines to be nonpartisan, even though they were intervening on behalf of one party to a conflict—that is, the party in power—and thus had partisan aims that would stoke at least some resistance from the political opposition.[55] To maintain otherwise was sheer fiction. Further, the manual admonished commanders to recruit the local constabulary on the recommendations of eminent local officials—despite the partisan leanings of the officials and the possibility that their actions had fanned the flames of insurgency in the first place. And, closely related, the manual urged the occupying force to cooperate closely with the local authorities, which probably bore some responsibility for the insurgents' disaffection.

Yet the decision to side with a potentially unsavory regime was a calculation that rested not with marine commanders but with the political leadership in Washington. As the manual itself noted, "Formulation of foreign policy in our form of government is not a function of the military." Under the U.S. Constitution, civilian officials, and ultimately the president, were chiefly responsible for gauging the wisdom of U.S. military action—that is, for determining whether the salvation of a local government merited the use of U.S. military might. To blame the marines for the political and moral shortcomings of their masters would be unfair. Given the uncertainties intrinsic to small wars, marine officers crafted a strategy that, while imperfect, was nonetheless a sure guide to international police action.[56]

10

CONCLUSIONS

"My endeavor was not only to assert these rights, but frankly and fully to acknowledge the duties that went with these rights."

Theodore Roosevelt, *Autobiography*

What Theodore Roosevelt proposed in his corollary to the Monroe Doctrine was little short of a general power of legislation and regulation, limited in execution to be sure, that was to be entrusted to the advanced powers. This was a makeshift solution pending the emergence of a multinational League of Peace. Given the immaturity of the early-twentieth-century international order, which was riven by competition among the great colonial powers and by other frictions, Roosevelt doubted whether a muscular international body able to deploy the police power could be formed any time soon. The members of such a body would simply continue to pursue their parochial interests—interests that would clash, much as they did in the current anarchic international system—within its confines and stymie the activities of the league. For the time being, the best that could be achieved was policing by the great powers within their geographic spheres of interest, or, at most, temporary coalitions where great-power interests converged. The Boxer Rebellion comes to mind as an example of a joint constabulary operation in the Rooseveltian mold.

Over the long term, however, TR prophesied that international loyalties and a waxing spirit of cooperation—a kind of international fellow-feeling—would augment if not supplant patriotism, making possible a world organization endowed with the international police power. Such a league should exercise the police power sparingly, when corrupt or ineffectual national governments were unable or unwilling to discharge their sovereign obligations to their citizens or foreign countries. Local matters were best left to national governments to which, purged of corruption and impotence, would presumably have

221

a better grasp of their own affairs than could some remote international body. TR believed there had to be some remedy of last resort for governments' failure to discharge their duties. A limited supervisory authority, operating in a quasi-federal international system, constituted his prescription for world order.

Summary of Findings

Theodore Roosevelt stayed remarkably true to his ideals. From time to time, however, Roosevelt, as befitted a man Henry Adams labeled "pure act," overstepped the bounds he himself had set—fanning fears among the U.S.'s Latin American neighbors and forcing Washington into damage-control mode. Thus his handling of diplomatic and military affairs, while praiseworthy in many respects, also serves as a cautionary tale. TR's police-power concept represents a useful analytical tool for gauging the wisdom of military intervention in beleaguered nations. Contemporary statesmen, however, should also reflect on Roosevelt's shortcomings before they act—lest they be tempted to simply ape the mode of statecraft practiced by a great man.

Civilized Status Confers the Police Power

A nation's maturity determined whether it could justly undertake constabulary missions or might itself be subject to police action. The advanced nations were not subject to police action, and they should make every effort to resolve their differences through pacific means. They could with a clear conscience carry out police actions in their geographic neighborhoods, so long as they hewed to the beneficent policy of uplift espoused by Theodore Roosevelt. Roosevelt considered the international police power an instrument of stewardship, not a pretext for self-aggrandizement. The European powers, Japan, and the United States were entitled to take up the mantle of international constable. Certain lesser powers were also suited to exercise the police power, consonant with TR's notion of civilization and the sovereign-equality doctrine.

In the New World, for example, the "great and prosperous civilized commonwealths, such as the Argentine, Brazil, and Chile, in the Southern half of South America, have advanced so far that they no longer stand in any position of tutelage toward the United States. . . . My view was that there was no more necessity for asserting the Monroe Doctrine than there was to assert it in regard to Canada. They were competent to assert it for themselves."[1] It followed that these countries could undertake the kind of preventive actions contemplated in the Roosevelt Corollary. The nature of the doctrine, as a uniquely American foreign-policy statement, ruled out a joint declaration prohibiting European intervention. Yet, since the police power derived from the principle of sovereignty and the right of self-defense, it was accessible to all members of the fraternity of civilized nations.

Police Duty as a Legal Prerogative

The United States invoked a legal right of intervention in all of the cases examined in chapter 8. Roosevelt, Root, and other administration spokesmen readily conceded that the Monroe Doctrine was not international law; thus the international police power was not an appendage of the doctrine. Rather, the police power was inferred from precepts of international law. Constabulary action need not involve actual fighting; exploiting *potential* force was preferable. Wherever possible the United States negotiated the terms of its supervisory authority with the government targeted for a constabulary mission. If the parties could be coaxed or browbeaten into giving their consent, which was usually the case, then the American constabulary mission could be a bloodless affair. And so it was. In all of the cases except for that of Venezuela, President Roosevelt founded his actions on treaty law — and even the Venezuelan dispute was settled by arbitration, another of his favorite tools. Sometimes the powers claimed by the United States were sweeping indeed. "The Philippines, Cuba, and Porto Rico," wrote Roosevelt in his autobiography, "came within our own sphere of governmental action" under the terms of the Treaty of Paris. Generally speaking, though, the United States sought to minimize the extent of its intrusion into the affairs of foreign states. American troops never fired a shot in anger in any constabulary mission during the Roosevelt presidency, with the sanguinary exception of the Philippine War.

Responsibilities accompanied the legal authority claimed by the United States, which under TR's tutelage "asserted certain rights in the Western Hemisphere under the Monroe Doctrine. My endeavor was not only to assert these rights, but frankly and fully to acknowledge the duties that went with these rights." Among these duties were maintaining order and nurturing republican self-government in the Caribbean Basin. While the doctrine was not international law, then, it was "a cardinal principle of our foreign policy" from which flowed certain legal benefits and obligations.[2] Warding off European territorial encroachment, and in the bargain freeing the American republics to pursue their own paths to self-rule, was thus not only a moral imperative but also a virtual precept of international law. Consequently, the Roosevelt Corollary, which purported to generalize the police power, held out the possibility of acting without the target state's consent—just as government might act without the consent of each individual citizen in domestic affairs.

Preemptive Outlook

U.S. motives, maintained TR, were intelligent self-interest and altruism. Heading off great-power actions that might threaten vital sea-lanes in the Caribbean was in the U.S. national interest. Since the United States, under the Monroe Doctrine, had placed the New World off-limits to European territorial aggrandizement, it was incumbent on Washington to step in preemptively when a Caribbean government failed to fulfill its responsibilities to foreign nationals. This outlook culminated in the Roosevelt Corollary, unveiled for the first time in the case of Santo Domingo. Roosevelt foretold that constabulary missions of this kind would bring salutary effects to the inhabitants of nations subjected to U.S. supervision.

Jurisdiction Stems from Power, Interest, and Geographic Proximity

Judging by the cases examined in chapter 8, Theodore Roosevelt believed the United States could establish "jurisdiction" for constabulary missions in a few different ways. First, there was war. The United States had obtained title to the former Spanish colonies by right of conquest in 1898 and thus inherited the police power in the islands. The Treaty of Paris led the McKinley and Roosevelt administrations to impose the municipal police power far beyond the Western Hemisphere. TR seemed to believe that there should be stringent geographic constraints on police operations, both for reasons of national power and interest and because the other civilized powers were capable of policing their own geographic neighborhoods. As a result the United States tended to refrain from constabulary action outside the Western Hemisphere except in unusual circumstances. The Spanish-American War, when the Philippine archipelago was won by virtue of military defeat of a great power in the Western Hemisphere, and the 1905–6 Morocco affair, which engaged the U.S. national interest while requiring only circumspect diplomatic intervention by President Roosevelt, were two such circumstances.

Second, as noted previously, the great civilized powers were entitled to conduct international police actions in their geographic vicinities, both to defend their own interests and to promote the well-being of states suffering from governmental corruption or impotence.

The extent of a great power's jurisdiction depended on the magnitude of the interest engaged by an instance of chronic wrongdoing or impotence and on its ability to project force to the afflicted state. Third, in his meditations on the Armenian genocide, Roosevelt hinted that flagrant humanitarian abuses would warrant international police action. Here again, the nearest great power would be expected to step in to head off the egregious abuses—but Roosevelt also suggested, in the context of the Turkish pogroms, that *any* nation with the wherewithal to intervene in such cases could do so, regardless of whether it was in the region of interest or whether its own interests were engaged. In this respect he seemed to envisage a sort of universal jurisdiction.

Multinational Police Actions

The example of the Boxer Rebellion notwithstanding, Theodore Roosevelt doubted whether, as a general rule, governments could cooperate effectively in constabulary operations, especially once military operations gave way to public administration. Roosevelt believed that world organization was not an immediate prospect, for the formation of a universal body awaited the coalescence of a sort of fellow-feeling akin to the patriotic affinity that united the American nation despite sharp ethnic, national, and religious cleavages. While such an evolution of world order was not unthinkable, then, it was too remote to guide policy in the here-and-now.

In the meantime Roosevelt hoped the other civilized powers, within their own spheres of interest, would adopt the vision of international policing he proposed for the United States in the Americas. He explicitly called on Europe to police adjacent territories, notably the Ottoman Empire. However, this was not a permanent but an interim solution, pending the emergence of a world body or League of Peace capable of performing constabulary duties. Once such a body was in place, national armed forces would be freed up for constabulary work within the confines of the nation-state. General arms limitations and reductions could follow, enhancing prospects for a durable peace.

Dispassionate Public Administration, the Lodestar of Constabulary Missions

Nations that embarked on constabulary operations, said TR, would be judged by the benefits their policies bestowed on native populations—not by how effectively they advanced their parochial interests. Implanting good government was the paramount goal. The constabulary function's overriding purpose was to prepare indigenous peoples for self-rule by equipping them with a political culture and institutions geared to ordered liberty, as well as the physical infrastructure needed to provide a decent life for their citizens. Roosevelt, a vocal advocate of good government throughout his public career, defined the constabulary function largely in terms of weeding out corruption from the target nation's administrative bodies. Only thus, he maintained, could the populace be spared the emergence of an oligarchy. Dispassionate execution of the constabulary function was the best way to achieve this laudable goal. He pointed to the representative institutions erected in the Philippines and Cuba, as well as the dramatic improvement in Dominican finances under American supervision, as some of his administration's proudest accomplishments.

Self-Denying Police Authority

Preserving the good name of the United States was a crucial element in Roosevelt's conception of the international police power. Once given, U.S. word must be kept. Refraining from self-aggrandizement was the key to sustaining America's credibility. TR, consequently, was fond of recalling the circumstances under which American forces had been pulled out of Cuba. "The Filipinos," he contended, "were quite incapable of standing by themselves when we took possession of the islands, and we had made no promise concerning them. But we had explicitly promised to leave the island of Cuba, had explicitly promised that Cuba should be independent. Early in my administration that promise had been redeemed." The Roosevelt administration did not take advantage of the Caribbean states' weakness to seize territory for itself. (Small parcels of land in Cuba and Panama were transferred to U.S. administration by treaty.) This was a welcome contrast with the behavior of the other great powers. Great Britain, for example, had made, and subsequently broken, a similar promise to withdraw from Egypt. And "though it is necessary for her to do so, the fact of her doing so has meant the breaking of a positive promise and has been a real evil."[3] Japan's treatment of Korea, proclaimed Roosevelt, had wrought similar misery among the Korean populace, betokening the wrong that often flowed from amoral realpolitik.

Variegated Strategy

Preparing a host country for self-government could be a laborious process, involving the use of all implements of American power:

diplomacy, naval and ground forces, law enforcement, civil administration, economic reform, and finance. In the early phases, when the
United States was likely to encounter armed resistance, constabulary
duty would exhibit a strong military flavor; witness the drawn-out
counterinsurgency effort in the Philippines. The American presence
should be as low-key as possible, especially during the high-tempo
military operations phase, to avoid conveying the impression to the
natives that an alien power had subjugated their nation.

Military government, then, should give way to something resembling normal civil government as soon as feasible. Roosevelt backed
turning over authority in the Philippines to civilian administrators,
headed by William Howard Taft, at the earliest possible date, and
thence gradually to Filipino officials and assemblymen. In Cuba, by
contrast, Leonard Wood, an army officer, oversaw the military government, but the U.S. occupation there was so fleeting that the intricate process of turning over the executive power to civil servants would
likely have been more disruptive than helpful. In Santo Domingo, the
American presence amounted to little more than a customs official
stationed on the island to oversee Dominican revenues and a U.S. Navy
warship in the harbor as a deterrent. The U.S. role, concluded Theodore
Roosevelt, was to inculcate the habits of self-rule among native populations, and that could be accomplished only by letting them progres-
sively take responsibility for their own affairs.

Expeditionary Forces for Constabulary Duty

Expeditionary capabilities, as opposed to heavy forces, were the
best tools for international constabulary duty. Depending on the circumstances, the United States would rely on the joint action of the
army, navy, and marines in international police missions. In many cases
military action would dominate the operation before giving way to
the exertions of civil servants. Order must be reestablished sufficiently
to permit the U.S. expeditionary force to organize a native constabulary and take on the executive functions of government. The marines
and army, transported by naval vessels and supported by naval gun-
fire, pacified the Philippine Islands; the army administered Cuba; and
the navy thwarted Colombian intervention in Panama, oversaw the
restoration of Dominican finances, and deterred excessive punitive
action against Venezuela by European warships. Theodore Roosevelt
used the best tool available to implement U.S. policy.

Now for the differences among the cases:

Breach of Self-Restraint in Panama

The Panama case is clearly the outlier among the six cases because Theodore Roosevelt cast off the admirable restraint that characterized his handling of the other cases (Santo Domingo excepted, of which more below). In essence he warped the text of a treaty concluded between the United States and a Latin American government beyond recognition in the service of the U.S. national interest. Under its interpretation of the treaty with Colombia, the Roosevelt administration could have stood aside and let events take their course in Panama; there was no real domestic or foreign threat to transit across the isthmus. The administration could have landed troops to safeguard the transit rights conferred by treaty. What it could not lawfully do was intervene militarily on behalf of a revolutionary faction that was warring against the very government whose sovereignty the United States had vowed to uphold. Yet that is precisely what it did.

Invoking the police power granted by the 1846 accord to justify military intervention that precisely contravened the letter and spirit of that accord was an especially audacious form of hypocrisy. Small wonder that the Latin American brethren of the United States were suspicious of Roosevelt's assertive foreign policy or that the president later felt the need to send his secretary of state on a mission to allay their apprehensions. While President Roosevelt attained his short-term goal, namely securing the fledgling Panamanian government's permission to proceed with construction of the canal, the misgivings spawned by his intemperate actions worked against American hemispheric leadership over the long haul. In short, Roosevelt's opportunism in the Panamanian intervention made a poor template for American constabulary action. Patient negotiation would have better served the goals of the administration's Latin America policy.

Breach of Self-Restraint in Santo Domingo

In the context of tumult in Santo Domingo, President Roosevelt exhibited the same troubling willingness to overlook explicit limitations on his authority and even to deploy force to implement his vision of the greater good. The Roosevelt administration trod lightly, deploying U.S. Navy warships to back up its modus vivendi, a modest arrangement that involved little more than placing a customs agent on the island to administer Dominican finances and repay the government's foreign debt. To be sure, Roosevelt's sins in the Dominican case were minor relative to his actions during the revolution in Panama: pursuant to the modus vivendi, he directed the on-scene navy commander to suppress revolution on the island until the Senate acted on the accord entrusting control of the customs facilities to the United States. True to his Lincoln-Jackson philosophy of executive power, he acted unless specifically forbidden to do so.

Breach of Self-Restraint in Drafting the Roosevelt Corollary

The language employed in President Roosevelt's 1904 message to Congress, replete with lordly references to "chronic wrongdoing," "impotence," and intervention by a "civilized"—and by implication superior—power was bound to raise hackles among the other Western Hemisphere republics. And Roosevelt, who preached a refreshing gospel of tactful yet forceful diplomacy, clearly should have known better. Indifference to cultural differences was Roosevelt's Achilles heel, on display in his treatment not only of China but also of Latin Americans who for cultural reasons were already primed to take offense at hints of Anglo-Saxon superiority. TR would have been better advised to heed his own advice and conduct himself with the circumspection that characterized his handling of the Cuban, Philippine, and Venezuelan cases. His own Big Stick philosophy was a sure guide to diplomacy.

Conception of the Police Power Less Heavy-Handed over Time

Roosevelt's international police-power concept had its genesis in the mid-1890s when he enthusiastically endorsed Richard Olney's theory of practical U.S. sovereignty over the New World. From time to time he mused about a U.S. protectorate over the Americas. But the basic trend in his thinking was toward a more limited vision of international police duty, in which international negotiation and mediation were the instruments of choice, supplemented as necessary by civil administration and backed up by shows of force. The police terminology appeared for the first time as early as Roosevelt's 1901 message, but his vision of the police power did not fully mature until the Santo Domingo case, which inspired his corollary to the Monroe Doctrine. The United States had extended the federal government's police powers to Cuba and the Philippines by right of conquest, enshrined in the terms of the Treaty of Paris. While President McKinley had made the decision to administer the islands, Roosevelt no doubt applauded his predecessor's choice. But the Spanish-American War was a singular event that conferred singular powers on the U.S. government.

The blockade of Venezuela persuaded TR that an expansive sort of protectorate over Latin America was in order. The episode inspired him to graft the principles of 1823 onto the quasi-protectorate he contemplated, giving his corollary both an offensive and a defensive flavor. In the end the standoff over Santo Domingo impelled him to proclaim a limited and transitory police power whose foundations lay in the legal concepts of national sovereignty and self-defense. For Roosevelt the Monroe Doctrine was not a license to assert de facto sovereignty over Latin America. It simply explained that the United States would exercise the international police power preemptively to head off European territorial encroachment.

Morocco Demonstrates Continuing Importance of Great-Power Politics

The Morocco affair, a dissimilar case, demonstrated that, for TR, internal police mechanics took second place to great-power equilibrium. In 1905–6 European peace and, by extension, the safety of the New World, seemed to hang in the balance. For Roosevelt, preserving the West against a great-power conflagration that would imperil the demesnes of peace and justice superseded relatively trivial concerns, such as thrashing out which European power should be authorized to oversee the Moroccan police in which Mediterranean seaport. It seems, then, that TR's "second corollary"—which enjoined U.S. intervention in great-power politics to arrest confrontations before they could degenerate into fratricidal war—trumped the Roosevelt Corollary when the security of the civilized world and, thus, the prospects for international peace and justice were at stake.

Principles of International Constabulary Duty

In general Roosevelt merits high marks for consistency. The fundamental themes underlying the police power boil down to the following:

- The civilized powers could lawfully intervene in countries unable or unwilling to discharge the responsibilities that went along with national sovereignty. For example, a government culpable for chronic wrongdoing, one justification offered for international police action, might have failed to live up to its sovereign responsibilities by refusing to pay off foreign loans or protect foreign nationals residing on its soil. Governmental impotence signaled an inability to maintain internal order, to discharge obligations to foreign nationals and governments, or to carry out the host of obligations that accompanied the privileges of sovereignty.

- The international police power ultimately resided in the community of civilized states, a community which proponents of the republican peace hoped would ultimately span the globe. Thus Roosevelt seemed to believe individual states, regional organizations, ad hoc multilateral coalitions, or a universal international organization, should one emerge, could lawfully intervene in cases of governmental impotence or chronic wrongdoing. He found legal justification for diplomatic and military intervention in the principles of national self-defense and sovereignty, as well as a deficiency of international law—namely, the lack of a multinational police force.

- Because the international police power was rooted in fundamental precepts of international law, civilized nations needed not seek the approval of other nations before embarking on constabulary missions. Indeed, the want of a central authority commanding a monopoly on legitimate force demanded that great powers such as the United States, Europe, Japan, and the advanced Latin American republics act in its stead to buoy world order. Pending the coalescence of wider feelings of kinship than patriotism, without which a muscular international organization would be untenable, the great powers must shoulder the responsibility for maintaining order and promoting uplift in their geographic spheres of interest.

- While constabulary operations would inevitably foster concrete national interests such as regional balances of power, defense of vital sea-lanes, and the integrity of the Western Hemisphere—neither nations nor individuals could be realistically expected to ignore their own self-interest—international constabulary missions must be visibly altruistic in execution. Their aims must benefit the interests and well-being of nations subjected to great-power intervention, as well as the parochial interests of policing nations. Otherwise the missions would spark a backlash of the less-developed world against the civilized powers and could lead to debilitating warfare.

- Physical power must underwrite international police actions. Ideally, forceful diplomacy—the exploitation of potential force—would lead to pacific great-power adjustment of the dispute, in the bargain avoiding actual bloodshed. Expeditionary military capabilities were the foundation of international police operations. The strategy underpinning international constabulary duty involved introducing military forces to stabilize the country, to erect an indigenous constabulary, to put the country's finances on a sound footing, and to support the many nonmilitary tasks necessary to prepare the citizenry for republican self-rule. This could be a long, painstaking process. The constabulary function, then, involved far more than military strategy.

Final Thoughts on Roosevelt's Police-Power Doctrine

The analysis undertaken here has demonstrated that an international police power existed in Theodore Roosevelt's worldview, that Roosevelt regarded the police power as an instrument of international Progressivism, and that it had a life both independent of the Monroe Doctrine and rooted in international law. Mentions of the police power appeared in TR's correspondence throughout his public life and, indeed, were often so casual as to suggest that he thought the police power was a routine, even self-evident, component of American statecraft. Certain conditions demanded that an advanced nation take on military and constabulary duty beyond its borders, even if such action meant a trial of arms. But should the major powers of today's world resuscitate the police power as a device to promote world order?

Yes and no. Consider the negatives. First, reviving the police power in connection with Roosevelt's legacy would be a tall order, if only because of the stigma attached to American imperialism. Imperialism is regarded as the supreme iniquity in policy circles and on campuses throughout the West, and the relatively mild American strain is typically grouped with that practiced by the European powers. At the very least, then, explicitly founding a new foreign-policy doctrine on TR's diplomacy would involve burnishing his reputation as a diplomat in the halls of Washington and on campus. Making inroads against the orthodox view of Rooseveltian diplomacy would be a slow, uncertain process of little immediate utility.

Second, judging by their own words, even Roosevelt's intimates did not share his full-fledged vision of an international police power implemented under the guise of the Monroe Doctrine. That should give latter-day observers pause. In his learned discussions of the doctrine, for instance, Elihu Root never mentioned the police power by name, preferring to premise his arguments on self-defense and sovereignty. Never did he embrace Roosevelt's notion that a power of legislation and regulation inhered in the international community. While they loudly supported the doctrine, neither did Henry Cabot Lodge, William Howard Taft, John Bassett Moore, or Leonard Wood come out in support of constabulary duty. Had TR simply outpaced the thinking of his contemporaries? Perhaps. Whatever the case, the legal and academic literature of his day provides scant sustenance for Roosevelt's international police-power theory. It would be difficult to justify reviving a doctrine that seemingly commanded tepid support even among TR's more worshipful associates.

Third, and most importantly, a resuscitated international police power could lend itself to abuse by the great powers, much as similar claims of authority did for the European powers in the nineteenth century. The sleight-of-hand by which Roosevelt converted the police power on the isthmus into a justification for intervening against Colombia, in clear contradiction of U.S. treaty obligations, provides grounds for concern. Indeed, the Panama episode sparked the ire even of Samuel Flagg Bemis, ordinarily a redoubtable defender of American diplomacy. And Roosevelt's order to the U.S. Navy to suppress revolution on Santo Domingo while Congress dithered over the treaty illuminated the ease with which consent sometimes blends into coercion in international politics. Scrupulous fidelity to international agreements would do much to ease the doubts of nations that fear they might become the targets of unjust military action. In shackling the pretensions of later generations of statesmen, the Founding Fathers had wisely declined to entrust arbitrary power to anyone and, indeed, deliberately devised a political system that checked the ambitions of demagogues. Some sort of barrier to self-aggrandizement would be needed before the police power could be deployed by the great powers today.

What of endowing the United Nations with the police power? Some of the First World War–era correspondence between Roosevelt and his intimates suggests how TR would have regarded a universalized police power. Judging by his commentary on the League of Nations, he would have opposed the creation of an international body able to thwart the liberty of action enjoyed by the United States, impair the nation's sovereignty, or infringe on the Monroe Doctrine. Henry Cabot Lodge put it best: In 1918, just after the armistice ending the First World War, and as the haggling over the postwar order heated up, Senator Lodge confided to TR, "One very dangerous thing is this League of Peace. It is easy to state the name. Everybody wants peace preserved; but the details are vital, and I do not believe the United States will consent or ought to consent to join any international body which would . . . control the Monroe Doctrine or our actions in our own hemisphere, or have power to order our army or navy." Lodge welcomed the ex-president's support for the Republican fight to amend the Versailles Treaty: "I know indeed how you are backing us up in every way, and it is of vast importance to us to have your sympathy and support."[4] The view summarized by Lodge accorded closely with TR's patriotic internationalism, as well as his belief that enlightened great powers should police their own geographic neighborhoods and cooperate to enforce peace and spread civilization's blessings. A world organization could not be allowed to subvert America's freedom of action.

None of this is to say that Theodore Roosevelt's vision of the constabulary function lacked merit. Far from it. Roosevelt provided an appealing vision of a brawny America that, while jealous of its own national interests, had responsibilities abroad commensurate with its growing power. His political thought stands as a rebuke both to those who insist that interest is the keystone of American diplomacy and to those who maintain that American policy should be purely idealistic. Unlike politicians who shroud their programs in unvarnished idealism, TR readily admitted that self-interest is indispensable to any diplomatic or military endeavor worth undertaking. Integrating altruism into American foreign policy in an age when realpolitik remained the dominant strain of international politics was a striking innovation. In line with his vehement Americanism, moreover, Roosevelt refused to subordinate patriotism to multilateralism. Since he prophesied that allegiance to a broader political entity was "eons distant," abandoning patriotism would have been fruitless. In the meantime, the civilized powers' patriotic action was the only realistic substitute for an international police force. Thus the international police-power doctrine conformed admirably to both the realities of world politics of his day and to an American political culture that prized patriotic sentiment.

And Roosevelt, it seems, sincerely meant his professions of benevolence. Great responsibilities went along with great power. TR declared adamantly that government was a beneficent force in society, equipped to nurture civilization and moral virtue both at home and abroad. His advocacy of helping countries beset with incompetent or tyrannical governments realize republican self-government makes a useful prism through which to scrutinize international military operations today. Roosevelt's argument that the corollary, by foreclosing European meddling in the affairs of the Americas, would advance both U.S. and Latin American interests rang true. During his presidency the United States abstained from interfering in countries outside the Caribbean littoral, assuaging Latin American misgivings on that score. With a couple of exceptions, TR refrained from labeling countries that displeased him as "savage" or using the specter of military intervention to strong-arm their leaders. Only the most serious cases of wrongdoing or governmental incompetence triggered U.S. interference. TR's palpable reluctance to interfere in Dominican affairs helped matters, while his circumspect yet firm diplomacy ensured that the operations in Santo Domingo and Panama remained bloodless and therefore fairly uncontroversial (despite the other qualms his actions in those two cases inspire). The Rooseveltian diplomatic enterprise, then, serves as an effective reminder to keep moral virtue in mind and to exercise restraint when deploying American power.

The international police power's self-denying character warns posterity to avoid the pitfalls of European imperialism. The United States could act to prevent the great powers from using the chronic wrongdoing and impotence by the Caribbean republics, alarmingly close to vital sea-lanes, as an excuse to seize New World territory. It could not wrest away new holdings of its own under the rubric of self-defense. Excluding great-power intrigues from the Western Hemisphere was a boon not only for the United States but also for Latin Americans, who thus remained free to find their own path to ordered liberty. Nourishing order in the Caribbean Basin, and implicitly throughout the Western Hemisphere, promised to expand the advanced world in keeping with the doctrine of the republican peace. Thus Rooseveltian diplomacy furthered U.S. humanitarian aims while holding out the prospect of ultimately enhancing the Republic's tangible interests, such as defending the approaches to the Panama Canal, searching out new foreign markets, and keeping defense spending at a fairly low level. TR's formula, alloying idealism with realism, makes an attractive model for contemporary American statecraft.

The notion of geographical spheres of interest reminds statesmen of the limitations of physical power. No great power can hope to police the world indefinitely without exhausting itself materially and morally. Nor should it try, for fear of needlessly angering the countries whose cooperation is crucial to preserving world order. Because of its unrivaled military might, the twenty-first-century United States should be prepared to lead operations that directly infringe its national interests or offend the humanitarian sentiments of the American people. Short of that, it should be prepared to yield pride of place to local great powers such as Europe, Japan, Russia, and India. Extrapolating from Roosevelt's commentary on international policing, it seems probable that TR would applaud the European Union's effort to develop an expeditionary capability that would allow Brussels to take up the burden of policing the European periphery. Japan, Argentina, Brazil, and Chile also earned his endorsement. For its part, the United States should husband its own resources to intervene in the most egregious cases of wrongdoing or impotence.

Perhaps the most important lessons of Roosevelt's experience with international constabulary missions concern "nation building." TR preferred that military action give way to civil administration at the earliest opportunity. Civil authorities were far better suited for building infrastructure, erecting local governments, and tackling the many other tasks involved in preparing durable republics. Roosevelt's enthusiasm for Taft's work in the Philippine Islands testified to the importance the president attached to good government. Cultivating a culture of self-rule would consume time. Roosevelt, consequently, believed that the United States should not fix arbitrary deadlines for the completion of police missions. He declined to promise the Filipinos their independence, and he seemed prepared to carry on with administering Dominican finances indefinitely. He insisted that the United States would pull out of a country once it was satisfied that its political objectives there had been met, usually when Americans had stabilized the government and, in more far-reaching cases such as Cuba and the Philippines, instilled the habits and institutions necessary for republican self-government. If an operation was worth undertaking, then, the United States should be prepared to stay the course.

In the final analysis, Theodore Roosevelt's international police-power doctrine is better suited for use as an analytical tool than as a direct template for twenty-first-century statecraft. Roosevelt furnishes guidance for evaluating potential candidates for intervention and instructs contemporary statesmen on many of the particulars involved with international constabulary duty. And his invocation of moral virtue as the foundation of American diplomacy, combined with attention to the national interest, is a useful reminder in an age when American foreign policy seems to fluctuate erratically between do-goodism and a barren devotion to "vital national interests." Both Roosevelt's faults and virtues, then, suggest how international police work ought to be done. Roosevelt bade Americans to do good works in the service of world order and the national interest, while his example at times illustrates the temptations and pitfalls that accompany bold endeavor. In short, his example enjoins statesmen to dexterously interweave idealism and hardheaded practicality. Returning practical wisdom to its rightful place in American statecraft would be no mean accomplishment—especially for a relic of the Progressive Era.

NOTES

Chapter 1

1. United Nations, *Charter of the United Nations and Statute of the International Court of Justice* (New York: United Nations, 1945; reprint, New York: UN Department of Public Information, 1993), 5, 29–30.

2. Hugo Grotius, *The Law of War and Peace*, trans. Louise R. Loomis (Paris, 1625; reprint, New York: Walter J. Black, 1949), 262–63.

3. Theodore Roosevelt, "Message of the President to the Senate and the House of Representatives," December 6, 1904, in U.S. Department of State, *Foreign Relations of the United States, 1904* (Washington, DC: Government Printing Office, 1905), xli. (Hereafter *FRUS: 19xx*.)

4. The term "international police power" is used here to refer to the quasi-legal authority Roosevelt invoked to justify diplomatic action in certain circumstances. When discussing the strategies used to execute international police actions, however, the author frequently refers to a "constabulary function," namely the use of the implements of national power to carry out such police actions. Military and police functions are elements in this broader mode of international intervention. A new term seemed necessary to escape commentators' use of the term "police action" to describe everything from full-scale war in Korea to the use of law enforcement to round up members of al Qaeda.

5. Howard K. Beale, *Theodore Roosevelt and the Rise of America to World Power* (Baltimore: Johns Hopkins Press, 1956); Frederick W. Marks III, *Velvet on Iron: The Diplomacy of Theodore Roosevelt* (Lincoln: University of Nebraska Press, 1979); Richard H. Collin, *Theodore Roosevelt, Culture, Diplomacy, and Expansion: A New View of American Imperialism* (Baton Rouge: Louisiana State University Press, 1985); and *Theodore Roosevelt's Caribbean: The Panama Canal, the Monroe Doctrine, and the Latin American Context* (Baton Rouge: Louisiana State University Press, 1990).

6. Kissinger later claimed that TR, unlike Wilson, had "rejected the supposed efficacy of international law." Henry Kissinger, *Diplomacy* (New York: Simon & Schuster, 1994), 54, and *Does America Need a*

Foreign Policy? Towards a Diplomacy for the 21st Century (New York: Simon & Schuster, 2002), 240–43.

7. Another possible reason for this oversight is that many historians adhere to the Progressive tradition, which was closely associated with U.S. imperialism. This association understandably inspires discomfort. Richard Hofstadter writes of the "curiously persistent association between democratic politics and nationalism, jingoism, or war." Richard Hofstadter, *The Age of Reform: From Bryan to F. D. R.* (New York: Knopf, 1955), 272–75. Walter A. McDougall also affirms the Progressive roots of imperialism, crediting the Spanish-American War, America's first foray into imperialism, with launching the Progressive Era at home. Walter McDougall, *Promised Land, Crusader State: The American Encounter with the World since 1776* (Boston: Houghton Mifflin, 1997). Finally, Andrew J. Birtle (*U.S. Army Counterinsurgency and Contingency Operations Doctrine, 1860–1941* [Washington, DC: Center of Military History, 1998], 101–103) observes that the U.S. Army had derived from its experiences in the American West and in overseas ventures in Cuba and the Philippines "a rough blueprint for social engineering in which well-meaning experts, in the guise of Army officers, would bestow on a grateful society a host of social, political, and economic reforms designed to produce a more efficient and honest government and a more modern, rational, and organized society . . . the Army not only implemented the Progressive impulse, but blazed new trails in government activism that Progressives at home were destined to follow."

8. Alan K. Henrikson, *Defining a New World Order: Toward a Practical Vision of Collective Action for International Peace and Security* (Medford, MA: The Fletcher School of Law and Diplomacy, Tufts University, 1991).

9. Theodore Roosevelt, *The Letters of Theodore Roosevelt*, ed. Elting E. Morison and others, 8 vols. (Cambridge: Harvard University Press, 1951–54). (Hereafter *Letters*)

10. Theodore Roosevelt, *Memorial Edition: Works of Theodore Roosevelt*, ed. Hermann Hagedorn, 24 vols. (New York: Charles Scribner's Sons, 1923–26). (Hereafter *Works: Memorial*); Theodore Roosevelt, *National Edition: Works of Theodore Roosevelt*, ed. Hermann Hagedorn, 20 vols. (New York: Charles Scribner's Sons, 1926) (hereafter *Works: National*).

11. *FRUS:1901–8*.

12. Carl Schurz, "'American Imperialism,' The Convocation Address, Delivered on the Occasion of the Twenty-seventh Convocation of the University of Chicago, January 4, 1899" (Sanford, NC:

Microfilming Corp. of America, 1982); "'For American Principles and American Honor,' An Address by Hon. Carl Schurz Delivered in Cooper Union, New York, May 24, 1900" (New York: Anti-Imperialist League of New York, 1900; reprint, Sanford, NC: Microfilming Corp. of America, 1982); *Reminiscences of Carl Schurz*, 3 vols. (London: John Murray, 1909). See also William Jennings Bryan, *The Memoirs of William Jennings Bryan, By Himself and His Wife Mary Baird Bryan* (Port Washington, NY: Kennikat Press, 1971); and Robert L. Beisner, *Twelve against Empire: The Anti-Imperialists, 1898–1900* (New York: McGraw-Hill, 1968).

13. Theodore Roosevelt, "Message of the President to the Senate and the House of Representatives," December 8, 1908, in *FRUS: 1908*, XLIV.

Chapter 2

1. See for example TR's account of "The Spread of the English-Speaking Peoples," in Roosevelt, *Works: Memorial*, vol. 10, *The Winning of the West*, 1–26.

2. Theodore Roosevelt, *Theodore Roosevelt: An Autobiography* (New York: Macmillan, 1913; reprint, with intro. by Elting E. Morison, New York: Da Capo, 1985), 7.

3. Theodore Roosevelt to Hamlin Garland, July 19, 1903, in *Letters*, vol. 3, 520.

4. Although he was not outspokenly religious, religious principles clearly underlay much of TR's philosophy. For instance, he often invoked the Golden Rule and declared that the eighth and ninth commandments should be the two cardinal principles for public officials. Theodore Roosevelt, "The Eighth and Ninth Commandments in Politics," *Outlook*, May 12, 1900, in *Works: National*, vol. 13, *The Strenuous Life: Essays and Addresses*, 387–90.

5. Theodore Roosevelt to Edward Sanford Martin, November 26, 1900, in *Letters*, vol. 2, 1443.

6. Asked to list the "kinds of books one ought to read," TR disgorged dozens of titles. The nonfiction titles included works by Herodotus, Polybius, Thucydides, Aristotle, and Lincoln. The exercise of virtue was common to these works. Theodore Roosevelt to Nicholas Murray Butler, November 4, 1903, in *Letters*, vol. 3, 642–44.

7. Roosevelt, *Autobiography*, 29.

8. Theodore Roosevelt to Martha Baker Dunn, September 6, 1902,

in *Letters*, vol. 3, 324–25. He also lauded the *Saga* in his autobiography and urged American parents to use children's literature as a tool of moral instruction. Roosevelt, *Autobiography*, 18.

9. Howard Beale declares of TR that it is "a little hard to define from his speeches and writings" the attributes of the superior Western civilization he extolled. A "strong mixture of manly virtues, of industrial development, of power to defend oneself effectively" was part of it, along with "an ability to provide orderly government, an inherited set of political institutions superior to those of anyone else, and respect for free individuals, and for the various freedoms won through the centuries by Western Europeans." These elements were readily apparent in the *Saga of King Olaf*. Beale, *Rise of America*, 46–47. See also Collin, *Theodore Roosevelt, Culture, Diplomacy, and Expansion*.

10. Henry Wadsworth Longfellow, *The Complete Poetical Works of Henry Wadsworth Longfellow*, ed. Horace E. Scudder (Boston: Houghton Mifflin, 1893), 218, 226–27.

11. In his autobiography TR proudly noted that his great-great-grandfather, Archibald Bulloch, had been the first president of revolutionary Georgia. He recounted the Civil War exploits of two uncles who had served in the legendary Confederate raider *Alabama*. The young TR staunchly backed the Union cause; he nonetheless embraced the gallantry of his uncles and of the Confederate armies at large. Roosevelt, *Autobiography*, 1–12.

12. Theodore Roosevelt to William Gibbs McAdoo, November 17, 1903, in *Letters*, vol. 3, 655. The terminology TR used in this letter foreshadowed his approach to constitutional law. Like other "broad constructionists," he refused to let the letter of the Constitution impede his pursuit of his vision of social justice and other overriding goods.

13. Roosevelt admired what he called the "Lincoln-Jackson" school of presidential decision making, which favored strong executive action. As he admitted, his views exhibited a strong Southern flair. Eugene D. Genovese, "The Chivalric Tradition in the Old South," *Sewanee Review*, Spring 2000: 188–205. See also Eugene D. Genovese, *The Southern Tradition: The Achievement and Limitations of an American Conservatism* (Cambridge: Harvard University Press, 1994); Walter Russell Mead, "The Jacksonian Tradition and American Foreign Policy," *The National Interest* 58 (Winter 1999/2000): 5–29; and Walter Russell Mead, *Special Providence: American Foreign Policy and How It Changed the World* (New York: Knopf, 2003), especially 3–29, 218–63.

14. Writing in the 1940s, W. J. Cash documented the romantic views elite and ordinary white Southerners entertained about their past. W. J. Cash, *The Mind of the South* (New York: Knopf, 1941), 82–83, 122–30.

15. Thomas Roderick Dew, in Genovese, "Chivalric Tradition," 203.

16. William Henry Holcombe, in Genovese, "Chivalric Tradition," 197.

17. Theodore Roosevelt Sr., in Carleton Putnam, *Theodore Roosevelt: The Formative Years, 1858–1886* (New York: Charles Scribner's Sons, 1958), 33.

18. Roosevelt, *Autobiography*, 7–10.

19. Roosevelt to Martin, November 26, 1900, 1443.

20. Roosevelt, *Autobiography*, 27–28.

21. Theodore Roosevelt, in Elting E. Morison, intro. to *Letters*, vol. 8, xvi.

22. Theodore Roosevelt to Edward Sanford Martin, July 30, 1903, in *Letters*, vol. 3, 535–36. President Roosevelt, writes Edward Renehan, viewed the Four Hundred as "a self-indulgent collection of elitist snobs 'with whom other members of the family have exceedingly few affiliations.'" Edward J. Renehan Jr., *The Lion's Pride: Theodore Roosevelt and His Family in Peace and War* (New York: Oxford University Press, 1998), 47.

23. Theodore Roosevelt to Robert Bacon, April 5, 1898, in *Letters*, vol. 2, 811.

24. Theodore Roosevelt to John Campbell Greenway, October 5, 1903, in *Letters*, vol. 3, 618.

25. Theodore Roosevelt, "The Enforcement of Law," *Forum* 20 (September 1895): 10.

26. Theodore Roosevelt, "True Americanism," *Forum* 17 (April 1894), in *Works: National*, vol. 13, *American Ideals*, 13–26.

27. Theodore Roosevelt, "Character and Success," *Outlook*, March 31, 1900, in *Works: National*, vol. 13, 381–86.

28. Roosevelt, "True Americanism," 25.

29. Theodore Roosevelt, "Fellow-Feeling as a Political Factor," *Century*, June 1900, in *Works: National*, vol. 13, 355–68.

30. Theodore Roosevelt, "What Americanism Means," *Forum* 17 (April 1894): 196–206.

31. Roosevelt, "True Americanism," 13–26.

32. Theodore Roosevelt to George Ferdinand Becker, September 6, 1899, in *Letters*, vol. 2, 1067–68.

33. Theodore Roosevelt to Frederic René Coudert, July 3, 1901, in *Letters*, vol. 3, 105.

34. Roosevelt, "True Americanism," 15.

35. Theodore Roosevelt to Franklin Woodruff Moulton, April 12, 1899, in *Letters*, vol. 2, 987.

36. TR quoted Burke—the only political philosopher so distinguished—in two of his annual messages. The Irish parliamentarian, the president declared, belonged to the same pantheon as Demosthenes, Cicero, and Lincoln. Theodore Roosevelt to Nicholas Murray Butler, October 29, 1903, in *Letters*, vol. 3, 642; Theodore Roosevelt to Richard Watson Gilder, April 1, 1893, in *Letters*, vol. 1, 311–12.

37. Theodore Roosevelt to John St. Loe Strachey, March 8, 1901, in *Letters*, vol. 3, 8.

38. Edmund Burke, "Letter to the Sheriffs of Bristol," in David P. Fidler and Jennifer M. Welsh, eds., *Empire and Community: Edmund Burke's Writings and Speeches on International Relations* (Boulder, CO: Westview Press, 1999), 160.

39. Fidler and Welsh, *Empire and Community*, 160–62.

40. The aspiring politician "must sacrifice somewhat of his own opinions . . . if he ever hopes to see his ideas take practical shape." Theodore Roosevelt, "The Manly Virtues and Practical Politics," *Forum* 17 (April 1894): 551–57.

41. Theodore Roosevelt to Cecil Arthur Spring Rice, August 12, 1899, in *Letters*, vol. 2, 1054.

42. Theodore Roosevelt, "Message of the President to the Senate and the House of Representatives," December 8, 1908, in *FRUS, 1908*, XVII.

43. Theodore Roosevelt, "The Best and the Good," *Churchman*, March 17, 1900, http://www.bartleby.com/58/8.html (accessed November 15, 1998).

44. As a New York Republican assemblyman, for example, TR cooperated with Grover Cleveland, then the Democratic governor, to push civil-service reform legislation that was unpopular with both machines. Edmund Morris, *The Rise of Theodore Roosevelt* (New

York: Ballantine Books, 1979; reprint, New York: Modern Library, 2001), 176–79.

45. Theodore Roosevelt to George Otto Trevelyan, March 9, 1905, in *Letters*, vol. 4, 1132.

46. Theodore Roosevelt to Cecil Arthur Spring Rice, December 27, 1904, in *Letters*, vol. 4, 1083.

47. Theodore Roosevelt to Preble Tucker, October 22, 1895, in *Letters*, vol. 1, 490–92.

48. Theodore Roosevelt to Theodore Roosevelt Jr., October 4, 1903, in Theodore Roosevelt, *Theodore Roosevelt's Letters to His Children*, ed. Joseph Bucklin Bishop (New York: Charles Scribner's Sons, 1923), 61–66.

49. Theodore Roosevelt to Anna Roosevelt Cowles, July 16, 1896, in *Letters*, vol. 1, 550.

50. Theodore Roosevelt to Thomas Collier Platt, May 8, 1899, in *Letters*, vol. 2, 1005.

51. Theodore Roosevelt to James S. Clarkson, May 27, 1903, in *Letters*, vol. 3, 482.

52. Theodore Roosevelt to James Bryce, November 25, 1898, in *Letters*, vol. 2, 889.

53. Roosevelt to Platt, May 8, 1899, 1004–1009.

54. Theodore Roosevelt to Henry L. Sprague, January 16, 1900, in *Letters*, vol. 2, 1141.

55. On one occasion TR admonished the staff of *McClure's*, arguing that profiling abuses by the wealthy while neglecting those of the poor fostered a mindset similar to that which had led to the Terror in France. Theodore Roosevelt to Samuel Sydney McClure, October 4, 1905, in *Letters*, vol. 5, 45.

56. Theodore Roosevelt, "Message of the President to the Senate and the House of Representatives," December 5, 1905, in *FRUS: 1905*, XXIII.

57. Theodore Roosevelt to George Otto Trevelyan, September 12, 1905, in *Letters*, vol. 5, 22–25.

58. William Allen White, "Roosevelt: A Force for Righteousness," *McClure's* 28 (January 1907): 393.

59. Theodore Roosevelt to William Howard Taft, March 15, 1906, in *Letters*, vol. 5, 183–84.

60. TR prescribed works such as Croly's *Promise of American Life*, one of the sacred texts of the Progressive movement, as an antidote to radical individualism. Roosevelt, *Autobiography*, 27.

61. Progressives worried about business combinations. Antitrust law was an effective check against corporate wrongdoing. For TR, however, conduct, not size, was the proper measure. "A combination should not be tolerated if it abuse the power acquired by combination to the public detriment." Theodore Roosevelt, "Message of the President to the Senate and the House of Representatives," December 3, 1907, in *FRUS: 1907*, xv.

62. Theodore Roosevelt, in Charles R. Kesler, "Teddy Roosevelt to the Rescue?" *The National Interest* 52 (Summer 1998): 108.

63. Hofstadter, *Age of Reform*, 239–71.

64. Theodore Roosevelt, "True American Ideals," *Forum* 18 (February 1895): 746–47.

65. Theodore Roosevelt to Edgar Brackett, March 17, 1900, in *Letters*, vol. 2, 1230–31.

66. Roosevelt decried the amoral legalism he encountered at Columbia Law School. The doctrine of caveat emptor, or let-the-buyer-beware, he said, encouraged deceptive practices. Roosevelt, *Autobiography*, 55.

67. Theodore Roosevelt to Leonard Wood, April 9, 1900, in *Letters*, vol. 2, 1251.

68. Theodore Roosevelt to Henry Loomis Nelson, April 8, 1901, in *Letters*, vol. 3, 44.

69. Roosevelt, "1908 Annual Message," xxvi–xxvii.

70. Roosevelt to Nelson, April 8, 1901, 44.

71. Theodore Roosevelt to John Davis Long, December 9, 1897, in *Letters*, vol. 1, 727. His engineering perspective exemplified the Progressive movement's faith in the power of technical experts to solve social problems.

72. Theodore Roosevelt, in Kesler, "Teddy Roosevelt to the Rescue?" 108.

73. Hofstadter, *Age of Reform*, 242.

Chapter 3

1. Owen J. Roberts, *The Court and the Constitution: The Oliver Wendell Holmes Lectures* (Cambridge: Harvard University Press, 1951), 37.

2. *Gibbons v. Ogden*, 22 U.S. (9 Wheat.) 1, 202 (1824).

3. *Barbier v. Connolly*, 113 U.S. 27; 5 S. Ct. 357 (1884). See also John Randolph Tucker, *The Constitution of the United States: A Critical Discussion of Its Genesis, Development, and Interpretation*, ed. Henry St. George Tucker (Chicago: Callaghan, 1899), 859–60. Says Westlaw, the legal research service, "The police power embraces the protection of the lives, health, and property of citizens, the maintenance of good order, and the preservation of good morals."

4. That is, the clause mandating that no state "shall deprive any person of life, liberty, or property without due process of law, nor deny to any person within its jurisdiction the equal protection of the laws."

5. *Barbier v. Connolly*, 113 U.S. 27; 5 S. Ct. 357.

6. *Barbier v. Connolly*, 113 U.S. 27; 5 S. Ct. 357.

7. Roberts, *Court and the Constitution*, 1–2.

8. Roberts, *Court and the Constitution*, 37–38. As the New Deal got underway in the 1930s, the Supreme Court declared, "the authority of the federal government over interstate commerce does not differ in extent or character from that retained by the states over intrastate commerce." *United States v. Rock Royal Co-operative*, 307 U.S. 533, 569 (1939). The Court defined "commerce" as equivalent to the phrase "intercourse for the purpose of trade," defined as transportation, purchase, sale, and exchange of commodities between the citizens of the different states. *Carter v. Carter Coal Co.*, 298 U.S. 238, 298 (1936). "Regulation," finally, was defined as the declaring of the rule by which commerce is to be governed. It embraced measures intended to foster and protect commerce between the states, including those that prohibited commerce in certain commodities. *Gibbons v. Odgen*, 9 Wheat. 1, 196 (1824); *The Daniel Ball*, 10 Wall. 557, 564 (1871); *Mobile County v. Kimball*, 102 U.S. 691 (1880); *Second Employers' Liability Cases*, 223 U.S. 1 (1912); *United States v. Carolene Products Co.*, 304 U.S. 144 (1938).

9. A list of such statutes and the decisions upholding them can be found in *Kentucky Whip and Collar Co. v. Illinois Central R.R.*, 299 U.S. 334, at 346 (1937).

10. See, for example, *Standard Oil Co. v. United States*, 221 U.S. 1 (1911).

11. Roberts, *Court and the Constitution*, 39–41.

12. Roberts, *Court and the Constitution*, 38–42.

13. *Shreveport* case, 234 U.S. 342 (1914).

14. See, for example, *Kidd v. Pearson*, 128 U.S. 1, 20, 21, 22 (1888);

United States v. E. C. Knight Co., 156 U.S. 1, 12, 13 (1895); *Hopkins v. United States*, 171 U.S. 578 (1898). By the Franklin Roosevelt era, the Court had cleared away many of the obstacles to federal action in areas formerly thought to be the exclusive domain of state and local governments.

15. Roosevelt to Trevelyan, March 9, 1905, 1132–35. (See ch. 2, n. 47.)

16. Theodore Roosevelt to Ray Stannard Baker, August 27, 1904, in *Letters*, vol. 4, 908. In a much earlier letter, TR defied critics of the Civil Service Commission, then under his direction, to unearth any evidence that his staff had engaged in partisan politics or discriminated by race or creed. Theodore Roosevelt to Alexander Monroe Dockery, May 24, 1894, in *Letters*, vol. 1, 380.

17. Theodore Roosevelt to Joseph Bucklin Bishop, April 11, 1900, in *Letters*, vol. 2, 1256–57.

18. Theodore Roosevelt to Henry White, October 28, 1895, in *Letters*, vol. 1, 492.

19. Theodore Roosevelt to Francis B. Delahunty, April 19, 1900, in *Letters*, vol. 2, 1267.

20. Theodore Roosevelt to Henry Cabot Lodge, September 9, 1900, in *Letters*, vol. 3, 141.

21. For TR, lynching embodied the mob spirit. In wording that evoked his corollary, he declared, "lynching represents by just so much a loosening of the bands of civilization." Theodore Roosevelt, "Message of the President to the Senate and the House of Representatives," December 3, 1906, in *FRUS: 1906*, xiv–xvi.

22. Theodore Roosevelt to Jacob E. Bausch, January 12, 1897, in *Letters*, vol. 1, 575.

23. Roosevelt to Platt, May 8, 1899, 1005. (See ch. 2, n. 52.)

Chapter 4

1. Robert V. Friedenberg, *Theodore Roosevelt and the Rhetoric of Militant Decency* (New York: Greenwood, 1990).

2. Roosevelt, "1908 Annual Message," xii–xiii. "On the other hand," TR pointed out, this cut both ways: "those who advocate proper control on behalf of the public, through the State, of these great corporations, and of the wealth engaged on a giant scale in business operations, must ever keep in mind that unless they do scrupulous justice

to the corporation, unless they permit ample profit, and cordially encourage capable men of business so long as they act with honesty, they are striking at the root of our national wellbeing."

3. Roosevelt, "1908 Annual Message," x.

4. Roosevelt, "1908 Annual Message," xiv.

5. Roosevelt, "1908 Annual Message," xvi.

6. Theodore Roosevelt to the State Board of Mediation and Arbitration, April 17, 1900, in *Letters*, vol. 2, 1265.

7. Theodore Roosevelt to Henry Cabot Lodge, April 17, 1900, in *Letters*, vol. 2, 1264–65. TR's 1907 message urged Congress to create "the machinery for compulsory investigation of such industrial controversies as are of sufficient magnitude and of sufficient concern to the people of the country as a whole to warrant the Federal Government in taking action." Roosevelt, "1907 Annual Message," xxvii.

8. Theodore Roosevelt to Jacob A. Riis, May 2, 1900, in *Letters*, vol. 2, 1283–84.

9. Senator Platt voiced alarm at the governor's tendency to be "a little loose on the relations of capital and labor, on trusts and combinations." Thomas Collier Platt to Theodore Roosevelt, May 6, 1899, in *Letters*, vol. 2, 1004n1.

10. TR reminded Senator Platt that "masses of these representatives of enormous corporate wealth have themselves been responsible for a portion of the conditions against which Bryan is in ignorant, and sometimes wicked, revolt." Republicans needed to correct the ills diagnosed by Bryan's populists, heading off extreme solutions that would make conditions worse. Roosevelt to Platt, May 8, 1899, 1004–1009. (See ch. 2, n. 52.)

11. Theodore Roosevelt to Edward Oliver Wolcott, September 15, 1900, in *Letters*, vol. 2, 1397–1405.

12. Theodore Roosevelt to John Punnett Peters, April 4, 1899, in *Letters*, vol. 2, 979–80.

13. Theodore Roosevelt to Bird Sim Coler, April 23, 1900, in *Letters*, vol. 2, 1270–71.

14. Roosevelt, *Autobiography*, 476.

15. Roosevelt, "1904 Annual Message," x.

16. Roosevelt, *Autobiography*, 476–77.

17. Theodore Roosevelt to Henry John Right, April 5, 1900, in *Letters*, vol. 2, 1247.

18. Roosevelt, "1905 Annual Message," x–xi.

19. Roosevelt, "1905 Annual Message," xii–xxiv.

20. Theodore Roosevelt to Winthrop Murray Crane, August 19, 1902, in *Letters*, vol. 3, 316–17.

21. Theodore Roosevelt to George Bruce Cortelyou, August 11, 1904, in *Letters*, vol. 4, 886–87.

22. Theodore Roosevelt to Lyman Abbott, September 5, 1903, in *Letters*, vol. 3, 590–93.

23. Roosevelt, *Autobiography*, 478–79.

24. Roosevelt to Abbott, September 5, 1903, 590–93.

25. Theodore Roosevelt to George Haven Putnam, November 16, 1903, in *Letters*, vol. 3, 656–58.

26. Article IV, Section 4 of the Constitution reads: "The United States shall guarantee to every State in this Union a Republican form of Government, and shall protect each of them against invasion; and on application of the Legislature (or of the Executive when the Legislature cannot be convened) against domestic violence."

27. Theodore Roosevelt to Carroll Davidson Wright, August 5, 1904, in *Letters*, vol. 4, 882–83.

28. Roosevelt to Wright, August 5, 1904, 882–83.

29. Theodore Roosevelt to Edwin Warfield, February 12, 1904, in *Letters*, vol. 4, 726–28.

30. Roosevelt, *Autobiography*, 480.

31. Roosevelt to Abbott, September 5, 1903, 592.

32. Jacob Riis relayed the contents of a letter from Seth Low, mayor of New York City, to President Roosevelt, describing the gravity of the situation: "I cannot emphasize too strongly the immense injustice of the existing coal situation to millions of innocent people. The welfare of a large section of the country imperatively demands the immediate resumption of anthracite coal mining." Seth Low, in Riis, *Theodore Roosevelt the Citizen*, 374–75.

33. Roosevelt, *Autobiography*, 480.

34. Theodore Roosevelt to Robert Bacon, October 5, 1902, in *Letters*, vol. 3, 340–41.

35. TR lamented, "with a hundred and forty thousand workmen idle there is certain to be some disorder. . . . Do they not realize that they are putting a very heavy burden on us who stand against socialism; against anarchic disorder?" Theodore Roosevelt to Joseph Bucklin Bishop, October 13, 1902, in *Letters*, vol. 3, 349.

36. Roosevelt to Bacon, October 5, 1902, 339–41.

37. Roosevelt, *Autobiography*, 480–81.

38. Roosevelt to Abbott, September 5, 1903, 592.

39. Roosevelt, *Autobiography*, 479.

40. For more on the growth of executive power, see Fareed Zakaria, *From Wealth to Power: The Unusual Origins of America's World Role* (Princeton, NJ: Princeton University Press, 1998).

41. President Roosevelt heralded the commission's final report as "of lasting value as a textbook in which the principles of dealing in concrete instances with disputes between labor and capital are set down temperately, sanely, but clearly and forcefully." Theodore Roosevelt to the Anthracite Coal Strike Commission, October 23, 1902, in *Letters*, vol. 3, 367; Roosevelt to Abbott, September 5, 1903, 592.

42. Roosevelt, *Autobiography*, 487–92.

43. Theodore Roosevelt to Grover Cleveland, October 5, 1902, in *Letters*, vol. 3, 338–39.

44. Roosevelt, "True American Ideals."

45. Roosevelt, "1904 Annual Message," x.

46. Roosevelt, "1904 Annual Message," xiv.

47. Roosevelt, "1904 Annual Message," x.

48. Theodore Roosevelt to J. H. Woodward, October 19, 1902, in *Letters*, vol. 3, 357.

49. Refer to *Letters*, vols. 3 and 4.

Chapter 5

1. From May 1889 until May 1895. Theodore Roosevelt, "Six Years of Civil-Service Reform," *Scribner's Magazine*, August 1895, in *Works: Memorial*, vol. 15, *Citizenship, Politics and the Elemental Virtues*, 176–77.

2. Likewise, several years later Roosevelt told a reporter from the *Atlanta Journal* that "no police department could be successfully managed unless two conditions existed: First—It must have one head.

Second—Politics must never enter into its conduct." Theodore Roosevelt, in Walter Howard, "How Roosevelt Would Act Here," *Atlanta Journal*, June 25, 1896, Theodore Roosevelt Papers, 485 reels (Washington, DC: Library of Congress Microfilm, 1967–69), series 1, reel 1. (Hereafter Theodore Roosevelt Papers)

3. Roosevelt, "Six Years," 180.

4. Some fifty thousand federal employees had been added to the classified list by the time TR's term as U.S. Civil Service commissioner ended in 1895. Roosevelt, "Six Years," 181, 191.

5. Roosevelt, "Six Years," 182.

6. By 1890, reported TR proudly, some twenty-eight thousand federal employees, nearly a quarter of the total work force, had been "withdrawn from the degrading influences of the spoils system" under revised civil-service legislation. Theodore Roosevelt, "The Merit System Versus the Patronage System," *Century*, February 1890, in *Works: Memorial*, vol. 16, *Campaigns and Controversies*, 168.

7. Roosevelt, "Six Years," 178, 179.

8. Roosevelt, "Merit System," 158, 166, 167. Roosevelt commenced his battle against patronage during his New York Assembly days, when he learned that contracts for stonecutters were parceled out on the basis of politics—slighting masons in his district.

9. Roosevelt, "Merit System," 161–62, 191, 196.

10. Theodore Roosevelt to the Civil Service Commission, August 1, 1889, in *Letters*, vol. 1, 178–81. By 1891, however, political contributions were again—reportedly—being exacted in Baltimore. Theodore Roosevelt to John Wanamaker, May 16, 1892, in *Letters*, vol. 1. 281–85.

11. Roosevelt, "Six Years," 176–77.

12. Roosevelt, "Merit System," 170–71.

13. Roosevelt, "Six Years," 183–84.

14. As a New York assemblyman, TR had introduced a resolution creating a Special Committee to Investigate the Local Government and County of New York and had himself presided over the work of the committee. When he took up his duties on the police board, he found that little had changed in the decade since the Special Committee had published its damning report. H. Paul Jeffers, *Commissioner Roosevelt: The Story of Theodore Roosevelt and the New York City Police, 1895–1897* (New York: J. Wiley & Sons, 1994), 21–23.

15. Theodore Roosevelt, "Administering the New York Police Force," *Atlantic Monthly*, September 1897, in *Works: Memorial*, vol. 15, 151–52.

16. The press was fascinated with the infighting between Roosevelt and Chief Byrnes. The *Herald*, for instance, applauded TR's efforts, citing the "old saw, 'He reforms twice who reforms quickly.'" "Police Anxious about Changes," *Herald*, May 10, 1895; see also "A Slap at Byrnes," *Evening Sun*, May 10, 1895, and "Theodore Roosevelt," *New York Times*, May 11, 1895, Theodore Roosevelt Papers, series 1, reel 1.

17. In a hearing at the mayor's office, Roosevelt, who backed a rival reform bill, told Strong, "this bill, had it been drawn with the express object of perpetuating the abuses known to exist in the Police Department . . . would have been drawn in precisely the same manner as this has been drawn." Theodore Roosevelt, in "Vetoed by the Mayor," *New York Times*, May 11, 1895, Theodore Roosevelt Papers, series 1, reel 1.

18. He deplored the bipartisan law for allowing "the machine politicians, by their opposition outside the board, and by the aid of any tool or ally whom they can get on the board," to "hamper and cripple the honest members of the board, no matter how resolute and able the latter may be." Only "an aroused and determined" public opinion could carry the day against machine politics. Roosevelt, "New York Police Force," 158.

19. Roosevelt, "New York Police Force," 156–57.

20. Jeffers, *Commissioner Roosevelt*, 251.

21. TR acknowledged that the yellow press was a powerful weapon for enemies of reform. "Tammany of course found its best allies in the sensational newspapers. Of all the forces that tend for evil in a great city like New York, probably none are so potent as the sensational papers." Roosevelt, "New York Police Force," 157, 160.

22. Theodore Roosevelt, in Howard, "How Roosevelt Would Act Here."

23. Roosevelt, "New York Police Force," 161.

24. TR upbraided the legislature for giving police captains the authority to evaluate the credentials of applicants for appointment to and promotion within the police force. Such decisions, said TR, were better left to objective civil-service examinations. Theodore Roosevelt, in "Police Appointments: New Rules against Political Influences," *Evening Post*, May 14, 1895, Theodore Roosevelt Papers, series 1, reel 1.

25. Jeffers, *Commissioner Roosevelt*, 116.

26. Jeffers, *Commissioner Roosevelt*, 116–17.

27. Roosevelt, "New York Police Force," 170–71, 173.

28. Reform-minded reporters helped TR counter the yellow press. Like Jacob Riis, Lincoln Steffens of the *Post* was quick to publish stories profiling corruption and abetting civil-service reform. "Now, then, what'll we do?" Roosevelt asked the two newsmen after taking office. Joseph Lincoln Steffens, *The Autobiography of Lincoln Steffens* (New York: Harcourt, Brace, 1931), vol. 1, 255–65.

29. A headline in the *Evening Sun* said it all: "The President of the Police Board Does a Roundsman's Work: Caught the Force Napping: All the Offenders Hauled Up before Him at Headquarters," *Evening Sun*, June 7, 1895, Theodore Roosevelt Papers, series 1, reel 1.

30. The informal police trials were crucial for TR. He told Mayor Strong, "the vital point for breaking down corruption and purifying the police force lies in the power of removing officers for just cause. We ought to have the power of removing them without recourse to any court." Theodore Roosevelt, in "Vetoed by the Mayor." The board's trials proceeded apace. "When he asks a question," reported the *Advertiser*, "Mr. Roosevelt shoots it at the poor trembling policeman as he would shoot a bullet at a coyote. And when he asks a question he shows a set of teeth calculated to unnerve the bravest of the finest." "Pantatas Trembling," *Advertiser*, May 15, 1895, Theodore Roosevelt Papers, series 1, reel 1.

31. Roosevelt, "New York Police Force," 161–62. In mid-1896 TR told a group of police captains to "keep before your minds the military service of the department." He noted that five of them had served in the Civil War, giving them a special appreciation of the virtues needed to combat wrongdoing: honesty and mental and moral courage. Theodore Roosevelt, "The Commissioner's Advice to His Men, New York, July 16, 1896, to Newly Promoted Captains," *New York Tribune*, July 17, 1896, in *Works: Memorial*, vol. 16, *Campaigns and Controversies*, 301–302.

32. Steffens recalled urging TR to promote a young policeman who had dared to arrest Pat Callighan, an ally of Tammany, for keeping his saloon open after hours. Although the officer was not eligible for promotion, Roosevelt prevailed on his fellow commissioners to make an exception. Steffens, *Autobiography*, vol. 1, 264.

33. Roosevelt, "New York Police Force," 162–63.

34. Theodore Roosevelt, in "No Sunday Liquor: Mayor Strong

Declares to Kempner and Grosse That the Excise Law Must Be Upheld," *Herald*, June 30, 1895, Theodore Roosevelt Papers, series 1, reel 1.

35. Roosevelt, "New York Police Force," 166.

36. "After the Saloon Men: Must Answer to Both the Police and Excise Boards," *New York Times*, June 11, 1895, Theodore Roosevelt Papers, series 1, reel 1.

37. In September 1895 some fifteen thousand immigrants rallied against the crackdown on Sunday liquor sales. Asked in jest to preside over the demonstrators' parade, TR agreed, laughing uproariously at placards bearing slogans such as "Roosevelt's Razzle-Dazzle Reform Racket." "Turned Out for Beer: Big Demonstration for Liberal Sunday Laws," *Press*, September 24, 1895, Theodore Roosevelt Papers, series 1, reel 1.

38. Roosevelt, "New York Police Force," 167–70.

39. Roosevelt, "New York Police Force," 172.

40. Jacob A. Riis, *Theodore Roosevelt the Citizen* (New York: Outlook, 1914; reprint, St. Clair Shores, MI: Scholarly Press, 1970), 131.

41. Riis concluded that the city had a "tremendous, ever swelling crowd of wage-earners which it is our business to house decently" on "sanitary, moral, and economic grounds"; New Yorkers were falling short in this regard by virtue of "our own slothfulness." The "tenement has come to stay," demanding public efforts to renovate existing buildings, build new ones, and implement strict sanitary and safety regulations. Jacob A. Riis, *How the Other Half Lives: Studies among the Tenements of New York* (New York: Charles Scribner's Sons, 1890), 282–97.

42. Roosevelt, "New York Police Force," 153. In 1894, after the election of William Strong, TR wrote to Riis, "It is very important to the city to have a business man's Mayor, but it is more important to have a workingman's Mayor." Playgrounds and schools were as important as rapid transit and clean streets. Roosevelt, *Autobiography*, 172, 174; Theodore Roosevelt, "Reform as Social Work," *McClure's Magazine*, March 1901, in *Works: Memorial*, vol. 15, 200–11.

43. Riis, *Theodore Roosevelt the Citizen*, 132.

44. Roosevelt, *Autobiography*, 175.

45. Roosevelt, *Autobiography*, 205.

46. Jeffers, *Commissioner Roosevelt*, 172–74.

Chapter 6

1. Henry Cabot Lodge indirectly noted that Roosevelt's tenure at the New York Police Department had coincided with Secretary of State Richard Olney's modification of the Monroe Doctrine in 1895. On one occasion Lodge urged TR to "take time from the police" to weigh in on Americans' views of the standoff with Great Britain over Venezuela. The result was Roosevelt's 1896 article in the journal *Bachelor of Arts*, titled "The Monroe Doctrine." Henry Cabot Lodge to Theodore Roosevelt, August 10, 1896, in Theodore Roosevelt and Henry Cabot Lodge, *Selections from the Correspondence of Theodore Roosevelt and Henry Cabot Lodge, 1884–1918*, ed. Henry Cabot Lodge and Charles F. Redmond (New York: Charles Scribner's Sons, 1925; reprint, New York: Da Capo, 1971), vol. 1, 163. (Hereafter *Roosevelt-Lodge Correspondence*.) Theodore Roosevelt, "The Monroe Doctrine," *Bachelor of Arts* 2, no. 4 (March 1896): 437–65.

2. Theodore Roosevelt to Carl Schurz, September 8, 1905, in *Letters*, vol. 5, 16–17.

3. Theodore Roosevelt, "Municipal Administration: The New York Police Force," *Atlantic Monthly* 80 (September 1897): 289–300.

4. Thomas Bailey, for instance, labeled TR an "apostle of Mars." Yet TR was able to boast upon leaving the Oval Office that U.S. forces had not fired a shot in anger during his presidency. Thomas A. Bailey, *A Diplomatic History of the American People*, 10th ed. (Englewood Cliffs, NJ: Prentice-Hall, 1980), 527–28.

5. See for example TR's 1897 address at the Naval War College, in which he declared, "No triumph of peace is quite so great as the supreme triumphs of war." In peacetime this meant vigorous enterprise; yet "orderly liberty . . . can be gained only by men who are willing to fight for an ideal." Theodore Roosevelt, "'Washington's Forgotten Maxim,' Address as Assistant Secretary of the Navy, before the Naval War College, June, 1897," in *Works: National*, vol. 13, *American Ideals*, 182–84.

6. Howard Beale declared that the expansionists were "impelled by national pride," unalterably convinced of American rectitude, and animated by a sense of Anglo-Saxon superiority. Beale, *Rise of America*, 38–47.

7. In this case Roosevelt was referring to the Progressive project in the Philippine Islands. Theodore Roosevelt to William Howard Taft, March 12, 1901, in *Letters*, vol. 3, 11–12.

8. Frederick Jackson Turner, "'The Significance of the Frontier

in American History,' From Proceedings of the Forty-first Annual Meeting of the State Historical Society of Wisconsin" (Madison: State Historical Society of Wisconsin, 1894; reprint, Woodbridge, CT: Research Publications, 1975). As he promised, Roosevelt paid tribute to Turner's pamphlet in the third volume of *The Winning of the West*.

9. Theodore Roosevelt to Frederick Jackson Turner, February 10, 1894, in *Letters*, vol. 1, 363. Turner, like Roosevelt, traced the westward surge of the United States to previous centuries of Anglo-Saxon enterprise. Anglo-Saxon civilization had been preserved fundamentally intact and had been carried forward by a distinctive—and well-armed—American people. Alongside farmers and entrepreneurs, the soldier had been one of the "pioneers of civilization." *Works. Memorial*, vol. 10, *The Winning of the West*, 1–26.

10. Roosevelt to Wolcott, September 15, 1900, 1397–1405. (See ch. 5, n. 11.)

11. Samuel Flagg Bemis, *A Diplomatic History of the United States*, rev. ed. (New York: Henry Holt, 1942), 463–78. Bemis titled the relevant chapter "The Great Aberration of 1898."

12. Roosevelt to Wolcott, September 15, 1900, 1401. TR discerned two different models by which the West had been brought to heel: (1) the Southern template, prevalent in Tennessee, Kentucky, and the Southwestern tract of land, in which the private initiative of the settlers had led to furious warfare; and (2) the Northwestern model, carried out under the auspices of the Northwest Ordinance, in which government action had subdued the Indian nations, through the agency of the U.S. Army, and allowed the settlers to push West. *Works: Memorial*, vol. 10, *Winning of the West*, xv, 1–26.

13. Roosevelt to Wolcott, September 15, 1900, 1404.

14. Theodore Roosevelt to Joseph Gurney Cannon, September 12, 1904, in *Letters*, vol. 4, 921–23.

15. William T. Stead, "The Conference at The Hague," *Forum* 28 (September 1899): 3–4.

16. Miles, who led the fight against the Apaches, wrote that the essence of Indian warfare was to "find, follow, and defeat" the enemy. He drew on his experiences in the West, pioneering the use of counterinsurgency field exercises and forming elite scout units. Birtle, *U.S. Army Doctrine*, 69, 74–76.

17. Theodore Roosevelt to Elihu Root, February 18, 1902, in *Letters*, vol. 3, 232–33. Roosevelt applied his Progressive model to the Indian population as early as 1891, urging the Harrison administra-

tion to eradicate patronage in the Bureau of Indian Affairs, to set the most capable Indians to diffusing the culture of self-rule among their fellows, and to "extend the present system of paid Indian judges and police." Morris, *Rise of Theodore Roosevelt*, 441.

18. Theodore Roosevelt to William Bayard Cutting, April 18, 1899, in *Letters*, vol. 2, 990–91.

19. Theodore Roosevelt to Frederick Courteney Selous, March 19, 1900, in *Letters*, vol. 2, 1233–34.

20. Theodore Roosevelt to Alexander Monroe Dockery, January 8, 1894, in *Letters*, vol. 1, 346–47. The Progressive project, TR made clear, applied equally to U.S. cities and to the islands acquired from Spain. The Progressive movement warred on barbarism at home and abroad, using a variety of policy instruments. Theodore Roosevelt to Lyman Abbott, July 15, 1901, in *Letters*, vol. 3, 119.

21. Theodore Roosevelt to Finley Peter Dunne, January 16, 1900, in *Letters*, vol. 2, 1134.

22. Immanuel Kant, *Perpetual Peace, and Other Essays on Politics, History, and Morals*, trans. Ted Humphrey (reprint, Indianapolis: Hackett Publishing, 1983).

23. Theodore Roosevelt, "Expansion and Peace," *Independent*, December 21, 1899, in *Works: National*, vol. 13, *The Strenuous Life: Essays and Addresses*, 336.

24. Theodore Roosevelt, "Message of the President to the Senate and the House of Representatives," December 3, 1901, in *FRUS: 1901*, xxxvi.

25. While wary of conflict with the world's preeminent sea power, Roosevelt wished Great Britain well and predicted that its efforts would on the whole help spread enlightenment. Theodore Roosevelt to Alfred Thayer Mahan, March 18, 1901, in *Letters*, vol. 3, 23; Roosevelt, "Monroe Doctrine," 448.

26. Roosevelt, "1907 Annual Message," LXI–LXII.

27. Serge Ricard, "Theodore Roosevelt: Principles and Practice of a Foreign Policy," *Theodore Roosevelt Association Journal* 18 (Fall–Winter 1992): 2–6.

28. Roosevelt, "Monroe Doctrine," 444–45. TR later engineered the invitation of the Latin American republics to the 1907 Hague conference, signifying their admission to the community of civilized nations.

29. "There are certain republics to the south of us," TR averred,

"which have already reached such a point of stability, order, and prosperity that they themselves, though as yet hardly consciously, are among the guarantors of this Doctrine. These republics we now meet not only on a basis of entire equality, but in a spirit of frank and respectful friendship, which we hope is mutual. If all of the republics to the south of us will only grow as those to which I allude have already grown, all need for us to be the especial champions of the Doctrine will disappear, for no stable and growing American Republic wishes to see some great non-American military power acquire territory in its neighborhood." Roosevelt, "1905 Annual Message," XXXIII–XXXIV.

30. Roosevelt to Mahan, March 18, 1901, 23.

31. Theodore Roosevelt to Cecil Arthur Spring Rice, August 11, 1899, in *Letters*, vol. 2, 1049–55.

32. Theodore Roosevelt to John Hay, April 2, 1905, Theodore Roosevelt Papers, series 1, reel 53.

33. "What wonderful people the Japanese are!" TR marveled. Japan "is now a great power and will be a greater power." TR urged the United States to "treat the Japanese in a spirit of all possible courtesy, and with generosity and justice," while also building up American naval power to discourage aggression. Theodore Roosevelt to Cecil Arthur Spring Rice, June 16, 1905, Theodore Roosevelt Papers, series 1, reel 55.

34. "The Japanese have won in a single generation the right to stand abreast of the foremost and most enlightened peoples of Europe and America," proclaimed TR; "they have won on their own merits and by their own exertions the right to treatment on a basis of full and frank equality." Roosevelt, "1906 Annual Message," XLI–XLII.

35. Theodore Roosevelt to Cecil Arthur Spring Rice, June 13, 1904, in *Letters*, vol. 4, 829–33.

36. TR, notes Beale, "used the term 'race' loosely," emphasizing not biology but "acquired characteristics and . . . the effect of geographic environment." Unlike "many promoters of racism of his day he did not regard the 'backward people' as permanently or inherently inferior." Indeed, "any particular Negro, Chinese, or Filipino who displayed qualities he admired was to him an admirable person and an equal." Beale, *Rise of America*, 43–45. See also Thomas G. Dyer, *Theodore Roosevelt and the Idea of Race* (Baton Rouge: Louisiana State University Press, 1980).

37. Indeed, he held up the Japanese as a Progressive ideal—at least in some respects: "I told [two visiting Japanese diplomats] that I

thought we had to learn from them many things, especially as to the misery in our great cities." Roosevelt to Rice, June 13, 1904, 831.

38. Theodore Roosevelt to Paul Estournelles de Constant, September 1, 1903, in *Letters*, vol. 3, 583–84.

39. Roosevelt, "Expansion and Peace," 339.

40. Roosevelt, "Expansion and Peace," 339.

41. Marks, *Velvet on Iron*, 20–21.

42. Theodore Roosevelt to F. B. Cunz, October 30, 1899, in *Letters*, vol. 2, 1092.

43. Roosevelt, "1904 Annual Message," XLVI–XLVII.

44. Roosevelt, "1904 Annual Message," XLVII.

45. The nature of the relationship between Mahan and Roosevelt has long been a matter of dispute. Richard W. Turk convincingly rebuts the standard view that Mahan profoundly influenced Roosevelt. "Clearly," maintains Turk, "Mahan did not, as some have suggested, enter the White House in the person of Theodore Roosevelt." Richard W. Turk, *The Ambiguous Relationship: Theodore Roosevelt and Alfred Thayer Mahan* (New York: Greenwood Press, 1987), 1–6, 101–107.

46. Theodore Roosevelt to Alfred Thayer Mahan, May 12, 1890, in *Letters*, vol. 1, 221–22. Refer to Alfred T. Mahan, *The Influence of Sea Power upon History, 1660–1783* (Boston: Little, Brown, 1890; reprint, New York: Dover Publications, 1987).

47. Roosevelt authored *The Naval War of 1812* soon after graduating from Harvard. In its pages he delivered an impassioned plea for the United States to build a modern navy to replace its creaky, largely Civil War–era fleet. As late as 1906, Roosevelt cited Mahan's interpretation of the War of 1812 approvingly in a discussion of that year's shipbuilding proposals. Theodore Roosevelt, *The Naval War of 1812, Or, The History of the United States Navy during the Last War with Great Britain* (New York: G. P. Putnam's Sons, 1882; reprint with intro. by Edward K. Eckert, Annapolis, MD: Naval Institute Press, 1987). Roosevelt, "1906 Annual Message," LVI.

48. Theodore Roosevelt to Alfred Thayer Mahan, May 3, 1897, in *Letters*, vol. 1, 607–608.

49. Theodore Roosevelt to John Hay, May 3, 1897, in *Letters*, vol. 1, 609. He also applauded Mahan's *The Interest of America in Sea Power, Present and Future* (Boston: Little, Brown, 1897; reprint, Freeport, NY: Books for Libraries Press, 1970). Theodore Roosevelt to William Astor Chanler, December 23, 1897, in *Letters*, vol. 1, 746–47.

50. Roosevelt to Mahan, March 18, 1901, 23.

51. Mahan reinforced TR's romantic view of war. "Though he valued the blessings of peace," points out Beale, "he craved the excitements of war. He therefore sought a big navy because it would prevent war, but also because it was such fun to have a big navy." Beale, *Rise of America*, 49–50.

52. Theodore Roosevelt to Arthur Hamilton Lee, July 25, 1900, in *Letters*, vol. 2, 1362.

53. Theodore Roosevelt to George Ferdinand Becker, July 8, 1901, in *Letters*, vol. 3, 111–12.

54. Alfred Thayer Mahan, *The Problem of Asia and Its Effect upon International Policies* (New York: Little, Brown, 1900; reprint, Port Washington, NY: Kennikat Press, 1970), 7.

55. Mahan, *Influence of Sea Power*, 71.

56. George W. Baer, *One Hundred Years of Sea Power: The U.S. Navy, 1890–1990* (Stanford, CA: Stanford University Press, 1994), 12.

57. Jon Tetsuro Sumida contends that Mahan has often been caricatured as a "rigid doctrinaire." "That is a widely held view, but it is faulty and unjust." And, to be sure, Mahan (like Roosevelt) acknowledged the limits on U.S. maritime interests. They were primarily concerned with controlling events in regions of vital interest, most notably the Caribbean Sea. Jon Tetsuro Sumida, *Inventing Grand Strategy and Teaching Command: The Classic Works of Alfred Thayer Mahan Reconsidered* (Washington, DC: Woodrow Wilson Center Press, 1997), xv–xviii, 81–98.

58. Roosevelt, "Washington's Forgotten Maxim," 183.

59. Mahan, *Problem of Asia*, 42.

60. Mahan, *Influence of Sea Power*, 26.

61. "The general character of England's foreign policy," wrote the British diplomat Eyre Crowe, was "inseparably bound up with the possession of preponderant sea power. The tremendous influence of such preponderance has been described in the classical pages of Captain Mahan. No one now disputes it." Eyre Crowe, "Memorandum on the Present State of British Relations with France and Germany, January 1, 1907," in G. P. Gooch and Harold Temperley, eds., *British Documents on the Origins of the War 1898–1914* (London: His Majesty's Stationery Office, 1927), vol. 3, *The Testing of the Entente, 1904–6*, 402. See also Holger H. Herwig, "The Influence of A. T. Mahan upon German Sea Power," in John B. Hattendorf, ed., *The Influence of*

History on Mahan (Newport, RI: Naval War College Press, 1991), 67–80; Rolf Hobson, *Imperialism at Sea: Naval Strategic Thought, the Ideology of Sea Power and the Tirpitz Plan, 1875–1914* (Boston: Brill Academic Publishers, 2002), 155–91; and James R. Holmes, "Mahan, a 'Place in the Sun,' and Germany's Quest for Sea Power," *Comparative Strategy* 23, no. 1 (January–March 2004): 27–62.

62. Theodore Roosevelt to Hermann Speck von Sternburg, January 17, 1898, in *Letters*, vol. 1, 763–64.

63. James Bryce, *The American Commonwealth*, 2d ed. (London: Macmillan, 1891), vol. 2, 414–16.

64. Carl Schurz, the editor of *Harper's Weekly*, dissected TR's address at the Naval War College. Schurz declared that TR, "in his combative ardor," had reasoned himself into a "logical quandary": "according to him a long peace has a tendency to make a people effeminate and unpatriotic, while war will invigorate a people and inspire patriotism. But he argues also that the building of a great fleet of war-ships will be a means not to bring on war, but to preserve peace. Ergo, the building of a great war fleet will effect that which promotes effeminacy and languishing patriotism." Instead "we should have a smart little navy enabling us to do our share of police duty on the seas." Otherwise the American people should content themselves with "enjoying an unarmed peace." Carl Schurz, "Armed or Unarmed Peace," *Harper's Weekly Magazine*, June 19, 1897, 603.

65. Roosevelt to Wolcott, September 15, 1900, 1397–1405.

66. In 1893, urging the annexation of Hawaii, TR admitted, "I am a bit of a believer in the manifest destiny doctrine. . . . I don't want to see our flag hauled down where it has been hauled up." Beale, *Rise of America*, 57.

67. Roosevelt, "Washington's Forgotten Maxim," 182–99. "The United States," declaimed TR in his ruminations on Washington and Lincoln, "has never once in the course of its history suffered harm because of preparation for war, or because of entering into war. But we have suffered incalculable harm . . . from a foolish failure to prepare for war or from reluctance to fight when to fight was proper." The need for turn-of-the-century America to build ships was "tenfold greater" than it had been in 1812. Building modern warships was a time-consuming process.

68. Theodore Roosevelt to William Astor Chanler, December 23, 1897, in *Letters*, vol. 1, 746–47.

69. Notes Howard Beale, "at the turn of the century when

America had to make her decision [whether to embark on an imperial path] the rival imperial powers were vigorously intensifying their rivalries and their chauvinisms in distant parts of the already crowded imperial world." Older powers such as Great Britain and France wanted to "retain the leading roles they had won," while newer powers such as Japan and Germany were looking for their own "place in the sun." Beale, *Rise of America*, 32, 63; Holmes, "Germany's Quest for Sea Power," 27–62.

70. Lodge summarized his and Roosevelt's views: "If England's title is good, we have no wish to disturb it." But if Britain could "extend her territory in South America without remonstrance from us, every other European power can do the same." Soon "you will see South America parceled out as Africa has been." Beale, *Rise of America*, 60.

71. Alfred T. Mahan, *Naval Strategy, Compared and Contrasted with the Principles and Practice of Military Operations on Land* (Boston: Little, Brown, 1911), 103.

72. Baer, *One Hundred Years*, 9–11.

73. Mahan, *Problem of Asia*, 16.

74. Mahan, *Problem of Asia*, 16–17.

75. Mahan, *Problem of Asia*, 29–30.

76. Mahan, *Problem of Asia*, 33.

77. During the First World War, Roosevelt told a Chicago audience that, because the "Monroe Doctrine will never be one particle stronger than the Navy," the navy was "the one most vitally important international asset to the nation." The "Navy stands foremost." Theodore Roosevelt, "'National Duty and International Ideals,' Speech of Theodore Roosevelt before the Illinois Bar Association at Chicago, April 29, 1916" (New York: Allied Print, 1916).

78. Theodore Roosevelt to Henry White, March 30, 1896, in *Letters*, vol. 1, 523.

79. Foreign policy in a liberal democracy, lamented TR, was necessarily somewhat opportunistic. Only ingrained traditions such as the Monroe Doctrine could withstand factional squabbling. Roosevelt to Rice, December 27, 1904, 1082–88. (See ch. 2, n. 48.)

80. Theodore Roosevelt to William Sheffield Cowles, April 5, 1896, in *Letters*, vol. 1, 524.

81. Henry Cabot Lodge to Theodore Roosevelt, March 30, 1901, in *Roosevelt-Lodge Correspondence*, vol. 1, 486–87.

82. Lodge to Roosevelt, March 30, 1901, 486–87.

83. William Howard Taft, "Address before the Board of Trade of Columbus, Ohio, April 2, 1908," in *Present Day Problems* (Freeport, NY: Books for Libraries Press, 1908; reprint, 1967), 81.

84. While "no nation can afford to disregard proper considerations of self-interest, any more than a private individual can do so," for TR it was "equally true that the average private individual in any really decent community does many actions . . . in which he is guided, not by self-interest, but by public spirit, by regard for the rights of others, by a disinterested purpose to do good to others, and to raise the tone of the community as a whole." The nation was no more than an aggregation of such individuals. Roosevelt, "1906 Annual Message," XL.

85. Roosevelt to Wolcott, September 15, 1900, 1400.

86. Theodore Roosevelt, in William Harbaugh, *Power and Responsibility: The Life and Times of Theodore Roosevelt* (New York: Farrar, Straus and Cudahy, 1961), 513.

87. Roosevelt, "Expansion and Peace," 332.

88. Roosevelt, "Expansion and Peace," 333.

89. Roosevelt, *Autobiography*, 518.

90. Theodore Roosevelt to Corinne Roosevelt Robinson, June 15, 1898, in *Letters*, vol. 2, 843.

91. Theodore Roosevelt to William Wirt Kimball, November 19, 1897, in *Letters*, vol. 1, 716–17.

92. Theodore Roosevelt to William Pierce Frye, March 31, 1898, in *Letters*, vol. 2, 806–807.

93. Theodore Roosevelt to Paul Dana, April 18, 1898, in *Letters*, vol. 2, 816–17. The *Sun*, under Dana's direction, had editorialized applauding the sense of chivalry that had impelled TR to volunteer for military service in Cuba.

94. Theodore Roosevelt to Elihu Root, April 5, 1898, in *Letters*, vol. 2, 812–13.

95. Theodore Roosevelt to James Bryce, March 31, 1898, in *Letters*, vol. 2, 807.

Chapter 7

1. *De Lima v. Bidwell*, 182 U.S. 1 (1901).

2. *Dooley v. United States*, 183 U.S. 151, 154 (1901).

3. *Downes v. Bidwell*, 182 U.S. 244 (1901).

4. Beisner, *Twelve against Empire*, 216.

5. A confrontation with Chile in 1891, says Beale, made "Roosevelt's heart swell with pride," providing "a model in their eyes and in the eyes of 'backward people' like the Chileans for future action by the United States." It "never occurred to Roosevelt that there could be any justice in a backward country's objecting to its resources' being exploited for foreign profit by foreigners who did not treat natives as equals but as backward people." Beale, *Rise of America*, 54–55.

6. Walter LaFeber identifies five factors spurring U.S. intervention: (1) great-power encroachment that seemed to imperil the Monroe Doctrine; (2) U.S. public sentiment; (3) commercial interests; (4) worries about control of the mouth of the Orinoco River, the gateway to the South American interior; and (5) personalities. Walter LaFeber, *The New Empire: An Interpretation of American Expansion, 1860–1898* (Ithaca, NY: Cornell University Press, 1963), 242–57.

7. Olney's message was "right and good," affirmed TR, who predicted that Europeans would now "recognize that the Monroe Doctrine is a living entity" underwritten by American power. Beale, *Rise of America*, 59–64.

8. Richard Olney to Thomas F. Bayard, July 20, 1895, in Ruhl J. Bartlett, ed., *The Record of American Diplomacy: Documents and Readings in the History of American Foreign Relations*, 4th ed. (New York: Knopf, 1964), 341–45.

9. Olney pointed to the European partition of Africa, then ongoing. A preventive stance, he maintained, would allow the United States to fend off European encroachment without constructing large military forces. Olney to Bayard, July 20, 1895, 345.

10. It should be noted that Olney was not exceeding Cleveland's wishes in his message. Venezuela was, said Cleveland, the "most distinct of home questions." LaFeber, *New Empire*, 253, 259–60, 267–69.

11. Theodore Roosevelt to Henry Cabot Lodge, December 20, 1895, in *Letters*, vol. 1, 500. President Roosevelt and Secretary of State Elihu Root eventually backtracked from Olney's formula. Root told the American Society of International Law that his predecessor had spoken rhetorically.

12. Lodge reprimanded the *New York Times*, which had editorialized that there was no general interest among the American populace in upholding the Monroe Doctrine and no public objection to British actions in the Venezuela controversy. Henry Cabot Lodge to Theodore Roosevelt, August 10, 1895, in *Roosevelt-Lodge Correspondence*, vol. 1, 163.

13. For an assessment of Anglo-American relations in the Caribbean, see William N. Tilchin, *Theodore Roosevelt and the British Empire: A Study in Presidential Statecraft* (New York: St. Martin's Press, 1997), 25–36.

14. Lord Salisbury to Sir Julian Pauncefote, November 26, 1895, in Bartlett, *Record of American Diplomacy*, 346–47.

15. Theodore Roosevelt to Henry Cabot Lodge, December 27, 1895, in *Letters*, vol. 1, 503–504.

16. Roosevelt to Lodge, December 27, 1895, 509. Roosevelt maintained that "a political speech was not an etching or an arrangement of pastels but a poster." Elting E. Morison, intro. to Roosevelt, *Autobiography*, ix.

17. Theodore Roosevelt to the editors of the *Harvard Crimson*, January 2, 1896, in *Letters*, vol. 1, 505–506.

18. Roosevelt, "Monroe Doctrine," 441.

19. Theodore Roosevelt to William Sheffield Cowles, February 26, 1900, in Theodore Roosevelt, *Letters of Theodore Roosevelt to Anna Roosevelt Cowles, 1870–1918* (New York: Charles Scribner's Sons, 1924), 237.

20. Roosevelt, "Monroe Doctrine," 441.

21. In 1910 he told an audience at the University of Berlin, "One of the prime dangers of civilization has always been its tendency to cause the loss of the virile fighting qualities, of the fighting edge." "The barbarian," by contrast, was "forced to keep and develop certain hardy qualities." Theodore Roosevelt, "Address before the University of Berlin, May 12, 1910," in Theodore Roosevelt, *Roosevelt, His Life, Meaning, and Messages* (New York: Current Literature Publishing, 1919), vol. 3, *Newer Roosevelt Messages*, 1066.

22. Roosevelt, "Monroe Doctrine," 443.

23. Theodore Roosevelt to James Brander Matthews, May 21, 1894, in *Letters*, vol. 1, 379.

24. Roosevelt to Mahan, May 3, 1897, 607.

25. Theodore Roosevelt to Henry Cabot Lodge, June 19, 1901, in *Roosevelt-Lodge Correspondence*, vol. 1, 494.

26. Roosevelt to Mahan, May 3, 1897, 607–608. (See ch. 6, n. 48.)

27. Theodore Roosevelt to Henry Cabot Lodge, March 27, 1901, in *Roosevelt-Lodge Correspondence*, vol. 1, 484–85.

28. Roosevelt to Lodge, June 19, 1901, 494.

29. "Prophetically, too," observes Beale, "the anti-imperialists foretold that . . . subject peoples . . . would one day rise and throw the foreign rulers out." Beale, *Rise of America*, 33–35.

30. Beisner, *Twelve against Empire*, 18–34.

31. Carl Schurz, "American Principles and American Honor," 4. McKinley's words gave Schurz fodder for his anti-imperialist brief.

32. The American Anti-Imperialist League's platform, approved in 1899, proclaimed that "the subjugation of any people is 'criminal aggression' and open disloyalty to the distinctive principles of our government." A "self governing state cannot accept sovereignty over an unwilling people." "Platform of the Anti-Imperialist League, Adopted at Chicago, October 18, 1899," *Liberty Tracts* 10, 2, in Bartlett, *Record of American Diplomacy*, 388–90.

33. Beisner, *Twelve against Empire*, 19.

34. Schurz railed against the "unconstitutional assumption of power, betrayal of the fundamental principles of our democracy, wanton sacrifice of our soldiers for an unjust cause, cruel slaughter of innocent people, and thus of horrible blood guiltiness without parallel in the history of republic." Carl Schurz to Charles Francis Adams, n.d. [October 7, 1900?], in Schurz, *Reminiscences*, vol. 3, 446–47.

35. Schurz offered the most thoughtful and comprehensive assessment of any of the anti-imperialists. The cases put forth by William Jennings Bryan, Andrew Carnegie, William James, Mark Twain, and other prominent anti-imperialists were in effect a subset of Schurz's work. See for instance William Jennings Bryan, "'Imperialism,' Address Delivered in Indianapolis, Ind., on Aug. 8, 1900, in Accepting the Democratic Nomination for the Presidency," in William Jennings Bryan, *Speeches of William Jennings Bryan*, intro. Mary Baird Bryan (New York: Funk & Wagnalis, 1909), vol. 2, 23–27.

36. Schurz, "American Imperialism," 3–5, 7. By the 1900 presidential campaign, Schurz had jettisoned much of the racial and climatological determinism of his University of Chicago speech. He hammered away instead at the imperialists' supposed betrayal of American principles, the perfidy of the plutocracy and its Republican allies, and the McKinley administration's treachery toward Aguinaldo. Schurz, "American Principles and American Honor," 1–5.

37. Schurz, "American Imperialism," 5–6, 8.

38. In his 1900 Cooper Union address, an increasingly strident Schurz tied the administration's duplicity to the concept of sovereignty. "Congress not only positively disclaimed any intention to annex" Cuba,

but also proclaimed that "the people of Cuba 'are, and of right ought to be, free and independent'—in other words, that Spain, by her oppressive misrule, had not only morally but actually forfeited her sovereignty over that country." Schurz reasoned that exactly the same principle applied to the archipelago. Yet McKinley had "issued the notorious 'benevolent assimilation order,'" which had left the United States "in possession of stolen goods—goods obtained by fraud, treachery, and brutal force." Schurz, "American Principles and American Honor," 1–5, 7.

39. Schurz, "American Imperialism," 10, 17.

40. Schurz, "American Imperialism," 14.

41. Schurz, "American Imperialism," 11–14.

42. Schurz, "American Imperialism," 10–11, 15.

43. Schurz, "American Imperialism," 10, 29–34.

44. Schurz, "American Imperialism," 23.

45. Walter Lippmann neatly analyzes the mismatch between ends and means. Walter Lippmann, *U.S. Foreign Policy: Shield of the Republic* (Boston: Little, Brown, 1943).

46. Echoing Mark Twain, Schurz characterized some of Roosevelt's utterances on foreign policy as the "symptom of an unbalanced mind." Asked by the Democratic campaign to rebut Hay's and Root's speeches defending the administration, Schurz labeled the president "an exceedingly interesting, picturesque, and forcible character, who would have found a most congenial and glorious field of action at the time of the Crusades." His "is a master nature, but this Republic does not want in the Presidency a master—least of all one who cannot master himself." In Claude M. Fuess, *Carl Schurz: Reformer* (New York: Dodd, Mead, 1932), 370–71.

47. Carl Schurz to Theodore Roosevelt, September 6, 1905, in *Roosevelt-Lodge Correspondence*, vol. 2, 195–200.

48. Roosevelt to Schurz, September 8, 1905, 16–17. (See ch. 6, n. 2.)

49. Roosevelt, "1901 Annual Message," xxxii.

50. A disarmed America might "avoid bloodshed," but would be unable to secure "the real peace for which the most law-abiding and high-minded men must at times be willing to fight." Roosevelt, "1905 Annual Message," xxx–xxxi.

51. Theodore Roosevelt to Joseph Bucklin Bishop, February 23, 1904, in *Letters*, vol. 4, 734–35.

52. John Lewis Gaddis, *Surprise, Security, and the American Experience* (Cambridge: Harvard University Press, 2004).

53. Roosevelt, "True Americanism," 17.

54. Roosevelt, "Monroe Doctrine," 437–54.

55. Dexter Perkins, *A History of the Monroe Doctrine* (Boston: Little, Brown, 1963), 228–75.

56. Theodore Roosevelt, "'Grant,' Speech Delivered at Galena, Illinois, April 27, 1900," in *Works: National*, vol. 13, 430–41.

57. Roosevelt, "1904 Annual Message," XL. "As yet there is only a partial and imperfect analogy between international and internal or municipal law, because there is no sanction of force for executing the former while there is in the latter. The private citizen is protected in his rights by the law, because the law rests in the last resort upon force exercised through the forms of law. A man does not have to defend his rights with his own hand, because he can call upon the police, upon the sheriff's posse, upon the militia, or in certain extreme cases upon the Army, to defend him. But there is no such sanction of force for international law." Roosevelt, "1905 Annual Message," XXX–XXXI.

58. Roosevelt, "1904 Annual Message," XL–XLI.

59. Roosevelt, "1904 Annual Message," XLI.

60. Roosevelt, "1904 Annual Message," XL–XLII.

61. "When the next Hague Conference is held," Roosevelt remarked to Lyman Abbott in 1905, "I trust that all the nations there represented will join in framing a general arbitration treaty. . . . It is neither possible nor desirable in the present stage of the world's progress to agree to arbitrate all questions that may come up. . . . But it is entirely possible and exceedingly desirable to limit the classes of cases which it is not possible definitely to promise beforehand to arbitrate." Theodore Roosevelt to Lyman Abbott, June 8, 1905, Theodore Roosevelt Papers, series 1, reel 55.

62. Roosevelt, "1905 Annual Message," XXXII.

63. Roosevelt, *Autobiography*, 1–28.

64. Roosevelt, "1904 Annual Message," XXXVIII, XLII. Uplifting indigenous Americans remained a concern. "The Alaskans" were "kindly, intelligent, anxious to learn, and willing to work. Those who have come under the influence of civilization . . . have proved their capability of becoming self-supporting, self-respecting citizens, and ask only for the just enforcement of law and intelligent instruction and supervision."

65. Roosevelt, "1904 Annual Message," XLII.

66. Roosevelt, "1904 Annual Message," XLII, XLIII.

67. Theodore Roosevelt to Corinne Roosevelt Robinson, June 15, 1898, in *Letters*, vol. 2, 843.

68. Roosevelt to Root, April 5, 1898, 812–14. (See ch. 6, n. 17.)

69. Theodore Roosevelt to Cecil Arthur Spring Rice, July 20, 1900, in *Letters*, vol. 2, 1358–59.

70. Roosevelt to Rice, June 13, 1904, 829–33. (See ch. 6, n. 35.)

71. To two visiting Japanese dignitaries, TR joked that his own ancestors had been part of a "white terror" during the tenth century; "and as we had outgrown the position of being a White Terror I thought that in similar fashion such a civilization as they had developed entitled them to laugh at the accusation of being part of the Yellow Terror." Roosevelt to Rice, June 13, 1904, 829–33.

72. Theodore Roosevelt to Francis Cruger Moore, February 9, 1898, in *Letters*, vol. 1, 771–72.

73. A "disaster to the British Empire" would compel the United States to choose between "abandoning the Monroe doctrine and submitting to the acquisition of American territory by some great European military power, or going to war." Theodore Roosevelt to Elihu Root, January 19, 1900, in *Letters*, vol. 2, 1151.

74. Roosevelt to Rice, June 13, 1904, 829.

75. Roosevelt to Rice, June 13, 1904, 829–33.

76. Indeed, TR privately fantasized about launching a "crusade" to chastise Turkey but recognized that the American people would never support such a venture. Theodore Roosevelt to George Otto Trevelyan, May 13, 1905, in *Letters*, vol. 4, 1173–76.

77. Roosevelt, "1905 Annual Message," XXXII–XXXIII.

78. Roosevelt, "1901 Annual Message," XXXVI.

79. Roosevelt, "Expansion and Peace," 332–40.

80. Walter Lippmann credited Roosevelt with narrowing the gap between expansive foreign commitments and meager means. Lippmann, *Shield of the Republic*.

81. Elihu Root, "'The Monroe Doctrine,' Address at the Ninety-Ninth Annual Banquet of the New England Society of New York, December 22, 1904," in *Miscellaneous Address, By Elihu Root*, eds. Robert Bacon and James Brown Scott (Cambridge: Harvard University Press, 1917), 267–70.

82. Root echoed Roosevelt's vehement denials that the 1823 principles had acquired the status of international law: "No one," he said, "ever pretended that Mr. Monroe was declaring a rule of international law or that the doctrine which he declared has become international law. . . . The doctrine is not international law but it rests upon the right of self-protection and that right is recognized by international law. The right is a necessary corollary of independent sovereignty." The United States was justified in enunciating a general doctrine that upheld its interests. The European powers had consented to the doctrine. The Duke of Devonshire, to cite just one example, had bluntly declared, "Great Britain accepts the Monroe Doctrine unreservedly." Root's comments on self-protection had preventive overtones. Every state had "the right . . . to protect itself by preventing a condition of affairs in which it will be too late to protect itself." Elihu Root, "'The Real Monroe Doctrine,' Presidential Address at the Eighth Annual Meeting of the American Society of International Law, Washington, April 22, 1914," in *Addresses on International Subjects, By Elihu Root*, eds. Robert Bacon and James Brown Scott (Cambridge: Harvard University Press, 1916), 109–11.

83. Root, "Real Monroe Doctrine," 106–107. Root reminded the American Society of International Law that the Latin American republics had been "received into the Second Conference at The Hague" at TR's behest and had "joined in the conventions there made upon the footing of equal sovereignty, entitled to have the territory and independence respected under that law of nations which formerly existed for Europe alone."

84. Root, "Monroe Doctrine," 270–71.

85. Elihu Root, in Philip C. Jessup, *Elihu Root* (New York: Dodd, Mead, 1938), vol. 1, 470.

86. Root, "Monroe Doctrine," 271.

87. Root, "Monroe Doctrine," 272.

88. So popular was Root's message, in fact, that on one memorable occasion Brazilian students had to be prevented from unharnessing the horses drawing his carriage and pulling the carriage through the streets of Rio themselves. Similar acclaim greeted TR during a postpresidential tour in 1913. Marks, *Velvet on Iron*, 182–85.

89. Roosevelt, "1906 Annual Message," VII–LIX.

90. Roosevelt, "1906 Annual Message," XLVII–XLVIII.

91. Root, "Real Monroe Doctrine," 117.

92. Root, "Real Monroe Doctrine," 118–19.

93. Root, "Real Monroe Doctrine," 119–21.

94. Root, "Real Monroe Doctrine," 123.

95. Theodore Roosevelt to William Carey Brown, March 12, 1901, in *Letters*, vol. 3, 13. Roosevelt was congratulating Brown, an army major, on killing an insurgent leader, or "bandit chief," as he put it.

96. Roosevelt, *Autobiography*, 521.

97. Marks, *Velvet on Iron*.

98. Alberto R. Coll, "Normative Prudence as a Tradition of Statecraft," *Ethics & International Affairs* 5 (1991): 33. Lippmann, *U.S. Foreign Policy*.

99. Roosevelt, *Autobiography*, 560–63.

100. Theodore Roosevelt to Cecil Arthur Spring Rice, November 1, 1905, in *Letters*, vol. 5, 61–64.

101. Roosevelt to Schurz, September 8, 1905, 16–17.

102. He interpreted this maxim as making "all foreign powers understand that when we have adopted a line of policy we have adopted it definitely, and with the intention of backing it up with deeds as well as words." Roosevelt to Lodge, March 27, 1901, 31–32. See also Beale, *Rise of America*, 51.

103. Theodore Roosevelt to Henry Cabot Lodge, October 5, 1903, in *Letters*, vol. 3, 616.

104. Woodrow Wilson, said TR, was one of the worst offenders. "Instead of speaking softly and carrying a big stick, President Wilson spoke bombastically and carried a dishrag," he informed one audience in 1916. Theodore Roosevelt, "Speech Delivered at Louisville, October 19, 1916," in *Roosevelt, His Life*, vol. 3, *Newer Roosevelt Messages*, 1073.

105. Theodore Roosevelt to George Kennan, May 6, 1905, in *Letters*, vol. 4, 1168–69.

106. Roosevelt, "Expansion and Peace," 3.

107. "It is out of the question," he insisted, "to claim a right and yet shirk the responsibility for its exercise. Not only we, but all American Republics who are benefited by the existence of the Doctrine, must recognize the obligations each nation is under as regards foreign peoples." Scrupulously executing commitments to foreign creditors and governments would deny the European great powers any excuse for occupying American territory. In any case, "the Monroe Doctrine does not force us to interfere to prevent punishment" of a tort com-

mitted by one nation against another, "save to see that the punishment does not assume the form of territorial occupation in any shape." Roosevelt, "1905 Annual Message," xxxiii–xxxiv.

108. Roosevelt, "1901 Annual Message," xxxvii.

109. Roosevelt to Taft, March 12, 1901, 11–12. (See ch. 6, n. 7.) At the time Taft was governor of the Philippines, a post Roosevelt had coveted before being nominated for national office.

110. Theodore Roosevelt, "'International Peace,' Address before the Nobel Prize Committee, Delivered at Christiania, Norway, May 5, 1910," in *Works: Memorial, vol. 18, American Problems*, 410–11.

111. Roosevelt, "International Peace," 412.

112. Roosevelt, "International Peace," 413–14.

113. Roosevelt, "International Peace," 414–15.

114. Theodore Roosevelt, "The Management of Small States Which Are Unable to Manage Themselves," *Outlook*, July 2, 1910, reprinted in *Works: Memorial*, vol. 18, *American Problems*, 387.

115. Roosevelt, "Management of Small States," 389–90.

116. Roosevelt, "Management of Small States," 395, 400–401.

117. Roosevelt, "Management of Small States," 395, 400–401.

118. Theodore Roosevelt to John Bassett Moore, January 6, 1904, in *Letters*, vol. 3, 690–91.

119. John Bassett Moore, "'Law and Organization,' Presidential Address at the Eleventh Annual Meeting of the American Political Science Association, at Chicago, in December, 1914," in *International Law and Some Current Illusions and Other Essays* (New York: Macmillan, 1924), 289–315.

120. Moore, "Law and Organization," 302. Moore went further than Roosevelt, who spoke only of judicial and executive functions.

121. Moore, "Law and Organization," 302–304.

122. Moore, "Law and Organization," 309–11.

123. Theodore Roosevelt, "'Uncle Sam's Only Friend Is Uncle Sam,' Address Delivered in June 1917," in *Roosevelt, His Life*, vol. 3, *Newer Roosevelt Messages*, 842–45.

124. Theodore Roosevelt, "The League of Nations," *Metropolitan Magazine*, January 1919, in *Roosevelt, His Life*, vol. 3, *Newer Roosevelt Messages*, 1046–47. Roosevelt repeated many of the themes he had introduced in his 1916 Chicago address, "National Duty and Interna-

tional Ideals," and in another address titled "The League of Nations" (1918), Theodore Roosevelt Collection, Harvard University, Cambridge, MA.

125. Roosevelt, "League of Nations," *Metropolitan*, 1047.

126. Roosevelt, "League of Nations," *Metropolitan*, 1047–48.

127. Roosevelt, "League of Nations," *Metropolitan*, 1047–49.

128. Roosevelt, "League of Nations," *Metropolitan*, 1050–51.

129. Roosevelt, "1908 Annual Message," XLIV.

Chapter 8

1. Roosevelt, *Autobiography*, 520.

2. The Platt Amendment, attached by Congress to the March 2, 1901, Army Appropriation Bill, authorized the president "to 'leave the government and control of the island of Cuba to its people' [quoting the Teller Amendment] so soon as a government shall have been established in said island under a constitution" that prohibited Cuba from alienating its sovereignty to an external power (with the limited exceptions granted to the United States) and contracting excessive foreign debt, and incorporated several other U.S. demands. U.S. Congress, "The Platt Amendment," in Bartlett, *Record of American Diplomacy*, 535–37.

3. "Basis for Establishment of Peace," Spain, signed Washington August 12, 1898, *Consolidated Treaty Series* 8728, ed. Clive Parry (Dobbs Ferry, NY: Oceana, 1969–81), vol. 11, 613–14.

4. "Treaty of Peace (Treaty of Paris)," Spain, signed Paris December 10, 1898, *Consolidated Treaty Series* 8728 (1974), vol. 11, 615–16. See also Howard C. Hill, *Roosevelt and the Caribbean* (Chicago: University of Chicago Press, 1927), 69–70.

5. "Treaty of Peace (Treaty of Paris)," 619–20.

6. Jessup, *Elihu Root*, vol. 1, 423.

7. Elihu Root, "'The Principles of Colonial Policy: Porto Rico, Cuba and the Philippines,' Extract from the Report of the Secretary of War for 1899," in *The Military and Colonial Policy of the United States: Addresses and Reports by Elihu Root*, eds. Robert Bacon and James Brown Scott (Cambridge: Harvard University Press, 1916), 161.

8. Root, "Colonial Policy," 162.

9. Root, "Colonial Policy," 162.

10. Root, "Colonial Policy," 163.

11. Root, "Colonial Policy," 164.

12. Root, "Colonial Policy," 164–65.

13. Root, "Colonial Policy," 165–67.

14. Root, "Colonial Policy," 170–71.

15. Root, "Colonial Policy," 172–73.

16. Root, "Colonial Policy," 173–75.

17. TR grouped U.S. activities taken under the settlement with Spain with those justified by the Monroe Doctrine. "The Philippines, Cuba, and Porto Rico came within our own sphere of governmental action. In addition to this we asserted certain rights in the Western Hemisphere under the Monroe Doctrine." Roosevelt, *Autobiography*, 519.

18. The historical background for the Philippines case comes primarily from Bemis, *Diplomatic History*, 479–502.

19. Bernhard von Bülow to Theodor von Holleben, July 1, 1898, in German Foreign Ministry, *Die Grosse Politik der Europäischen Kabinette, 1871–1914: Sammlung der Diplomatischen Akten des Auswärtigen Amtes, Im Auftrage Des Auswärtigen Amtes*, eds. Johannes Lepsius and others (Berlin: Deutsche Verlagsgesellschaft für Politik und Geschichte, 1922–27), vol. 15, 44–45.

20. Birtle, *U.S. Army Doctrine*, 108.

21. Theodore Roosevelt to Henry Cabot Lodge, May 25, 1898, in *Roosevelt–Lodge Correspondence*, vol. 1, 299–301.

22. McKinley, observes Ernest May, "appeared to be jumping aboard a vehicle he could not brake" during the debate over annexing the Philippines. First, there was the element of interest. The import of Dewey's naval victory at Manila Bay quickly sank in. On May 5, 1898, the president wrote Henry White, "We hold the other side of the Pacific and the value to this country is almost beyond imagination." Second, and more importantly in May's view, popular and elite sentiment increasingly came to favor annexing the entire archipelago. Japan and Britain made it known that they wanted the Philippines if the United States opted not to stay, Mahan and the other expansionists played up the strategic benefits of an outpost so close to China, and the American populace seemed gripped by a sense of mission. "In the end," says May, "there was no alternative" for President McKinley but to follow the drift of public opinion. Declared the *Journal des Débats* perceptively, "Let us remember how McKinley, who has no will of his

own, came to annex the Philippines. Public opinion demanded it, and he was about as much master of the situation as a log drifting downstream." Ernest R. May, *Imperial Democracy: The Emergence of America as a Great Power* (New York: Harcourt, Brace & World, 1961), 243–66.

23. William McKinley, in C. S. Olcott, *Life of William McKinley* (New York: AMS Press, 1972), vol. 2, 108–11.

24. One of the most remorseless anti-imperialists, however, arose from the ranks of the Republican Party. Massachusetts senator George F. Hoar broke with the McKinley administration over annexation of the Philippine Islands. Hoar told one audience that the United States was at risk of being transformed into "a vulgar, commonplace empire founded upon physical force, controlling subject races and vassal states, in which inevitably one class must forever rule and other classes must forever obey." Annexing the Philippines, moreover, would vitiate the Monroe Doctrine, exposing the Western Hemisphere anew to European machinations. Beisner, *Twelve against Empire*, 139–64.

25. Bemis, *Diplomatic History*, 482.

26. Rufus S. Tucker, "A Balance Sheet of the Philippines," *Harvard Business Review* 8 (October 1929): 10–23.

27. Roosevelt to Wolcott, September 15, 1900, 1400–1401. (See ch. 4, n. 11.)

28. Theodore Roosevelt to Eugene A. Philbin, September 10, 1904, in *Letters*, vol. 4, 922–23.

29. Theodore Roosevelt to Adelbert Moot, February 13, 1900, in *Letters*, vol. 2, 1183.

30. Roosevelt to Wolcott, September 15, 1900, 1404.

31. Roosevelt to Wolcott, September 15, 1900, 1403.

32. Roosevelt to Dunne, January 16, 1900, 1134. (See ch. 6, n. 21.) Indiana senator Albert J. Beveridge, for instance, told the Senate, "We will not renounce our part in the mission of our race, trustee, under God, of the civilization of the world." Filipinos were "not capable of self-government. . . . How shall they, in the twinkling of an eye, be exalted to the heights of self-governing peoples which required a thousand years for us to reach, Anglo-Saxon though we are?" Bartlett, *Record of American Diplomacy*, 385–87.

33. Theodore Roosevelt to Raymon Reyes Lala, June 27, 1900, in *Letters*, vol. 2, 1343.

34. Theodore Roosevelt to Rudyard Kipling, November 1, 1904, in *Letters*, vol. 4, 1007.

35. Roosevelt to Coudert, July 3, 1901, 105. (See ch. 2, n. 35.)

36. Roosevelt to Cannon, September 12, 1904, 939. (See ch. 6, n. 14.)

37. Taft, TR told Senator Hoar, had urged him not to promise the Filipinos independence for fear of producing a "feeling of unrest" among the population. Nonetheless, "when and if the Filipinos attained a degree and capacity for self-government . . . then we should leave it to them to decide whether or not they would be independent of us or continue knit to us by some form less of dependence than of interdependence." Theodore Roosevelt to George Frisbie Hoar, June 16, 1902, in *Letters*, vol. 3, 276–77.

38. Roosevelt to Moot, February 13, 1900, 1183.

39. Roosevelt to Wolcott, September 15, 1900, 1403.

40. Roosevelt to Wolcott, September 15, 1900, 1403–1404.

41. Roosevelt to Wolcott, September 15, 1900, 1404–1405. Indeed, Roosevelt himself coveted the post of governor general of the Philippines: "The one position that I should like to have had," he told Lt. H. K. Love in 1900, "was that of Governor General of the Philippines with proper power." Theodore Roosevelt to H. K. Love, November 24, 1900, in *Letters*, vol. 2, 1441.

42. Roosevelt to Taft, March 12, 1901, 11. (See ch. 6, n. 7.)

43. Roosevelt to Cannon, September 12, 1904, 938–39.

44. Theodore Roosevelt to Henry Cabot Lodge, February 24, 1903, in *Letters*, vol. 3, 432.

45. Theodore Roosevelt to Edward Everett Hale, December 17, 1901, in *Letters*, vol. 3, 209.

46. The McKinley and Roosevelt administrations generally preferred to institute civil government as speedily as possible. U.S. Army officers objected to the civil-military divide, as they had in the American West, when the federal government created a civil authority to oversee Indian affairs. Birtle, *U.S. Army Doctrine*, 122–23.

47. William Howard Taft, "'The Army of the United States,' Address before the Board of Trade of Columbus, Ohio, April 2, 1908," in *Present Day Problems*, 77.

48. Taft, "Army of the United States," 76–78.

49. Taft, "Army of the United States," 78.

50. Taft, "Army of the United States," 80–82.

51. Taft, "Army of the United States," 83–89.

52. William Howard Taft, "Inaugural Address as Civil Governor of the Philippines, Manila, Philippines, July 4, 1901," in *Present Day Problems*, 1.

53. Taft, "Inaugural Address as Civil Governor," 4–5.

54. Taft, "Inaugural Address as Civil Governor," 4–10.

55. By 1907 Taft could claim that the constabulary was "conceded to be discharging with efficiency the function which it was chiefly created to perform, of . . . aiding the provincial governors and municipal authorities . . . in maintaining the peace of each province and each municipality." William Howard Taft, "Address at the Inauguration of the Philippine Assembly, Manila, Philippines, October 16, 1907," in *Present Day Problems*, 25.

56. Taft, "Inaugural Address as Civil Governor," 4–7.

57. Taft, "Inaugural Address as Civil Governor," 5–6.

58. The hopes of TR and Taft for a reciprocity arrangement along the lines of the one created for Puerto Rico went unfulfilled because of the objections of U.S. agricultural interests, mostly tobacco and sugar planters. Taft decried "the delay in this much-needed relief [that] has greatly retarded the coming of prosperous times." Taft, "Philippine Assembly Address," 18–20.

59. Taft, "Philippine Assembly Address," 33. Taft also reminded the assembly that such a sale would have to be executed by treaty and thus, during ratification proceedings in Congress, exposed to the full light of public scrutiny.

60. Taft reproached anti-imperialists who had urged the U.S. administration to return the islands to their inhabitants for prolonging the war and alienating Filipinos from their government. Taft, "Philippine Assembly Address," 19.

61. In 1906 President Roosevelt told Congress, "We are constantly increasing the measure of liberty accorded the islanders, and . . . we shall take a great stride forward in testing their capacity for self-government by summoning the first Filipino legislative assembly; and the way in which they stand this test will largely determine whether the self-government thus granted will be increased or decreased." The nation had "no more imperative duty" than to manage "the affairs of all the islands under the American flag . . . so as to make it evident that it is in every way to their advantage that the flag should fly over them." Roosevelt, "1906 Annual Message," xxxviii.

62. Taft, "Philippine Assembly Address," 11–13, 36–37, 41. Filipinos, said Taft, now had "a right to initiate legislation, to modify, amend, shape or defeat legislation proposed by the Commission." This would compel Filipinos to "investigate not only the theoretical wisdom of proposed measures, but also the question of whether they can be practically enforced, and whether, where expense is involved, they are of sufficient value to justify the imposition of a financial burden upon the people." He concluded that the key to governing a country was to strike the "golden mean" of providing for the public welfare without levying crushing taxes.

63. Roosevelt, "1908 Annual Message," XLVI.

64. The campaigns against Confederate partisans, and especially against rebellious American Indian tribes, shaped the outlook of U.S. Army officers on imperial constabulary operations. The analogy to warfare in the American West appears repeatedly in the writings and statements of officers posted to the Philippines. The Filipinos, wrote one, were in "the same position as the Indians of our country have been for many years, and in my opinion must be subdued in much the same way." The army had never developed a formal doctrine for Indian warfare. It had, however, developed "a theory that blended conventional with unconventional techniques to attack the social and economic resources upon which Indian power rested." In the Philippines this theory manifested itself in parallel policies of "attraction" and "chastisement." Birtle, *U.S. Army Doctrine*, 58–92, 112–13.

65. Birtle, *U.S. Army Doctrine*, 136.

66. The Western experience taught U.S. Army officers that "force was the sine qua non" of this kind of warfare. This view, says Birtle, "stemmed less from vindictiveness than from acceptance of the brutal fact" that the tribes were bound to forcibly resist the disruption of their culture and traditions. Acculturation could begin once victory was in hand. Civil measures—preeminently public education—were the catalysts for the acculturation process. The "most permanent and satisfactory way" to resolve these problems, wrote one veteran of the campaign against the Apaches, was "to raise and elevate the condition of the Indian himself." Birtle, *U.S. Army Doctrine*, 79, 83, 85, 119.

67. The army's "long experience in wrestling with the Indian question," writes Birtle, "endowed it with . . . a loose body of principles, assumptions, and beliefs," including "the necessity of close civil-military coordination of a pacification campaign (preferably under military control), the establishment of a firm-but-fair paternalistic government, and the introduction of economic and educational reforms." Birtle, *U.S. Army Doctrine*, 85.

68. William McKinley to Elihu Root, December 21, 1898, in U.S. Army, *Correspondence Relating to the War with Spain* (Washington, DC: Government Printing Office, 1902), vol. 2, 858–59; Brian McAllister Linn, *The U.S. Army and Counterinsurgency in the Philippine War, 1899–1902* (Chapel Hill: University of North Carolina Press, 1989), 9–11.

69. The objective of the insurgency, explained Gen. Francisco Macabulos, "was not to vanquish [the U.S. Army] . . . but to inflict on them constant losses, to the end of discouraging them and convincing them of our rights." Brian Linn points out, however, that they had adopted "a strategy suited for a protracted war to achieve an immediate goal: to convince the American public to repudiate McKinley and elect the anti-imperialist Bryan in November 1900." Aguinaldo's supporters began to lose heart when McKinley won reelection. Brian McAllister Linn, *The Philippine War, 1899–1902* (Lawrence: University Press of Kansas, 2000), 187–88.

70. Linn, *Army and Counterinsurgency*, 16–18.

71. William Howard Taft, in Linn, *Philippine War*, 195–97.

72. Army officers shared the Progressive ethos of turn-of-the-century America. Progressivism gave officers a fundamental philosophy about society and reform; it also spurred them to take an active hand in social and political affairs, beyond their purely military function. These "Armed Progressives," to use the term applied to Gen. Leonard Wood, rejected the traditionally rigid separation of military and civil affairs. Birtle, *U.S. Army Doctrine*, 92, 98.

73. The army's twin approach to pacification derived in large part from General Orders (GO) 100, *Instructions for the Government of Armies of the United States in the Field* (1863). GO 100 was based on a pamphlet by Francis Lieber, a noted legal scholar, titled *Guerrilla Parties Considered with Reference to the Laws and Usages of War* (New York: D. Van Nostrand, 1862). *Guerrilla Parties* prescribed treatment for rebel irregulars based on the degree to which they abided by the laws of war. Partisans merited the protections accorded prisoners of war, while "war-rebels" and "bushwhackers," who wore civilian dress and hid among civil populations, could be treated summarily as brigands or pirates. The relationship between soldier and civilian, moreover, was a reciprocal one. If a populace repaid the occupier's benevolence with violent resistance, the occupier was entitled to apply stern repressive measures. See also Birtle, *U.S. Army Doctrine*, 32–35, 100–101, 113, 120, 126–28.

74. General Otis assumed that Filipinos would welcome the ben-

efits of American rule. Otis downplayed military operations in favor of municipal government, health, education, physical infrastructure, and police. For him these were the tangible expression of "benevolent assimilation." Textbooks such as William E. Birkhimer's *Military Government and Martial Law*, 3d ed. rev. (Kansas City, MO: F. Hudson, 1914) conveyed the same basic message. Linn, *Philippine War*, 200; Birtle, *U.S. Army Doctrine*, 101–102.

75. General MacArthur speedily ordered the arming of the Filipino police and the raising of indigenous "constabulary bodies." Despite some growing pains, local constabularies proved to be some of the most effective forces available to the U.S. administration. Linn, *Philippine War*, 204.

76. This dual-pacification scheme closely resembled the one implemented on the American frontier under GO 100. Military and civil functions mingled freely. One directive from Manila observed, "not even those left on duty with troops can wholly escape the character of civil administrators. . . . The performance of civil duties must become more and more exacting and ultimately assume a first importance." Linn, *Philippine War*, 199.

77. Linn contends that the dispersal of American forces throughout Luzon was a blessing in disguise. Regional commanders enjoyed wide latitude for independent action. "Indeed," says Linn, "the key to the Army's success was its lack of adherence to rigid doctrines or theories and the willingness of its officers to experiment with novel pacification schemes." Linn, *Army and Counterinsurgency*, 20–21, 163–70.

78. Many Americans likened the Filipino tactics to those "of the Indian or the guerrilla." For Brig. Gen. Samuel B. M. Young, army policy was too soft; what was required was "the remedial measures that proved successful with the Apaches." Linn, *Philippine War*, 186–87, 211.

79. Taft had MacArthur replaced with Maj. Gen. Adna R. Chaffee, who had fought partisans in the Civil and Indian wars and commanded troops during the Boxer intervention. Linn, *Philippine War*, 217; Birtle, *U.S. Army Doctrine*, 77, 82–83, 133.

80. Linn, *Philippine War*, 213–14.

81. Linn, *Army and Counterinsurgency*, 23–25.

82. The amount of fighting varied widely from village to village and province to province. In thirty-four of seventy-seven provinces, there was no fighting at all. Soldiers in one town might face constant attack while their comrades a few miles away seldom came under guerrilla attack. Linn, *Philippine War*, 185.

83. "Report of General MacArthur," in U.S. Department of War, *Annual Report of the War Department: 1900* (Washington, DC: Government Printing Office, 1900), vol. 1, pt. 4, 345 (hereafter *ARWD:1xxx*); "Dispatch of Colonel Gardner," in *ARWD: 1900*, vol. 1, pt. 4, 394; "Report of the Secretary of War," in *ARWD: 1899*, vol. 1, pt. 1, 63–73; "Report of the Lieutenant General Commanding the Army," in *ARWD: 1900*, vol. 1, pt. 4, 211.

84. Reconcentration meant ordering local inhabitants to bring all of their belongings into specified neighborhoods in an attempt to cut off the insurgents' supplies. Although schools and medical care were provided, the close quarters fostered sickness and malnutrition. Linn, *Army and Counterinsurgency*, 27.

85. Linn, *Army and Counterinsurgency*, 26–27. The end of the war did not come, however, without some brutal counterinsurgency tactics. After a sanguinary battle between insurgents and the U.S. garrison at Balangiga, in Samar, General Smith directed his subordinates, "I wish you to kill and burn, the more you kill and the more you burn the better you will please me." Asked to set an age limit for the slaughter, Smith replied, "Ten years." The general's methods brought results; but he was later court-martialed for war crimes. Max Boot, *The Savage Wars of Peace: Small Wars and the Rise of American Power* (New York: Basic Books, 2002), 120–21.

86. Linn concludes that no district commander—with "Hell-Raising Jake" Smith being a possible exception—"ever implemented a counterinsurgency policy based on extralegal repression." Still, commanders increasingly tolerated some stretching of official policy, especially in remote villages and towns. Linn, *Philippine War*, 220, 224.

87. Linn, *Army and Counterinsurgency*, 168.

88. Keith B. Bickel, *Mars Learning: The Marine Corps Development of Small Wars Doctrine, 1915–1940* (Boulder, CO: Westview Press, 2001), 37.

89. Birtle, *U.S. Army Doctrine*, 154.

90. "Old frontier hands," observes Birtle, "recognized that the native soldiers' familiarity with the terrain, people, and language . . . gave them an edge over American troops in constabulary operations." Recalled Capt. John Bigelow, author of *The Principles of Strategy, Illustrated Mainly from American Campaigns*, 2d ed. (Philadelphia: J. D. Lippincott, 1894; reprint, New York: Greenwood Press, 1968), Indian auxiliaries were trained not as soldiers but as "more formidable Indians." Some fifteen thousand Filipino auxiliaries were organized into light infantry (the Philippine Scouts), paramilitary police (the Philippine Con-

stabulary), and local police and militias. Birtle, *U.S. Army Doctrine*, 70, 116–17.

91. Birtle, *U.S. Army Doctrine*, 155–56.

92. Linn, *Philippine War*, 327.

93. Both Secretary Root and his military subordinates believed that a lack of civic responsibility among the Filipino populace was the chief obstacle to reform. Because this was not "a matter of intellectual apprehension, but of character and of acquired habits of thought and feeling," Root maintained that it would take years, if not decades, of "tuition under a strong and guiding hand" to modify the Filipino temperament. The key was to impart self-restraint without trampling indigenous customs and traditions. Birtle, *U.S. Army Doctrine*, 103–104.

94. The U.S. authorities believed that public education was the best way to prepare Filipinos for the rigors of republican self-government. By August 1900, accordingly, the army had established some one thousand schools, spending $100,000 on facilities and teaching supplies. General MacArthur characterized these expenditures as "an adjunct to military operations, calculated to pacify the people and procure and expedite the restoration of tranquility throughout the archipelago." Birtle, *U.S. Army Doctrine*, 121.

95. Bickel, *Mars Learning*, 33–35.

96. Bickel, *Mars Learning*, 34–35.

97. The Platt Amendment authorized the United States to "exercise the right to intervene for the preservation of Cuban independence, the maintenance of a government adequate for the protection of life, property, and individual liberty, and for discharging the obligations . . . imposed by the treaty of Paris." U.S. Congress, "The Platt Amendment," in Bartlett, *Record of American Diplomacy*, 535–37.

98. Stead, "Conference at The Hague," 3–4.

99. Howard C. Hill, a frequent critic of Roosevelt, applauded the president's handling of ties between the United States and Cuba. "In striking and pleasing contrast to Roosevelt's dealings with Colombia are his relations with Cuba," says Hill. TR "assumed toward the island republic an attitude which on the whole resembles that of a father who takes pride in the achievements of his child but who does not hesitate, if need arises, to admonish and discipline his offspring." Hill, *Roosevelt and the Caribbean*, 69.

100. The first military governor, Maj. Gen. John R. Brooke, preferred to rule through civil channels. General Brooke placed Cubans in charge of most of the executive agencies. In keeping with the army's

emphasis on incremental reform, he gradually modified Cuban law and governance. The McKinley administration quickly tired of Brooke's cautious approach, dispatching Leonard Wood, a leading "Armed Progressive," to turn Cuba into a "workshop for American progressivism." Birtle, *U.S. Army Doctrine*, 104–105.

101. Leonard Wood, *Leonard Wood on National Issues*, ed. Evan J. David (Garden City, NY: Doubleday, Page, 1920), 3.

102. The "Cubans [were] reestablished in complete possession of their own beautiful island. . . . There are plenty of occasions in our history when . . . we have not been as scrupulous as we should have been as regards the rights of others. But I know of no action by any other government in relation to a weaker power which showed such disinterested efficiency . . . as was true in connection with our intervention in Cuba." Roosevelt, *Autobiography*, 519.

103. Hill, *Roosevelt and the Caribbean*, 70.

104. Provisions of the constitution relating to future ties between Cuba and the United States aroused consternation at the Cuban constitutional convention that convened in 1900. The delegates, observes Hill, were understandably reluctant to acknowledge formally that their nation was "under the tutelage or oversight of its powerful neighbor to the north." The Platt Amendment was "heartily disliked" by the Cuban delegates, who insisted "that the stipulations violated the very object that they were supposed to guarantee, namely, the independence of Cuba." When Congress adopted the amendment anyway, a Cuban delegation traveled to Washington to protest in person. While President McKinley and Secretary of War Root informed the Cubans that no changes could be made, they did promise to lobby Congress to enact favorable commercial relations between the United States and Cuba. A subsequent statement relayed by General Wood said, "the intervention described in the third clause of the Platt Amendment referred not to wanton meddling but rather to the preservation of Cuban independence and to the maintenance of a government able to secure life, liberty, and property for Cuban citizens and discharge the obligations codified in the Treaty of Paris." Thus reassured, the convention duly incorporated the Platt Amendment into the draft constitution. Hill, *Roosevelt and the Caribbean*, 71–78.

105. "Relations with Cuba," Cuba, signed Havana May 22, 1903, *Treaties and Other International Acts Series* 8549 (1971), 1116–19.

106. Bemis, *Diplomatic History*, 504–505.

107. Wood and Roosevelt had jointly organized the First U.S. Volunteer Cavalry, or Rough Riders, for the campaign against Spain.

Morris, *Rise of Theodore Roosevelt*, 642–49. See also Jack C. Lane, *Armed Progressive: General Leonard Wood* (San Rafael, CA: Presidio Press, 1978).

108. Herminio Portell-Vilá, "Paper Presented to the American Historical Association, Urbana, Ill., 1933," citing a letter from Leonard Wood to Theodore Roosevelt, October 29, 1901, footnote in Bemis, *Diplomatic History*, 505.

109. Roosevelt to Cannon, September 12, 1904, 923.

110. Wood, *National Issues*, 1–4.

111. The U.S administration enjoyed wide discretion. "The powers of the Military Governor," noted Wood, "were absolute in every particular, and yet there was but one instance of a reversal of the action of the native court." Otherwise, the "courts have been untrammeled in the exercise of their authority, and the municipalities have been governed by officials elected by the people at the polls." Wood, *National Issues*, 11–12, 13.

112. Wood, *National Issues*, 4–6. Hill points out that the U.S. military administration's effort to eradicate tropical disease on the island excited "keen interest in the world at large." The U.S. Army medical corps, for instance, instituted a vigorous campaign against mosquitoes, managing to virtually wipe out yellow fever. Strict quarantine regulations and sanitary works were two keys to this achievement. A lapse in the enforcement of sanitary measures was the chief irritant in relations between the two countries after the U.S. pullout. Unable to push through legislation satisfying Washington's complaints, President Tomas Estrada Palma ended up implementing sanitary measures by presidential decree. Hill, *Roosevelt and the Caribbean*, 82–86.

113. Wood, *National Issues*, 7–12, 14.

114. Wood, *National Issues*, 12–15.

115. Wood, *National Issues*, 16–17.

116. While Birtle hails the army's achievements during the brief occupation of Cuba, he also observes that military government had been unable to do more than superimpose "a thin veneer of American-style institutions for which there was very little support from within Cuban society itself." Leonard Wood moved too quickly; soldiers all too often rode roughshod over Cuban culture; legal reforms distilled from the Anglo-Saxon tradition proved to be a poor fit with Roman law; and even health and sanitation programs that went against Cuban habits were abandoned once the army withdrew. Compounding these difficulties, the American populace had little appetite for a sustained occupation. "Steeped in the principles of liberty and self-

determination, much of the American people felt uncomfortable at the prospect of maintaining the type of lengthy stewardship necessary to fundamentally change Cuban society." Birtle, *U.S. Army Doctrine*, 106–108.

117. "The Cubans," declares Hill, "had good reason for gratitude to the United States. During the four years of the American occupation order had been maintained, public revenues had been honestly collected and wisely expended, public health had been improved through medical research and sanitation, capital had been attracted, free schools had been established, public works had been constructed, and the Cubans had received training in administration and self-government." The sugar tariff was one major stumbling block. TR pled with Congress to cut the tariff on Cuban sugar "in a spirit of large generosity." "We have rightfully insisted upon Cuba adopting toward us an attitude differing politically from that she adopts toward any other power; and in return, as a matter of right, we must give to Cuba a different—that is, a better—position economically in her relations with us than we give to other powers." Only after a two-year struggle did lawmakers finally approve an arrangement giving Cuban exporters a 20 percent advantage on sales of sugar and other agricultural and industrial products. Hill, *Roosevelt and the Caribbean*, 77–82.

118. TR repeatedly advocated a compromise settlement between the contending Cuban factions. Even when the president did decide to step in, he instructed Taft to emphasize that the intervention was primarily to protect U.S. interests, to convey the temporary nature of the occupation, to avoid using the term "intervention," and to make clear that the U.S. force would stay only long enough to erect a permanent government. Hill, *Roosevelt and the Caribbean*, 99–100.

119. The impasse resulted in large part from the actions of the Cuban Congress, which, dominated by the Moderate Party, refused to pass legislation implementing a constitutional mandate making municipal offices elective. The executive retained the power to appoint and dismiss local officials, as well as judges. The opposition Liberals boycotted the December 1905 elections and took up arms, prompting American observers on the island to decry the islanders' "natural tendency to insurrection." Badly outnumbered and outgunned, the Cuban military was unable to subdue the revolt. Deteriorating conditions placed U.S. property and the sugar crop at risk, prodding the Roosevelt administration to step in. Hill, *Roosevelt and the Caribbean*, 87–93.

120. Roosevelt, "1906 Annual Message," XLIV–XLV; Hill, *Roosevelt and the Caribbean*, 104.

121. Theodore Roosevelt to William Howard Taft, January 22, 1907, in *Letters*, vol. 5, 560.

122. While taking control of Cuba was a last resort, declared TR, "I do not care in the least for the fact that such an agreement [establishing a provisional government] is not constitutional." Hill, *Roosevelt and the Caribbean*, 101.

123. Roosevelt to Taft, January 22, 1907, 560.

124. Roosevelt authorized intervention only after he became convinced that the alternative was anarchy. After President Palma resigned, evidently in a bid to compel U.S. intervention, the U.S. consul general informed Washington that chaos would ensue "unless the United States Government will adopt the measures necessary to avoid this danger." TR dispatched Taft and Robert Bacon, the acting secretary of state, to Cuba to inspect the situation firsthand. "Our interest in Cuban affairs," wrote TR, "will come only if Cuba herself shows that she has fallen into the insurrectionary habit, that she lacks the self-restraint necessary to secure peaceful self-government, and that her contending factions have plunged the country into anarchy." Hill, *Roosevelt and the Caribbean*, 94–96.

125. Keith Bickel observes that both Cuban factions had an interest in U.S. military intervention because they both believed American involvement would work in their favor. In the end, both sides stood down, giving way to the U.S.-sponsored provisional government. Bickel, *Mars Learning*, 33.

126. Roosevelt, "1906 Annual Message," XLV.

127. William Howard Taft, *The United States and Peace* (New York: Charles Scribner's Sons, 1914), 14–15.

128. In 1901 Roosevelt told Henry Cabot Lodge that German military preparations, combined with U.S. lassitude, would force the United States to "put up or shut up on the Monroe doctrine." Theodore Roosevelt to Henry Cabot Lodge, March 17, 1901, in *Letters*, vol. 3, 31–32.

129. Hill, *Roosevelt and the Caribbean*, 106–107.

130. American Business Man, "Is the Monroe Doctrine a Bar to Civilization?" *North American Review* 176 (April 1903): 520. Francis B. Loomis, the American minister in Caracas, agreed. In January 1901 he informed Secretary Hay confidentially, "The talk about the constitution is bosh. . . . This is not a constitutional government. General Castro is a dictator, and does pretty much as he pleases." Hill, *Roosevelt and the Caribbean*, 108.

131. Hill, *Roosevelt and the Caribbean*, 106–107.

132. The British government estimated that Caracas had been in default of its British debt for nearly forty years. For this reason, concludes Hill, Great Britain, not Germany, pushed hardest for coercive measures vis-à-vis Castro's government. Hill, *Roosevelt and the Caribbean*, 108–11, 115.

133. Theodore Roosevelt to Hermann Speck von Sternburg, July 12, 1901, in *Letters*, vol. 3, 115–16. Germany's principal demands on Caracas were (1) the recovery of interest on Venezuelan bonds seven years in arrears; (2) the payment of dividends guaranteed by the Venezuelan government on a railroad built in Venezuela by a German firm; and (3) indemnity for German losses in the late Venezuelan revolution. Hill, *Roosevelt and the Caribbean*, 109.

134. While he toned down his rhetoric, Roosevelt never entirely outgrew this attitude. As late as 1905, after proclaiming his corollary to the Monroe Doctrine, TR told his brother-in-law, "Some time soon I shall have to spank some little brigand of a South American republic." He did, however, push the 1907 Hague convention to embrace the Drago Doctrine, which would have strictly forbidden the use of force to collect debts. Beale, *Rise of America*, 47.

135. Roosevelt backed away from this sort of overblown rhetoric. He exempted the "ABC" countries of South America from the corollary. These great Latin American nations had matured sufficiently to withstand European coercion on their own. They were so remote from the United States, moreover, that Washington had little need to worry about a breach of the doctrine. Roosevelt engineered their attendance at the 1907 Hague conference, testifying to their "grown-up" status. Taft, *United States and Peace*, 18–19.

136. Roosevelt to Speck von Sternburg, July 12, 1901, 115–16.

137. TR gave several different accounts of the Venezuelan episode over the years, remaining remarkably closemouthed about it while in office. "Only after leaving the White House," says Edmund Morris, "did he reveal, at first in strict confidence, that in November and December of 1902 'the United States was on the verge of war with Germany.'" Nearly a century elapsed before it became apparent that he had done so "to spare the vanity of an emperor." Edmund Morris, "'A Matter of Extreme Urgency': Theodore Roosevelt, Wilhelm II, and the Venezuela Crisis of 1902," *Naval War College Review*, spring 2002; available from http://www.nwc.navy.mil/press/Review/2002/spring/art5-sp2.htm (accessed January 31, 2004).

138. Hay replied to the German communiqué, quoting Roosevelt's 1901 message to Congress. The president told Congress, "We do not guarantee any State against punishment if it misconducts itself, provided that punishment does not take the form of the acquisition of territory by any non-American power." This was the consistent U.S. policy. The British government insisted that it intended only to pursue a "warlike blockade." Hill, *Roosevelt and the Caribbean*, 111–12, 116–17. Roosevelt, "1901 Annual Message," xxxvi.

139. British statesmen and journalists were the first to claim that the Monroe Doctrine contained a right of positive interference. Eager to reduce the foreign commitments that had overtaxed the Royal Navy, they urged Washington to adopt a policy that would amount to safe guarding British interests in the Western Hemisphere. During the Venezuela border crisis of 1895–96, Lord Salisbury had suggested that the United States could not protect Latin Americans from the consequences of their own misconduct unless it asserted some kind of control over them. Lord Salisbury to Sir Julian Pauncefote, November 26, 1895, in Bartlett, *Record of American Diplomacy*, 346–50.

140. Theodore Roosevelt to William Roscoe Thayer, August 21, 1916, in Joseph Bucklin Bishop, *Theodore Roosevelt and His Time, Shown in His Own Letters* (New York: Charles Scribner's Sons, 1920), vol. 1, 221–25. Time may have clouded his memory, or, suggests Hill, animosity toward Germany during World War I may have colored his account. Hill, *Roosevelt and the Caribbean*, 125–38.

141. Hill, *Roosevelt and the Caribbean*, 141.

142. German Foreign Ministry Communiqué, March 3, 1903, in Perkins, *Monroe Doctrine*, 235. Olney's 1895 exchange of notes with Lord Salisbury fueled talk of a protectorate, and thus Latin American anxieties. Roosevelt and his successors, notably Taft, were quick to distance themselves from the notion that the United States intended to enforce "suzerainty" over the New World, as Olney had seemed to imply.

143. Theodore Roosevelt to John Hay, March 13, 1903, Theodore Roosevelt Papers, series 1, reel 33.

144. Theodore Roosevelt to John Hay, April 22, 1903, Theodore Roosevelt Papers, series 1, reel 33.

145. Rear Adm. Henry Clay Taylor, chief of the U.S. Navy's Bureau of Navigation, secretly warned President Roosevelt that the German flotilla would bombard Venezuela and demand an indemnity. Venezuela could "offer nothing but territory, or she could mortgage her revenue in such a way as to place herself in complete political

dependence on Germany. The United States could not allow either of these. . . . The only courses open to the United States [would be] payment of the indemnity taking such security as she can from Venezuela or war." Henry Clay Taylor to Theodore Roosevelt, late November 1902, Theodore Roosevelt Papers, series 1, reel 31. A sentence in Berlin's written commitment to the blockade declared, "We would consider the temporary occupation on our part of different Venezuelan harbor places." "The adjective 'temporary,'" observes Morris, "reminded TR that in 1898 Kaiser Wilhelm II had 'temporarily' acquired Kiaochow in China, on a lease that His Majesty had somehow lengthened to ninety-nine years." Morris, "A Matter of Extreme Urgency."

146. Theodore Roosevelt to Charles Evans Hughes, August 28, 1916, in *Letters*, vol. 8, 1108.

147. Hill, *Roosevelt and the Caribbean*, 30.

148. Theodore Roosevelt, "How the United States Acquired the Right to Dig the Panama Canal," *Outlook*, October 7, 1911, 314–18.

149. Concludes Samuel Flagg Bemis, "Public opinion [in Latin America] began to brand the sponsor-nation of the Monroe Doctrine with the accusation of conquest in that part of the world which it professed to have liberated from European interference. 'Have I defended myself?' asked Roosevelt after explaining his actions to the cabinet. 'You certainly have,' replied a brave Elihu Root. 'You have shown that you were accused of seduction and you have conclusively proved that you were guilty of rape.'" In 1912 the U.S. minister to Bogotá informed Secretary of State Philander Chase Knox that the breach opened by Roosevelt's intervention "has been growing wider since that hour . . . the indignation of every Colombian, and millions of other Latin-Americans, was aroused and is still most intensely active." Bemis, *Diplomatic History*, 517; Walter LaFeber, *The Panama Canal: The Crisis in Historical Perspective* (Oxford: Oxford University Press, 1979), 57; Hill, *Roosevelt and the Caribbean*, 68.

150. Hill, *Roosevelt and the Caribbean*, 31.

151. Roosevelt to Hale, December 17, 1901, 209.

152. Says Beale, Roosevelt's "excited outbursts over the refusal of Colombian senators to ratify the canal treaty we had dictated were akin to the behavior of the recognized leader of a group of small boys whom some smaller boy had successfully defied." Declared William James in 1900, "He is still mentally in the *Sturm und Drang* period of early adolescence." Beale, *Rise of America*, 48.

153. The Roosevelt administration demanded that the treaty be

ratified "exactly in its present form, without any modifications whatever." TR ascribed any sign of resistance to ill faith. Hill, *Roosevelt and the Caribbean*, 52–53.

154. Roosevelt scoffed at the notion that Colombia was entitled to the same treatment accorded civilized powers such as Denmark and Switzerland. TR believed that Marroquin controlled the Senate and could easily have secured approval of the treaty. Roosevelt to Kipling, November 1, 1904, 1008.

155. Hay had written Roosevelt that he had three options in the crisis: (1) to stand by and let events take their course, (2) to take a direct hand in the affair, or (3) to begin negotiations with Nicaragua. TR ruled out remaining aloof. Hill, *Roosevelt and the Caribbean*, 57; Bishop, *Roosevelt and His Time*, vol. 1, 278.

156. Theodore Roosevelt to John Hay, September 15, 1903, Theodore Roosevelt Papers, series 1, reel 37.

157. John Bassett Moore, "Considerations on the Present Situation with Respect to the Canal Treaty with Colombia," Theodore Roosevelt Papers, series 1, reel 37.

158. Theodore Roosevelt to John Hay, August 19, 1903, Theodore Roosevelt Papers, series 1, reel 36.

159. If the Panamanians "had not revolted," Roosevelt said some years later, "I should have recommended Congress to take possession of the isthmus by force of arms." Bemis, *Diplomatic History*, 514–15; Bishop, *Roosevelt and His Time*, vol. 1, 289; Hill, *Roosevelt and the Caribbean*, 63.

160. Hill analyzes the treaty: Did the clause empowering the United States to maintain transit "guarantee to New Granada the possession of the isthmus against all attack, domestic as well as foreign?" If unrest threatened, "did the treaty give the right to and place the obligation upon the United States to maintain peace?" Could the United States use force "without the request or permission of New Granada?" Could the United States use force to prevent New Granada from putting down "a riot or an insurrection?" Hill, *Roosevelt and the Caribbean*, 40.

161. In his letter transmitting the treaty to the Senate for advice and consent, President James K. Polk told lawmakers that the "guaranty of the sovereignty of New Granada over the isthmus" was "a natural consequence of the guaranty of its neutrality," which itself was the only "practical mode of securing the neutrality of this territory." In 1866, Secretary of State William Seward declared, "The United States

have always abstained from any connection with questions of internal revolution in the State of Panama . . . and will continue to maintain a perfect neutrality in such domestic controversies." Hill, *Roosevelt and the Caribbean*, 40–43.

162. Early in September, Roosevelt invited Moore to Oyster Bay to discuss the memorandum. TR later said that Moore's visit to Sagamore Hill had inspired his course of action. Hill, *Roosevelt and the Caribbean*, 58.

163. Theodore Roosevelt to Kermit Roosevelt, November 4, 1903, in *Letters*, vol. 3, 644.

164. Moore, "Considerations on the Present Situation."

165. "Treaty of Amity, Commerce, and Navigation Concluded December 12, 1846," in U.S. Department of State, *Treaties and Conventions Concluded between the United States of America and Other Powers since 1776*, rev. ed. (Washington, DC: Government Printing Office, 1873), 177–88.

166. To show that the parties to the treaty had foreseen a U.S.-built canal, Moore reproduced a statement by James K. Polk that contemplated the construction of a canal. Moore, "Considerations on the Present Situation."

167. Moore pointed out that an 1879 protocol had explicitly extended U.S. transit rights on the isthmus to military personnel and extradited fugitives. Moore, "Considerations on the Present Situation."

168. Moore, "Considerations on the Present Situation."

169. Roosevelt recalled rejecting proposals to foment secession. "I should be delighted if Panama were an independent State . . . but for me to say so publicly would amount to an instigation of a revolt, and therefore I cannot say it." Theodore Roosevelt to Albert Shaw, October 10, 1903, in *Letters*, vol. 3, 628.

170. Hill contends, "There is no question that both the attitude and the actions of the administration during the weeks which followed the rejection of the treaty gave encouragement, at least indirectly, to the leaders of the insurrection." TR himself indirectly confirmed this assessment, observing that, while Bunau-Varilla had received "no assurances in any way" from Roosevelt or Hay, he was "a very able fellow. . . . He would have been a very dull man had he been unable to make such a guess." Bunau-Varilla correctly surmised that the revolutionaries would get no direct help from Washington but that Roosevelt would not permit Colombian troops to intervene. Hill, *Roosevelt and*

the Caribbean, 54–56, 59. See also Bishop, *Roosevelt and His Time,* vol. 1, 279, 288–89, 295-96, 299.

171. U.S. warships were directed to "Proceed with all possible dispatch to Panama. . . . Maintain free and uninterrupted transit. If interruption is threatened by armed force, occupy the line of railroad. Prevent landing of any armed force, either Government or insurgent, with hostile intent." Hill, *Roosevelt and the Caribbean,* 61.

172. The Panamanian populace evidently strongly favored the canal. Indeed, the newly installed governor informed his superiors in Bogotá that, should the province revolt to secure the canal, he would stand with the revolutionaries. Hill, *Roosevelt and the Caribbean,* 55.

173. Until 1902, however, American sailors and marines had landed on the isthmus only with the approval or consent of the Co-lombian authorities. Concludes Hill, U.S. policy from 1846–1902 had been to (1) protect Panama against foreign aggression, (2) intervene in internal upheavals only on request of the Colombian authorities, and (3) refrain from interfering with Colombian troop movements. Hill, *Roosevelt and the Caribbean,* 43–46.

174. Theodore Roosevelt, "Message of the President to the Senate and the House of Representatives," December 7, 1903, in *FRUS: 1903,* XXXIII–XLII. Roosevelt delivered a special message to Congress making three claims: First, the primary object of the 1846 treaty had been to assure the construction of a canal. Colombia had breached its treaty obligations to the United States when it repudiated the Hay-Herrán Treaty. Second, the interminable delays wrought by the Co-lombian Congress would have tempted France to step in on behalf of the French-owned New Panama Canal Company. Third, the United States had a virtual mandate to act in the interest of civilization. Hill disputes Roosevelt's claim that the 1846 treaty sought to bring about the construction of a canal and derides the necessity-knows-no-law logic underpinning the president's arguments. Hill, *Roosevelt and the Caribbean,* 64–67.

175. Roosevelt to Cannon, September 12, 1904, 922–23.

176. Once the new, more pliant Panamanian government was in place, Roosevelt reverted to his tactful mode of diplomacy. He gave way when Panama insisted that its law apply in the Canal Zone: "Of course I entirely agree with you that we can do nothing without Panama's consent," he told John Hay while the two sides were negoti-ating this question. Theodore Roosevelt to John Hay, December 22, 1903, Theodore Roosevelt Papers, series 1, reel 39.

177. "Isthmian Canal Convention," Panama, signed Washington November 18, 1903, *Consolidated Treaty Series* 8642 (1972), vol. 10, 663–64.

178. "Isthmian Canal Convention," 664–65.

179. "Isthmian Canal Convention," 665.

180. "Isthmian Canal Convention," 666.

181. "Isthmian Canal Convention," 666, 669.

182. "Isthmian Canal Convention," 670–71.

183. TR hoped to parley the Santo Domingo case into a broader supervisory authority. Asked to defuse a dispute over Costa Rican finances, he told John Hay, "It is to our advantage to gain by the free offer of these republics just that power over their finances the lack of which is causing us such trouble at this moment in San Domingo and Venezuela." Theodore Roosevelt to John Hay, January 14, 1905, Theodore Roosevelt Papers, series 1, reel 52.

184. Hill, *Roosevelt and the Caribbean*, 148–49.

185. Jacob H. Hollander, "The Convention of 1907 between the United States and the Dominican Republic," *American Journal of International Law* 1, vol. 2 (April 1907): 288.

186. "Like Venezuela," notes Hill, "Santo Domingo had long been a prey to ambitious, self-seeking adventurers and a victim of disorders and insurrections usually originating in the efforts of rival leaders to obtain possession of the resources of the republic and, more especially, of the customs-houses, the chief source of governmental revenue." Hill, *Roosevelt and the Caribbean*, 149–54.

187. The arbitrators awarded a monthly payment of $40,000 to the Improvement Company, in default of which the customs house at Puerto Plata would be delivered to an American representative of the company along with a lien on the duties collected at Monte Christi, Sanchez, and Samana. Unable to make the prescribed payments, the Morales government surrendered Puerto Plata to the American agent in October 1904—threatening immediate disaster to the government. The handover of Puerto Plata provoked a strong response from the Italian, French, and Belgian representatives, who realized they would not be able to recover their claims.

188. *FRUS: 1904*; Perkins, *Monroe Doctrine*, 234–40. Some legal theorists of Roosevelt's day connected governmental powerlessness with great-power aggrandizement. The editors of the *American Journal of International Law* noted a popular belief "that but for the Monroe

doctrine and the danger of its enforcement goodly tracts of America would be under foreign dominion instead of enjoying the blessings of self-government." James Brown Scott, "Editorial Comment," *American Journal of International Law* 1, no. 1 (January 1907): 138.

189. Indeed, in 1901 France and Belgium had acquired a mortgage on the revenues of the ports of Santo Domingo and Macoris, the chief sources of revenue for the government. Under the arrangement the French and Belgian governments could demand control of the customs houses there if the Dominican government failed to pay their claims. This left Santo Domingo in an impossible situation, since the government would be forced to choose between honoring its foreign obligations and having enough revenue for normal operations. In July 1903 the Italian, German, and Spanish governments made matters worse by demanding that the Dominican government sign protocols agreeing to pay specified monthly sums to their creditors. Hill, *Roosevelt and the Caribbean*, 154–57.

190. Theodore Roosevelt to Theodore Roosevelt Jr., February 10, 1904, in *Letters*, vol. 4, 724.

191. Bishop, *Roosevelt and His Time*, vol. 1, 431.

192. *FRUS: 1904*; Perkins, *Monroe Doctrine*, 234–40.

193. Henry F. Pringle, *Theodore Roosevelt: A Biography* (New York: Harcourt, Brace, 1931), 294.

194. Theodore Roosevelt to Elihu Root, June 7, 1904, in *Letters*, vol. 4, 821–23.

195. "Arbitration of San Domingo Improvement Company Claim," Dominican Republic, signed Santo Domingo January 31, 1903, *Consolidated Treaty Series* 8566 (1971), 189–92.

196. House, *House Executive Documents*, vol. 1, *Annual Reports of the War Department*, 59th Cong., 1st sess., 1905 (Washington, DC: Government Printing Office, 1906), 298.

197. *House Executive Documents*, 59th Cong., 1st sess., vol. 1, 298.

198. Hill, *Roosevelt and the Caribbean*, 160–61.

199. In 1908 Roosevelt listed the modus vivendi among his most notable accomplishments as president, claiming that it had "put the affairs of the island on a better basis than they have been for over a century." Bishop, *Theodore Roosevelt and His Time*, vol. 2, 130. See also Roosevelt, *Autobiography*, 510.

200. Theodore Roosevelt to Alvey Augustus Adee, March 28,

1905, in *Letters*, vol. 4, 1148–49.

201. Hill, *Roosevelt and the Caribbean*, 160.

202. Roosevelt's detractors argued that only the presence of American warships allowed Colonel Colton and his assistants to collect duties. TR's supporters in the Senate agreed. Hill, *Roosevelt and the Caribbean*, 162.

203. Theodore Roosevelt to William Howard Taft, April 8, 1905, in *Letters*, vol. 4, 1158–59.

204. Theodore Roosevelt to Charles Joseph Bonaparte, September 4, 1905, in *Letters*, vol. 5, 10.

205. Theodore Roosevelt to William Howard Taft, July 29, 1905, in *Letters*, vol. 4, 1290–91.

206. "Without question," concludes Hill, "the presence of American warships in Dominican waters discouraged insurrections." Senators feared that the president meant to defend the current Dominican government against all revolution, thus establishing the protectorate to which they so vehemently objected. Once Elihu Root became secretary of state, however, the administration's attitude seemingly shifted. When Morales was overthrown and fled the country in January 1906, Root stated that U.S. forces would be used only upon specific request of the Dominican government and only for "temporary protection of life of American citizens," including the U.S. agents administering the customs houses. Hill, *Roosevelt and the Caribbean*, 165–66.

207. "Power when wielded by abnormal energy is the most serious of facts, and all Roosevelt's friends know that his restless and combative energy was more than abnormal . . . he was pure act." Henry Adams, *The Education of Henry Adams*, intro. James Truslow Adams (New York: Modern Library, 1931), 417.

208. By no means was Roosevelt alone in his forward-leaning outlook on the exercise of power. He consulted the Senate after Morales "asked us to take over the custom houses pending action by the Senate." Senator Gorman, an outspoken Democratic critic of the administration, "told me that he had taken it for granted that I would have to take such action" as imposing the modus vivendi "and believed it necessary." Both men understood this to be "merely his unofficial opinion, and that officially he is going to condemn our action as realizing his worst forebodings." Theodore Roosevelt to John Hay, March 30, 1905, Theodore Roosevelt Papers, series 1, reel 53.

209. The modus vivendi proved satisfactory to the European

claimants and to the Dominicans. First, during the twenty-eight months the arrangement was in place, the Dominican treasury went from being empty to having $3.2 million on hand. The government had not only been able to meet its routine expenses but to fund an array of public infrastructure. The senators, however, struck the provision in which the United States pledged "to respect the complete territorial integrity of the Dominican Republic," arguing that there was no difference between respecting and guaranteeing the integrity of the Dominican Republic. Second, the treaty made no mention of U.S. involvement in the island's domestic affairs. Third, the treaty left it up to the Dominican government, not the United States, to evaluate foreign claims. Hill, *Roosevelt and the Caribbean*, 166–69.

210. "Modus Vivendi," Dominican Republic, signed Santo Domingo April 1, 1905, *Consolidated Treaty Series* 8566 (1971), vol. 7, 194–95.

211. Hollander, "The Convention of 1907," 289–90.

212. "Collection and Application of Customs Revenues," Dominican Republic, signed Santo Domingo February 8, 1907, *Consolidated Treaty Series* 8566 (1971), vol. 7, 197.

213. "Collection and Application of Customs Revenues," 197–98.

214. Theodore Roosevelt, "Message from the President of the United States, Transmitting a Protocol of an Agreement between the United States and the Dominican Republic, Providing for the Collection and Disbursement by the United States of the Customs Revenues of the Dominican Republic, Signed on February 4, 1905," in *The Works of Theodore Roosevelt: Executive Edition* (New York: P. F. Collier, n.d. [1908?]), vol. 3, 241–42.

215. Roosevelt, "Dominican Republic Protocol," 241–43.

216. Roosevelt, "Dominican Republic Protocol," 246.

217. Roosevelt, "Dominican Republic Protocol," 241–44.

218. "Our own Government," declared TR in his 1905 message to Congress, "has always refused to enforce . . . contractual obligations on behalf of its citizens by an appeal to arms." In his instructions to the American delegates to the Third International Conference of American Republics, held at Rio de Janeiro in July–August 1906, he added, "We have not considered the use of force for such a purpose consistent with that respect for the independent sovereignty of other members of the family of nations, which is the most important principle of international law and the chief protection of weak nations against the oppression of the strong." The Rio conference recom-

mended that the American nations press the upcoming Hague conference to consider "the question of the compulsory collection of public debts." Roosevelt, "1905 Annual Message," xxxiv; Hill, *Roosevelt and the Caribbean*, 171–72.

219. Roosevelt, "Dominican Republic Protocol," 244–46.

220. Roosevelt, "Dominican Republic Protocol," 244–46.

221. Roosevelt, "Dominican Republic Protocol," 248.

222. Roosevelt, "Dominican Republic Protocol," 248–50.

223. Roosevelt, "Dominican Republic Protocol," 256–59.

224. Roosevelt, "Dominican Republic Protocol," 258–60.

225. Theodore Roosevelt to William Bayard Hale, February 26, 1904, in *Letters*, vol. 4, 740.

226. Roosevelt to Roosevelt Jr., February 10, 1904, 723–24.

227. Theodore Roosevelt to Elihu Root, September 14, 1905, in *Letters*, vol. 5, 25–26.

228. Roosevelt to Hale, December 17, 1901, 209.

229. Roosevelt to Bishop, February 23, 1904, 734–35. (See ch. 7, n. 50.)

230. Roosevelt to Roosevelt Jr., February 10, 1904, 723–24.

231. Theodore Roosevelt to John Hay, April 2, 1905, in *Letters*, vol. 4, 1156–57.

232. Theodore Roosevelt to John Hay, May 6, 1905, Theodore Roosevelt Papers, series 1, reel 54.

233. Roosevelt to Bishop, February 23, 1904, 734–35.

234. Roosevelt attributed his successes to the Big Stick, which he described as a policy of humor, combined with absolute inflexibility on matters of principle. Marks, *Velvet on Iron*; Frederick W. Marks III, "Morality as a Drive Wheel in the Diplomacy of Theodore Roosevelt," *Diplomatic History* 2, no. 1 (Winter 1978): 43–62.

235. Roosevelt to Hay, April 2, 1905, in *Letters*, vol. 4, 1157. His modus vivendi was so effective, chortled TR, that "the public is now paying no heed to the matter whatever." Theodore Roosevelt to Henry Cabot Lodge, May 20, 1905, in *Letters*, vol. 4, 1181.

236. Roosevelt to Hay, April 2, 1905, Theodore Roosevelt Papers, series 1, reel 53.

237. Roosevelt, "1905 Annual Message," xxxiii.

238. Roosevelt, "1905 Annual Message," xxxiv.

239. Roosevelt, *Autobiography*, 520.

240. Roosevelt, "1905 Annual Message," xxxiv.

241. Roosevelt, "1905 Annual Message," xxxiv.

242. Roosevelt, "1906 Annual Message," xlvii–xlviii.

243. Elihu Root, *Latin America and the United States: Addresses by Elihu Root*, eds. Robert Bacon and James Brown Scott (Cambridge: Harvard University Press, 1917), xiv–xv.

244. Scott, "Editorial Comment," 143.

245. The basic historical facts for this case come from Bemis, *Diplomatic History*, 571–89.

246. Theodore Roosevelt to Whitelaw Reid, April 28, 1906, in Bishop, *Theodore Roosevelt and His Time*, vol. 1, 468–69.

247. Roosevelt to Reid, April 28, 1906, 472.

248. Roosevelt to Reid, April 28, 1906, 472–75.

249. Roosevelt to Reid, April 28, 1906, 468–70.

250. Elihu Root to Hermann Speck von Sternburg, January 29, 1906, in Bishop, *Roosevelt and His Time*, vol. 1, 489–91.

251. Hermann Speck von Sternburg to Theodore Roosevelt, February 22, 1906, in Bishop, *Roosevelt and His Time*, vol. 1, 492.

252. Elihu Root to Hermann Speck von Sternburg, March 7, 1906, in Bishop, *Roosevelt and His Time*, vol. 1, 494–95.

253. Elihu Root to Hermann Speck von Sternburg, March 17, 1906, in Bishop, *Roosevelt and His Time*, vol. 1, 497–99.

254. Wilhelm II, in Hermann Speck von Sternburg to Theodore Roosevelt, March 14, 1906, in Bishop, *Roosevelt and His Time*, vol. 1, 496–97.

255. Beale, *Rise of America*, 387–89; Ricard, "Theodore Roosevelt," 2–6.

256. "Algeciras Convention," Morocco, signed Algeciras April 7, 1906, *Major Peace Treaties of Modern History, 1648–1967*, ed. Fred L. Israel, intro. Arnold Toynbee (New York: Chelsea House Publishers, 1967), vol. 2, 1160–61.

257. "Algeciras Convention," 1161.

258. "Algeciras Convention," 1160–63.

259. "Algeciras Convention," 1167, 1171.

260. "Algeciras Convention," 1173.

261. "Algeciras Convention," 1189.

262. Theodore Roosevelt to Whitelaw Reid, April 26, 1906, in Bishop, *Roosevelt and His Time*, vol. 1, 502.

263. The American diplomatic correspondence surrounding the Algeciras conference is found in *FRUS: 1905*, 668–88.

Chapter 9

1. Callwell defined small wars as "the partisan warfare which usually arises when trained soldiers are employed in the quelling of sedition and of insurrections in civilised countries; they include campaigns of conquest when a Great Power adds the territory of barbarous races to its possessions; and they include punitive expeditions against tribes bordering upon distant colonies." He nowhere considered the kind of altruistic police efforts prescribed by Theodore Roosevelt. Callwell admitted that campaigns "to establish order in some foreign land" usually developed "into campaigns of conquest." Charles E. Callwell, *Small Wars: Their Principles and Practice*, 3d ed. (London: HMSO, 1906; reprint with intro. by Douglas Porch, Lincoln: University of Nebraska Press, 1996), 22, 27.

2. Roosevelt to Butler, November 4, 1903, in *Letters*, 642–44. (See ch. 2, n. 6.)

3. An army veteran of the Boer War, Callwell also examined how control of the sea influenced military operations ashore, emphasizing the role of joint warfare to a degree unusual for his day. Charles E. Callwell, *Military Operations and Maritime Preponderance: Their Relations and Interdependence* (Edinburgh: William Blackwood and Sons, 1905; reprint with intro. by Colin Gray, Annapolis, MD: Naval Institute Press, 1986), xii–lxi.

4. Speaking of the Russian and French practice of "cattle lifting and village burning" in colonial campaigns, Callwell observed that the "United States troops used to retaliate upon the Red Indians in similar fashion." Callwell, *Small Wars*, 10.

5. Colin Gray postulates that the U.S. Marines were familiar both with *Military Operations and Maritime Preponderance* and with *Small Wars*. By the 1920s, says Gray, "Callwell already was well known to them as the leading practical theorist on small wars. Indeed, the "U.S. Marines' 1940 manual on small wars drew on Callwell explicitly." Colin Gray, "Introduction: Sir Charles E. Callwell, KCB—An 'Able Theorist'

of Joint Warfare," in Callwell, *Military Operations and Maritime Preponderance*, xvi–xvii.

6. Douglas Porch, "Introduction to the Bison Books Edition," in Callwell, *Small Wars*, v, xii.

7. Drawing on the lessons of the Spanish-American War, among other evidence, Callwell declared that naval operations had been "a prominent part of the struggle," although "the question of final maritime control" had "been decided by land operations." To borrow from Julian Corbett, Callwell was one of the architects of the notion that the army was a projectile to be fired by the navy. Callwell, *Military Operations and Maritime Preponderance*, 128; Julian S. Corbett, *Some Principles of Maritime Strategy* (London: Longmans, Green, 1911; reprint, Annapolis, MD: Naval Institute Press, 1988).

8. The "great principle which regular troops must always act upon in small wars" was to "overaw[e] the enemy by bold initiative and by resolute action." Callwell, *Small Wars*, xiii–xiv, 24, 40, 42.

9. Britain's weak performance in the Boer War perplexed TR. "Many of my friends need to understand that if the British Empire suffer a serious disaster, I believe in five years it will mean a war between us and some one of the great European military nations, unless we are content to abandon the Monroe doctrine for South America." Theodore Roosevelt to Hermann Speck von Sternburg, November 27, 1899, in *Letters*, vol. 2, 1098; Theodore Roosevelt to Anna Cowles Roosevelt, December 17, 1899, in *Letters*, vol. 2, 1112–13; Theodore Roosevelt to John St. Loe Strachey, January 27, 1900, in *Letters*, vol. 2, 1444–45; Theodore Roosevelt to Arthur Hamilton Lee, January 30, 1900, in *Letters*, vol. 2, 1151–53; Theodore Roosevelt to Cecil Arthur Spring Rice, March 12, 1900, in *Letters*, vol. 2, 1216–17.

10. Boot, *Savage Wars of Peace*, 69–74.

11. Boot, *Savage Wars of Peace*, 74–78.

12. From the Boxer affair General Chaffee drew the lesson that stern measures were needed to subdue rebellious Asian populaces. Only after the masses were subdued could U.S. officials pursue a benign policy. Birtle, *U.S. Army Doctrine*, 152.

13. Birtle, *U.S. Army Doctrine*, 148–50.

14. Boot, *Savage Wars of Peace*, 78–97.

15. John Hay to Charles V. Herdliska, July 3, 1900, in *FRUS: 1900*, 299.

16. Roosevelt to Lee, July 25, 1900, 1362. (See ch. 6, n. 16.) De-

spite his qualms about Wilhelmine diplomacy, Roosevelt voiced "a very strong hope that Germany, England and the United States will more and more be able to act together. They surely ought to." Theodore Roosevelt to Hermann Speck von Sternburg, November 19, 1900, in *Letters*, vol. 2, 1428.

17. Theodore Roosevelt to George Ferdinand Becker, July 8, 1901, in *Letters*, vol. 3, 111–12.

18. Roosevelt to Wolcott, September 15, 1900, 1404. (See ch. 4, n. 11.)

19. Theodore Roosevelt to Hermann Speck von Sternburg, March 8, 1901, in *Letters*, vol. 3, 5–6. The Japanese contingent had performed best. "What natural fighters they are!" The Russians were "the worst for plundering and murdering," while "the Americans had a tendency to get drunk and to plunder but never killed either women or children." Roosevelt to Speck von Sternburg, November 19, 1900, 1428.

20. Theodore Roosevelt, "Management of Small States," 387.

21. Indeed, years later Roosevelt reported telling two Japanese dignitaries that he "would gladly welcome any part played by Japan which would tend to bring China forward along the road which Japan trod, because I thought it for the interest of all the world that each part of the world should be prosperous and well policed." Roosevelt to Rice, June 13, 1904, 830. (See ch. 6, n. 35.)

22. The U.S. State Department reviewed the leases for Port Arthur and Kiaochow, concluding that "the control over all of these leased ports has, during the existence of the lease, passed as absolutely away from the Chinese government as if the territory had been sold outright, and that they are as thoroughly under jurisdiction of the lessee governments as any portion of their home territory." Since "these ports have practically passed from the control of an uncivilized people to civilized," the United States could spare itself the expense of exercising extraterritorial jurisdiction. Alvey A. Adee to E. H. Conger, August 25, 1899, in *FRUS: 1900*, 382–85; E. H. Conger to John Hay, December 11, 1899, in *FRUS: 1900*, 385–86.

23. Roosevelt described the Monroe Doctrine as a kind of Open Door for Latin America. He insisted he did "not want the United States or any European power to get territorial possessions in South America but to let South America gradually develop on its own lines, with an open door to all outside nations." The Roosevelt administration "would not interfere with transitory intervention on the part of any State outside of South America, when there was a row with some State in South

America." The president wished "the same policy could be pursued in China. That is, if the Chinese could be forced to behave themselves—not permitted to do anything atrocious, but not partitioned, and with the ports kept open to all comers, as well as having the vexatious trade restrictions which prevent inter-Chinese trade in the interior, abolished." Theodore Roosevelt to Hermann Speck von Sternburg, October 11, 1901, in *Letters*, vol. 3, 172–73.

24. Bickel, *Mars Learning*, 43–44, 47. Bickel notes that, of twenty-nine journal articles written by veterans of the army's small wars, only four dealt with civil pacification measures.

25. U.S. Department of War, *Field Service Regulations, 1905* (Washington, DC: Government Printing Office, 1905), 39, 217; Bickel, *Mars Learning*, 48–50.

26. The U.S. military lacked military police units until the 1940s. This helps explain the failure to differentiate between the military and police functions. An analyst writing during the 1990s observed that international police missions exhibited three main dimensions: (1) monitoring and supervising local law-enforcement organizations; (2) training and mentoring local police forces; and, on rare occasions, (3) actually performing law-enforcement functions themselves. Erwin A. Schmidl, "Police Functions: A Historical Overview," in Robert Oakley and Michael Dziedzic, eds., *Policing the New World Disorder* (Washington, DC: National Defense University, 1996), 19–25.

27. U.S. Army, U.S. Army Field Manual 27–5, *Military Government* (Washington, DC: Government Printing Office, 1940); U.S. Army, U.S. Army Field Manual 27–10, *The Law of Land Warfare* (Washington, DC: Government Printing Office, 1956), 10–11.

28. U.S. Army, *Law of Land Warfare*, 10, 138–143.

29. U.S. Army, *Law of Land Warfare*, 158–59.

30. U.S. Army, *Law of Land Warfare*, 138–39.

31. Bickel, *Mars Learning*, 51.

32. Jack Shulimson, *The Marine Corps' Search for a Mission, 1880–1898* (Lawrence: University Press of Kansas, 1993), 206.

33. Bickel, *Mars Learning*, 52.

34. Bickel, *Mars Learning*, 58–59.

35. Tension between the missions of conventional war fighting and constabulary duty pervaded the turn-of-the-century U.S. Army. Wrote 1st Lt. John Bigelow as the Indian wars wound down, "the so-

called Army is but a police force" if distracted with constabulary missions; "to prepare for war should in time of peace, be the constant effort of our Army." The U.S. Army was also stung by public criticism for its sometimes-brutal tactics. The constabulary mission fell to the U.S. Marine Corps almost by default. Birtle, *U.S. Army Doctrine*, 86–87, 181–82. See also Bigelow, *Principles of Strategy*, 228–33.

36. Ronald Shaffer, "The 1940 Small Wars Manual and the 'Lessons of History,'" in U.S. Marine Corps, *Small Wars Manual: United States Marine Corps 1940*, 2d ed. (Washington, DC: Government Printing Office, 1940; reprint, Manhattan, KS: Sunflower University Press, 1972), v–xv. (Although published under one cover, the *Small Wars Manual* is arranged into separately numbered chapters. Subsequent footnotes from the manual will follow the format *Small Wars Manual*, chapter no., page no.)

37. U.S. Marine Corps, *Small Wars Manual*, chap. 1, 12.

38. U.S. Marine Corps, *Small Wars Manual*, chap. 1, 11–14.

39. U.S. Marine Corps, *Small Wars Manual*, chap. 1, 12–13, 17–34.

40. U.S. Marine Corps, *Small Wars Manual*, chap. 1, 28–29, 32.

41. U.S. Marine Corps, *Small Wars Manual*, chap. 1, 5, 8–9.

42. U.S. Marine Corps, *Small Wars Manual*, chap. 1, 5–6.

43. U.S. Marine Corps, *Small Wars Manual*, chap. 1, 26–28.

44. The powers entrusted to the new force were legion. "Among the police duties of the constabulary are the prevention of smuggling and the control of the importation, sale, and custody of arms, ammunition, and explosives. It is also empowered to arrest offenders for infractions of local laws, not only of the state, but also of the territorial subdivisions and municipalities. It is charged with the protection of persons and property, the control of prisons, and the issuance of travel permits and vehicular licenses. The constabulary provides guards for voting places and electoral records, and exerts plenary control during natural disasters, such as floods and earthquakes." To this imposing list was appended an additional host of civil duties. U.S. Marine Corps, *Small Wars Manual*, chap. 12, 8–9.

45. U.S. Marine Corps, *Small Wars Manual*, chap. 1, 5–6.

46. U.S. Marine Corps, *Small Wars Manual*, chap. 1, 26–27.

47. U.S. Marine Corps, *Small Wars Manual*, chap. 1, 43.

48. U.S. Marine Corps, *Small Wars Manual*, chap. 1, 43–44.

49. U.S. Marine Corps, *Small Wars Manual*, chap. 1, 44.

50. U.S. Marine Corps, *Small Wars Manual*, chap. 1, 11–16; chap. 2, 1–3.

51. U.S. Marine Corps, *Small Wars Manual*, chap. 1, 1–7.

52. U.S. Marine Corps, *Small Wars Manual*, chap. 1, 5.

53. U.S. Marine Corps, *Small Wars Manual*, chap. 1, 7.

54. U.S. Marine Corps, *Small Wars Manual*, chap. 14, 29–35.

55. U.S. Marine Corps, *Small Wars Manual*, chap. 1, 42.

56. U.S. Marine Corps, *Small Wars Manual*, chap. 1, 54–55.

Chapter 10

1. Roosevelt, *Autobiography*, 520.

2. Roosevelt, *Autobiography*, 519.

3. Roosevelt, *Autobiography*, 518.

4. Henry Cabot Lodge to Theodore Roosevelt, November 26, 1918, in *Roosevelt-Lodge Correspondence*, vol. 2, 547.

BIBLIOGRAPHY

Manuscript Collections

Theodore Roosevelt Collection, Harvard University, Cambridge, MA.

Theodore Roosevelt Papers. 485 reels. Library of Congress Microfilm, Washington, DC.

Published Primary Sources

Bartlett, Ruhl J., ed. *The Record of American Diplomacy: Documents and Readings on the History of American Foreign Relations*. 4th ed. New York: Knopf, 1964.

Bigelow, John. *The Principles of Strategy, Illustrated Mainly from American Campaigns*. 2d ed. Philadelphia: J. D. Lippincott, 1894. Reprint, New York: Greenwood Press, 1968.

Birkhimer, William E. *Military Government and Martial Law*. 3d ed. rev. Kansas City, MO: F. Hudson, 1914.

Bishop, Joseph Bucklin, ed. *Theodore Roosevelt and His Time, Shown in His Own Letters*. 2 vols. New York: Charles Scribner's Sons, 1920.

Bryan, William Jennings. *The Memoirs of William Jennings Bryan, By Himself and His Wife Mary Baird Bryan*. Port Washington, NY: Kennikat Press, 1971.

———. *Speeches of William Jennings Bryan*. Introduction by Mary Baird Bryan. 2 vols. New York: Funk and Wagnales, 1909.

Fidler, David P., and Jennifer M. Welsh, eds. *Empire and Community: Edmund Burke's Writings and Speeches on International Relations*. Boulder, CO: Westview Press, 1999.

Funston, Frederick. *Memories of Two Wars: Cuban and Philippine Experiences*. New York: Charles Scribner's Sons, 1911.

German Foreign Ministry. *Die Grosse Politik der Europäischen Kabinette, 1871–1914: Sammlung der Diplomatischen Akten des Auswärtigen Amtes, Im Auftrage Des Auswärtigen Amtes*. Edited by Johannes Lepsius and others. 40 vols. Berlin: Deutsche Verlagsgesellschaft für Politik und Geschichte, 1922–27.

Gooch, G. P. and Harold Temperley, eds. *British Documents on the Origins of the War 1898–1914*. Vol. 3: *The Testing of the Entente, 1904–6*. London: His Majesty's Stationery Office, 1927.

Graff, Henry F. *American Imperialism and the Philippine Insurrection: Testimony Taken from Hearings on Affairs in the Philippine Islands before the Senate Committee on the Philippines—1902.* Boston: Little, Brown, 1969.

Hollander, Jacob H. "The Convention of 1907 between the United States and the Dominican Republic." *American Journal of International Law* 1, vol. 2 (April 1907).

Hooker, Mary. *Behind the Scenes in Peking.* London: John Murray, 1911.

Leary, John J. *Talks with TR, from the Diaries of John J. Leary, Jr.* Boston: Houghton Mifflin, 1920.

Lejeune, John A. *The Reminiscences of a Marine.* Philadelphia: Dorrance, 1930.

Lieber, Francis. *Guerrilla Parties Considered with Reference to the Laws and Usages of War.* New York: D. Van Nostrand, 1862.

Lodge, Henry Cabot. "Address of Senator Henry Cabot Lodge of Massachusetts in Honor of Theodore Roosevelt." Washington, DC: Government Printing Office, 1919.

Mahan, Alfred T. *The Influence of Sea Power upon History, 1660–1783.* Boston: Little, Brown, 1890. Reprint, New York: Dover Publications, 1987.

———. *The Interest of America in Sea Power, Present and Future.* Boston: Little, Brown, 1897. Reprint, Freeport, NY: Books for Libraries, 1970.

———. *Letters and Papers of Alfred Thayer Mahan.* Edited by Robert Seager II and Doris D. Maguire. Annapolis, MD: Naval Institute Press, 1975.

———. *Naval Strategy, Compared and Contrasted with the Principles and Practice of Military Operations on Land.* Boston: Little, Brown, 1911.

———. *The Problem of Asia and Its Effect upon International Policies.* New York: Little, Brown, 1900. Reprint, Port Washington, NY: Kennikat Press, 1970.

Robinson, Corinne R. *My Brother, Theodore Roosevelt.* New York: Charles Scribner's Sons, 1921.

Roosevelt, Nicholas. *Theodore Roosevelt: The Man as I Knew Him.* New York: Dodd, Mead, 1967.

Roosevelt, Theodore. *Administration: Civil Service.* New York: G. P. Putnam's Sons, 1900.

———. *America and the World War.* New York: Charles Scribner's Sons, 1919.

———. *American Ideals, and Other Essays, Social and Political, by Theodore Roosevelt.* New York: G. P. Putnam's Sons, 1897.

———. *American Problems.* New York: Charles Scribner's Sons, 1926.

———. "The Best and the Good." *Churchman*, March 17, 1900. http://www.bartleby.com/58/8.html (accessed November 15, 1998)

———. *Campaigns and Controversies.* New York: Charles Scribner's Sons, 1926.

———. "The Enforcement of Law." *Forum* 20 (September 1895): 1–10.

———. *Essays on Practical Politics by Theodore Roosevelt*. New York: G. P. Putnam's Sons, 1888.

———. *Fear God and Take Your Own Part, by Theodore Roosevelt*. New York: George H. Doran, 1916.

———. *The Foes of Our Own Household, by Theodore Roosevelt*. New York: George H. Doran, 1917.

———. *The Great Adventure, Present-Day Studies in American Nationalism*. New York: Charles Scribner's Sons, 1918.

———. *Hero Tales from American History*. New York: Charles Scribner's Sons, 1926.

———. "How the United States Acquired the Right to Dig the Panama Canal." *Outlook*, October 7, 1911, 314–18.

———. *International Peace: An Address before the Nobel Committee of the Norwegian Parliament by Mr. Theodore Roosevelt*. Stockholm: P. A. Norstedt and Soner, 1910.

———. "'The League of Nations,' Address Delivered in 1918." Theodore Roosevelt Collection, Harvard University, Cambridge, MA.

———. *The Letters of Theodore Roosevelt*. Edited by Elting E. Morison and others. 8 vols. Cambridge: Harvard University Press, 1951–54.

———. *Letters of Theodore Roosevelt to Anna Roosevelt Cowles, 1870–1918*. New York: Charles Scribner's Sons, 1924.

———. *Literary Essays*. New York: Scribner, 1926.

———. "The Manly Virtues and Practical Politics." *Forum* 17 (April 1894): 551–57.

———. *Memorial Edition: Works of Theodore Roosevelt*. Edited by Hermann Hagedorn. 24 vols. New York: Charles Scribner's Sons, 1923–26.

———. "The Monroe Doctrine." *Bachelor of Arts* 2, no. 4 (March 1896): 437–65.

———. "Municipal Administration: The New York Police Force." *Atlantic Monthly* 80 (September 1897): 289–300.

———. "'National Duty and International Ideals,' Speech of Theodore Roosevelt before the Illinois Bar Association at Chicago, April 29, 1916." New York: Allied Print, 1916.

———. *National Edition: Works of Theodore Roosevelt*. Edited by Hermann Hagedorn. 20 vols. New York: Charles Scribner's Sons, 1926.

———. *National Strength and International Duty*. Princeton, NJ: Princeton University Press, 1917.

———. *The Naval War of 1812, Or, The History of the United States Navy during the Last War with Great Britain*. 2 vols. New York: G. P. Putnam's Sons,

1882. Reprint with an introduction by Edward K. Eckert. Annapolis, MD: Naval Institute Press, 1987.

———. *The New Nationalism*. Englewood Cliffs, NJ: Prentice-Hall, 1961.

———. *New York, by Theodore Roosevelt*. New York: Longmans, Green, 1891.

———. *Oliver Cromwell*. New York: Charles Scribner's Sons, 1926.

———. "Our Policy and Our Work in the Philippines." Theodore Roosevelt Collection, Harvard University, Cambridge, MA.

———. *Outlook Editorials*. New York: Outlook, 1909.

———. *Presidential Addresses and State Papers and European Addresses*. 8 vols. New York: Review of Reviews, 1910.

———. *Progressive Principles: Selections from Addresses Made during the Presidential Campaign of 1912*. Edited by Elmer H. Youngman. New York: Progressive National Service, 1913.

———. *Realizable Ideals: The Early Lectures by Theodore Roosevelt*. San Francisco: Whittaker and Ray-Wiggin, 1912.

———. Review of *The Law of Civilization and Decay*, by Brooks Adams. *Forum* 22 (September 1896): 575–589.

———. Review of *Social Evolution*, by Isaac Kidd. *North American Review* 161, no. 464 (July 1895): 94–109.

———. *Roosevelt, His Life, Meaning, and Messages*. 4 vols. New York: Current Literature Publishing, 1919.

———. *The Rough Riders*. New York: Charles Scribner's Sons, 1899.

———. *Selected Works of Theodore Roosevelt*. 8 vols. Vol. 8, *The Strenuous Life: Essays and Addresses*. New York: Century, 1900.

———. *State Papers as Governor and President, 1899–1909*. New York: Charles Scribner's Sons, 1926.

———. *Theodore Roosevelt: An Autobiography*. New York: Macmillan, 1913. Reprinted with an introduction by Elting E. Morison. New York: Da Capo Press, 1985.

———. *Theodore Roosevelt's Letters to His Children*. Edited by Joseph Bucklin Bishop. New York: Charles Scribner's Sons, 1923.

———. "True American Ideals." *Forum* 18 (February 1895): 746–47.

———. "What Americanism Means." *Forum* 17 (April 1894): 196–206.

———. *The Winning of the West*. 4 vols. Lincoln: University of Nebraska Press, 1995.

———. *The Works of Theodore Roosevelt: Executive Edition*. 16 vols. New York: P. F. Collier, n.d. [1908?].

——— and Henry Cabot Lodge. *Selections from the Correspondence of Theodore Roosevelt and Henry Cabot Lodge, 1884–1918*. Edited by Henry Cabot

Lodge and Charles F. Redmond. 2 vols. New York: Charles Scribner's Sons, 1925. Reprint, New York: Da Capo, 1971.

Root, Elihu. *Addresses on International Subjects, By Elihu Root.* Edited by Robert Bacon and James Brown Scott. Cambridge: Harvard University Press, 1916.

――――. *Latin America and the United States: Addresses by Elihu Root.* Edited by Robert Bacon and James Brown Scott. Cambridge: Harvard University Press, 1917.

――――. *The Military and Colonial Policy of the United States: Addresses and Reports by Elihu Root.* Edited by Robert Bacon and James Brown Scott. Cambridge: Harvard University Press, 1916.

――――. *Miscellaneous Address, By Elihu Root.* Edited by Robert Bacon and James Brown Scott. Cambridge: Harvard University Press, 1917.

Schurz, Carl. "'American Imperialism,' The Convocation Address, Delivered on the Occasion of the Twenty-seventh Convocation of the University of Chicago, January 4, 1899." Sanford, NC: Microfilming Corp. of America, 1982.

――――. "Armed or Unarmed Peace." *Harper's Weekly Magazine,* June 19, 1897: 603.

――――. "'For American Principles and American Honor,' An Address by Hon. Carl Schurz Delivered in Cooper Union, New York, May 24, 1900." New York: Anti-Imperialist League of New York, 1900. Reprint, Sanford, NC: Microfilming Corp. of America, 1982.

――――. *Reminiscences of Carl Schurz.* 3 vols. London: John Murray, 1909.

Steffens, Joseph Lincoln. *The Autobiography of Lincoln Steffens.* 2 vols. New York: Harcourt, Brace, 1931.

Stout, Ralph, ed. *Roosevelt in the Kansas City Star: War-Time Editorials by Theodore Roosevelt.* Boston: Houghton Mifflin, 1921.

Taft, William Howard. *Present Day Problems.* Freeport, NY: Books for Libraries Press, 1908. Reprint, 1967.

――――. *The United States and Peace.* New York: Charles Scribner's Sons, 1914.

Taylor, John R. M., ed. *The Philippine Insurrection against the United States: A Compilation of Documents with Notes and Introductions.* Washington, DC: Government Printing Office, 1906.

Turner, Frederick Jackson. "'The Significance of the Frontier in American History,' From Proceedings of the Forty-first Annual Meeting of the State Historical Society of Wisconsin." Madison: State Historical Society of Wisconsin, 1894. Reprint, Woodbridge, CT: Research Publications, 1975.

United Nations. *Charter of the United Nations and Statute of the International Court of Justice.* New York: United Nations, 1945. Reprint, New York: UN Department of Public Information, 1993.

U.S. Army. *Correspondence Relating to the War with Spain and Conditions Growing Out of Same Including the Insurrection in the Philippine Islands and the China Relief Expedition, Between the Adjutant-General of the Army and Military Commanders in the United States, Cuba, Porto Rico, China, and the Philippine Islands from April 15, 1898 to July 30, 1902.* Washington, DC: Government Printing Office, 1902.

———. U.S. Army Field Manual 27-5, *Military Government.* Washington, DC: Government Printing Office, 1940.

———. U.S. Army Field Manual 27-10, *The Law of Land Warfare.* Washington, DC: Government Printing Office, 1956.

U.S. Congress. House. *House Executive Documents.* 59th Congress, 1st Session, 1905. Vol. 1, *Annual Reports of the War Department.* Washington, DC: Government Printing Office, 1906.

———. *The Declaration of Independence and the Constitution of the United States of America.* Reprint, Washington, DC: Cato Institute, 1998.

U.S. Congress. Senate. Select Committee on Haiti and Santo Domingo. *Inquiry into Occupation and Administration of Haiti and Santo Domingo.* 2 vols. Washington, DC: Government Printing Office, 1922.

U.S. Department of the Navy. *Annual Report of the Navy Department, 1898–1909.* Washington, DC: Government Printing Office, 1898–1909.

U.S. Department of State. *Foreign Relations of the United States, 1901–1908.* Washington, DC: Government Printing Office, 1902–9.

———. *Treaties and Conventions Concluded between the United States of America and Other Powers since 1776.* Rev. ed. Washington, DC: Government Printing Office, 1873.

———. *Treaties and Other International Agreements of the United States of America, 1776–1949.* Washington, DC: Government Printing Office, 1969–74.

U.S. Department of War. *Annual Report of the War Department, 1898–1908.* Washington, DC: Government Printing Office, 1898–1908.

———. *Field Service Regulations, 1905.* Washington, DC: Government Printing Office, 1905.

U.S. Marine Corps. *Small Wars Manual: United States Marine Corps 1940.* 2d ed. Washington, DC: Government Publishing Office, 1940. Reprint with an introduction by Ronald Shaffer. Manhattan, KS: Sunflower University Press, 1972.

Wood, Leonard. *Leonard Wood on National Issues.* Edited by Evan J. David. Garden City, NY: Doubleday, Page, 1920.

Secondary Sources

Abbot, Lawrence F. *Impressions of Theodore Roosevelt.* Garden City, NY: Doubleday, Page, 1919.

Adams, Brooks. *America's Economic Supremacy*. New York: Macmillan, 1900.

——. *The Law of Civilization and Decay: An Essay on History*. Introduction by Charles A. Beard. New York: Macmillan, 1895. Reprint, New York: Books for Libraries Press, 1971.

——. *The New Empire*. New York: Macmillan, 1903.

Adams, Henry. *The Education of Henry Adams*. Introduction by James Truslow Adams. New York: Modern Library, 1931.

Alfonso, Oscar M. *Theodore Roosevelt and the Philippines, 1897–1909*. New York: Oriole Editions, 1974.

American Business Man. "Is the Monroe Doctrine a Bar to Civilization?" *North American Review* 176 (April 1903): 520.

Baer, George W. *One Hundred Years of Sea Power: The U.S. Navy, 1890–1990*. Stanford, CA: Stanford University Press, 1994.

Bailey, Thomas A. *A Diplomatic History of the American People*. 10th ed. Englewood Cliffs, NJ: Prentice-Hall, 1980.

——. *Theodore Roosevelt and the Japanese-American Crises: An Account of the International Complications Arising from the Race Problem on the Pacific Coast*. Stanford, CA: Stanford University Press, 1934.

Beale, Howard K. *Theodore Roosevelt and the Rise of America to World Power*. Baltimore: Johns Hopkins Press, 1956.

Beede, Benjamin R. *Intervention and Counterinsurgency: An Annotated Bibliography of the Small Wars of the United States, 1898–1984*. New York: Garland, 1985.

Beisner, Robert L. *Twelve against Empire: The Anti-Imperialists, 1898–1900*. New York: McGraw-Hill, 1968.

Bemis, Samuel Flagg. *A Diplomatic History of the United States*. Rev. ed. New York: Henry Holt, 1942.

——. *The Latin-American Policy of the United States*. New York: Harcourt, Brace, 1943.

Berman, Jay S. *Police Administration and Progressive Reform: Theodore Roosevelt as Police Commissioner of New York*. New York: Greenwood Press, 1987.

Bickel, Keith B. *Mars Learning: The Marine Corps Development of Small Wars Doctrine, 1915–1940*. Boulder, CO: Westview, 2001.

Birtle, Andrew J. *U.S. Army Counterinsurgency and Contingency Operations Doctrine, 1860–1941*. Washington, DC: Center of Military History, 1998.

Blum, John M. *The Republican Roosevelt*. Cambridge: Harvard University Press, 1967.

Boot, Max. *The Savage Wars of Peace: Small Wars and the Rise of American Power*. New York: Basic Books, 2002.

Brands, H. W. *Bound to Empire: The United States and the Philippines*. Oxford: Oxford University Press, 1992.

———. *TR: The Last Romantic.* New York: Basic Books, 1997.

Brinkley, Douglas, and others. "C-SPAN Survey of Presidential Leadership." C-SPAN, 1999. http://www.americanpresidents.org/survey (accessed January 15, 2002).

Bryce, James. *The American Commonwealth.* 2d edition. 2 vols. London: Macmillan, 1891.

———. "British Feeling on the Venezuelan Question." *North American Review* 162, no. 471 (February 1896): 145–53.

Burton, David H. *Theodore Roosevelt: Confident Imperialist.* Philadelphia: University of Pennsylvania Press, 1969.

Cadenhead, I. E., Jr. *Theodore Roosevelt: The Paradox of Progressivism.* Woodbury, NY: Barron's Educational Series, 1974.

Callwell, Charles E. *Military Operations and Maritime Preponderance: Their Relations and Interdependence.* Edinburgh: William Blackwood and Sons, 1905. Reprint with an introduction by Colin Gray. Annapolis, MD: Naval Institute Press, 1996.

———. *Small Wars: Their Principles and Practice.* 3d ed. London: HMSO, 1906. Reprint with an introduction by Douglas Porch. Lincoln: University of Nebraska Press, 1996.

Campbell, A. E. *America Comes of Age: The Era of Theodore Roosevelt.* New York: American Heritage Press, 1971.

Carnegie, Andrew. "The Venezuelan Question." *North American Review* 162, no. 471 (February 1896): 129–44.

Cash, W. J. *The Mind of the South.* New York: Knopf, 1941.

Chessman, G. Wallace. *Governor Theodore Roosevelt: The Albany Apprenticeship, 1898–1900.* Cambridge: Harvard University Press, 1965.

———. *Theodore Roosevelt and the Politics of Power.* Boston: Little, Brown, 1969.

Coll, Alberto R. "Normative Prudence as a Tradition of Statecraft." *Ethics & International Affairs* 5 (1991): 33–51.

Collin, Richard H. *Theodore Roosevelt, Culture, Diplomacy, and Expansion: A New View of American Imperialism.* Baton Rouge: Louisiana State University Press, 1985.

———. *Theodore Roosevelt's Caribbean: The Panama Canal, the Monroe Doctrine, and the Latin American Context.* Baton Rouge: Louisiana State University Press, 1990.

Collins, John M. *America's Small Wars: Lessons for the Future.* Washington, DC: Brassey's, 1991.

Cooper, John M., Jr. *The Warrior and the Priest: Woodrow Wilson and Theodore Roosevelt.* Cambridge: Harvard University Press, 1983.

Corbett, Julian S. *Some Principles of Maritime Strategy.* London: Longmans, Green, 1911. Reprint, Annapolis, MD: Naval Institute Press, 1988.

Davis, Oscar K. *Released for Publication: Some Inside Political History of Theodore Roosevelt and His Times, 1898–1918*. Boston: Houghton Mifflin, 1925.

Dennett, Tyler. *Roosevelt and the Russo-Japanese War: A Critical Study of American Policy in Eastern Asia in 1902–5, Based Primarily upon the Private Papers of Theodore Roosevelt*. Garden City, NY: Doubleday, Page, 1925.

Dyer, Thomas G. *Theodore Roosevelt and the Idea of Race*. Baton Rouge: Louisiana State University Press, 1980.

Ellsworth, Harry Allanson. *One Hundred Eighty Landings of United States Marines 1800–1934*. Washington, DC: History and Museums Division, Headquarters, U.S. Marine Corps, 1934. Reprint, 1974.

Esthus, Raymond A. *Theodore Roosevelt and Japan*. Seattle: University of Washington Press, 1967.

——. *Theodore Roosevelt and the International Rivalries*. Waltham, MA: Ginn-Blaisdell, 1970.

Friedenberg, Robert V. *Theodore Roosevelt and the Rhetoric of Militant Decency*. New York: Greenwood, 1990.

Fuess, Claude M. *Carl Schurz: Reformer*. New York: Dodd, Mead, 1932.

Gaddis, John Lewis. *Surprise, Security, and the American Experience*. Cambridge: Harvard University Press, 2004.

Gardner, Joseph L. *Departing Glory: Theodore Roosevelt as Ex-President*. New York: Charles Scribner's Sons, 1973.

Garner, Bryan A. *Black's Law Dictionary*. St. Paul, MN: West Publishing Company, 1996.

Genovese, Eugene D. "The Chivalric Tradition in the Old South." *Sewanee Review*, Spring 2000: 188–205.

——. *The Southern Tradition: The Achievement and Limitations of an American Conservatism*. Cambridge: Harvard University Press, 1994.

Godkin, E. L. "Diplomacy and the Newspaper." *North American Review* 160, no. 462 (May 1895): 570–79.

Gould, Lewis L. *The Presidency of Theodore Roosevelt*. Lawrence: University Press of Kansas, 1991.

Griffith, William, ed. *The Roosevelt Policy*. 3 vols. New York: Current Literature Publishing, 1919.

Grotius, Hugo. *The Law of War and Peace*. Translated by Louise R. Loomis. Paris, 1625. Reprint, New York: Walter J. Black, 1949.

Harbaugh, William H. *Power and Responsibility: The Life and Times of Theodore Roosevelt*. New York: Farrar, Straus and Cudahy, 1961.

Healy, David. *Drive to Hegemony: The United States in the Caribbean, 1898–1917*. Madison: University of Wisconsin Press, 1988

Henrikson, Alan K. *Defining a New World Order: Toward a Practical Vision of*

Collective Action for International Peace and Security. Medford, MA: The Fletcher School of Law and Diplomacy, Tufts University, 1991.

Herwig, Holger H. *Germany's Vision of Empire in Venezuela, 1871–1914.* Princeton, NJ: Princeton University Press, 1986.

———. "The Influence of A. T. Mahan upon German Sea Power." In John B. Hattendorf, ed., *The Influence of History on Mahan.* Newport, RI: Naval War College Press, 1991.

———. *Luxury Fleet: The Imperial German Navy, 1888–1918.* London: Allen and Unwin, 1980.

———. *Politics of Frustration: The United States in German Naval Planning, 1889– 1941.* Boston: Little, Brown, 1976.

Hill, Howard C. *Roosevelt and the Caribbean.* Chicago: University of Chicago Press, 1927.

Hobson, Rolf. *Imperialism at Sea: Naval Strategic Thought, the Ideology of Sea Power and the Tirpitz Plan, 1875–1914.* Boston: Brill Academic Publishers, 2002.

Hofstadter, Richard. *The Age of Reform: From Bryan to F. D. R.* New York: Knopf, 1955.

Holmes, James R. "Mahan, a 'Place in the Sun,' and Germany's Quest for Sea Power." *Comparative Strategy* 23, no. 1 (January–March 2004): 27–62.

Israel, Fred L., ed. *Major Peace Treaties of Modern History, 1648–1967.* Introduction by Arnold Toynbee. New York: Chelsea House Publishers, 1967.

Jeffers, H. Paul. *Commissioner Roosevelt: The Story of Theodore Roosevelt and the New York City Police, 1895–1897.* New York: J. Wiley and Sons, 1994.

Jessup, Philip C. *Elihu Root.* 2 vols. New York: Dodd, Mead, 1938.

Johnson, Paul. *A History of the American People.* New York: HarperCollins, 1997.

Kant, Immanuel. *Perpetual Peace, and Other Essays on Politics, History, and Morals.* Translated by Ted Humphrey. Reprint, Indianapolis: Hackett Publishing, 1983.

Karnow, Stanley. *In Our Image: America's Empire in the Philippines.* New York: Random House, 1989.

Keller, Morton, ed. *Theodore Roosevelt: A Profile.* New York: Hill and Wang, 1967.

Kesler, Charles R. "Teddy Roosevelt to the Rescue?" *The National Interest* 52 (Summer 1998): 108.

Kissinger, Henry. *Diplomacy.* New York: Simon & Schuster, 1994.

———. *Does America Need a Foreign Policy? Toward a Diplomacy for the 21st Century.* New York: Simon & Schuster, 2002.

Knight, Melvin M. *The Americans in Santo Domingo.* New York: Vanguard, 1928.

LaFeber, Walter. *The American Age: United States Foreign Policy at Home and Abroad since 1750*. New York: W. W. Norton, 1989.

———. *The New Empire: An Interpretation of American Expansion, 1860–1898*. Ithaca, NY: Cornell University Press, 1963.

———. *The Panama Canal: The Crisis in Historical Perspective*. Oxford: Oxford University Press, 1979.

Lane, Jack C. *Armed Progressive: General Leonard Wood*. San Rafael, CA: Presidio Press, 1978.

Langley, Lester D. *The Banana Wars: An Inner History of American Empire, 1900–1934*. Lexington: University Press of Kentucky, 1983.

———. *The United States and the Caribbean in the Twentieth Century*. 4th ed. Athens: University of Georgia Press, 1989.

Linn, Brian McAllister. *The Philippine War, 1899–1902*. Lawrence: University Press of Kansas, 2000.

———. *The U.S. Army and Counterinsurgency in the Philippine War, 1899–1902*. Chapel Hill: University of North Carolina Press, 1989.

Lippmann, Walter. *U.S. Foreign Policy: Shield of the Republic*. Boston: Little, Brown, 1943.

Lodge, Henry Cabot. "England, Venezuela, and the Monroe Doctrine." *North American Review* 160, no. 462 (May 1895): 651–58.

Lynch, Cecilia. "Kant, the Republican Peace, and Moral Guidance in International Law." *Ethics & International Affairs* 8 (1994): 23–28.

Marks, Frederick W., III. "Morality as a Drive Wheel in the Diplomacy of Theodore Roosevelt." *Diplomatic History* 2, no. 1 (Winter 1978): 43–62.

———. *Velvet on Iron: The Diplomacy of Theodore Roosevelt*. Lincoln: University of Nebraska Press, 1979.

May, Ernest R. *Imperial Democracy: The Emergence of America as a Great Power*. New York: Harcourt, Brace and World, 1961.

McCaleb, Walter F. *Theodore Roosevelt*. New York: A. and C. Boni, 1931.

McCullough, David. *Mornings on Horseback*. New York: Simon & Schuster, 1981.

McDougall, Walter A. "Editor's Column." *Orbis*, Summer 1999: 345–54.

———. *Promised Land, Crusader State: The American Encounter with the World since 1776*. Boston: Houghton Mifflin, 1997.

Mead, Walter Russell. "The Jacksonian Tradition and American Foreign Policy." *The National Interest* 58 (Winter 1999/2000): 5–29.

———. *Special Providence: American Foreign Policy and How It Changed the World*. New York: Knopf, 2003.

Miller, Nathan. *The Roosevelt Chronicles*. Garden City, NY: Doubleday, 1979

———. *Theodore Roosevelt: A Life*. New York: Quill, 1992.

Miller, Stuart C. *"Benevolent Assimilation": The American Conquest of the Philippines, 1899–1903*. New Haven, CT: Yale University Press, 1982.

Millett, Allan R. *The Politics of Intervention: The Military Occupation of Cuba, 1906–1909*. Columbus: Ohio State University Press, 1968.

Moore, John Bassett. *International Law and Some Current Illusions and Other Essays*. New York: Macmillan, 1924.

———. *The Principles of American Diplomacy*. New York: Harper and Brothers Publishers, 1918.

Morris, Edmund. *"'A Matter of Extreme Urgency': Theodore Roosevelt, Wilhelm II, and the Venezuela Crisis of 1902." Naval War College Review*, Spring 2002. http://www.nwc.navy.mil/press/Review/2002/spring/art5-sp2.htm (accessed January 31, 2004).

———. *The Rise of Theodore Roosevelt*. New York: Ballantine Books, 1979. Reprint, New York: Modern Library, 2001.

Mowry, George E. *The Era of Theodore Roosevelt and the Birth of Modern America, 1900–1912*. New York: Harper and Brothers, 1958.

———. *Theodore Roosevelt and the Progressive Movement*. Madison: University of Wisconsin Press, 1946.

Murray, Williamson, MacGregor Knox, and Alvin Bernstein, eds. *The Making of Strategy: Rulers, States, and War*. Cambridge: Cambridge University Press, 1994.

Musicant, Ivan. *The Banana Wars: A History of United States Military Intervention in Latin America from the Spanish-American War to the Invasion of Panama*. New York: Macmillan, 1990.

Neu, Charles E. *An Uncertain Friendship: Theodore Roosevelt and Japan, 1906–1909*. Cambridge: Harvard University Press, 1967.

Oakley, Robert and Michael Dziedzic, eds. *Policing the New World Disorder*. Washington, DC: National Defense University, 1996.

Offutt, Milton. *The Protection of Citizens Abroad by the Armed Forces of the United States*. Baltimore: Johns Hopkins University Press, 1928.

O'Gara, Gordon C. *Theodore Roosevelt and the Rise of the Modern Navy*. New York: Greenwood Press, 1969.

Olcott, C. S. *Life of William McKinley*. 2 vols. New York: AMS Press, 1972.

Paullin, Charles O. *Paullin's History of Naval Administration, 1775–1911: A Collection of Articles from the U.S. Naval Institute Proceedings*. Annapolis, MD: U.S. Naval Institute, 1968.

Perkins, Dexter. *A History of the Monroe Doctrine*. Boston: Little, Brown, 1963.

Preston, Diana. *The Boxer Rebellion: The Dramatic Story of China's War on Foreigners That Shook the World in the Summer of 1900*. New York: Walker, 2000.

Pringle, Henry F. *Theodore Roosevelt: A Biography*. New York: Harcourt, Brace, 1931.

Putnam, Carleton. *Theodore Roosevelt: The Formative Years, 1858–1886*. New York: Charles Scribner's Sons, 1958.

Ragin, Charles C. *Constructing Social Research*. Thousand Oaks, CA: Pine Forge Press, 1994.

Reckner, James R. *Teddy Roosevelt's Great White Fleet*. Annapolis, MD: Naval Institute Press, 1988.

Renehan, Edward J., Jr. *The Lion's Pride: Theodore Roosevelt and His Family in Peace and War*. New York: Oxford University Press, 1998.

Rhodes, James F. *The McKinley and Roosevelt Administrations, 1897–1909*. New York: Macmillan, 1922.

Ricard, Serge. "Theodore Roosevelt: Principles and Practice of a Foreign Policy." *Theodore Roosevelt Association Journal* 18 (Fall–Winter 1992): 2–6.

Riis, Jacob A. *How the Other Half Lives: Studies among the Tenements of New York*. New York: Charles Scribner's Sons, 1890.

———. *Theodore Roosevelt the Citizen*. New York: Outlook, 1914. Reprint, St. Clair Shores, MI: Scholarly Press, 1970.

Roberts, Owen J. *The Court and the Constitution: The Oliver Wendell Holmes Lectures*. Cambridge: Harvard University Press, 1951.

Roth, Russell. *Muddy Glory: America's "Indian Wars" in the Philippines, 1899–1935*. West Hanover, MA: Christopher Publishing House, 1981.

Scott, Hugh Lenox. *Some Memories of a Soldier*. New York: Century, 1928.

Scott, James Brown. "Editorial Comment." *American Journal of International Law* 1, no. 1 (January 1907): 138–44.

Segovia, Lazaro. *The Full Story of Aguinaldo's Capture*. Translated by Frank de Thomas. Manila, 1902. Reprint, Manila: MCS Enterprises, 1969.

Shulimson, Jack. *The Marine Corps' Search for a Mission, 1880–1898*. Lawrence: University Press of Kansas, 1993.

Smythe, Donald. *Guerrilla Warrior: The Early Life of John J. Pershing*. New York: Charles Scribner's Sons, 1973.

Stead, William T. "The Conference at The Hague." *Forum* 28 (September 1899): 3–4.

Sumida, Jon Tetsuro. *Inventing Grand Strategy and Teaching Command: The Classic Works of Alfred Thayer Mahan Reconsidered*. Washington, DC: Woodrow Wilson Center Press, 1997.

Thayer, William R. *Theodore Roosevelt*. Boston: Houghton Mifflin, 1919.

Tilchin, William N. "The Rising Star of Theodore Roosevelt's Diplomacy:

Major Studies from Beale to the Present." *Theodore Roosevelt Association Journal* 15, no. 3 (Summer 1989): 2–24.

———. *Theodore Roosevelt and the British Empire: A Study in Presidential Statecraft*. New York: St. Martin's Press, 1997.

Tilly, Charles. *Big Structures, Large Processes, Huge Comparisons*. New York: Russell Sage Foundation, 1984.

Train, Eugene P. *The Treaty of Portsmouth: An Adventure in American Diplomacy*. Lexington: University of Kentucky Press, 1969.

Tucker, John Randolph. *The Constitution of the United States: A Critical Discussion of Its Genesis, Development, and Interpretation*. Edited by Henry St. George Tucker. Chicago: Callaghan, 1899.

Tucker, Rufus S. "A Balance Sheet of the Philippines." *Harvard Business Review* 8 (October 1929): 10–23.

Turk, Richard W. *The Ambiguous Relationship: Theodore Roosevelt and Alfred Thayer Mahan*. New York: Greenwood Press, 1987.

Van Evera, Stephen. *Guide to Methods for Students of Political Science*. Ithaca, NY: Cornell University Press, 1997.

Wagenknecht, Edward. *The Seven Worlds of Theodore Roosevelt*. New York: Longmans, Green, 1958.

Welles, Sumner. *Naboth's Vineyard: The Dominican Republic, 1844–1924*. 2 vols. Mamaroneck, NY: Paul P. Appel, 1926. Reprint, 1966.

White, William Allen. "Roosevelt: A Force for Righteousness." *McClure's* 28 (January 1907): 393.

Wilcox, Marrion. *Harper's History of the War in the Philippines*. New York: Harper and Brothers, 1900.

Wister, Owen. *Roosevelt: The Story of a Friendship*. New York: Macmillan, 1930.

Zakaria, Fareed. *From Wealth to Power: The Unusual Origins of America's World Role*. Princeton, NJ: Princeton University Press, 1998.

INDEX

ABOUT THE AUTHOR

James R. Holmes is a senior research associate at the University of Georgia Center for International Trade and Security. A former navy surface warfare officer, he served in the engineering and weapons departments on board the battleship *Wisconsin*, taught engineering at the Surface Warfare Officers School Command, and served as professor of strategy at the Naval War College. James was decorated for combat leadership in Desert Storm. His work has appeared in a variety of scholarly, professional, and news outlets, ranging from *Comparative Strategy* to the *Los Angeles Times*. He is a Phi Beta Kappa graduate of Vanderbilt University and earned graduate degrees from Salve Regina University, Providence College, and the Fletcher School of Law and Diplomacy at Tufts University. He finished first in the class of 1994 at the Naval War College, earning the Naval War College Foundation Award.